离散华人之界线与连线
实证与理论研究
Boundaries and Bonds of the Chinese Diaspora
Empirical and Theoretical Studies

离散华人之界线与连线
实证与理论研究

主编：游俊豪・刘宏・张慧梅・王纯强・周陶沫

南洋理工大学，新加坡

Boundaries and Bonds of the Chinese Diaspora
Empirical and Theoretical Studies

Chief Editors

Cheun Hoe Yow • Hong Liu • Huimei Zhang
Soon Keong Ong • Taomo Zhou

Nanyang Technological University, Singapore

NEW JERSEY · LONDON · SINGAPORE · BEIJING · SHANGHAI · TAIPEI · CHENNAI

Published by

World Scientific Publishing Co. Pte. Ltd.
5 Toh Tuck Link, Singapore 596224
USA office: 27 Warren Street, Suite 401-402, Hackensack, NJ 07601
UK office: 57 Shelton Street, Covent Garden, London WC2H 9HE

British Library Cataloguing-in-Publication Data
A catalogue record for this book is available from the British Library.

BOUNDARIES AND BONDS OF THE CHINESE DIASPORA
Empirical and Theoretical Studies

Copyright © 2025 by Singapore Chinese Cultural Centre and Chinese Heritage Centre, Nanyang Technological University

All rights reserved.

ISBN 978-981-127-552-4 (hardcover)
ISBN 978-981-127-921-8 (ebook for institutions)
ISBN 978-981-127-922-5 (ebook for individuals)

For any available supplementary material, please visit
https://www.worldscientific.com/worldscibooks/10.1142/13388#t=suppl

Desk Editors: Lai Ann/Sia Geng Jie
Artist: Amy Lee

Typeset by Stallion Press
Email: enquiries@stallionpress.com

Contents

Introduction   vii

Part 1 (第一辑)   1

Chapter 1: Upriver and Overseas: Revisiting Boundaries in the Study of Nineteenth-Century Cantonese Migration   3

Steven B. Miles

Chapter 2: Paradox of Superdiversity: Contesting Racism and "Chinese Privilege" in Singapore   29

Hong Liu and Lingli Huang

Chapter 3: Post-1978 Chinese Migration to Brazil: The *Qiaoxiang* Migration Models and the Rite of Passage   55

Changsheng Shu

Chapter 4: Homeland, Host Country, and Beyond: Identity Transformation among Chinese Migrants in Singapore   79

Shaohua Zhan

Chapter 5: "Finding the Distant Homeland Here": Contemporary Indonesian Poetry in Chinese   101

Josh Stenberg

Chapter 6: The Participation of Malaysian Chinese Women in the Workforce: Traditional Values and Choices   125

Jee Yin Chin, Yee Mun Chin and Hooi San Noew

Chapter 7: Revolutionary Cosmopolitanism and its Limits: The Chinese Communist Party and the Chinese in Singapore, Medan and Jakarta Compared (1945–1949) 149

Guo-Quan Seng

Chapter 8: The Patriarchy of Diaspora: Race Fantasy and Gender Blindness in Chen Da's Studies of the Nanyang Chinese 179

Rachel Leow

Part 2 (第二辑) 203

第九章： 人力资本跨国流动及其融资网络 205
龙登高

第十章： 20世纪"文化中国"的再展演：侨乡与海外华人社会的社区节日 241
蔡志祥

第十一章： 跨界连结：论华侨银行战时发展策略 (1938–1945年) 263
杨妍

第十二章： 传统与嬗变：华侨华人慈善事业新发展 295
邢菁华、张洵君

第十三章： 区域华文文学的越界、跨国与主体解/构：以旅台马华文学为例 311
朱崇科

第十四章： 鲁迅木刻思想的马来亚传播 325
胡星灿

第十五章： 隐形宣传与友联出版社：从亚洲基金会档案 (1955–1970) 看纯文艺期刊《蕉风》 351
许维贤

Reconstruction and Beyond:
An Introduction of Diasporic Chinese Boundaries and Bonds

Yow Cheun Hoe

There are many cities, towns, and villages across the globe that witness a significant Chinese diaspora presence, or people of Chinese origins. Some are ethnic Chinese communities that have been established over generations with traceable roots from China as well as other places. Others are individuals and organizations of recent immigrants who have left China after 1978 when it embarked on an open-door policy and economic reform. Over time, they have formed groupings and positionings in the process of reconstructing networks and identification within the Chinese diaspora and beyond.

The origin of this book lies in a webinar conference on the theme of "Boundaries and Bonds: Empirical and Theoretical Studies of Chinese Diaspora", which featured 18 distinguished speakers from Asia, North and South Americas, Australia, and Europe, and attracted more than 1,000 participants from across the globe for two days, on 2–3 October 2021. In the hope of getting a better understanding of realities embedded in ethnic Chinese communities, there were three keynote speeches and four panels of papers presented. The panels include: (i) Identities and Concepts; (ii) Transnationalism and Governance; (iii) Terrains and Representation; and (iv) Literature and Publications. Some of these papers were presented in English, while others were in Chinese.

The conference was the result of a successful collaboration between three institutions as the main organizers: the Singapore Chinese Cultural Centre (SCCC); the School of Social Sciences (SSS), Nanyang Technological University (NTU), Singapore; and the Chinese Heritage Centre (CHC), NTU. It also had solid working relations with the Singapore Society of Asian Studies (SSAS), which played the role of supporting organizer. These four institutions share a passion and interest in diasporic Chinese studies.

This book is a collection of the conference's papers. With the discussion and exchange of ideas made during the conference, the authors have revised, updated, and expanded upon their papers. We have decided to keep the papers in the languages they were originally written in without translation. Another note is that, after the conference, some of the papers were selected and featured as special issues in the *Journal of Chinese Overseas*, Vol. 18, No. 2 (2022) and *Huaren Yanjiu Guojie Xuebao* (《华人研究国际学报》, *International Journal of Diasporic Chinese Studies*), Vol. 14, No. 1 (2022), two of the key journals for the studies of ethnic Chinese, Chinese migrants, and their descendants.

The three keynote speeches provide a wide horizon for us to contemplate how the Chinese diaspora has transcended boundaries and cultivated bonds. Steven B. Miles uncovers how Cantonese upriver migration in the 19th century provided future migrants with the experience to develop overseas networks. Liu Hong and Huang Lingli highlight issues surrounding superdiversity taking place in Singapore involving Chinese communities and migrants. Long Denggao shows how transnational flows of migrants have determined the form of culmination of capital in networks.

Besides the keynote papers, the English section of this volume also contains six papers, offering a wide range of case studies. Shu Changsheng examines how Chinese migrants in Brazil have constituted a *qiaoxiang* (literally hometown for Chinese sojourners) model with linkages with China after 1978. Zhan Shaohua investigates Chinese migrants in Singapore and how they relate to their homeland, host country, and beyond. Josh Stenberg's research is on contemporary Indonesian poetry in Chinese and the search for their homeland. The paper by Chin Jee Yin, Chin Yee Mun, and Noew Hooi San presents findings on how Malaysian Chinese women participate in the workforce. Seng Guo-Quan studies the relations between the Chinese Communist Party and ethnic Chinese in Singapore, Medan, and Jakarta. Rachel Leow revisits Chen Da's studies of the Nanyang Chinese to trace the patriarchy of the diaspora.

The Chinese section of this book includes six other papers that also provide various perspectives to look at diasporic Chinese ethnicity and networks. Choi Chi Cheung sheds light on festival celebrations in *qiaoxiang* areas and how it has evolved in diasporic Chinese communities. Yang Yan traces how overseas Chinese banks had strategically hinged upon transnational connections during the Second World War. Xing Jinghua and Zhang Xunhua map new trends in diasporic Chinese philanthropy. Zhu Chongke uncovers transnational subjectivity of Malaysian Chinee literature with writers based in Taiwan. Hu Xingcan explores how Lu Xun's wood carving was disseminated into Malaya. Hee Wai Siam examines how the Malaysian Chinese literary magazines *Chao Foon* was involved in Cold War propaganda.

This book and October 2021 conference would not have been possible without the joint effort made by the CHC, NTU; SSS, NTU; as well as the SCCC and the SSAS. These four organizations have provided intellectual inputs to the conference, which was funded by CHC, SSS, NTU Strategic Initiative (#04INS000136C430), and SCCC.

My heartfelt gratefulness goes to co-editors for this book — Prof Liu Hong, Dr Zhang Huimei, Assoc Prof Zhou Taomo, and Asst Prof Ong Soon Keong. I would also like to thank Frederica Lai and Shaun Choh who have given administrative support from CHC and SCCC, respectively, for this book and the conference.

The views of the chapters represent those of the respective authors and do not necessarily reflect the views of the editors, organizers, funders and publishers.

构建与跨越：
有关离散华人界线与连线的导言

游俊豪

全球各地许多城市、小镇、乡村，都有离散华人的踪影与存在。当中，有的华人族群与社区，已然经过数个代际的繁衍，根源可以追溯至中国，以及其他地方。有的是新移民，1978年中国改革开放后，来到其他国家的个人，以及合群所组的团体。随着时间的推移，这些新旧离散华人的凝聚与定位，其实是通过族裔内部与超越族裔之外，不断在重组网络，调整认同。

这本论文集，始于"界线与连线：离散华人的实证与理论研究"的国际会议。这一场会议，在2021年10月2日至3日举行，共有18名来自亚洲、北美、南美、澳洲、欧洲的著名学者提呈论文，吸引了超过一千名全球观众参与。为了增进对华人族群实况的认识，会议呈现了三份主题演讲、四个议题小组。小组的议题为：（一）身份认同与概念、（二）跨国主义与治理、（三）发展脉络与再现、（四）文学书写与出版。这些论文分别以英文或中文报告。

会议的成功举行，见证了三个机构的有效合作。其中一个是新加坡华族文化中心，另外两个是新加坡南洋理工大学里的社会科学学院、华裔馆。此外，会议也获得新加坡亚洲研究学会的支持，对于华人族群领域与课题，这四个单位都拥有热忱与兴趣。

这本书，汇集了该国际会议的论文。在会议上进行讨论和收集意见之后，作者们对论文作出了修改、更新、拓展。我们决定保留论文原来使用的原文，并没有翻译。另外需要指出的是，在会议结束之后，我们选了一些论文在 *Journal of Chinese Overseas*（第18卷，第2期，2022年）、

《华人研究国际学报》（第14卷，第1期，2022年），分别作为专辑发表。这两份都是华侨、华人、华裔研究领域的重要期刊。

三篇主题论文提供了广阔的视野，有助于我们思考离散华人如何跨越界线、建构连线。麦哲维（Steven B. Miles）揭示，19世纪广东人沿着江河的迁徙，给随后的海外网络的拓展累积了经验。刘宏（Liu Hong）和黄伶俐（Huang Lingli）探索新加坡的超级多元性，以及置身其中的华人社群与移民。龙登高（Long Denggao）梳理人口的跨国流动，如何影响了网络当中的资本储存。

除主题论文之外，英文部分还包含六篇文章，提供了繁复多元的案例。束长生（Shu Changsheng）检阅1979年后抵达巴西的中国移民，审视他们跟中国侨乡建构的网络与模式。占少华（Zhan Shaohua）观照新加坡的中国新移民，分析他们如何跟家乡、所在国、他处维持并发展联系。石峻山（Josh Stenberg）的研究，投射在印度尼西亚的中文诗歌，探索这些书写如何寻找家乡。陈子莹（Chin Jee Yin）、陈亿文（Chin Yee Mun）和梁傌珊（Noew Hooi San）的文章，揭示马来西亚华人女性在职场的参与情况。成国泉（Seng Guo-Quan）梳理中国共产党跟新加坡、棉兰、雅加达华人的关系。廖彩亿（Rachel Leow）回顾陈达对于南洋华侨的研究，追溯其中有关父权在离散华人的形构。

中文部分也收录了另外六篇文章，对离散华人的族群性与网络，也呈现了多重视角。蔡志祥论述传统节庆如何在侨乡形成，如何在离散华人社区延异。杨妍分析华侨银行，如何在二战期间调整发展策略。邢菁华与张洵君追踪华侨华人慈善事业，揭示其最新的发展趋势。朱崇科的研究显示，旅台马华作家参与了跨国文学主体性的重构。胡星灿探讨了鲁迅木刻思想的马来亚传播。许维贤检阅马华文学杂志《蕉风》在冷战宣传当中的角色与运作。

这本书得以编辑并出版，归功于新加坡华族文化中心、新加坡南洋理工大学社会科学学院、华裔馆、新加坡亚洲研究学会四个单位对于2021年10月国际会议的投入。华裔馆、南洋理工大学社会科学学院、南洋理工大学科研经费（04INS000136C430）、新加坡华族文化中心提供了经费支持。

我谨此对这本书的合作编辑，刘宏教授、张慧梅博士、周陶沫副教授、王纯强助理教授，表示衷心感谢。我也要感谢华裔馆的赖净慈、新加坡华族文化中心的曹世明，他们给国际研讨会和这本书提供了行政协助。

本书各章代表相关作者的观点，文责自负，与本书的编者、组织者、资助机构和出版机构无关。

About the Publishers
出版机构简介

School of Social Sciences

The School of Social Sciences (SSS) is home to research and education in the social sciences. SSS offers study programmes in a range of subjects at both undergraduate and graduate levels, from a BSocSci (Hons) in a Single or Double Major and MSc (by coursework) to MA (by research) and PhD. SSS has around 1,700 undergraduates and close to 400 graduate students across our degree programmes. Presently, SSS offers four subject majors at the undergraduate level — Economics, Psychology, Public Policy and Global Affairs, and Sociology. Undergraduates also have the opportunity to choose interdisciplinary studies in Economics and Data Science, or double majors such as Economics and Media Analytics, Economics & Public Policy and Global Affairs. Meanwhile, at the graduate level, SSS offers PhD and MA programmes in all four subject majors as well as MSc in Applied Economics and Applied Gerontology. In line with the strategic goals of NTU 2025 and the evolving concerns of human society, the School has formed four interdisciplinary research clusters — Aging, Inclusion and Healthcare; Cognitive and Behavioural Science; Environment and Sustainability; and Policy and Society. In addition, we have the Economic Growth Centre (EGC) that supports research by the Economics division.

南洋理工大学社会科学学院简介

南洋理工大学社会科学学院（SSS）是开展社会科学研究和教育的所在院系，为本科生和研究生提供一系列学科的学习课程，包括单专业或双专业的社会科学荣誉学位、修课型硕士学位和研究型硕士学位、博士学位。学院有约1700名本科生和近400名研究生修读这些学位课程。目前，社会科学学院为本科生提供经济学、心理学、公共政策和全球事务、社会学四个学科专业，他们也有机会选择经济学和数据科学的跨学科学习，或者是经济学与媒体分析、经济学与公共政策和全球事务等双专业。在研究生阶段，学院则提供所有四个学科专业的博士和硕士课程，以及应用经济学和应用老年学硕士课程。为配合"南大2025年战略"目标以及对人类社会不断变化的关注，社会科学学院形成了四个跨学科研究群，即乐龄化、包容性和医疗保健、认知和行为科学、环境和可持续性。此外，学院也设立了经济增长中心（EGC），以支持经济学科的研究。

Chinese Heritage Centre

The Chinese Heritage Centre (CHC) at Nanyang Technological University (NTU) is unique in the world. Founded as a non-profit organisation in 1995 and guided by an international Board of Governors, CHC aims to advance knowledge and understanding of the ethnic Chinese communities in different parts of the globe. Since 2011, CHC has been reconstituted as an autonomous institute of NTU. It has remained self-sustaining, depending on fundraising from private donors and government matching grants. In a globalising world, CHC functions as a three-in-one institution, serving as a research centre, a library, and a museum. Its work is crucial in three ways:

- CHC addresses the insufficient public acknowledgement of the tremendous contributions that the Chinese overseas have made to local communities around the world.
- CHC stems the tide of gradual identity and cultural detachment among Chinese youths by reconnecting them to their roots.
- CHC leverages on the strategic location in Singapore at a major research university, at the crossroad of East and West, and at the centre of the greater Chinese diaspora to create, advance, and curate the global body of knowledge concerning the Chinese overseas.

华裔馆简介

华裔馆成立于1995年，坐落前南洋大学行政楼（该建筑于1998年被列为国家文物古迹），是集研究中心、图书馆和博物馆三位一体的非营利机构。2011年,华裔馆并入南洋理工大学,成为南大的一个自治及自给自立的机构,也是全球除中国大陆以外,唯一一个专注于海外华人研究的多功能大学研究中心。在世界日益全球化的今天,华裔馆为弘扬和传承历史悠久的华族文化不遗余力,其目标集中在以下三个方面:

- 向世人昭示全球五千万海外华人对世界和各所在国做出的巨大贡献。
- 扭转华裔后代华人身份认同感的弱化及失根现象。
- 充分利用新加坡融贯东西文化的优势,依托南洋理工大学的研究平台和资源,促进海外华人研究,保护华族物质和精神遗产,传承和弘扬华族文化。

Singapore Chinese Cultural Centre

The Singapore Chinese Cultural Centre (SCCC) collaborates with arts and cultural groups and community partners to promote and develop local Chinese culture. By continuing to create innovative and engaging content, we strive to nurture a greater appreciation of our multi-cultural identity and sense of belonging. Opened by our Patron PM Lee Hsien Loong on 19 May 2017, our Centre located in the heart of Singapore, encourages everyone to connect with our unique Chinese Singaporean culture through exhibitions, fairs, performances, seminars, talks, workshops, and other cultural activities, available both online and at our centre throughout the year.

新加坡华族文化中心简介

为推广本土华族文化,新加坡华族文化中心长年与多个文化艺术团体及社区伙伴合作。中心通过新颖有趣的内容,让大众了解本土文化的多元性,同时培养对国家的归属感。新加坡华族文化中心于2017年5月19日由赞助人李显龙总理主持开幕。矗立市中心的文化中心,通过线上线下的形式为公众举办展览、表演、市集、讲座、工作坊、研讨会等丰富多彩的文化活动,让大家可以更深入地了解本土华族文化。

Part 1
(第一辑)

Upriver and Overseas: Revisiting Boundaries in the Study of Nineteenth-Century Cantonese Migration

上游与海外:重探十九世纪广府移民研究的界线

Steven B. Miles 麦哲维 | ORCID: 0000-0002-6203-7517
Division of Humanities, The Hong Kong University of Science and Technology, Hong Kong
hmsbmiles@ust.hk

Abstract

Inspired by one of the themes of the "Boundaries and Bonds: An International Conference on Chinese Diaspora," hosted by Nanyang Technological University in October 2021, this article explores conceptual boundaries in the study of Cantonese migration during the pivotal nineteenth century. Based on research on internal Cantonese migration along the West River, but set in a comparative framework of overseas Cantonese migration, I consider in turn natural or topographical barriers, political boundaries, regional and class discrepancies, and gendered imaginings and practices of migration. Focusing on villages and townships along the West River, I show that emigrant communities with prior access to a long, navigable, and commercially important river readily adapted to new experiences of overseas migration after the mid-nineteenth century.

Keywords

boundaries – Cantonese – migration – overseas – Qing – riverine

摘要

受到 2021 年 10 月由南洋理工大学主办的"界线与连线:华侨华人研究国际学术研讨会"的议题的启发,本文对研究 19 世纪这个关键时期的广府移民的概念性的界线作一探讨。以西江流域的内部广府移民为核心,基于海外广府移民的比较性构思,我将考察自然和地形障碍、政治界限、地域以及阶级的差异、性别化的想象和移民实践。此文以西江流域的村庄和乡镇为主，展示对一条悠长、可通航的、商业上有重要价值的河脉有着便利通行的外出移民群体在19世纪中叶之后轻而易举地适应了向海外移民这样的新实践。

关键词

界线 – 广府人 – 移民 – 海外 – 清代 – 河域

1   Introduction[1]

Twenty years ago, Adam McKeown suggested that the boundary separating China from neighboring regimes "may not be the most useful point at which to make a distinction between different kinds of migration" (McKeown 2001: 65).[2] Since then, despite the pioneering work of Lucille Chia (2006) and Philip Kuhn (2008), historians of Ming and Qing China have only slowly come around to engaging scholarship on overseas Chinese migration. Studies of overland migration across Qing China's southwestern (Giersch 2006) and Inner Asian frontiers (Schlesinger 2017) present opportunities for fruitful comparative work with trade and migration across the empire's maritime frontier. The newest scholarship on Central China's Huizhou Prefecture, homeland of the most renowned internal trade diaspora, has begun to engage literature on maritime frontiers and overseas Chinese (Guo 2022: 194–95). Meanwhile, historians of overseas migration from southeastern China during the late nineteenth and early twentieth centuries have produced a series of studies that reveal unique dynamics of particular locales, whether *qiaoxiang* (Williams 2018; Macauley 2021) or transit points such as Hong Kong (Sinn 2013) and Xiamen (Ong 2021). Though not the central focus of these studies, they share the implication that the relationship between internal and external migration during the nineteenth and twentieth centuries varied by place and time.

---

1   This essay was initially conceived as a keynote address for "Boundaries and Bonds: An International Conference on Chinese Diaspora," hosted by Nanyang Technological University, October 2–3, 2021. I thank the conference organizers and participants, as well as two anonymous reviewers for the *Journal of Chinese Overseas*.
2   Although McKeown's research focuses on the early twentieth century, his discussion here is more general, referring to the "border of the Chinese empire" (not the nation-state per se), citing works that cover the Qing period or both the late nineteenth and early twentieth centuries.

All such communities in southeastern China were linked to networks of both coastal and riverine trade. Nonetheless, most rivers in Fujian and Guangdong had a limited reach into the interior. In contrast, the West River (Xijiang 西江), one of the most important conduits for trade in China, originated in tributaries whose headwaters reached to Guizhou, Yunnan, and Vietnam, covered most of Guangxi, and emptied into the sea via multiple distributaries in Guangdong's Pearl River delta. Accordingly, delta townships and villages along the main trunk of the West River were emigrant communities for upriver migrants before they produced overseas migrants. That is, for delta communities close to the West River – in Shunde and Nanhai counties on the northwestern bank, and in Xinhui and Heshan on the southwestern bank – emergent patterns of migration within the borders of Qing China created cultures of migration (Pieke, Nyíri, Thunø, and Ceccagno 2004: 51–56, 194) readily adaptable to new overseas trajectories after 1850. Moreover, this upriver orientation continued to be important even as overseas migration expanded dramatically starting in the 1850s. The experience with trade and migration along a major river differentiated these communities from other emigrant communities in southeastern China, including the Hokkien homeland in Fujian and the communities in the Tan River basin that formed the core of the Four Counties (Si Yi, See Yap 四邑) in Guangdong.

Boundaries, one of the themes of the conference for which the present essay was originally written, provide a conceptual tool for exploring the ways in which Cantonese migration within the delta and along the West River basin both prefigured and paralleled trajectories of migration to destinations beyond the borders of Qing China. The following essay focuses on riverine communities on either side of West River and is framed around different kinds of boundaries: natural boundaries, political boundaries, and boundaries of region, class, gender. The mid-nineteenth century was undoubtedly a period of profound transformation due to factors ranging from domestic unrest to global forces such as industrialization and imperialism. Like Michael Williams (2018: 2, 4, 6, 25), in his bottom-up approach, I center my analysis on how migrants and their families in communities along the West River perceived, navigated, and manipulated these boundaries, discovering a less disruptive history than is often assumed. In other words, residents of communities with long-standing patterns of riverine trade and migration readily adapted to the dramatically changed circumstances of the nineteenth century. Viewing history from their perspective allows us to perceive resonances between internal and external migration and continuities across the mid-nineteenth century divide.

2 "Natural" Boundaries: River and Sea

Topographical features could channel migration. Such was the case with the riverine Cantonese diasporic trajectory that largely followed the contours of the West River and its tributaries, across political boundaries, through western Guangdong into Guangxi, southern Guizhou, eastern Yunnan, and northern Vietnam. In upriver areas, mountains largely separated the West River basin from coastal networks of trade and migration shaped by island chains and monsoon winds.

When Qing-era residents of the Pearl River delta wrote about their world, however, they did not always make a sharp distinction between river and sea. This, in turn, should compel us to reconsider the conceptual boundary between internal, upriver and external, overseas migration.

Take for example a poem (Zhao N.d.: 2:20a) written in the late 1830s by a Nanhai County resident during his journey up the West River to recover the coffins of two nephews who had died of illness while trading at a market town in far northern Guangxi. When the boat shipping their remains back home broke apart at Wuzhou, near the Guangdong border, the crew placed the coffins on the riverbank and fled. The poet recounts the progress of his boat, pulled by trackers through Lingyang Gorge, a place that was some two hundred kilometers from the mouth of the river and a symbol to riverine travelers that they were leaving the delta for mountainous, upriver areas. "Stones appear," he wrote, "making an obstruction across the sea" (*hai* 海).

Cantonese writers imagined the West River as a sea not only when writing poems. Compilers of a gazetteer of Jiujiang, a township lying on the northeastern bank of the river in Nanhai County, refer to the West River as the "West Sea" (Xi Hai 西海) (*Jiujiang Rulin xiang zhi* 1883: 1:43b). The Deng lineage, based across the river in Gulao township, Heshan County, compiled a genealogy in 1850; in it, a map labels the river as "Great Sea" (Da Hai 大海) (*Nanyang shipu* 1850). This conflation of river and sea makes sense: before the accelerated diking of rivers and reclamation of sands in the several centuries before these texts were written, communities like Jiujiang and Gulao had been islands surrounded by the sea (Marks 1998: 67–68).

Cantonese writers also conceived of the Pearl River, the stretch of river that ran past Guangzhou, connected to the West River through distributaries in the delta, as a "sea." In his diary on the day of the Dragon Boat Festival in 1829, the literatus Xie Lansheng 谢兰生 observed the impact of a recent deluge. "Commoners' homes along the sea shore" (*binhai minfang* 滨海民房) in the densely populated and highly commercialized western suburb of Guangzhou had been flooded, while crews of dragon boats designed to race on the sea (*haimian longchuan* 海面龙船) dared not venture out from creeks for fear of drowning (Xie: DG9.5.5).[3]

When these Cantonese writers traveled through the Pearl River delta, they did so by boat, and their progress was influenced by both river currents and coastal tides. Readers of Xie Lansheng's diary learn that the author's movements were shaped by this ebb and flow. For example, one day in February 1820 he abandoned plans to visit the flower gardens upriver at Huadi 花地 because the tide was not rising. A rising tide on a hot summer day in 1828 made a trip to Huadi possible, after which Xie returned home with the receding tide (Xie: JQ24.12.21 and DG8.6.25). There were of course important distinctions between upriver and overseas travel, of which these writers were keenly aware. Long before his nephews left to trade in northern Guangxi, the poet composed a poem for another kinsmen. The poem's title, "Sending a Merchant out to Sea," and content make clear that the subject of the poem is heading across the South China Sea into areas of maritime Southeast Asia that were by the early nineteenth century common destinations for Cantonese merchants (Zhao 1815: 2:6b). That said, for Qing-era delta residents of the Pearl River delta, the distinction between upriver journeys and overseas journeys was not as stark as we might imagine.

For residents of emigrant communities along the delta portion of the West River, then, migration both upriver and overseas fit into family strategies for socioeconomic maintenance. Consider the range of destinations among three Jiujiang families of the Guan surname. Around the outset of the nineteenth century, two brothers from one of six dominant Guan lineages in Jiujiang, both married to women from the prominent Zhu surname in Jiujiang, sought their fortunes outside the township. One brother made enough money trading between Guangdong and Guangxi to earn a reputation for selfless philanthropy. The other brother "in his youth sojourned" in Vietnam, where he won over the "uncouth" natives with his honesty, and was conceivably involved in one of the nine businesses owned by Nanhai Guans who patronized Hanoi's Yuedong huiguan 粤东会馆 (Guangdong native-place association) in 1803. Both brothers lived out their last days in Jiujiang, whereas the younger brother's sons in turn had Vietnamese concubines who were buried in their native country (*Guan Shudetang jiapu*: 6:53a–54a, 17:36a–37b; *Corpus of Ancient Vietnamese Inscriptions*: no. 195 and 196).

---

3 I consulted two versions of Xie Lansheng's diary, *Changxingxingzhai riji*, citing by date of diary entry ("JQ" for Jiaqing 嘉庆 and "DG" for Daoguang 道光).

In 1896, Guan Shizong 关栻宗 (b. 1859), member of another Jiujiang Guan lineage, passed the lowest level of the civil service examinations, earning him *shengyuan* 生员 status. He did so not in his native Nanhai County, but rather in the central Guangxi county of Wuxuan, where he was registered under the name Guan Fengji 关逢吉 (*Shixi lu*: 74–79).[4] Two of Shizong's sons later moved to Hong Kong, where, like many of their fellow townsmen, they went into banking. One of Shizong's grandsons, Stanley Kwan (1925–2011), would go on to help found the Hang Seng Index before migrating to Toronto, Canada (Kwan 2009: 4–6).

Finally, we have Cuan Sun, featured in Robert Chao Romero's *The Chinese in Mexico, 1882–1940*. "Cuan" is an alternative romanization of "Guan," and the Nanhai County "village" where he was born in 1900, Kiukon, was almost certainly Jiujiang. In the early 1910s, after a brother-in-law who owned a grocery store in the northern Mexican state of Sonora paid a return visit to Jiujiang, he brought Cuan Sun with him, presumably as an apprentice, though Cuan also attended school in Mexico. Later, Cuan Sun, now also known as Ricardo Cuan, moved to southern Mexico to open a perfume shop with a nephew, Pablo Cuan, before moving back to northern Mexico in 1927 to join six partners in running a general merchandise store. In 1940, although Ricardo was a Mexican citizen, his mother, then residing in Hong Kong, arranged a marriage by proxy to a woman, presumably in Hong Kong or Nanhai, whom he had never met (Romero 2010: 47, 70, 107).[5] These three Jiujiang Guan families created distinct migrant trajectories – to Guangxi, to Vietnam, to Hong Kong, and to Mexico – by establishing themselves in particular lines of work. The range of destinations that these individuals targeted and the particular entrepreneurial niches (Kuhn 2008: 46) that they developed were shaped by larger forces, ranging from the emergence of a unified Nguyen regime in Vietnam to Chinese exclusion laws in the United States that factored into the growth of a Chinese community in northern Mexico. Yet entrepreneurial migrants from Jiujiang readily adapted to changing circumstances as they navigated borders separating provinces, empires, and nations.

---

4 Many thanks to Cheuk Kwan for sharing the genealogy.
5 I take the native places of "Kow Kong," "Jiu Jang," "Kaw Kong," and "Kau Kong," which appear in studies of Chinese in Mexico that draw on US and Mexican immigration archives (Romero 2010; Schiavone Camacho 2012), to refer to Jiujiang.

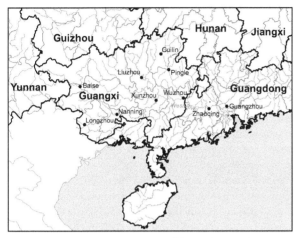

MAP 1   The West River Basin (adapted from Miles 2017: 3)

3   Political Boundaries: Gaming the Examination System

Political boundaries were an important factor in shaping diasporic formations, and in determining the range of likely career options available to migrants in given destinations. Nonetheless, migrants were able to navigate political boundaries and adapt to state policies, even turning policies to their own advantage. A good example of this involves Qing China's household registration and civil service examination systems. Men who wished to take the examinations were required to do so in their native place, the county (*xian* 县) or department (*zhou* 州) in which their household was registered as a tax-paying unit. Cantonese men often acquired civil examination degrees as registered residents of locales outside their native place. Most commonly, they did so in different counties within Guangzhou Prefecture, which largely overlapped with the Pearl River delta. Thus, a native of one county would somehow gain residential registration in another county, pass the lowest level of the examinations, and become a *shengyuan* in the second county's government school. This practice often required some obfuscation, adopting a new given name (as in the case of Guan Shizong), taking an examination under a different surname, or passing oneself off as a resident of a county without meeting legal requirements of length of residence and property ownership, a practice that the state categorized as "fraudulent registration" (*maoji* 冒籍) (Rowe 1984: 235–36; Du 2015: 184–85).

When Cantonese men took examinations in locales outside the Pearl River delta but within Guangdong, they mostly targeted destinations in the western part of the province. When outside Guangdong, they almost always aimed further west, in Guangxi. One factor explaining this pattern is that many Cantonese families already had commercial interests and kinship connections along the West River basin. Another reason is that, in general, examinations were less competitive in Guangxi than in Guangdong. Depending upon the locale, it was sometimes easier to become a *shengyuan* in Guangxi than in Guangdong, and, having achieved this credential, it was certainly easier to pass the provincial examinations and achieve the *juren* 举人 degree in Guangxi than in Guangdong (Elman 2000: 664).

Within Guangxi, Cantonese generally avoided Guilin Prefecture, the province's cultural and political center, where competition was intense. Instead, migrants targeted areas in southeastern Guangxi where Cantonese commercial influence was heaviest, in such river ports as Wuzhou and Xunzhou. But a surprising number went far upriver, into the frontiers of western and southern Guangxi. This practice was most prevalent before a state crackdown in 1760, as migrants took advantage of state policies designed to consolidate imperial control in frontier areas of the southwest by fostering the growth of a local scholar-official elite (*Zhupi zouzhe*: 0073–043; Miles 2017: 99–103).

In the first half of the nineteenth century, the practice of Cantonese sitting for examinations in Guangxi gradually reemerged, then increased markedly during the consolidation of Qing control following mid-century rebellions: first of the famous Taiping regime and then the less well-known Da Cheng 大成 state, a Cantonese Triad regime based in Xunzhou. Because both county-level and provincial-level examinations were repeatedly postponed or cancelled during the 1850s, the state inflated quotas for examinations in the 1860s. One incentive for doing so was to raise money for ongoing military operations against the Da Cheng regime and its allies. Unlike his predecessor a century before, the Guangxi education commissioner in the early 1860s eagerly encouraged sons of migrant merchant families to take examinations in Guangxi, in exchange for paying a fee. Among several examples of temporarily inflated quotas, in 1866, ten times the normal quota of *shengyuan* were entered into the government school of Taiping Prefecture, in southwestern Guangxi. The quota in the provincial examinations was in the 1860s doubled, to roughly a hundred new *juren* in one sitting (*Chongshan xian zhi* 1937: 354, 377).

Some Cantonese families were quick to take advantage of these new opportunities. For the Mo lineage, based at the Nanhai County township of Shatou, winning degrees in Guangxi appears to have been a temporary strategy. In one branch of the lineage, Mo Xieqian 莫燮乾 acquired registration in Pingnan

County, passed the Guangxi provincial examination in 1875, and went on to win the *jinshi* 进士 degree as a Guangxi resident in 1880. Mo Xieqian appears in the Shatou Mo genealogy as Mo Jiayou 莫嘉祐, the genealogy explaining that he became a student in the Xunzhou Prefecture school under the name Xieqian. A distant cousin in the same branch became a *shengyuan* in Yangli Department, in southwestern Guangxi (*Julu xianchengtang chongxiu jiapu*, ce 2:39b, 111a–b). From another branch of the lineage, Mo Ruzhen 莫汝贞 gained registration in Laibin County and was entered into the county school by coming first in the county examinations, eventually earning a higher degree in 1873. Yet Ruzhen maintained connections with Nanhai, marrying a woman born into a prominent lineage in a township neighboring Shatou. The editor of the 1936 Laibin gazetteer, himself a descendant of an eighteenth-century Cantonese migrant, writes of Mo Ruzhen that, even though he acquired registration in a village just outside the Laibin county seat, he was originally registered in Nanhai County, and therefore was "actually not a [Laibin] county man" (*shi fei xianren* 实非县人) (*Laibin xian zhi* 1936: 237–38; *Gesheng xuanba tongnian mingjing tongpu: Tongzhi guiyou ke*: Guangxi:4a; *Julu xianchengtang chongxiu jiapu*, 2:149a). The overall impression conveyed by the biographies of these Mo lineage members is that they aggressively pursued opportunities in Guangxi during the second half of the nineteenth century, but that the focus of their activities was largely centered back in the delta township of Shatou.

This western strategy was particularly important for some communities, even wealthy ones whose native sons competed effectively in Guangdong examinations. Take for example Longjiang township, in Shunde County near the Nanhai County townships of Jiujiang and Shatou. Based on the list of examination degree-winners in the 1926 Longjiang gazetteer, the township produced two *shengyuan* via Guangxi residential registration in 1858, two in 1862, and one in 1863. In 1864, three of seven Longjiang men who became *shengyuan* did so under "western registration" (*xiji* 西籍) or in a "western school" (*xixiang* 西庠). In 1865 all ten native sons who became *shengyuan* were registered Guangxi residents, typically in locales where Cantonese were the dominant merchants. This practice continued through the end of the century (*Shunde Longjiang xiang zhi* 1926: 2:53b–56b; Miles 2021: 243–60).

Thus, the revival of civil examinations represented not simply a recovery of the Qing order in the aftermath of the Taiping and Triad rebellions but also unprecedented opportunities for migrants and their families to achieve gentry status through Guangxi examinations. They did so through what Michael Szonyi (2017: 59) in another context calls regulatory arbitrage, by crossing administrative boundaries, seeking advantageous quotas, adopting alternative names, and otherwise turning state policies to their own advantage. Conditions in

Guangxi, where elite Cantonese merchants were aligned with a re-conquering Qing state in the 1860s, were far different from those in California and British Columbia, where Cantonese migrants dealt with racist exclusion laws in part by means of "paper sons" (Hsu 2000: 74–85; Mar 2010: 6, 25, 27). The creative use of kinship and native-place affiliations to navigate political boundaries and state policies, however, was a feature of migration in both contexts.

4 Social Boundaries: Class and Region

One widely known distinction in studies of overseas Cantonese migration is between the respective emigrant communities of two main groups of Cantonese migrants: the Three Counties (Sanyi, Sam Yap 三邑) and the Four Counties. Less commonly stressed is that the West River divided the Three Counties of Nanhai, Panyu, and Shunde to the northeast from the Four Counties of Xinhui, Xinning (later renamed Taishan), Kaiping, and Enping to the southwest. The latter category sometimes included Heshan County, also south of the West River, to comprise the Five Counties.[6]

Nanhai, Panyu, and Shunde were the core counties of Guangzhou Prefecture, and by extension the Pearl River delta. In the nineteenth century, Nanhai and Panyu shared jurisdiction of the prefectural seat and provincial capital, Guangzhou; however, Nanhai and Shunde, lying on the north bank of the West River, were more important than Panyu in upriver migration. All three counties consistently produced the most degree-holders in the prefecture (see table 3, in appendix), and by most measures that we have were its wealthiest counties (*Shunde xian zhi* 1674: 7:3a; Luo 1988: 49–50; Faure 2007: 80).

To varying degrees, four of the Five Counties were administratively derivative of the first county, Xinhui. Both Enping County and Xinning County traced their origins to the late fifteenth century, when they were separately created in part out of territory originally under Xinhui jurisdiction. In 1649, the new Qing state founded the inland county of Kaiping by combining parts of Xinhui, Xinxing, and Enping. Finally, in the wake of Hakka immigration and land reclamation, in 1732 Heshan County was created out of portions of Kaiping and Xinhui that abutted the southwestern bank of the West River (*Mingshi* 2003: 1135, 1137; *Heshan xian zhi* 1754: 4:2a).

---

6 My focus here is on emigrant communities along one stretch of the West River. I thus do not consider other counties in the delta that were important in overseas Cantonese migration, for example, Dongguan and Xiangshan.

By the latter half of the nineteenth century, the distinction between these two clusters of counties was intertwined with class boundaries. This had not always been the case. As far as I have been able to determine, the Three Counties and Four/Five Counties appellations are products of the nineteenth century, emerging in the context of mass migration overseas. At the very least, in my research on Cantonese migration upstream along the West River basin between the late-sixteenth and mid-nineteenth centuries, I have not seen any sources that categorize Cantonese migrants into Three Counties natives and Four (or Five) Counties natives. On the contrary, sources give the impression that Xinhui was one of the wealthy and powerful counties of the delta, along with Nanhai, Shunde, and Panyu. To give just one example, during the 1660s, local elites in the neighboring, remote western Guangdong counties of Dongan and Xining complained about outsiders acquiring local residential registration and filling the two counties' quotas of *shengyuan*, to the detriment of Dongan and Xining natives. The leader of this protest identified the main offenders as migrants from the "five big counties of Guangzhou Prefecture" (*Guang shu zhi wu da xian* 广属之五大县). Based on gazetteer records of degree-winners in Dongan and Xining, he was surely referring to Nanhai, Panyu, Shunde, Dongguan, and Xinhui. In other words, proximity to the West River, rather than location on one side or the other, determined a community's access to wealth (Miles 2017: 92–93).

Nonetheless, examining the first half of the nineteenth century, we can begin to discern different niches in the larger Cantonese commercial economy, with the Three Counties tending to produce migrant merchants, if only petty merchants or even just aspiring merchants, and the Four Counties producing migrant laborers, including skilled laborers. There were of course laborers in both the Three Counties and the Four/Five Counties, but labor migrants from each region exhibited different patterns of geographic mobility. In both regions, commercialization and the proliferation of periodic markets spurred migration to urban places, including market towns and county seats. The larger urban destinations, however, were in the Three Counties: the provincial capital and global port, Guangzhou, and the industrial and commercial center, Foshan. Anecdotal evidence paints a picture of Four/Five Counties laborers and craftsmen working in the Three Counties, not the other way around. For example, Heshan County natives have a large presence on an 1829 stone inscription for a new temple in Foshan for silk-hat makers, while a document in the Guangdong provincial archives contains the testimony of two Heshan men hired to work at a tea store in Guangzhou's southern suburb in the 1850s ("Dingjian maoling hang miao beiji" 1829; FO 931/0971). Likewise, the Republican-era Enping gazetteer describes peasants leaving Enping as soon as the autumn harvest was in, heading to places such as Jiujiang to work as hired laborers, and only returning at the end of the year. The compilers add that this practice became rare after the middle of the Guangxu reign (1875–1908), from which fact we may deduce that it was a common practice in the decades leading up to the 1890s (*Enping xian zhi* 1934: 4:12b; Chen 1997: 537).[7]

The Three Counties produced their own migrant laborers, who gravitated toward Three Counties cities like Foshan and Guangzhou or sought their fortunes upriver in Guangxi, but not commonly in the Four Counties. Among the numerous Nanhai County men who appear in Qing records of Triad activities in Guangxi during the first two decades of the nineteenth century are peddlers and small-time entrepreneurs, but also one man who worked as a porter in Teng County, another who worked as a hired laborer in Shanglin County, and a third who was a hired laborer in Yishan County (*Tiandihui*: 279, 206, 330–31). Although one can certainly find examples of Three Counties laborers and Four Counties merchants, the relationship between place, migration, and economic niche leads Yong Chen to conclude that the Four/Five Counties "entered the region's commercial network as suppliers of labor" (Chen 1997: 537). These dynamics – Four/Five Counties migrant laborers gravitating toward urban settlements in the Three Counties, which in turn sent entrepreneurial migrants upriver – resonate with what the anthropologist Julie Chu (2010: 42, 243) finds in her study of a township outside Fuzhou in the 1990s: Fujianese locals seeking work in New York while migrants from western Chinese provinces like Sichuan moved in to occupy the lower echelons of work and housing in the township.

In upriver destinations, then, although the Three Counties-Four Counties distinction does not appear in written sources, Three Counties migrants had relatively more wealth and influence than their Four/Five Counties counterparts. Engraved lists of donors commemorating construction projects for Cantonese *huiguan* 会馆 (native-place associations) give a sense of the relative commercial importance of different emigrant communities in the delta. Selecting inscriptions and projects as evidence can be somewhat arbitrary, because merchants from particular places had more or less influence in specific locales upriver. Nonetheless, the three examples that I provide here convey a fair sense of the relative weight of county cohorts within this upriver Cantonese trade diaspora around the turn of the nineteenth century.

At the inter-provincial rice emporium of Rongxu, a 1788 inscription marks renovation of the Yuedong huiguan. In the list of patrons, among shippers docking at Rongxu, shop owners based there, and delta institutions with interests there, the important native places (in some cases indicated more generally

---

7 The historian Yong Chen cites this source without noting Jiujiang as a specific destination.

TABLE 1   Largest native-place cohorts on 1788 Yuedong huiguan inscription, Rongxu

County	Township	Total number of donors
Nanhai 21	Foshan 15, Jiujiang 7	43
Shunde 30	Longjiang 5	35
Xinhui 18	Jiangmen 9	27
Panyu 10	Yuangang 8	18
Heshan 3		3

only by county, and in others more specifically by sub-county township) are listed in table 1 ("Chongjian Yuedong huiguan timing beiji" 1788).

Further upstream on a West River tributary in southeastern Guangxi, Cantonese merchants in Beiliu County were based at a complex composed of the Yuedong huiguan and the General's Temple (Jiangjun miao 将军庙). Donors on a list partially reconstructed from two fragmented temple stelae, apparently belonging to a set and dated winter of 1785–86, are grouped by native county in Guangdong. Nanhai has the largest group of donors, at 170 or more, followed by Shunde at about half that number, and Xinhui with roughly two-thirds the size of the Shunde contingent. Heshan County constitutes a tiny but distinct group of two, possibly three, donors ("Juanzhu yinliang timing bei" 1785/86; "Ye benjie ji ge" N.d.).

Finally, the list of donors for the 1803 construction of the Yuedong huiguan in Hanoi reveals an even more pronounced dominance of two of the Three Counties, Nanhai and Shunde (see table 2) (*Corpus of Ancient Vietnamese Inscriptions*, no. 195).

The Cantonese merchants who appear on these inscriptions as donors moved along the same trajectories and traded in the same places, broadly speaking. Merchants from the two delta counties on the northeastern bank of the West River – Nanhai and Shunde – are consistently the most prominent. That said, Xinhui does not seem out of its league when compared to the Three Counties. None of the other Four Counties appears, however, and the fifth county, Heshan, despite its strategic placement on the West River, is markedly less important.

The divergent influence and reputations of delta communities on either side of the West River became solidified during the mid-nineteenth-century rebellions and the Qing reconquest of Guangxi. The largest rebellion was of course the Taiping Rebellion, which originated in the central prefecture of Xunzhou. Nonetheless, after the Taiping army moved into Hunan in 1852 and

TABLE 2 Largest native-place cohorts on 1803 Yuedong huiguan inscription, Hanoi

County	Number of donors
Shunde	74
Nanhai	68
Xinhui	14
Heshan	7
Panyu	2

on toward Jiangnan, the main conflict in the West River basin was between Qing loyalist forces and an evolving coalition of Triads, river pirates, and local bandits known in English-language scholarship as the Red Turbans (Wakeman 1966: 139–48). Unrest began with riverine piracy in the late 1840s, in the Pearl River delta culminated with the 1854–55 Red Turban occupation of Foshan and siege of Guangzhou, and continued with the rebel retreat upriver and establishment of the Da Cheng regime at Xunzhou, from 1855 to 1861.

The most notorious pirate, Triad, and Da Cheng leaders were identified with delta communities on the southwest side of the river, especially Gulao township in Heshan County. From the sparse and sometimes conflicting information that we have about them, they emanated from a geographically mobile underclass. A postwar Guangxi account describes the earliest pirate leaders, Zhang Zhao 张钊 and Tian Fang 田芳, as boat hands from Gulao, while a Guangxi literatus asserted that Zhang had led a band of mercenaries at Wuzhou during the Opium War. Liang Peiyou 梁培友, the Gulao pirate who emerged after the demise of Zhang Zhao and Tian Fang in 1853, was already active in Xunzhou Prefecture as a seller of protection to the riverine traffic that he would eventually turn to plundering (FO 931/1372; Su 1889: 3:3a, 9a; Miles 2021: 65–69, 80–81).

The two most prominent leaders of the 1854 Triad uprising were Gulao migrants working in Foshan. One leader, Li Wenmao 李文茂, was a professional actor who brought his theatrical martial skills to actual combat. Conflicting accounts about the background of the central figure in the uprising, Chen Kai 陈开, identify him as a gambler, a hired laborer, a boatman, or a cooper. The most detailed account explains that Chen was hired to work in a Foshan shop owned by a Gulao native ([Heshan Mai genealogy]: 1908; *Heshan xian zhi weicheng gao* 1944: 343). Triad leaders who spread the rebellion across the river to Heshan and Xinhui already had records of criminal activity along the river into Guangxi (e.g., FO 931/1474). After failing to capture Guangzhou and then losing control of Foshan, Chen Kai and Li Wenmao led their forces upriver into

Guangxi, where they joined with Liang Peiyou and at Xunzhou established the relatively stable, largely Cantonese-led Da Cheng regime. Their retreat into Guangxi fit into an existing pattern of riverine migration.

The leaders and most of the followers about whom we know were Cantonese from both sides of the West River. Nonetheless, in the postwar era, gentry-led militias and literati-authored accounts glossed over the ambiguous and fluid loyalties of the mid-century conflict, identifying "good" and "bad" people to conquering Qing forces and producing texts that celebrated Qing loyalists among the elites of Jiujiang, Foshan, and other communities in the Three Counties (*Jiujiang Rulin xiang zhi* 1883: 2:44b–45a, 40a–b, 42b; *Foshan Zhongyi xiang zhi* 1926: 350, 589). That Heshan men had comprised the upper crust of the rebel regime reinforced the notoriety of Gulao pirates.

Because I have found no reference to the Three Counties or Four/Five Counties in sources for upriver Cantonese migration, or in any sources produced before the 1850s, I am led to a tentative conclusion emphasizing historical contingency: These categories were created in the context of the mid-century rebellions and the upsurge in overseas migration from parts of the Four/Five Counties that had not played a prominent role in upriver migration before this period. If the Three Counties–Four/Five Counties dichotomy is a product of the mid-nineteenth century, however, a general trend of divergent economic niches and migration strategies between the two regions was already apparent before 1850. In this sense, research from the West River basin confirms Yong Chen's findings that, overseas, the economic relationship between the two regions in some ways reproduced that relationship within southern China.

5 Gendered Boundaries: Women as Anchors and Commodities

As with overseas Cantonese migration in the late nineteenth century, upriver migration was gendered: most migrants were male, as the patrilineal system encouraged Cantonese mothers, wives, and daughters to remain at home. In extant historical records, female travelers most often appear as relatives of male migrants, their tales of riverine travel interwoven with the lives of their husbands, fathers, or sons, for example, a Shunde County woman honored as a chaste widow in 1847 who had personally traveled far into Guangxi to retrieve her deceased husband's coffin (*Shunde xian zhi* 1853: 29:32a). Such stories only reinforced the ideal practice of male mobility anchored by female domesticity, for successful migrants with a primary wife in the delta and one or more concubines upriver. This ideal was encapsulated in a legend surrounding a prominent landmark that Cantonese migrants encountered on riverine journeys. At Lingyang Gorge, a boulder known as the Husband-Awaiting Stone (Wangfushi

望夫石) reminded travelers that they were leaving the familiar world of their delta homes. Nineteenth-century travelers were familiar with a legend pairing this landmark with another, far upriver near Nanning, this one known as the Man-Detaining Grotto (Liurendong 留人洞). The legend recounted a Cantonese merchant with a Cantonese primary wife in the delta and an exotic, magic- or poison-wielding native woman – as temporary lover or concubine – in Guangxi. Drawing on written accounts that were over a century old in his time, the early nineteenth-century Cantonese literatus Chen Tan 陈昙 explained the legend's rationale: "when easterners are 'sojourners' in the west, westerners grow fond of us, and so we marry uxorilocally and do not return…. The Husband-Awaiting Stone in the east is transformed from a yearning wife, whose spirit and soul have coagulated to form objects" (Chen 1829: 6:12a–b).[8] The fact that several European travelers in the late nineteenth century relate versions of the legend suggest that it was one familiar not only to literati but also to the merchants, boatmen, and translators who must have been their informants (Legge, Palmer, and Tsang 1866: 19; Colquhoun 1883: 34–35).

The various iterations of this legend play on the family ideals that supported male migration. In reality, some wives remarried after migrant husbands failed to return or to send remittances; however, in this legend a solidly loyal Cantonese primary wife in the delta anchors a family threatened by excessive male attention to temporary economic and sexual bonds with exotic women upriver. These dynamics will be familiar to scholars of gendered migration and family practices in southern China during the modern era (Szonyi 2005: 44; Shen 2012: 100). In this gendered imagination of migration, the male migrant alone crosses boundaries separating two immobile women. At its core, the legend describes a split family, an institution that allowed for geographically dispersed individuals to retain membership in families as unified ritual and economic entities with pooled resources. Male migration, whether upstream along the West River basin or overseas, was most often a family strategy (Chen 1997: 546).

To my knowledge, no extant letters document split families that supported upriver Cantonese migration in the nineteenth century.[9] But other sources provide glimpses into the role of Cantonese wives as delta anchors of split families. Legal records reporting home robberies include such details as the occupants at home during a crime. In a sample of 471 home invasions in

---

[8] The earliest Cantonese-inflected iteration of this legend is found in a late seventeenth-century text. See Qu 1997: 181–82.

[9] For letters to and from overseas migrants, see Shen 2012: 85–86; Benton, Zhang and Liu 2020. Occasional mention of letters to or from riverine migrants indicates that they existed. E.g., *Xingke tiben*, 1746–1/QL51.10.19; *Guoshi zupu* 1879: unpaginated; Jian 1903: 7:30a.

Nanhai County from the 1850s to the mid 1880s, in a third (32.91%) of these cases an adult male was away on business. If one adds cases involving a male away for other reasons (working as an official, working as a clerk, taking civil service examinations, serving in the military, unstated), nearly half of the cases involved an absent adult male. In the rare instances when these records indicate where these absent men pursued their careers, the destination is almost always in Guangxi.[10] One example involves Née Wu. With her son in Guangxi trading, she and her daughter-in-law were awoken one night in 1879 when robbers scaled the roof of their home and came down into the interior courtyard to plunder silver and jewelry (*Like tiben*, 02-01-03-11939-014/GX5.12.10).

The genealogy biography of one Cantonese woman extols her role as a financial manager. It describes a family of three brothers from a Nanhai township west of Guangzhou who operated as a single economic unit. The eldest brother in his prime had been a merchant in Guangxi, before retiring to his village in the 1850s. After his death in 1873, his wife, Née Ye (1813?–1912), managed the family enterprise at their rural base for more than forty years, coordinating with one brother-in-law conducting commerce in Wuzhou and another running a shop in Guangzhou (*Nanhai Dali Longfuxiang Zhongshi jiapu* 1921/1928: *shixi*:19a, *jiazhuanpu*: 1b–2a). Such cases suggest that the transition from wife to widow tended to be a smoother one when the new widow had gained experience as de facto head of household in a family with a migrant husband upriver.[11] For many Cantonese families, at least in communities with high rates of male migration, the idea and practice of the split family was not a new development created by overseas male migration in the modern era.

Although they were surely a small proportion of migrants along the West River basin, Cantonese women and upriver women were parts of a larger circulatory migration regime. In genealogical records, at least, concubines, as more purely commodified women, appear to have been more mobile than primary wives. That said, Cantonese concubines of the most prominent upriver Cantonese migrants and their descendants may have served as markers of

---

10 First Historical Archives of China, *Like tiben* 吏科題本, results from search terms "Xianfeng" and "Nanhai," results from search terms "Tongzhi" and "Nanhai," and the first 300 results from search terms "Guangxu," "Nanhai," and "*jie*" (robbery). I use routine memorials from the Board of Personnel; the main concern of these documents was to assess and possibly punish officials for failing to apprehend perpetrators of armed robbery within a statutory deadline (*shufang* 疏防). Accordingly, the memorials contain detailed information on the location of robberies, the time that the crime occurred, the number of victims, and the value of items lost. See Miles 2021: 200–01.

11 The sometimes thin line between wife of a migrant and widow is seen in a term that southern Fujianese used to describe the condition of migrants' wives: "preserving [chastity] as a widow of the living" (*shou sheng gua* 守生寡, or *shou huo gua* 守活寡). See Shen 2012: 81.

prestige back in the delta, where they were often buried (while husbands and primary Guangxi wives would be buried in Guangxi). Wu Cailue 吴才略, born in Gui County in 1753, was the son of a Nanhai County man who had been trading there since the 1740s. Cailue was raised by his Guangxi local mother in Guiping but apprenticed in a paternal uncle's business there. Making his own fortune in tax collection and the pawn trade, Cailue acquired multiple wives including two from Nanhai County. He married the youngest, Concubine Li 黎 (1786–1870), at his ancestral home in Nanhai in 1802 (*Guiping Wushi zhipu* 1887/88: 3:10b–11a and *nianpu*, 5:9a). This seems a reversal of the pattern whereby wealthy first-generation migrants in California purchased concubines from Guangdong (Sinn 2013: 239). Instead, a second-generation migrant, raised by one upriver woman and married to another, maintained a concubine back in his ancestral place. Lin Tingxuan 林廷宣 (1814–1873), a member of a Cantonese family that built its fortune in the rice and pawn trade at Gui County, married a Gui County woman, but his concubine Cao 曹 (1849–1923) was from Foshan, where she was eventually buried (*Lin Guangyuan tang zupu* 1930: 47a–b). Other Cantonese concubines were moved upriver, for example a Foshan concubine, married at age eighteen, who committed suicide at Wuzhou when that city fell to rebels in 1857 (*Cangwu xian zhi* 1874: 16:44b).

In genealogies of delta lineages, the more common direction in which concubines moved was downriver, as Cantonese merchants brought or sent back women acquired upriver. Examples of delta men with Guangxi concubines with no other evidence of upriver activity raises the possibility of a long-distance market in concubines. For example, a Nanhai County man who lived from 1798 to 1853 married as primary wives (in turn, after the preceding primary wife died) two women from Zhejiang's Shaoxing Prefecture, which had a significant presence in the salt and administrative sectors of the urban Guangzhou economy (Miles 2006: 29–34). One of this man's concubines (1803–1873) was a native of Lingui County, at Guilin (*Nanhai Huangshi zupu* 1899: 2:2a–3a). A native of Foshan, Huo Wensheng 霍文胜 (1812–1886), had a primary wife Pan 潘 (1817–1839) from Nanhai and, from Guangxi, a concubine Mo 莫 (1819–1886) (*Shitou Huoshi zupu* 1902: 9:47b). When people like Huo Wensheng settled Guangxi concubines, not all of whom we would likely classify as Han Chinese, in their delta homes, the experience of these women surely in some ways resonated with that of Mexican women whom migrant men from Jiujiang brought back following anti-Chinese ethnic violence in the early 1930s and discovered that they were not their husbands' primary wives (Schiavone Camacho 2012: 105, 108, 111). The Guangxi women would not have been stateless, unlike the Mexican women who had lost citizenship after marrying their Chinese husbands. Nonetheless, it is easy to imagine that they were forced to adapt to new circumstances of reduced status, vis-à-vis their husbands' Cantonese primary wives, in an unfamiliar environment. Conversely, we might conclude that when Cantonese families encountered Mexican wives in the early 1930s, the particular origins of these women would have been novel, but the general circumstances of successful male migrants bringing back secondary wives from migration destinations were familiar. Male migration, split families, and intermarriage between male migrants and female residents in migration destinations are phenomena that will sound familiar to many readers, whether they work on China or the Chinese overseas (Cohen 1976: 59–64; Hsu 2000: 109–11; Kuhn 2008: 14–15, 25–26).

6 Conclusion: Upriver and Overseas

By the outset of the nineteenth century, Cantonese families in communities along the West River below Lingyang Gorge already had deep experience of long-distance migration as a socioeconomic strategy. Places like Jiujiang, Longjiang, and Gulao, with easy access to riverine trade, were relatively prosperous communities within southeastern China. Aside from those involved in the warfare of the 1850s, most migrants from these communities, whether heading upriver or, later, overseas, do not seem to have been "pushed" by economic deprivation or political disruption. Rather, they appear as enterprising migrants building on established networks of trade and cultures of migration. This access to a long, navigable, and commercially important river set these communities apart from otherwise similar *qiaoxiang* elsewhere in southeastern China. For residents of places like Jiujiang, unlike their counterparts in interior parts of the Four Counties, overseas migration after 1850 was not the first viable alternative to remaining immobile.

Cantonese migrants who ventured upriver during the nineteenth century operated in a different environment from that which their peers encountered overseas. Migrant elites in Guangxi enjoyed a generally mutually beneficial relationship with the Qing state (and arguably the Nguyen regime in Vietnam). Through commercial taxes they supported Qing administration in Guangxi. Though subtly subverting the state's goals of fostering an indigenous degree-holding gentry on the southwestern frontier, migrant elites' enthusiasm for civil-service examination degrees bolstered the legitimacy of imperial institutions. Even the founders of the rival Da Cheng regime embraced (ultimately fleeting) opportunities for state building in Guangxi that were not available elsewhere.

At the same time, from the perspective of these communities along the West River, the ways in which migrants and their families readily adapted to new opportunities overseas confirm the doubts that McKeown raised about political boundaries as the most important analytical divide in the study of migration. Nineteenth-century Cantonese migrants crossed provincial and imperial borders (whether upriver or overseas) with relative ease, responding to shifting state regulations. In an area where writers conceived of the river as a sea, choosing between upriver and overseas destinations was not necessarily the most fundamental factor in the experience of potential migrants. Other kinds of boundaries mattered more. One's gender was of primary importance, expanding or limiting options for upriver or overseas migration. Class and regional boundaries led to divergent experiences of migration. The successful entrepreneurs from Jiujiang who married "concubines" in Guangxi, Vietnam, and Mexico at either end of the nineteenth century shared more with each other than they did with migrant laborers from elsewhere in the delta. Finally, taking the perspective of migrants and their families may lead us to revisit another analytical boundary, the chronological divide of the mid-nineteenth century. Certainly, new power relations, new modes of transportation, and new means of production and economic organization led to an unprecedented expansion of migration to a far greater range of overseas destinations; however, with a vast experience of long-distance migration, Cantonese migrants from the communities described in this essay who left on these journeys were not unprepared for the challenge.

References

Primary Sources[12]

Cangwu xian zhi 苍梧县志 (Cangwu County Gazetteer). 1874. Held at Harvard-Yenching Library.

Chen Tan 陈昙. *Kuangzhai zaji* 邝斋杂记 (Miscellaneous Notes from the Kuang Studio). 1829. Held at Sun Yat-sen Library of Guangdong Province.

"Chongjian Yuedong huiguan timing beiji" 重建粤东会馆碑记 (Stele Record of the Renovation of the Yuedong Huiguan). 1788. Yuedong huiguan, Longxu (Rongxu), Wuzhou, Guangxi.

Chongshan xian zhi 崇善县志 (Chongshan County Gazetteer). 1937. In *Zhongguo fangzhi congshu, Huanan difang*, volume 203. 1975. Taibei: Chengwen chubanshe.

Colquhoun, Archibald R. 1883. *Across Chrysé: Being the Narrative of a Journey of Exploration through the South China Border Lands from Canton to Mandalay*. London: Sampson, Low, Marston, Searle, and Rivington.

---

12   Titles of most primary sources that I use in this article are written in Traditional Chinese characters. I have converted them to Simplified Chinese to match the conventions of this journal.

Corpus of Ancient Vietnamese Inscriptions. 2005. Hanoi: Vien Nghien Cu Nom. Volume 1.

"Dingjian maoling hang miao beiji" 鼎建帽绫行庙碑记 (Stele Record of the Establishment of the Silk-hat Guild's Temple). 1829. Zumiao, Foshan, Guangdong.

Enping xian zhi 恩平县志 (Enping County Gazetteer). 1934. In *Zhongguo difangzhi jicheng, Guangdong fu xian zhi ji*, volume 35. 2003. Shanghai: Shanghai shudian.

FO (Foreign Office): Kwangtung Provincial Archives. Held at the National Archives, Kew, London, Great Britain.

Foshan Zhongyi xiang zhi 佛山忠义乡志 (Foshan Zhongyi Township Gazetteer). 1926. In *Zhongguo difangzhi jicheng, Xiangzhen zhi zhuanji*, volume 30. 1992. Shanghai: Shanghai shudian.

Gesheng xuanba tongnian mingjing tongpu: Tongzhi guiyou ke 各省选拔同年明经通谱:同治癸酉科 (Record of Special Tribute Students Selected in 1873). Held at Harvard-Yenching Library.

Guan Shudetang jiapu 关树德堂家谱 (Guan Shude Hall Genealogy). 1897. Held at Sun Yat-sen Library of Guangdong Province.

Guangzhou fuzhi 广州府志 (Guangzhou Prefecture Gazetteer). 1879. In *Zhongguo fangzhi ku*. 2009. Beijing: Beijing Airusheng shuzihua jishu yanjiu zhongxin.

Guiping Wushi zhipu 桂平吴氏支谱 (Branch Genealogy of the Wu Surname of Guiping). 1887/88. Held at Library of Guangxi Zhuang Autonomous Region.

Guoshi zupu 郭氏族谱 ([Guangzhou] Guo Lineage Genealogy). 1879. Held at Sun Yat-sen Library of Guangdong Province.

[Heshan Mai 麦 Genealogy]. 1908. Untitled manuscript. Held at Sun Yat-sen Library of Guangdong Province.

Heshan xian zhi 鹤山县志 (Heshan County Gazetteer). 1754. In *Zhongguo difangzhi jicheng, Guangdong fu xian zhi ji*, volume 33. 2003. Shanghai: Shanghai shudian.

Heshan xian zhi weicheng gao 鹤山县志未成稿 (Uncompleted manuscript of the Heshan County Gazetteer). 1944. In *Guangdong shengli Zhongshan tushuguan cang xijian fangzhi congkan*, volume 27. 2011. Beijing: Guojia tushuguan chubanshe.

Jian Chaoliang 简朝亮. 1903. *Dushutang ji* 读书堂集 (Collected Writings from the Hall of Study). 1903. Held at the Joseph Regenstein Library, University of Chicago.

Jiujiang Rulin xiang zhi 九江儒林乡志 (Jiujiang Rulin Township Gazetteer). 1883. In *Zhongguo difangzhi jicheng, Xiangzhen zhi zhuanji*, volume 31. 1992. Shanghai: Shanghai shudian.

"Juanzhu yinliang timing bei" 捐助银两题名碑 (Stele list of Donors and Their Contributions in Silver Taels). 1785/86. Jingsulou, Beiliu, Guangxi.

Julu xianchengtang chongxiu jiapu 钜鹿显承堂重修家谱 (New edition of the Julu Xiancheng Hall Genealogy [Shatou, Nanhai Mo Lineage]). Compiled 1869, reprinted 1873. Held at Sun Yat-sen Library of Guangdong Province.

Laibin xian zhi 来宾县志 (Laibin County Gazetteer). 1936. In *Zhongguo fangzhi congshu, Huanan difang*, volumeь201. 1975. Taibei: Chengwen chubanshe.

Legge, James, Palmer, John Linton and Kwei-hwan Tsang. 1866. *Three Weeks on the West River of Canton*. Hong Kong: De Souza & Co.

Like tiben 吏科题本 (Board of Personnel Routine Memorials). Held at First Historical Archives of China, Beijing.

Lin Guangyuan tang zupu 林光远堂族谱 (Lin Guangyuan Hall Genealogy). 1930. Held at Library of Guangxi Zhuang Autonomous Region.

Mingshi 明史 (Ming History). 2003. Beijing: Zhonghua shuju.

Nanhai Dali Longfuxiang Zhongshi jiapu 南海大沥龙腹乡钟氏家谱 (Longfu Village, Dali, Nanhai Zhong Family Genealogy). 1921/1928. Held at Sun Yat-sen Library of Guangdong Province.

Nanhai Huangshi zupu 南海黄氏族谱 (Nanhai Huang Lineage Genealogy). 1899. Held at Sun Yat-sen Library of Guangdong Province.

Nanyang shipu 南阳世谱 ([Poshan, Gulao, Heshan Deng lineage] Nanyang Genealogy). Compiled 1850, transcribed 1874. In FamilySearch Chinese Genealogies collection.

Qu Dajun 屈大均. 1997. *Guangdong xinyu* 广东新语 (New Comments on Guangdong). Beijing: Zhonghua shuju.

Shitou Huoshi zupu 石头霍氏族谱 ([Nanhai] Shitou Huang Lineage Genealogy). 1902. Held at Sun Yat-sen Library of Guangdong Province.

Shixi lu 世系录 ([Nanhai Jiujiang Guan family] Genealogical Records). 1934, appended 1984. Privately held by Cheuk Kwan.

Shunde Longjiang xiang zhi 顺德龙江乡志 (Gazetteer of Longjiang Township, Shunde). 1926. In *Zhongguo fangzhi congshu, Huanan difang*, volume 51. 1967. Taibei: Chengwen chubanshe.

Shunde xian zhi 顺德县志 (Shunde County Gazetteer) 1674. In *Zhongguo difangzhi jicheng, Guangdong fu xian zhi ji*, volume 31. 2003. Shanghai: Shanghai shudian.

Shunde xian zhi 顺德县志 (Shunde County Gazetteer) 1853. In *Zhongguo fangzhi congshu, Huanan difang*, volume 4. 1966. Taibei: Chengwen chubanshe.

Su Fengwen 苏凤文. 1889. *Gufei zonglu* 股匪总录 (General Record of Ganged Bandits). Hathi Trust Digital Library.

Tiandihui 天地会 (Heaven and Earth Society). 1988. Edited by Zhongguo renmin daxue Qingshi yanjiusuo 中国人民大学清史研究所 and Zhongguo diyi lishi dang'anguan 中国第一历史档案馆. Beijing: Zhongguo renmin chubanshe. Volume 7.

Xie Lansheng 谢兰生. 2014. *Changxingxingzhai riji* 常惺惺斋日记 (Diary from the Studio of Constant Awareness). Transcribed and punctuated by Li Ruoqing 李若晴. Guangzhou: Guangdong renmin chubanshe.

Xie Lansheng 谢兰生. 2015. *Changxingxingzhai riji* 常惺惺斋日记 (Diary from the Studio of Constant Awareness). Original manuscript. Reprinted in *Guangzhou dadian*, volume 192. Guangzhou: Guangzhou chubanshe.

Xingke tiben 刑科題本 (Board of Punishments Routine Memorials). Held at First Historical Archives of China, Beijing.

"Ye benjie ji ge" 业本街暨各 (Enterprises on this Street and Each). No date. Jingsulou, Beiliu, Guangxi.

Zhao, Jiansheng 招健升. 1815. *Ziyitang cao* 自怡堂草 (Manuscripts from the Hall of Self Content). Held at Sun Yat-sen Library of Guangdong Province.

Zhao, Jiansheng 招健升. No date. *Ziyitang xiaocao xuji* 自怡堂小草续集 (Continuation of *Little Manuscripts from the Hall of Self Content*). Held at Sun Yat-sen Library of Guangdong Province.

Zhupi zouzhe 硃批奏折 (Imperially Rescripted Palace Memorials). Held at First Historical Archives of China, Beijing.

Other Sources

Benton, Gregor, Zhang, Huimei and Hong Liu ed. 2020. *Chinese Migrants Write Home: A Dual-Language Anthology of Twentieth-Century Family Letters*. New Jersey: World Scientific.

Chen, Yong. 1997. "The Internal Origins of Chinese Emigration to California Reconsidered." *Western Historical Quarterly*, 28: 520–46.

Chia, Lucille. 2006. "The Butcher, the Baker, and the Carpenter: Chinese Sojourners in the Spanish Philippines and Their Impact on South Fujian (Sixteenth-Eighteenth Centuries)." *Journal of the Economic and Social History of the Orient* 49(4): 509–34.

Chu, Julie Y. 2010. *Cosmologies of Credit: Transnational Mobility and the Politics of Destination in China*. Durham: Duke University Press.

Cohen, Myron L. 1976. *House United, House Divided: The Chinese Family in Taiwan*. New York: Columbia University Press.

Du, Yongtao. 2015. *The Order of Places: Translocal Practices of the Huizhou Merchants in Late Imperial China*. Leiden: Brill.

Elman, Benjamin A. 2000. *A Cultural History of Civil Examinations in Late Imperial China*. Berkeley: University of California Press.

Faure, David. 2007. *Emperor and Ancestor: State and Lineage in South China*. Stanford: Stanford University Press.

Giersch, C. Patterson. 2006. *Asian Borderlands: The Transformation of Qing China's Yunnan Frontier*. Cambridge: Harvard University Press.

Guo, Qitao. 2022. *Huizhou: Local Identity and Mercantile Lineage Culture in Ming China*. Oakland: University of California Press.

Hsu, Madeline Y. 2000. *Dreaming of Gold, Dreaming of Home: Transnationalism and Migration between the United States and South China, 1882–1943*. Stanford: Stanford University Press.

Kuhn, Philip A. 2008. *Chinese Among Others: Emigration in Modern Times*. Lanham: Rowman & Littlefield Publishers, Inc.

Kwan, Stanley S.K., with Nicole Kwan. 2009. *The Dragon and the Crown: Hong Kong Memoirs*. Hong Kong: Hong Kong University Press.

Luo, Yixing 罗一星. 1988. "Shilun Qingdai qianqi Lingnan shichang zhongxindi de fenbu tedian" 试论清代前期岭南市场中心地的分布特点 (A Tentative Discussion of the Characteristic Distribution of Market Centers in Lingnan during the Early Qing). *Guangzhou yanjiu* 9: 48–53.

Macauley, Melissa. 2021. *Distant Shores: Colonial Encounters on China's Maritime Frontier*. Princeton: Princeton University Press.

Mar, Lisa Rose. 2010. *Brokering Belonging: Chinese in Canada's Exclusion Era, 1885–1945*. New York: Oxford University Press.

Marks, Robert B. 1998. *Tigers, Rice, Silk, and Silt: Environment and Economy in Late Imperial South China*. New York: Cambridge University Press.

McKeown, Adam. 2001. *Chinese Migrant Networks and Cultural Change: Peru, Chicago, Hawaii, 1900–1936*. Chicago: The University of Chicago Press.

Miles, Steven B. 2006. *Sea of Learning: Mobility and Identity in Nineteenth-Century Guangzhou*. Cambridge, MA: Harvard University Asia Center, 2006.

Miles, Steven B. 2017. *Upriver Journeys: Diaspora and Empire in Southern China, 1570–1850*. Cambridge, MA: Harvard University Asia Center.

Miles, Steven B. 2021. *Opportunity in Crisis: Cantonese Migrants and the State in Late Qing China*. Cambridge, MA: Harvard University Asia Center.

Ong, Soon Keong. 2021. *Coming Home to a Foreign Country: Xiamen and Returned Overseas Chinese, 1843–1938*. Ithaca: Cornell East Asia Series, Cornell University Press.

Pieke, Frank N., Pál Nyíri, Mette Thunø, and Antonella Ceccagno. 2004. *Transnational Chinese: Fujianese Migrants in Europe*. Stanford: Stanford University Press.

Romero, Robert Chao. 2010. *The Chinese in Mexico 1882–1940*. Tucson: The University of Arizona Press.

Rowe, William T. 1984. *Hankow: Commerce and Society in a Chinese City, 1796–1889*. Stanford: Stanford University Press.

Schiavone Camacho, Julia María. 2012. *Chinese Mexicans: Transpacific Migration and the Search for a Homeland, 1910–1960*. Chapel Hill: The University of North Carolina Press.

Schlesinger, Jonathan. 2017. *A World Trimmed with Fur: Wild Things, Pristine Places, and the Natural Fringes of Qing Rule*. Stanford: Stanford University Press.

Shen, Huifen. 2012. *China's Left-Behind Wives: Families of Migrants from Fujian to Southeast Asia, 1930s–1950s*. Honolulu: University of Hawai'i Press.

Sinn, Elizabeth. 2013. *Pacific Crossing: California Gold, Chinese Migration, and the Making of Hong Kong*. Hong Kong: Hong Kong University Press.

Szonyi, Michael. 2005. "Mothers, Sons and Lovers: Fidelity and Frugality in the Overseas Chinese Divided Family before 1949." *Journal of Chinese Overseas* 1(1): 43–64.

Szonyi, Michael. 2017. *The Art of Being Governed: Everyday Politics in Late Imperial China*. Princeton: Princeton University Press.

Wakeman, Frederic, Jr. 1966. *Strangers at the Gate: Social Disorder in South China, 1839–1861*. Berkeley: University of California Press.

Williams, Michael. 2018. *Returning Home with Glory: Chinese Villagers around the Pacific, 1849 to 1949*. Hong Kong: Hong Kong University Press.

Appendix

TABLE 3 Provincial degree-winners produced by counties in Guangzhou Prefecture in the Guangdong provincial examinations and the Guangxi provincial examinations, 3 sample years[a]

	1738		1798		1861 (1858)	
	Guangdong	Guangxi	Guangdong	Guangxi	Guangdong	Guangxi
Nanhai	4		9	1	25	3
Panyu	3		7		19	
Shunde	12	3	10		17	
Dongguan	2	1	2		6	
Zengcheng			1			
Longmen					1	
Xin'an	1				1	
Xinning					2	
Xiangshan	3		1		7	
Xinhui	3	1	4		13	
Sanshui	1				3	
Qingyuan					3	
Huaxian	1				3	

a *Guangzhou fuzhi* 1879: 43:23a–24a, 45:1a–2a, 46:17a–19b. The 1861 examination was intended to supplement the cancelled examination in 1858, due to warfare, and had an expanded quota.

Paradox of Superdiversity: Contesting Racism and "Chinese Privilege" in Singapore

超级多样性的悖论:解构新加坡的种族主义与 "华人优势"

Hong Liu (刘宏)[1] | ORCID: 0000-0003-3328-8429
Tan Lark Sye Chair Professor of Public Policy and Global Affairs,
School of Social Sciences, Nanyang Technological University, Singapore
LiuHong@ntu.edu.sg

Lingli Huang (黄伶俐)[2] | ORCID: 0000-0001-7965-1663
Affiliated fellow, Nanyang Centre for Public Administration,
Nanyang Technological University, Singapore
huanglingli@ntu.edu.sg

Abstract

Large-scale immigration has turned Singapore into a highly diverse setting, where migrants and local-born Singaporeans encounter one another on a daily basis. In the past decade, the city-state has seen rising debates and contestations over racism, despite being known as a racially harmonious society. This article situates the public discourse on racism and "Chinese privilege" in the context of superdiversity and examines its wider implications for theorization and policy. Approaching the paradox of superdiversity from a political economy perspective, we investigate how three sets of factors have contributed to the rising public discourse on racism not only between migrants and locals but also among local-born Singaporeans: i) immigration regime and the strategy toward a knowledge economy, ii) new patterns of electoral politics, and iii) the impacts of China's growing influences in Southeast Asia. This article offers

---

1 Hong Liu is Tan Lark Sye Chair Professor (Public Policy and Global Affairs) at School of Social Sciences, Nanyang Technological University, Singapore.
2 Dr Lingli Huang (Corresponding author) is an affiliated fellow at the Nanyang Centre for Public Administration, Nanyang Technological University, Singapore.

© HONG LIU AND LINGLI HUANG, 2022 | DOI:10.1163/17932548-12341468
This is an open access article distributed under the terms of the CC BY 4.0 license.

---

* This chapter was originally published as: Liu, H. and Huang, L. (2022). Paradox of Superdiversity: Contesting Racism and "Chinese Privilege" in Singapore. *Journal of Chinese Overseas*, 18(2), 287–311. Reprinted with kind permission from Brill.

This is an Open Access chapter published by World Scientific Publishing Company. It is distributed under the terms of the Creative Commons Attribution-NonCommercial-NoDerivatives 4.0 (CC BY-NC-ND) License which permits use, distribution and reproduction, provided that the original work is properly cited, the use is non-commercial and no modifications or adaptations are made.

two broader theoretical implications for the scholarship on migration and race relations in a context of superdiversity. First, the paradoxical co-existence of superdiversity and racism obtains not only between migrants and natives, as many studies have shown, but also between native races in the host society. Second, diversifications and new forms of contestations and racism are not only a result of the immigration regime and domestic politics of the host country, but are also shaped by the international political economy, as evidenced by the way in which the rise of China has intensified contestations on race relations in Singapore.

Keywords

superdiversity – racism – Chinese privilege – political economy – migration – Singapore

摘要

大规模移民使得新加坡成为了一个移民与本地居民互动频繁、人口构成高度多样性的国家。虽然新加坡一直以种族和谐社会而闻名，但是近十年来社会对种族问题的公共辩论越来越多。本文将新加坡关于种族主义与"华人优势"的公共讨论放在"超级多样性"这一理论架构下来研究。我们将从政治经济学的角度研究超级多样性的悖论现象，并分析三个方面的因素如何导致移民和本地居民之间以及本地居民内部之间种族歧视相关的公共讨论的增加。这三个因素包括新加坡的移民制度与建立知识型经济的国家战略，选举政治的新模式以及中国崛起的影响。

关键词

超级多样性 – 种族主义 – 华人优势 – 政治经济学 – 移民 – 新加坡

1 Introduction

Singapore is a multiracial society, where Chinese, Malays, Indians, and others have lived largely in peace since the nation's independence in 1965. The ruling party, the People's Action Party (PAP), promotes multiculturalism and multiracialism as key national values, while designing an array of policies to foster racial integration and harmony (Chua 2017). For example, the Ethnic Integration Policy proportionally mixes the four main races in public housing in order to prevent geographical segregation by race. The Singapore government launched the Racial Harmony Day in 1997 to celebrate a harmonious society. Paradoxically, in a social and political environment where racial harmony assumes paramount importance, the discussions on race, particularly racial grievances and tensions, were considered "sensitive issues" that ought not be publicly debated (Chua 2003; Goh 2013).

Over the past decade or so, however, public debates and contestations over race in Singapore have been rising. The contestations started with the backlash against immigration since the late 2000s, with some native Singaporeans expressing racist attitudes toward migrants. This was followed by the growing public debates on race relations among the locals. Alternative views have emerged to counter the official narrative by highlighting "un-harmonious" race relations, such as racial inequalities and racism (Ang and Chew 2021; Holman and Arunachalam 2015). The recent debate on "Chinese privilege" is a case in point. The debate centers around the question whether the Chinese, the majority race, enjoy social and institutionalized power and privilege over minorities (Goh and Chong 2020; Zainal and Abdullah 2021).

This essay introduces the term *paradox of superdiversity* to capture the puzzling rise of public discourse over racism in Singapore. The concept of superdiversity not only describes increasing diversities in terms of ethnicity and other parameters but also provides a useful lens through which to examine "power, politics and policy" (Meissner and Vertovec 2015). We will demonstrate how the new political economy, both as a cause *and* effect of diversifications, has interacted with multidimensional race relations in Singapore, fueling debates and contestations over racism and Chinese privilege. We focus on three sets of political economic factors: i) the strategy to build a knowledge-intensive economy, which requires the recruitment of foreign professionals and the constant skill-upgrading of the local labor force; ii) new patterns of electoral politics in the context of an immigration backlash; iii) the rise of China and its impacts for Singapore. These factors, furthermore, are either drivers or consequences of diversifications.

Most studies on superdiversity focus on the experiences in the West where diverse immigrant groups from the global South have transformed the White-dominant societies (Foner, Duyvendak and Kasinitz 2019). Asia has witnessed the fastest growth in international migration in the past two decades (McAuliffe, Bauloz, Nguyen and Qu 2019). Asian metropolitan centers such as Singapore have received large numbers of migrants, who mainly come from within Asia. Race relations in these cities are different from those in Western societies, where relations between Whites and non-Whites constitute the focus of research (Raghuram 2022). While a few scholars have employed the term of superdiversity to describe the changes in Singapore (Goh 2019; Vertovec 2015), there is a need to further investigate how diversifications interact with race relations, particularly in the context of the rising public discourse on racism.

Our inquiry focuses not only on national politics but also extends the scope of research to the international political economy, which has been largely neglected in the literature on migration.

Data for this study are drawn from government documents, local newspapers, online postings, and local survey reports. Government documents include policy compilations, ministers' speeches, and parliamentary debate records. We selected three major local newspapers that represent three main languages (English, Chinese, and Malay) in Singapore. We also employ materials from online blogs and discussion forums to understand opinions in cyber space, but these data are triangulated with other sources to ensure accuracy. These data have been supplemented by the authors' participatory observations by way of taking part in various social and cultural functions involving the multi-ethnic population in the country.

The remainder of this article is organized as follows. Section Two reviews the literature on the impacts of super-diversification on racism and race relations. Section Three documents how Singapore has been transformed into a society of superdiversity, followed by an overview of the public discourse on racism and "Chinese privilege." Section Four examines how the nation's new political economy has interacted with diversifications. Section Five analyses the new dynamics of state-society relations and its effects on the public discourse on racism. The article concludes with theoretical and policy implications.

2   Superdiversity and Racism: Paradoxical Co-existence

Since the 1990s increasingly complex patterns of global migration flows and settlement have emerged. The concept of superdiversity describes the heterogeneity of urban societies resulting from multidimensional diversifications due to immigration. These dimensions include, but are not limited to, country of origin, legal status, gender, age, religion, language, human capital, and diverse local responses (Meissner and Vertovec 2015; Vertovec 2007; 2019).

Vertovec, who coined the concept, does not suggest that superdiversity would reduce racism or inequality. He argues instead that superdiversity would lead to new patterns of inequality and prejudice including racism. However, he also notes that the "presence and everyday interaction of people from the world" may give rise to new cosmopolitan orientations and attitudes, which possibly yield positive benefits for intergroup relations (Vertovec 2007: 1045–6). The subsequent studies have found both positive and negative effects of superdiversity on race relations.

Examining the lived experience of localized social relationships in London, Wessendorf (2014) argues that the experience of diversity has become so ordinary that there is no direct hostility or conflict between different racial and ethnic groups, at least in public and semi-public places. Tran (2019) finds that young people who grow up in more diverse communities, such as in New York City, are more comfortable with diversity when they transition into adulthood. Padilla, Azevedo and Olmos-Alcaraz (2015: 632) demonstrate that people could get along well in a super-diverse context, where "heterogeneity is common and experienced on a daily basis, such that 'difference/otherness' is internalized and may be transformed into a quotidian positive feature." Other studies find that the presence of superdiversity does not necessarily mitigate intergroup tensions and would even give rise to new forms of racism. Mepschen (2019) shows that in the Netherlands diversifications give rise to a common notion that Dutch culture is threatened by outsiders. Research also reveals that superdiversity does not significantly alter the dominance of the mainstream groups in the host society and that racial inequalities and power imbalances are often reproduced in super-diverse settings (Alba and Duyvendak, 2019; Foner et al. 2019).

Back and Sinha (2016) highlight the paradoxical co-existence of racism and multi-culture. On the one hand, in the super-diverse setting young migrants are able to employ convivial tools to make "a liveable home in the micro-public space." On the other, superdiversity does not do away with existing racism and even gives rise to new forms of racism. Thus, migrants must find a way to navigate "barriers and limits of racism" in the host society (2016: 530).

We introduce the theme of *paradox of superdiversity* to refer to the persistence of tense race relations and the emergence of new forms of racism in a super-diverse society. It is a paradox for at least two reasons. First, superdiversity literally suggests a positive development toward the co-existence of diverse racial and ethnic groups in a society, but the process of diversification is often accompanied by heightened inter-racial or inter-ethnic tensions and conflicts. Second, the quotidian and commonplace existence of difference and diversity in society, which increases the awareness and acceptance of others, stands in parallel with racial and group discriminations.

In the case of Singapore, decades of immigration and racial mixes in marriages and living space have produced super-diverse public spaces in the city-state (Vertovec 2015; Ye 2017). But the city-state has witnessed a strong backlash against immigration in the past two decades (Ang 2018; Gomes 2014; Liu 2014; Ortiga 2015; Yeoh and Lam 2016; Zhan and Zhou 2020). With growing anti-migrant sentiment and xenophobia, migrants are racialized and targeted in online forums, media reports, and daily interactions. This even takes place between co-ethnics, as local-born Chinese and Indians discriminate against co-ethnic migrants (Ho and Kathiravelu 2022; Liu 2014; Ortiga 2015).

The case of Singapore offers a unique opportunity to examine new forms of racism. The focus of the literature has so far been mainly on the relations between natives and migrants. The rising contestations over racism among Singapore's native races thus presents a puzzle and warrants the investigation of whether and how this is a result of diversifications. Furthermore, Singapore is the only nation-state outside China with a Chinese majority. This provides a distinct angle from which to examine the impact of an ascending China on race relations in a receiving country, filling a crucial gap in the scholarship of superdiversity and race relations.

3 Contestations over Racism and Chinese Privilege

3.1 *Diversifications of the Host Society*

Singapore's population totaled 5.7 million in 2020, including 3.5 million citizens and 0.5 million permanent residents (PRs) and 1.7 million temporary migrants. The foreign-born population, including naturalized citizens, PRs and temporary migrants, accounted for 46 percent, which was among the highest in the world (DOS 2021a; United Nations 2019). Migrants in the city-state can be classified into two broad categories: foreign talent and foreign workers. Foreign talent refers to highly skilled professionals or middle-skilled workers, while foreign workers are low-wage transient workers who work in the sectors such as domestic service, construction, and marine shipyard. Within each category, migrants are differentiated and stratified based on salary, skill level, and occupation (Yang, Yang and Zhan 2017; Yeoh and Lam, 2016).

Migrants in Singapore come from a diverse range of source countries, mostly within Asia, with Malaysia, China, Indonesia, the Philippines, Bangladesh, India, Japan, and South Korea among the largest sources (United Nations 2019). The city-state intends to maintain the racial composition of the resident population (citizens and PRs), with 74 percent Chinese, 13 percent Malays, 9 percent Indians, and 3 percent other races. Thus, permanent residents and naturalized citizens are admitted roughly in line with this composition. However, within each race, migrants come from different countries and have diverse cultural orientations, and they may not identify themselves as the same race/group. For example, Chinese migrants come from Malaysia, mainland China, Hong Kong, Taiwan, and other countries or places. Malays come from Malaysia and Indonesia while Indians originate mainly in India, though they are also from overseas Indian diasporas, Pakistan, and Bangladesh.

Inter-racial and transnational marriages are another driving force of diversification. Interracial marriages refer to those in which spouses belong to different categories of race in terms of official classification. Transnational marriage means that a Singaporean citizen marries a person of another nationality. Currently, one in five marriages in Singapore is between two different races and nearly two in five marriages involve a foreign spouse (Strategy Group 2020; Yeoh, Chee, Anant and Lam 2021). These ratios are among the highest in the world. Interracial and transnational marriages have increased the proportion of mixed races, which fall outside the official CMIO categorization, i.e., Chinese, Malay, Indian and Others (Chua 2021; Rocha and Yeoh 2021).

3.2 Contestations over Racism in Singapore

Attaching paramount importance to racial harmony, the Singapore state discourages public discussions of racism and racist behavior as it believes that this would harm race relations. There were several racial incidents in the 1990s and 2000s, but the authority quickly intervened and punished the perpetrators to prevent prolonged public discussions. The state also uses the Sedition Act to penalize those whose actions "promote feelings of ill-will and hostility between different races or classes" (Neo 2011).

Nevertheless, the issues of race and racism were taken to the center of the public discourse in the course of the past decade, as evidenced by the frequency of racism as a topic in local newspaper articles and reports. We have searched for articles discussing racism in Singapore in three major local newspapers in three languages: English (*The Straits Times, ST*), Chinese (*Lianhe Zaobao*) and Malay (*Berita Harian* and *Berita Minggu*).[3] The results show an upward trend, particularly since 2015. The rising trend is the most remarkable in the *ST*, but it is also notable in the Chinese and Malay newspapers (Figure 1). In the *ST*, the number of articles discussing racism in Singapore increased from fewer than 30 before 2011 to 54 in 2012, and further to 85 in 2017 and 111 in 2019. In 2020 and 2021, the discussion of racism experienced an even more rapid growth, with the article count reaching 264 in the first 10 months of 2021 (Figure 1).

The content analysis of newspaper articles reveals that the discourse of racism in the early 2010s was partly driven by an immigration backlash. The anti-migrant and xenophobic sentiments intensified after the 2008 financial crisis as migrants, particularly highly skilled ones, were blamed for taking jobs from locals. Local-born Singaporeans vented their frustration with and hatred of migrants in online forums, often in racist terms, and these sentiments also spread from online space to personal interactions (Gomes 2014; Zhan and Zhou 2020). The situation had become so serious that twelve civil society groups released a statement in 2014 to voice concerns about the nation's surge in racism and xenophobia (Tai 2014).

---

3 We do not include the newspapers in Tamil as Singapore's only Tamil language newspaper, *Tamil Murasu*, has a rather small circulation compared with the other three languages. *Berita Minggu* is the Sunday edition of *Berita Harian*.

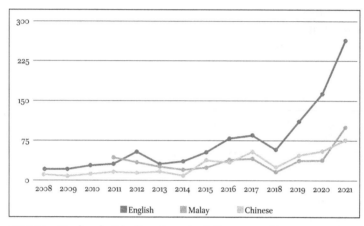

FIGURE 1 Number of articles discussing racism in Singapore: 2008–2021
Note: The Figure shows the numbers of media references to "Racism in Singapore" in three newspapers of the three languages via Factiva, an international news database. The database was accessed by 1 November 2021. All duplicate articles have been excluded in the search results. Data for the Malay newspaper before 2011 is unavailable.
SOURCE: AUTHORS' COLLATION FROM THE FACTIVA NEWSPAPER DATABASE

The immigration backlash and racism against migrants has also been observed in other countries (Amin 2013). What makes the case of Singapore different is that the rising public discourse on racism is also about tensions between native races, especially after 2015. This appears puzzling because it seems that the immigration backlash has the effect of strengthening interracial solidarity and reducing tensions among natives. For example, Chinese Singaporeans tend to identify more with local Malays and Indians than with new Chinese migrants, even though they are of the same race as the latter (Liu 2014).

During the pandemic in 2020–21, the heated debate on racism and several race-related incidents compelled the authorities to acknowledge that Singapore might not have been racially as harmonious as previously thought. The growing discussions of racism led the *ST* to publish a long opinion piece in December 2020, reporting on interviews with officials and civil society leaders of minority races about their own experience of racism in Singapore (Chua 2020). Several race-related incidents in 2021 triggered a wave of heated debates. For instance, in early May, a 55-year-old Indian Singaporean woman was allegedly assaulted and subjected to racial slurs by a Chinese Singaporean man, for not wearing a mask while doing brisk walking (Menon 2021). Also in May, a Malay/Muslim couple accused the People's Association (a government-sponsored grassroots organization) of racism for using their wedding photograph without permission to create a standee for the celebration of Hari Raya Puasa, a religious holiday marking the end of Ramadan. The Association apologized but denied any racist intention (Ang 2021). K. Shanmugam, Minister for Home Affairs and Law, commented on a viral video showing a man making racist remarks at an interracial couple, "I used to believe that Singapore was moving in the right direction on racial tolerance and harmony. Based on recent events, I am not so sure anymore" (Leo 2021). Prime Minister Lee Hsien Loong acknowledged the fragility of Singapore's racial harmony in his National Day Rally speech in August 2021.[4]

3.3 Debating "Chinese Privilege"

The contestations over racism in Singapore center on how minority races such as Malays and Indians are subjected to racial inequality and discrimination. Sangeetha Thanapal, a social activist, coined the term "Chinese privilege" to suggest that Singaporean Chinese have enjoyed institutionalized power and privilege over minority races (Koh and Thanapal 2015). The term has triggered heated debates in media and among scholars for at least three reasons.

First, the term suggests the existence of systemic and structural racism in Singapore, which echoes the debate over Critical Race Theory in the United States (Delgado and Stefancic 2017). However, Singapore has a very different history and racial composition from that in America (Zhou and Liu 2016). During the colonial period, all four races in Singapore were colonial subjects under British rule. After the nation's independence, the ruling PAP implemented policies designed to restrict Chinese culture and Chinese-language schools in the name of preventing Chinese chauvinism in the 1960s and 1970s (Lim 2021). In addition, the use of English as the working language and the transition to an export-oriented economy had rendered the Chinese-speaking population disadvantaged in education and the labor market. By 2015, nearly 20 percent of Chinese (aged 15 and over) could still speak only Mandarin or one or more Chinese dialect (DOS 2016: 17). This group of Chinese, mostly in their 50s and above, have to work in low-wage jobs due to language limitations. They are contrasted with English-speaking Chinese, who have been well positioned in Singapore's globalized economy since the 1970s.

Second, the notion of Chinese privilege challenges the ideology of meritocracy, which the state promotes as a national value. Studies find that there is a strong popular belief in meritocracy in Singapore (Chua 2017: 134–135; Mathews 2016). Advocates of the notion of Chinese privilege contend that the system often reproduces the power and privilege of Chinese and perpetuates

---

4 The speech can be found at: https://www.pmo.gov.sg/Newsroom/National-Day-Rally-2021-English.

racial inequalities between Chinese and minority races. This is against the principle of meritocracy (Zainal and Abdullah 2021).

Third, the concept of Chinese privilege challenges the state's ideology and policy of racial harmony. Through the lens of Chinese privilege, policies that were previously designed to promote racial harmony and racial integration might be viewed as measures to preserve Chinese privilege. For instance, the Ethnic Integration Policy regulates that the four official races must be proportionally mixed in public housing. Currently the maximum proportions in each neighborhood and each block are 84 and 87 percent for Chinese, 22 and 25 percent for Malays, and 12 and 15 percent for Indians and Others. Critics argue that the policy ensures a majority of Chinese in every neighborhood/block, so that minority races are in the minority in all neighborhoods (Neo 2017). In addition, the racial quotas have negatively affected minority property owners, as they might find it harder to sell their flats or be forced to sell below the market price due to policy restrictions (Lee 2021).

3.4 Rising Public Discourse on Racism

On 9 June 2021, *Lianhe Zaobao*, the most-widely circulated Chinese-language newspaper in Singapore, published an editorial suggesting three reasons for the intense contestations on race and racism (*Lianhe Zaobao* 2021). First, the Covid-19 pandemic puts a great stress on life and livelihood, which makes people look inward and become less tolerant of others. Second, social media provide the space for extreme views on race and racism, which often exaggerate interracial tensions. Third, foreign ideas such as Critical Race Theory have been imported into Singapore, and the use of terms such as "Chinese privilege" exacerbates anxiety regarding race relations. The editorial caused a backlash from scholars in Singapore and overseas, 271 of whom signed an open letter to the newspaper asserting that the editorial ignores structural racism and the history of racial stereotyping in Singapore.[5] The letter read: "We believe that the pandemic and social media have simply revealed long-standing fissures and the everyday discrimination experienced by racial minorities in Singapore."

Social media played an important role in driving the discourse of race and racism. Our examination of race-related incidents since 2011 shows that more than 90 percent of these incidents first attracted public attention in social media. Some incidents started with racist online postings while others drew public attention when videos or accounts of offline racist incidents were posted on social media.[6] It is also likely that social media has simply provided

---

5   The open letter can be accessed at http://bit.ly/ZBopenletter.
6   For a list of these racist incidents, see https://www.visakanv.com/sg/examples-of-racism/.

an alternative space for people to discuss existing racism and race-related problems, as the open letter points out. While the pandemic might be a catalyst for racial incidents, the public discourse over racism was on the rise even before the pandemic, as Figure 1 shows.

The editorial and the open letter both note how livelihood issues, including everyday stress, employment, and housing, have driven the discourse on race and racism. However, both sides limit their focus to the race-livelihood dynamics among native races. This overlooks how race relations and livelihood issues in Singapore have been profoundly transformed by immigration and the integration of the economy into the global economy. The paradox of superdiversity, which draws attention to new forms of racism due to immigration, and the political economy behind this paradox, will broaden our understanding of race-livelihood dynamics and contestations over racism. The next two sections examine how the new political economy, interacting with diversifications, has transformed state-society relations in Singapore, leading to rising contestations over racism.

4 The New Political Economy

The past decade has witnessed the emergence of a new political economy in Singapore, characterized by three significant changes: the efforts to build a knowledge-based economy; competitive electoral politics; and the impacts of China's ascendance. While the forces behind these changes date to the 1990s, it was not until the 2010s that they had coalesced and given rise to notable new patterns of political economy.

4.1 *Building a Knowledge Economy and the Immigration Backlash*

Singapore achieved rapid economic growth after 1965, rising to become one of the four Asian Tiger economies by the 1980s. After that, the country strove to move up the global value chains by concentrating greater effort on high value-added sectors. In the 1990s, particularly after the 1997 financial crisis, the government decided to build a knowledge-intensive economy, which entailed a policy to attract highly skilled migrants from abroad.

The declining fertility rate also contributed to the new immigration policy. In 2001, the total fertility rate decreased to 1.4, much lower than the replacement level of 2.1. Before the new millennium, Singapore had imported low-skilled and high-skilled migrants to fill job vacancies. The policy to attract foreign talent in the 2000s was different in that it encouraged the settlement of highly skilled migrants to replenish the population (Yeoh and Lam, 2016).

While the city-state wanted to maintain the racial composition of the permanent population (including citizens and PRs), co-ethnic natives and migrants differentiate themselves on the basis of their place of origin, language, culture, and other parameters.

Immigration and the diversifications of the host society have caused a backlash from natives. From 2000 to 2010, Singapore's total population grew from 4.0 to 5.1 million, largely due to immigration (DOS 2021a). Natives complained of migrants stealing jobs, driving down wages, buying up properties, and putting a stress on public resources such as transportation and education. They also accused migrants of lacking loyalty or not being integrated into the host society, thus diluting Singapore's identity and culture. Most of these accusations targeted high-skilled rather than low-skilled migrants (Yeoh and Lam 2016; Zhan, Huang and Zhou, 2022). The backlash grew in intensity in the late 2000s. Due to widespread discontent regarding immigration, the PAP had only received 60.1 percent of the popular vote in the 2011 general election, the lowest in its history (Thompson 2014). In 2013, a population white paper released by the government, which envisioned an increase in the population to 6.9 million by 2030, caused the largest public protest since the 1970s.

In response to the immigration backlash, the state tightened the inflow of highly skilled migrants, while giving priority to local citizens in areas such as employment, education, health care, and housing (Zhan, Huang and Zhou, 2022). The Fair Consideration Framework was launched in 2013 to urge employers to hire Singaporeans first. Since then, the government has further restricted hiring foreign professionals. The measures include imposing employment quotas on hiring middle-skilled foreign workers, increasing salary thresholds for granting work passes, and monitoring employers' hiring practices. Meanwhile, the state established the SkillsFuture Scheme to support the skills upgrading of Singaporean workers. Nevertheless, as the city-state's economy depends on a large migrant labor force, immigration continues to be a thorny issue in public debates and political campaigns.

4.2 *Competitive Electoral Politics*

The PAP has been the only ruling party in Singapore since 1965. From the 1960s to the 2000s, the party won majority votes and took almost all parliamentary seats in all elections, and opposition parties posed little or no threat. However, the political ground has been shifting in the past decade, characterized by increasingly competitive elections and the diminishing popular support for the PAP (Welsh and Chang 2019), largely due to the immigration backlash. Along with the PAP's poor electoral performance in 2011, the Workers' Party won six parliament seats, a landmark gain for an opposition party. In the presidential election held in August of the same year, Tony Tan, former Deputy Prime Minister, seen "as the preferred candidate" of the PAP, won by a slim margin of 7,269 votes out of over two million votes cast.

The PAP won a victory of 69.9 percent of votes in the 2015 general election partly because the public mourned the recent passing of Singapore's founding Prime Minister Lee Kuan Yew, who co-founded the PAP (Tan and Boey 2017). Nevertheless, the Workers' Party retained the six parliament seats it won in 2011. The 2020 general election, held amidst the Covid-19 pandemic, saw the PAP share of the popular votes decrease to 61.2 percent, with the Workers' Party unprecedentedly winning 10 out of 93 parliament seats. Furthermore, three other constituencies, which carry 11 parliament seats, were closely contested by opposition parties. The new normal of competitive elections has undermined the dominance of the PAP on race and racism and opened up a space for public debates and contestations, which will be discussed in the next section.

4.3 Rise of China

Previous studies on racism in a super-diverse context mainly focus on the host country's immigration regime and domestic dynamics. The case of Singapore, however, suggests that changes in the international political economy also shape race relations and the discourse on race. The rise of China is arguably the most important geopolitical event in contemporary Asia. Singapore has been greatly affected by China's growing economic influence. Economic relations between the two countries developed rapidly after 2001 when China joined the WTO, and even more so with the launching of China's Belt Road Initiative (BRI) in 2013. China has become Singapore's largest trade partner and the volumes of their bilateral trade have been steadily increasing since 2010 (Chiang 2019; Liu, Fan and Lim 2021). Singapore has been China's largest foreign investor country since 2013. In 2018, there were 998 Singaporean investment projects in China, and 24,869 Singaporean firms operated in China, while about 7,500 mainland Chinese enterprises conducted business in Singapore (Xinhua Silk Road 2019).

The rise of China has multiple impacts on Singapore. First, mainland China has become the second largest source of immigration, accounting for 18 percent of the foreign-born population in Singapore, second only to Malaysia (United Nations 2019). Many Chinese diasporas in Singapore have acquired permanent residency and citizenship, and constitute an integral part of the host society. Second, the ballooning volumes of trade and investment between the two countries have created ample well-paid job opportunities for both native Singaporeans and Chinese diasporas. The state's policy toward new Chinese immigrants is two-fold. It enacted policies to facilitate these immigrants' integration into the country's multiracial and multicultural society and develop Singaporean identity, which should be above their ethnic identity. Meanwhile, the state engages the immigrants and their associations to expand business networks with China (Liu 2021). In addition, Singaporean Chinese are encouraged to learn Mandarin and Chinese culture so that they have the necessary skills to conduct business in China or work for China-related businesses in Singapore. Third, Singapore has served as a springboard for Chinese enterprises to expand their businesses in the Southeast Asian region. The 7,500 Singapore-based Chinese enterprises established their regional headquarters, R&D, or manufacturing centers in the city-state (Lin 2018). This has not only amplified China's economic influence in the region but has also created business and employment opportunities for both local-born Singaporeans and new Chinese immigrants. However, economic opportunities deriving from China's impacts are not equally shared among all ethnic members of Singaporean society, and this has constituted a new source of inequality, as discussed below.

5   Beyond Diversity: Changing Dynamics of State-Society Relations

The peculiarity of the paradox of superdiversity in Singapore is that the coexistence of diversifications and racism not only manifests itself in native-migrant tensions but also takes place among native races. This section examines how three factors – livelihood pressure, new forms of inequality, and the politicization of racial discourse – have led to contestations over racism among native races. These factors are a result of the working of the new political economy, which has altered the dynamics of state-society relations in Singapore. In other words, it is not the diversity itself but the new political and economic forces that are responsible for new forms of racism and contestations over race.

5.1   *Heightened Livelihood Pressure*

The tightening of immigration since 2011 has not significantly reduced pressure on natives' livelihood. This is because building a knowledge-intensive economy requires the recruitment of a sufficient number of highly skilled foreign professionals. Although the growth of the migrant population slowed after 2011, its proportion in the total population has remained around 45 percent (United Nations 2019). The skill training program for natives, though helpful, puts further stress on members of the local workforce by urging them to constantly upgrade their skills. The livelihood pressure has amplified tensions among native races, particularly between Chinese and minority races, for at least two reasons.

First, natives must compete with migrants and with each other to find and retain a decent job. The immense stress on livelihood and intense competition in the labor market have made minority races increasingly sensitive to real or perceived discrimination in the workplace. The Institute of Policy Studies at the National University of Singapore conducted a survey on race, religion, and language in 2013 and 2018, surveying approximately 4,000 Singaporean citizens and permanent residents each time (Mathews, Lim and Selvarajan 2019). A striking finding of the two surveys is that perceived work-related discrimination among Malays and Indians, the two main minority races, had increased over the five-year period, while their perceived discrimination in public spaces or in receiving public services remained largely unchanged (Table 1). Minority races also reported much more discrimination than Chinese. In 2018, Malay respondents who reported discrimination at work, when applying for a job, and when seeking a job promotion, accounted for 35, 52, and 51 percent, respectively. The figures for Indians were 32, 47, and 45 percent. By contrast, the figures for Chinese respondents were only between 10 and 14 percent (Table 1).

Our analysis of social media postings also reveals that perceived discrimination over work-related issues was frequently voiced by members of minority races. It was reported in April 2016 that a manager in a chain bakery made racist remarks toward a Malay female during a job interview. The job interviewee posted the discriminatory experience on social media, causing the bakery to

TABLE 1 Frequency of respondents' perceiving discriminatory treatment in 2013 and 2018, percentage

		At work		When applying for a job		When seeking a job promotion	
		Sometimes	Often	Sometimes	Often	Sometimes	Often
Chinese	2018	8.5	2.2	9.7	2.5	11.0	2.7
	2013	12.2	3.4	12.7	3.8	13.6	3.9
Malay	2018	25.7	9.5	29.3	22.3	32.4	18.4
	2013	24.5	10.6	27.8	19.4	26.7	17.1
India	2018	22.6	9.4	26.2	20.8	25.5	19.7
	2013	20.5	9.5	23.3	18.2	22.3	17.5
Others	2018	8.0	**8.9**	15.9	13.3	24.6	10.5
	2013	22.3	5.8	25.2	15.1	25.2	12.6

Note: the numbers in 2018 are presented in bold if they are higher than those in 2013.
SOURCE: MATHEWS ET AL. (2019: 35–36)

fire the manager subsequently (Ho and Wei 2016). Many online postings by members of minority races claim that they could not even get an interview after the hiring company learnt about their race or religion. It should be noted that the issues of race and religion are often intertwined. Nearly all Malays in Singapore are Muslims, and most Indians practice Hinduism or another religion that originated in South Asia.

Second, the discrimination against migrants may spill over and escalate tensions among native races. Many migrants in Singapore belong to the same racial categories of natives. The discrimination against migrants of minority races, particularly Indian migrants, sometimes spreads to native Indians. Due to its advancement in high-tech industries, India has been a major source of highly skilled migrants. According to the UN data, the number of Indian migrants in Singapore increased to 150,082 in 2015, a nearly ten-fold increase over 14,019 in 1990 (Yang et al. 2017). The jobs that Indian professional migrants take carry high salaries and social prestige, which are also desired by natives. This has become a cause for the tension, particularly during economic downturns.

In August 2020, in the middle of the pandemic, Singaporean netizens posted the LinkedIn profiles of Indian employees of top investment and financial companies including the Temasek Holdings, DBS Bank, and Standard Chartered, alluding to how these firms had hired Indian migrants over native Singaporeans. The Temasek Holdings, the nation's sovereign wealth fund, accused these postings of being racist, divisive, and discriminatory. It also indicated that some of the targeted employees were Indian Singaporean citizens, though it was unclear whether they were local-born or foreign-born (Ng and Yong 2020). Another example is the controversy over the "Singapore-India Comprehensive Economic Cooperation Agreement (CECA)," a bilateral free-trade agreement signed in June 2005. Some natives suspected that the agreement led to the inflow of too many Indian migrants, demonstrated by the notable presence in the IT and financial sectors of the latter (Chua, Koay and Zhang 2021). Minister Shanmugam argued that xenophobia against Indian migrants had exacerbated racism toward native Indians because not all could distinguish between Indians born in Singapore and those born overseas (Abdullah 2021).

It should be noted that discrimination against migrants has not spread to native Chinese or Malays. Xenophobia toward Chinese migrants, which has also been intense in the recent decade, has not affected native Chinese, as they are the majority race. In the case of Malays, although Malaysia is the largest source of the foreign-born population in Singapore, migrants from the country, including both Chinese and Malays, have been much less discriminated against than their counterparts from China and India. This is because of cultural affinity and close people-to-people connections between Malaysia and Singapore, which were one country before Singapore's separation from the Federation of Malaysia in 1965.

5.2 New Forms of Inequalities

The new political economy has created new inequalities, which may enlarge the gulfs among native races. Singapore has implemented a highly selective immigration policy, which only allows the highly skilled to apply for permanent residency and citizenship while excluding low-skilled migrants. As a result, permanent immigrants, including new citizens and PRs, usually have a higher income than the general population. Although no statistics on the income gap between native citizens and immigrants is available, popular sentiment regarding such inequality is palpable, as natives often complain about how immigrants have taken away high-wage jobs in the finance and high-tech sectors and reside in upscale real estate and neighborhoods (Yeoh and Lam 2016; Zhan and Zhou 2020). The recruitment and naturalization of high-income Chinese and Indian migrants might have perpetuated income inequality among native races. For historical reasons, Malays on average earned lower income than Chinese and Indians in Singapore (Lee 2004). Between 2010 and 2020, the income gap between Malay and Chinese households in Singapore slightly increased while the income gap between Malays and Indians grew even wider (DOS 2021b: 13).

The impact of a rising China may have also created new inequalities because economic relations with China have only advantaged certain ethnic groups in Singapore. For instance, fluency in Mandarin gives native Chinese an edge in looking for jobs that require interactions with Chinese clientele or that handle investment in China. Our examination of social media postings reveals that a frequent complaint from members of minority races is that they are not considered for jobs that require Mandarin fluency.

The language advantage of native Chinese has been linked to the controversy over the Special Assistance Plan (SAP) schools in the debate on "Chinese privilege." Singapore implements a bilingual policy that requires students learning both English and the mother tongue: Chinese students learn Mandarin, Malay students learn Malay, while Indian students learn Tamil or another major Indian language. The rationale is that English will be used as the working language, while the mother tongue serves to preserve traditions and strengthen a person's sense of cultural belonging. Singapore greatly increased the significance of the mother tongue in the education system in 1979 (Sim 2016). For Chinese, the SAP was introduced to preserve traditional Chinese values, and students must study both English and Chinese as the first languages in such schools. The SAP schools have grown in significance with the strengthening of Sino-Singapore economic relations (Tan and Ng 2011), and these schools have received generous government support and are positioned to admit top students. However, minority races are practically excluded from admission due to the language barrier. This has become a key issue in the recent controversy over Chinese privilege (Zainal and Abdullah 2021).

Not all Singaporean Chinese benefit from the economic relations with China or from the SAP schools. People who can speak both English and Chinese may find it easier to get a job that requires fluency in Mandarin, but those who only speak Chinese are severely disadvantaged in the labor market. This is because most jobs, including those in Chinese firms or Singaporean firms that conduct businesses with China, require English fluency. In addition, Chinese who only speak English do not benefit much from the rise of China in terms of linguistic skills. This group has been expanding as English has become the most spoken language at home in Singapore (Ong 2021; Toh and Liu 2021).

5.3   The Politicization of Racial Discourses

Competitive electoral politics between the PAP and opposition parties undermined the former's dominance in the discourse over race. This has led to more political debates over race issues and the politicization of race. A search for the key words "racist" and "racism" in the database of Singapore's parliamentary debates reveals an increasing trend of debates on race and racism over the past decade.[7] Between 2011 and 2015, five parliamentary sessions discussed racist acts or racism, mainly in response to racism in online postings. Over the following five years (2016–2020), debates on racism occurred in eight parliamentary sessions. During these sessions, the opposition parties questioned whether the PAP's laws and policies were effective for dealing with racial discrimination, whereas the PAP stressed the importance of using laws to counter racism. In 2021, the debates on racism intensified, with twenty parliamentary sessions on racism from January to October. The most contentious debates centered around foreign-talent policy and racism. The opposition parties argued that the government's immigration policy reduced job opportunities for native Singaporeans, while the PAP accused members of the opposition of stirring xenophobia and racism. The heated debates in these parliamentary sessions suggest that the issue of race has been politicized in the context of competitive electoral politics, and race and racism are now openly debated in the political sphere, leading to contestations over racism in society at large.

---

7 The database is accessible at https://sprs.parl.gov.sg/search/home.

The race-based government policies, which the PAP argues are efforts to preserve a multi-culture and promote racial harmony, are also increasingly questioned and debated. An example is the CMIO framework and policies built on the framework. As noted earlier, there have been more and more calls for the state to revise the rigid model due to immigration and interracial marriages. Race-based policies such as the Ethnic Integration Policy are also subject to debates and even criticisms, forcing the PAP to clarify its stance on these issues. The PAP felt compelled to accommodate some popular demands from minority races for the purpose of winning electoral support (Abdullah 2016). The issue of the hijab is a case in point. The hijab is both a racial and a religious matter in Singapore, as almost all Malays are Muslims. The state disallowed hijab wearing by children in schools and employees in some uniformed public services, such as nursing, the police force, and the army. In the past decade, however, the PAP has softened its stance, and in 2021 it permitted female Muslim staff in public health care to wear the hijab at work (Low 2021).

6   Conclusion

Large-scale immigration has given rise to a society of superdiversity in Singapore. Despite frequent racial interactions and an emphasis on racial harmony, new forms of racism and contestations over racism have been rising in the course of the past decade. We have analyzed how this is related to the emergence of a new political economy in the city-state. The strategy toward a knowledge economy since the late 1990s has led Singapore to import large numbers of migrants. The immigration and settlement of migrants, particularly those who are highly skilled, caused a strong backlash from native citizens, giving rise to new forms of racism against migrants. Meanwhile, the immigration backlash eroded popular support for the PAP, which must now face competitive elections. This opens up public space for discussions and debates on race relations. The rise of China and the deepening of Sino-Singapore economic relations have advantaged some groups of native Chinese, which might have contributed to new forms of inequalities and further intensified the debate on Chinese privilege. These political economic factors, both as a cause and effect of the transition to a superdiverse society, have exposed existing fissures among native races, fueling the debates on race.

This paper offers two broader theoretical implications for the scholarship on migration and race relations in a context of superdiversity. First, the paradoxical co-existence of superdiversity and racism obtains not only between migrants and natives, as many studies have shown, but also between native races in the host society. Second, diversifications and new forms of contestations and racism are not only a result of the immigration regime and domestic politics of the host country, but are also shaped by the international political economy, as evidenced by the way in which the rise of China has intensified contestations on race relations in Singapore.

Our findings have policy implications. First, new forms of racism against migrants, despite having the effect of uniting native residents, may exacerbate racial problems and spread tensions widely in the host society, as diversifications have blurred the boundaries between migrants and natives. Thus, policy makers should make further interventions to mitigate racism against migrants. Second, immigration as a strategy of economic development or a demographic solution is likely to create new inequalities due either to the selectivity of migration policy or to changing international relations. Policy makers should be attentive to these new inequalities and implement measures to narrow the gaps in areas such as income, employment, and education.

Acknowledgements

The authors would like to acknowledge funding support from Nanyang Technological University Start-up Grant "Globalisation, Brain Circulation, and Competition for International Talents: A Comparative Study of Asian, European and North American Experiences and Policy Implications" (04INS000136C430) and the China Social Sciences Foundation (21 & ZD022). The views expressed in this article are solely those of the authors.

References

Abdullah, Ahmad Zhaki. 2021, 11 May. Singapore Will Fail if Racism and Xenophobia Take Root. Channel News Asia. https://www.channelnewsasia.com/singapore/singapore-will-fail-if-racism-and-xenophobia-take-root-shanmugam-1356431. Accessed on 3 September 2021.

Abdullah, Walid Jumblatt. 2016. "Managing Minorities in Competitive Authoritarian States: Multiracialism and the Hijab Issue in Singapore." *Indonesia and the Malay World* 44(129): 211–228.

Alba, Richard and Jan Willem Duyvendak. 2019. "What about the Mainstream? Assimilation in Super-diverse Times." *Ethnic and Racial Studies* 42(1): 105–124.

Amin, Ash. 2013. "Land of Strangers." *Identities* 20(1): 1–8.

Ang, Hwee Min and Hui Min Chew. 2021, 25 June. Singapore Right to be Concerned about Racist Incidents. *Channel News Asia*. https://www.channelnewsasia.com /singapore/racism-singapore-forum-ips-rsis-lawrence-wong-incidents-1942276. Accessed on 3 September 2021.

Ang, Jolene. 2021, 29 May. PA Apologises for Using Couple's Wedding Photo for Hari Raya Decorations without Permission. *The Straits Times*. https://www.straitstimes .com/singapore/pa-apologises-for-using-muslim-couples-wedding-photo-for -hari-raya-without-permission. Accessed on 3 September 2021.

Ang, Sylvia. 2018. "The 'New Chinatown': the Racialization of Newly Arrived Chinese Migrants in Singapore." *Journal of Ethnic and Migration Studies* 44(7): 1177–1194.

Back, Les and Shamser Sinha. 2016. "Multicultural Conviviality in the Midst of Racism's Ruins." *Journal of Intercultural Studies* 37(5): 517–532.

Chiang, Min-Hua. 2019. "China–ASEAN Economic Relations after Establishment of Free Trade Area." *The Pacific Review* 32(3): 267–290.

Chua, Beng Huat. 2003. "Multiculturalism in Singapore: An Instrument of Social Control." *Race & Class* 44 (3): 58–77.

Chua, Beng Huat. 2017. Liberalism Disavowed: Communitarianism and State Capitalism in Singapore. Ithaca, NY: Cornell University Press.

Chua, Mui Hoong. 2020, 25 December. Racism in Singapore: Time to Listen to Minorities' Concerns. *The Straits Times*. https://www.straitstimes.com/opinion/racism-in -singapore-time-to-listen-to-minorities-concerns. Accessed on 6 September 2021.

Chua, Mui Hoong. 2021, 16 July. Categorising Singapore by Race: The CMIO System is 100 Years Old and Needs An Update. *The Straits Times*. https://www.straitstimes .com/opinion/the-cmio-system-is-100-years-old-and-needs-an-update. Accessed on 10 October 2021.

Chua, Nigel, Koay, Andrew and Jane Zhang. 2021, 8 July What is CECA & are S'poreans Losing Out Because of It? *Mothership*. https://mothership.sg/2021/07/what-is-ceca -singapore/. Accessed on 10 October 2021.

Delgado, Richard and Jean Stefancic. 2017. *Critical Race Theory*. New York: New York University Press.

Foner, Nancy, Duyvendak, Jan Willem and Philip Kasinitz. 2019. "Introduction: Super-diversity in Everyday Life." *Ethnic and Racial Studies* 42(1): 1–16.

Goh, Daniel P.S. 2013. "Multicultural Carnivals and the Politics of the Spectacle in Global Singapore." *Inter-Asia Cultural Studies* 14(2): 228–251.

Goh, Daniel P.S. 2019. "Super-diversity and the Bio-politics of Migrant Worker Exclusion in Singapore." *Identities* 26(3): 356–373.

Goh, Daniel P.S. and Terence Chong. 2020. "'Chinese Privilege' as Shortcut in Singapore: A Rejoinder." *Asian Ethnicity*: 1–6.

Gomes, Catherine. 2014. "Xenophobia Online: Unmasking Singaporean Attitudes towards 'Foreign Talent' Migrants." *Asian Ethnicity* 15(1): 21–40.

Ho, Elaine Lynn-Ee and Laavanya Kathiravelu. 2022. "More Than Race: A Comparative Analysis of 'New' Indian and Chinese Migration in Singapore." *Ethnic and Racial Studies* 45(4): 636–655.

Ho, Olivia and Cheng Wei Aw. 2016, 29 April. PrimaDeli Apologises, Sacks Staff for Making Racist Remarks to Job Interviewee. *The Straits Times*. https://www.straitstimes.com/singapore/manpower/primadeli-apologises-sacks-staff-for-making-racist-remarks-to-job-interviewee. Accessed on 3 November 2021.

Holman, Joanna and Dharmalingam Arunachalam. 2015. "Representing Harmony and Diversity: Media Representations of Multiculturalism and Ethnicity in Singapore." *Asian Ethnicity* 16(4): 498–515.

Koh, Adeline and Sangeetha Thanapal. 2015. Chinese Privilege, Gender and Intersectionality in Singapore. https://www.boundary2.org/2015/03/chinese-privilege-gender-and-intersectionality-in-singapore-a-conversation-between-adeline-koh-and-sangeetha-thanapal/. Accessed on 3 September 2021.

Lee, Joshua. 2021, 9 July. 30 Years of Racial Quotas in HDB Estates & Blocks Later, Do We Still Need the Ethnic Integration Policy? *Mothership*. https://mothership.sg/2021/07/30-years-of-racial-quotas-in-hdb-estates-blocks-later-do-we-still-need-the-ethnic-integration-policy/. Accessed 3 September 2021.

Lee, William Keng Mun. 2004. "The Economic Marginality of Ethnic Minorities: An Analysis of Ethnic Income Inequality in Singapore." *Asian Ethnicity* 5(1): 27–41.

Leo, Lakeisha. 2021, 6 June. Shanmugam "Not So Sure" Singapore Moving in Right Direction on Racial Tolerance after Man's Racist Remarks Captured on Video. *Channel News Asia*. https://www.channelnewsasia.com/singapore/racist-viral-video-interracial-couple-shanmugam-racial-tolerance-1836196. Accessed on 3 September 2021.

Lianhe Zaobao. 2021, 9 June. Kuozhan gonggong kongjian cujin zhongzu hexie 扩展公共空间促进种族和谐 (Expand Public Space to Promote Racial Harmony). *Lianhe Zaobao*. https://www.zaobao.com.sg/forum/editorial/story20210609-1153760. Accessed on 3 September 2021.

Lim, Jason. 2021. "'A Tolerant Society Is the Way Forward': Exposing Chinese Chauvinism in Singapore, 1959–1979." *Translocal Chinese: East Asian Perspectives* 15(1): 67–92.

Lin, Jie Chen. 2018, 17 October. Singapore on the Belt and Road: Chinese Enterprises' New Springboard into the World. *Diyi Caijing Ribao*, p. A05. https://www.yicai.com/oldepaper/pc/201810/17/node_A05.html. Accessed on 10 October 2021.

Liu, Hong. 2014. "Beyond Co-ethnicity: The Politics of Differentiating and Integrating New Immigrants in Singapore." *Ethnic and Racial Studies* 37(7): 1225–1238.

Liu, Hong. 2021. "The New Chinese Diaspora in a Globalising Singapore." *Melbourne Asian Review* 8, https://melbourneasiareview.edu.au/the-new-chinese-diaspora-in-a-globalising-singapore/.

Liu, Hong, Fan, Xin and Guanie Lim. 2021. "Singapore Engages the Belt and Road Initiative: Perceptions, Policies, and Institutions." *Singapore Economic Review* 66(1): 219–241.

Low, Youjin. 2021, 29 August. NDR 2021: Muslim Staff in Public Healthcare Sector, including Nurses, Can Wear Tudung at Work from Nov 1. *Today*. https://www.today online.com/singapore/ndr-2021-muslim-staff-public-healthcare-sector-including-nurses-can-wear-tudung-work-nov-1. Accessed on 10 October 2021.

Mathews, Mathew. 2016. "Key Findings from the CNA-IPS Survey on Race Relations." Institute of Policy Studies, Singapore. https://lkyspp.nus.edu.sg/docs/default-source/ips/cna-ips-survey-on-race-relations_summary_190816.pdf. Accessed on 2 December 2021.

Mathews, Mathew, Leonard Lim and Shanthini Selvarajan. 2019. "IPS-OnePeople.Sg Indicators of Racial and Religious Harmony: Comparing Results from 2018 and 2013," (The Institute of Policy Papers Working Paper No.35, 1–72). Institute of Policy Studies, Singapore. https://lkyspp.nus.edu.sg/docs/default-source/ips/ips-working-paper-no-35_ips-onepeoplesg-indicators-of-racial-and-religious-harmony_comparing-results-from-2018-and-2013.pdf. Accessed on 2 December 2021.

McAuliffe, Marie, Céline Bauloz, Michelle Nguyen and Sophie Qu. 2019. "Migration and Migrants: A global Overview." In *World Migration Report 2020*, pp. 19–52. Geneva: International Organization for Migration.

Meissner, Fran and Steven Vertovec. 2015. "Comparing Super-diversity." *Ethnic and Racial Studies* 38(4): 541–555.

Menon, Malavika. 2021, 10 May. Police Investigating Man Accused of Using Racial Slur and Kicking 55-year-old Woman. *The Straits Times*. https://www.straitstimes.com/singapore/police-investigating-man-accused-of-using-racial-slur-and-kicking-55-year-old-woman. Accessed on 10 November 2021.

Mepschen, Paul. 2019. "A Discourse of Displacement: Super-diversity, Urban Citizenship, and the Politics of Autochthony in Amsterdam." *Ethnic and Racial Studies* 42(1): 71–88.

Neo, Jaclyn Ling-Chien. 2011. "Seditious in Singapore-free Speech and the Offence of Promoting Ill-will and Hostility between Different Racial Groups." *Singapore Journal of Legal Studies*: 351–372.

Neo, Jaclyn L. 2017. "Navigating Minority Inclusion and Permanent Division: Minorities and the Depoliticization of Ethnic Difference." http://juspoliticum.com/article/Navigating-Minority-Inclusion-and-Permanent-Division-Minorities-and-the-Depoliticization-of-Ethnic-Difference-1156.html. Accessed on 2 December 2021.

Ng, Keng Gene and Clement Yong. 2020, 15 August. Temasek Calls Out Racist Facebook Posts Targeting Its Indian Employees. *The Straits Times*. https://www.straitstimes.com/singapore/temasek-slams-racist-facebook-posts-targeting-its-indian-employees. Accessed on 3 November 2021.

Ong, Justin. 2021, 16 June. English Most Spoken at Home for Nearly Half of S'pore Residents: Population Census. *The Straits Times*. https://www.straitstimes.com/singapore/english-most-spoken-at-home-for-nearly-half-of-spore-residents-population-census. Accessed on 3 November 2021.

Ortiga, Yasmin Y. 2015. "Multiculturalism on its Head: Unexpected Boundaries and New Migration in Singapore." *Journal of International Migration and Integration* 16(4): 947–963.

Padilla, Beatriz, Azevedo, Joana and Antonia Olmos-Alcaraz. 2015. "Superdiversity and Conviviality: Exploring Frameworks for Doing Ethnography in Southern European Intercultural Cities." *Ethnic and Racial Studies* 38(4): 621–635.

Raghuram, Parvati. 2022. "New Racism or New Asia: What Exactly is New and How Does Race Matter?" *Ethnic and Racial Studies* 45(4):778–788.

Rocha, Zarine L. and Brenda S.A. Yeoh. 2021. "Managing the Complexities of Race: Eurasians, Classification and Mixed Racial Identities in Singapore." *Journal of Ethnic and Migration Studies* 47(4): 878–894.

Sim, Cheryl. 2016. "Bilingual Policy." *Singapore Inforpedia*. https://eresources.nlb.gov.sg/infopedia/articles/SIP_2016-09-01_093402.html. Accessed on 3 November 2021.

DOS (Singapore Department of Statistics). 2016. *General Household Survey 2015*. Singapore.

DOS (Singapore Department of Statistics). 2021a. *Population Trends 2021*. Singapore.

DOS (Singapore Department of Statistics). 2021b. *Census of Population 2020 Statistical Release 2*. Singapore.

Strategy Group. 2020. *Population in Brief 2020*. Singapore: Government of Singapore.

Tai, Janice. 2014, 28 May. Civil Society Groups "Alarmed" by Surge of Racism and Xenophobia. *The Straits Times*. https://www.straitstimes.com/singapore/civil-society-groups-alarmed-by-surge-of-racism-and-xenophobia. Accessed on 5 October 2021.

Tan, Charlene and Pak Tee Ng. 2011. "Functional Differentiation: A Critique of the Bilingual Policy in Singapore." *Journal of Asian Public Policy* 4(3): 331–341.

Tan, Kenneth Paul and Augustin Boey. 2017. "Singapore in 2016: Life after Lee Kuan Yew." *Southeast Asian Affairs*: 315–334.

Thompson, Eric C. 2014. "Immigration, Society and Modalities of Citizenship in Singapore." *Citizenship Studies* 18(3–4): 315–331.

Toh, Audrey Lin Lin and Hong Liu. 2021. "Language Ideologies, Chinese Identities and Imagined Futures: Perspectives from Ethnic Chinese Singaporean University Students." *Journal of Chinese Overseas* 17(1): 1–30.

Tran, Van C. 2019. "Coming of Age in Multi-ethnic America: Young Adults' Experiences with Diversity." *Ethnic and Racial Studies* 42(1): 35–52.

United Nations. 2019. "International Migrant Stock 2019." United Nations. https://www.un.org/en/development/desa/population/migration/data/estimates2/estimates19.asp. Accessed on 3 November 2021.

Vertovec, Steven. 2007. "Super-diversity and Its Implications." *Ethnic and Racial Studies* 30(6): 1024–1054.

Vertovec, Steven. 2015. *Diversities Old and New: Migration and Socio-spatial Patterns in New York, Singapore and Johannesburg*. Springer.

Vertovec, Steven. 2019. "Talking around Super-diversity." *Ethnic and Racial Studies* 42(1): 125–139.

Welsh, Bridget and Alex H. Chang. 2019. "PAP Vulnerability and the Singapore Governance Model: Findings from the Asian Barometer Survey." In *The Limits of Authoritarian Governance in Singapore's Developmental State*, eds., Lily Zubaidah Rahim and Michael D. Barr, pp. 195–216. Singapore: Palgrave Macmillan.

Wessendorf, Susanne. 2014. *Commonplace Diversity: Social Relations in a Super-diverse Context*. Springer.

Xinhua Silk Road. 2019. "Economic and Commercial Office of Chinese Embassy in Singapore: Mutual Investment between China and Singapore Goes Hand in Hand." https://www.imsilkroad.com/news/p/363115.html. Accessed on 3 October 2021.

Yang, Hui, Yang, Peidong and Shaohua Zhan. 2017. "Immigration, Population, and Foreign Workforce in Singapore: An Overview of Trends, Policies, and Issues." *HSSE Online* 6(1): 10–25.

Ye, Junjia. 2017. "Managing Urban Diversity through Differential Inclusion in Singapore." *Environment and Planning D: Society and Space* 35(6): 1033–1052.

Yeoh, Brenda S.A., Chee, Heng Leng, Anant, Rohini and Theodora Lam. 2021. "Transnational Marriage Migration and the Negotiation of Precarious Pathways beyond Partial Citizenship in Singapore." *Citizenship Studies* 25(7): 898–917.

Yeoh, Brenda S.A. and Theodora Lam. 2016. "Immigration and Its (Dis)Contents: The Challenges of Highly Skilled Migration in Globalizing Singapore." *American Behavioral Scientist* 60(5–6): 637–658.

Zainal, Humairah and Walid Jumblatt Abdullah. 2021. "Chinese Privilege in Politics: A Case Study of Singapore's Ruling Elites." *Asian Ethnicity* 22(3): 481–497.

Zhan, Shaohua, Huang, Lingli and Min Zhou. 2022. "Differentiation from Above and Below: Evolving Immigration Policy and the Integration Dilemma in Singapore." *Asian and Pacific Migration Journal* 31(1): 3–25.

Zhan, Shaohua and Min Zhou. 2020. "Precarious Talent: Highly Skilled Chinese and Indian Immigrants in Singapore." *Ethnic and Racial Studies* 43(9): 1654–1672.

Zhou, Min and Hong Liu. 2016. "Homeland Engagement and Host-society Integration: A Comparative Study of New Chinese Immigrants in the United States and Singapore." *International Journal of Comparative Sociology* 57(1–2): 30–52.

Post-1978 Chinese Migration to Brazil: The *Qiaoxiang* Migration Models and the Rite of Passage

1978 以来的巴西中国移民:侨乡移民模式与通过仪式

Changsheng Shu[1] (束长生) | ORCID: 0000-0001-9792-651X
University of São Paulo, São Paulo, Brazil
shu@usp.br

Abstract

The post-1978 migration of Chinese rural peasants to Brazil can be analyzed using the *qiaoxiang* (migrant-sending regions) models proposed by Woon Yuen-fong (1996), Minghuan Li and Diana Wong (2017) and by Min Zhou and Xiangyi Li (2014, 2018). From a sending-country perspective, we study two major models of Chinese migration in Brazil: one is the *Guangdong qiaoxiang* model, and the other, the *Zhejiang qiaoxiang* model. The first is based mainly on the catering services, especially *pastelarias* (snack bars), while the second is based mainly on the wholesale and retail business of light industrial imports from China. It is well known that transnational migrations contribute to *qiaoxiang* development while reinforcing the existing social structures of inequality and uneven development that stimulate further migrations. As a result, migration becomes deeply ingrained on the *qiaoxiang* culture, a "rite of passage" that young adults must experience in their life. Through the "rite of passage," *qiaoxiang* migrations are perpetuated and renovated.

---

1 Shu Changsheng is Associate Professor in the Department of Oriental Letters, the University of São Paulo, Brazil. I would like to thank Profs. Min Zhou and Hong Liu for valuable suggestions to improve the texts. Thanks are also due to two antonymous reviewers for their critical opinions. I am very grateful to the journal's Managing Editor Frederica Lai for her patience in reading the drafts and correcting the mistakes. I am responsible for all the remaining errors.

Keywords

qiaoxiang models of migration – boundaries – rite of passage – Chinese migration in Brazil

摘要

本文利用 Woon Yuen-fong (1996), Min Zhou and Xiangyi Li (2014, 2018), Minghuan Li and Diana Wong (2017) 的侨乡移民研究成果分析了 1978 年以来中国人移民巴西的现状。笔者认为，中国新移民向巴西移民的模式主要有两种：一是广东(粤) 侨乡模式，二是浙江(浙) 侨乡模式，来自粤侨乡的华侨华人移民的主要经济活动是餐饮服务，尤其是角仔店经济，而来自浙侨乡的华侨华人移民主要经营进口小商品的批发和零售业务。众所周知，跨国移民在促进侨乡发展的同时，也加强了旧有的不平等和发展不平衡的社会结构，从而刺激了更多的乡亲移民国外。因此，海外移民成为侨乡的根深蒂固的文化，对于侨乡的年青人来说，海外移民是他们生命中的一个"通过仪式"，由此"通过仪式"，侨乡移民模式得到了维持和更新。

关键词

侨乡移民模型 – 边界 – 通过仪式 – 巴西华人移民

1 Introduction

Unlike in developed countries, where post-1978 Chinese migrants are likely to be students, professionals and investors drawn from urban centers all over China, in Brazil, most Chinese migrants have been unskilled peasants from traditional rural areas of Guangdong (mainly Taishan and Wuyi), Fujian and Zhejiang provinces (mainly Qingtian and Wenzhou), i.e., the traditional *qiaoxiang* areas. For this reason, from a sending-country perspective, we study the post-1978 Chinese migration to Brazil using the *qiaoxiang* migration models proposed by Woon Yuen-fong (1996), Min Zhou and Xiangyi Li (2014, 2018), and Minghuan Li and Diana Wong (2017).

Woon Yuen-fong (1996) analyses Kaiping County's consistent development strategies around its Overseas Chinese connections since the early 1990s. Affluent Overseas Chinese have contributed to the revival of the qiaoxiang communities by making donations to development projects and by putting political pressure on the local state. The Overseas Chinese and the local leaders, by taking care of ancestors, seniors, and descendants in their home communities, accumulate merit (in the Confucian and Buddhist senses) by ensuring the continued success of their own direct descendants. Few have any plans to invest or retire to their ancestral community and yet they donate millions of dollars to set up public projects and endowment funds. They are eager to restore or rebuild magnificent schools in their native communities at a time of a drastic decrease in enrollment. They are anxious to erect elaborate village gates with the correct geomancy and to build huge community halls in their home villages, which in fact have been slowly depopulated because the Overseas Chinese themselves have sponsored many close relatives for emigration.

Min Zhou and Xiangyi Li (2014, 2018) analyze the "cultural remittances" of the Chinese overseas who have donated money to build symbolic structures, such as village gates, monuments, spiritual statues, and street altars, as well as cultural facilities including museums, cultural centers, libraries, and public parks, for "collective consumption." The authors assert that "cultural remittances" serve as a unique mechanism for social-status compensation and that this type of transnational practice is not merely caused by migrants' own initiatives or by state policies from above but also by the responses and actions of local governments and local societies in the migrant hometowns. It is the interaction of individual experiences at the micro level, such as felt or experienced social marginalization, and multi-level contextual factors, such as wage differential, currency exchange rates, and hometown reception, that affects the realization of social-status compensation and accounts for regional variations.

Minghuan Li and Diana Wong (2017) distinguish three *qiaoxiang* migration models: the first is the Cantonese *qiaoxiang* migration model, specifically the Taishan county (and the Wuyi counties as a whole) of Guangdong province; the second model is the Fujianese *qiaoxiang* migration model, specifically Fuqing, Fuzhou, Zhangzhou and Putian Prefectures of Fujian Province; the third is the Zhejiang *qiaoxiang* model, specifically the Qingtian and Wenzhou municipalities of southern Zhejiang province. Li and Wong argue that *qiaoxiang* migration is distinctive, based on its entrepreneurial self-organization of mobility, labor and capital. According to the authors, the migration economies of the homeland and hostland mutually reinforce each other and allow access to cheap labor, provide jobs, and generate capital to fund further migration. On the one hand, newly arrived migrants depend on these migrant-owned enterprises for a job. The migrant-owned businesses, on the other hand, depend on the continual inflow of cheap and trusted labor for their competitiveness and further expansion.

In this paper, we first analyze *qiaoxiang* emigration from China to Brazil since 1978 and the major economic activities in the host country that nourish the migrant inflows. We argue that, for the rural youth of Chinese *qiaoxiang*, emigration is a "rite of passage" that they must pass through. Our conclusion is that, in Brazil, the *qiaoxiang* migration models were in operation until 2016. Since then, Chinese migration has suffered as a result of economic crisis, and is suffering even more now as a result of the COVID pandemic that started in 2020.

Based on the concept of "diminutive causation" propounded by Godfried Engbersen (2013), we suggest that *qiaoxiang* migration model may decline in the long run. But for those who are determined to migrate, their "passages" will be made much easier, less perilous and more comfortable as a result of the greater financial resources available to them.

2   Methodology and Data

The principal methodology of my research is a combination of bibliographic analysis with some semi-structured interviews conducted in Rio de Janeiro and São Paulo, during the period 2019–2020. Ten immigrants I had known for some years were contacted and asked "why did you emigrate?." These immigrants, 3 from Guangdong and 7 from Zhejiang, aged 20 to 50, told me that in the *qiaoxiang* young people must emigrate for the following reasons. (1) In the villages, only the old, the disabled and children remain. "Your schoolmates, your neighbors, your friends, your uncles, cousins and even nephews, are all abroad. There is no reason for you to stay." (2) If you choose not to go abroad, village folks will think you as unwilling to endure hardship (*buken chiku*), which is synonymous of laziness – a capital sin in traditional Chinese morality. For this reason, if you don't emigrate, you may lose face, and cause your family members to lose face. (3) In China, there is no alternative. Even if you find a job and work hard, the salary is low, and the boss is always watching you. So it's better to emigrate. Besides, by going abroad, you will see new places and meet new people, it is an exciting experience. Of course, life is hard in foreign countries, but by emigrating, you have complied with the social rituals of *qiaoxiang*.

Based on the above information, I see *qiaoxiang* migration as a rite of passage. I know the period of liminality is too long to be in tune with the original conception of the rite of passage, but I am not the first researcher to use the term to highlight the importance of migration for rural youth raised in the traditional migrant-sending villages. Joshua Reichert argues that for Mexicans living near the US-Mexican border, "migration becomes a *rite of passage* [italics mine], and those who do not attempt to elevate their status through international movement are considered lazy, unenterprising, and undesirable"

(Reichert 1982, apud Massey et al. 1993). Alessandro Monsutti (2007) posits that in the Afghan-Iran border regions, migration to Iran had become a rite of passage for the young Afghans, in building masculinity and adulthood. Although China and Brazil do not share a border, the mentality and the daily practices of the Chinese *qiaoxiang* youth are similar to those of Mexicans and Afghans: migration is a stage in their lives through which they have to pass.

3 The *Qiaoxiang* Migration Model in Brazilian Contexts

By *qiaoxiang*, we mean "migrants' (*qiao*) home village (*guxiang* or *xiang*)," or migrant-sending places. It is a term widely used in Chinese academic literature to refer to rural sending areas characterized by a high percentage of transnational migrants with close ties to their hometowns or villages. Li Minghuan and Diana Wong (2017) delineate a distinctive pattern of peasant migration from the *qiaoxiang*, based on its entrepreneurial self-organization of mobility, labor and capital. According to the authors, "the migration economies of the homeland and hostland mutually reinforce each other, which allows access to cheap labor, provides jobs, and generates capital to fund further migration." On the one hand, newly arrived migrants depend on the ethnic economy for a job. The ethnic economy, on the other hand, depends on the continual inflow of cheap and trusted labor for its competitiveness and further expansion.

Adopting the arguments of Li and Wong (2017), I distinguish four *qiaoxiang* migration models in Brazil: the first is the Cantonese *qiaoxiang* migration model, specifically Taishan county (and Wuyi) in Guangdong province, the homeland of circa two-thirds of Chinese migrants in Brazil; the second is Zhejiang *qiaoxiang* model, i.e., the Qingtian and Wenzhou municipalities of Zhejiang province, homeland to more than one third of Chinese migrants in Brazil. We might also distinguish a third model, the Fujianese *qiaoxiang* migration model, i.e., the Fuqing, Fuzhou, Zhangzhou and Putian Prefectures of Fujian Province. But comparing with the first two models, the scale of Fujianese migration is relatively small. According to the research of Shi Xueqin, in 1997, there were only 31 Fuqing migrants in Brazil, 20 of whom were undocumented (Shi 2000). Besides that, the economic activities of the Fujianese immigrants are similar to those of Zhejiangese immigrants, so we will focus only on the Yue (Guangdong) and Zhe (Zhejiang) models. Due to its historical complexities, Taiwanese migration to Brazil (by Taiwanese, I mean both Taiwanese natives and mainlanders who migrated to Taiwan after 1945) will be discussed in separate papers (See Figure 1, below).

```
┌─────────────────────┐              ┌─────────────────────┐
│ Guangdong Qiaoxiang │              │  Zhejiang Qiaoxiang │
│      Migration      │              │      Migration      │
└─────────────────────┘              └─────────────────────┘
           ↓         ↘              ↓
    ┌──────────────┐         ┌──────────────────┐
    │  Restaurants │         │    Low-Price     │
    │ and Pastelarias│ ←──── │  Manufactured    │
    │              │         │ Goods Wholesale  │
    │              │         │   and Retail     │
    └──────────────┘         └──────────────────┘
           ↑                          ↑
┌─────────────────────┐      ┌─────────────────────┐
│   Fujian Qiaoxing   │      │       Taiwan        │
│      Migration      │      │      Migration      │
└─────────────────────┘      └─────────────────────┘
```

FIGURE 1   Qiaoxiang migration models in Brazil, author's elaboration

3.1 *Guangdong* Qiaoxiang *Migration and the Catering Services*

According to a report, many Chinese immigrants in Brazil come from the Haiyan Township (海宴镇) in Taishan municipality (台山市), Guangdong province. The latest census of Haiyan Town shows that 96,889 emigrants distributed across 60 countries and regions in the world. The favorite destination of Haiyan emigrants is the United States, while Brazil is the second favorite destination, having received 14,652 Haiyan migrants. It is said that among the total number of 200,000 Chinese immigrants living in Brazil, about 7 percent are originally from the same hometown, Haiyan Township (Shen and Huang 2016).

Haiyan has many "Brazilian Villages," among them Shige Village (石阁村). According to an official source, Shige Village has only 1,300 habitants actually living in the village but it also has nearly 3,000 expatriates, among them more than 2,000 living in Brazil. The migration story of Su Xinliang's family is a good example of how Shige Village became a "Brazil Village." Su's grandfather migrated to Brazil in 1922. He first worked as a laborer in a restaurant in São Paulo, later on, he opened his own *pastelaria* – a pastry food bar. After earning some money, he opened five more *pastelarias* and invited five brothers in China to work with him. Su's father has ten brothers and sisters (seven men and three women). In 1955, Su's fourth uncle migrated to São Paulo via Hong Kong. In 1970, Su's other three uncles migrated to Brazil after 5 years of working in Hong Kong. In 1986, Su's father also migrated to Brazil. In 1993, his father helped other relatives in the village to migrate to Brazil. Now, Su's family has only one relative still living in the village, taking care of the ancestral houses and the children left behind by their emigrant parents. So how many members of Su's clan are living in Brazil? Su Xinliang has only a rough idea. He says: "From my father and uncles to my grandsons, there are four generations, 85 persons in total" (Ouyang and Shen 2016).

Up until 2016, when one walked through the streets of Brazilian cities like São Paulo and Rio de Janeiro, one often saw *pastelarias*, (*jiaozi dian* in Chinese) operated by Chinese immigrants. The Cantonese migrants like to invest in *pastelarias*, because they are relatively simple and easy to operate and bring fast returns. The main product of *pastelarias* is the pastel, a kind of fast food that has many varieties and shapes. Some are triangular and some are rectangular, but all are dumpled with minced beef meat, chicken, beacon or cheese, etc. As fast-food shops, *pastelarias* are usually small in area (10–20 square meters in average). Besides selling pastels, *pastelarias* also earn money by selling sugarcane juice and other types of fruit juice. In Rio and São Paulo, pastel with sugarcane juice (or fruit juices) are the "standard" menu of the *pastelarias*.

To certain extend, running a *pastelaria* is quite a good economic occupation for Cantonese immigrants in Brazil. It is easy to invest in and easy to operate, with quick economic returns. It provides jobs for unskilled newcomers and generates capital to fund further migration. It depends on the continual inflow of cheap and trusted labor for its competitiveness and further expansion. Depending on its localization – especially if the store is located in the downtown commercial area – the business will be very profitable. According to estimates, there are approximately 20,000 Chinese in Rio de Janeiro, among them nearly 15,000 from Taishan in Guangdong province. There are about 2,000 *pastelarias* in the Rio State, about 70 percent of which are operated by Cantonese immigrants (Ouyang and Shen 2016).

3.2 *Zhejiang* Qiaoxiang *Migration and the Trade in Low-Price Products*

Qingtian is a famous migrant-sending place, the hometown of many overseas Chinese from Zhejiang. According to the Qingtian County Bureau of Statistics, the number of permanent inhabitants of Qingtian County was 358,700 in 2018. Qingtian has 330,000 emigrants distributed across more than 120 countries and territories. In the case of Brazil, according to official data from Qingtian municipal government, from 1986 to 2000, a total of 3,094 citizens were authorized immigrants (*Qingtian Huaqiao Shi* 2011: 94). Taking irregular Qingtianese emigration into consideration, the same source said that, up to 2003, there were about 10,000 Qingtianese migrants in Brazil (*Qingtian Huaqiao Shi* 2011:102). In 2020, it was estimated that there were 50,000 Qingtianese (and their descendants) living in Brazil, and the total number of the Zhejiang *qiaoxiang* migrants (and their descendants) could be around 60,000 thousand

(My wechat conversations with Mr Jiang of the Qingtian Association of São Paulo, 15–20 October 2020).

Before 1949, there were fewer than one hundred Qingtianese living in Brazil. The most successful migrant was Mr Zhou Jiwen (1902–1980), who migrated to Rio de Janeiro around 1926 (Guo 2005). He opened a store selling embroidered table cloths imported from China. Another Qingtian migrant, Chen Yuxing, arrived in Rio de Janeiro around 1928 and opened a jewelry store selling pearl necklaces made in China (his brother had a store in Paris, France). Besides pearl necklaces, his store also supplied Qingtianese street peddlers with Chinese artifacts, handcrafts, textiles, chinaware and jewelry, which was highly valued by Brazilians at the time (Guo 2005).

After its communist revolution in 1949, China gradually closed its door. From 1950 to 1978, very few Qingtianese migrated to Brazil, and those who did usually followed the example of their predecessors, living as street vendors. We may look at the case of Mr Ji Furen, who migrated from Qingtian to Rio de Janeiro in 1958. He worked first as a street vendor and then, in 1968, opened a store selling imported goods. He used to import embroidered tablecloths and chinaware from Hong Kong, but Brazil's import tax was 250 percent, which limited his business. In 1974 he suspended his import business and opened a restaurant. In 1982, the Brazilian government reduced the import taxes to 85 percent. In 1986, this tax was further reduced to 50 percent. Mr Ji decided to reopen his import business. In 1994, when the Brazilian government opened its economy and liberalized international trade, the average import tax was reduced to 34 percent, and in case of products of daily use, it was further reduced to 20 percent. In the same year, Brazil started its *Plano Real* and issued a new Real (currency) and stopped the galloping inflation. Around 1995, the Brazilian currency was stabilized but highly valorized in relation to the US dollar (one Real was equal to one Dollar). At this time, the Chinese currency was down in relation to the US dollar (one RMB yuan was equal to 1/8 of a US dollar). Taking this extremely favorable opportunity, Mr Ji Furen invested all his resources in international trade. As his business expanded, he started to sponsor relatives, friends and neighbors to emigrate to Brazil. He and his brother each sponsored more than one hundred co-villagers to migrate to Brazil (Guo 2005). One of his nephews engaged in migration networking and was said to have successfully brought to Brazil about 400 Qingtianese in the early 1990s. Under these extremely favorable conditions, the Chinese immigrants, especially Qingtianese, invested in the importation of cheap Chinese products to Brazil. Later, not only Qingtianese but also Cantonese and Fujianese also engaged in the import of Chinese products from Zhejiang and Guangdong provinces.

The 1990s and 2000s were the golden age of Chinese out-migration and Chinese business expansion throughout the world. As indicated by a research paper, "In the 1994–2007 period, trade flows between Brazil and China increased by more than 20 percent per year. The total volume of trade (i.e. the sum of exports and imports) between the two countries was equal to USD 1.8 billion in 1994. Thirteen years later this flow reached USD 25 billion. Both countries experienced an economic opening in which tariffs were cut and non-tariff measures became less common. Regarding the Chinese opening process, its integration into the World Trade Organization in 2001 was a milestone" (Santos and Zignago 2010).

In the 1990s, Qingtianese migrants established a presence in the popular commercial zone of Rio de Janeiro called the Saara, situated in the downtown area of Rio de Janeiro. The name "Saara" comes from *Sociedade de Amigos das Adjacências da Rua da Alfândega* (Society of the Friends of *Rua da Alfândega* and Nearby Streets), a voluntary organization responsible for keeping order in the business area. Until the end of 1960s, Saara was occupied by migrants from the Middle East and Jews, but since the 1970s, Korean and Japanese immigrants have started to enter the region, bringing manufactured goods from East and Southeast Asia. Around 1995, there were only 3 to 5 Chinese stores in that region, but the number increased very quickly. In 2007, there were at least 80 Qingtianese stores. These Qingtianese business establishments had a big impact on Zhejiang province's foreign trade. In Saara, one of the biggest Qingtianese importers was Chou Jinghua. At its peak, every week he brought 4 to 5 containers of daily-use goods from Yiwu market, including waist belts, caps, scarves, gloves, shirts, sandals, lighters, underwear, pyjamas, tools etc. It was calculated that Qingtianese business firms imported four hundred to five hundred containers of goods to Rio de Janeiro every month (Shu 2009). As Saara became saturated, newcomers established their businesses in a suburban commercial market called Shopping Madureira, where the booth rent was cheaper and the clients were more numerous. Qingtianese import enterprises supplied the Brazilian retailers a variety of cheap products and fueled local commerce.

In sum, the trade in low-price popular products conducted by Zhejiang migrants served as economic bases for the Zhejiang *qiaoxiang* migration model. It generates capital which finances the emigration, and it creates employment opportunities for Chinese migrants as well as for local Brazilians. The newcomers, in turn, will open new stores and expand the economic horizons of the popular products business. The overseas demand for homeland products stimulates hometown industrialization, contributing to China's transformation into a "factory of the world."

4 Homeland Dissimilation and Rite of Passage

Transnational migration contributes to hometown development, but also creates homeland dissimilation (FitzGerald 2012). Homeland dissimilation refers to the process of differentiation between migrants and non-migrants in the hometown of origin, between families with or without migrants in the same hometown, and between families in migrant-sending communities and those in non-migrant-sending areas in the homeland. According to Liang et al. (2008), homeland dissimilation at the community level took place through three main mechanisms. One is the fancy houses built by migrant households. Visitors to these migrant-sending communities are often stunned by the luxury houses built with remittances. Sometimes the houses are built for consumption, but more importantly they have a broader symbolic meaning – they indicate that these migrants "have made it" abroad. The second mechanism is donations to *qiaoxiang* philanthropic activities and contributions to hometown development projects, such as roads, bridges, schools, hospitals, etc. Often the names of theses donors are inscribed on a board along with the amount of money contributed. This significantly elevates the status of these migrant households in these communities. The third mechanism is the rebuilding of ancestral halls (*citang*) and reconstruction of family graves. In a land known for ancestor worship, the reconstruction of family graves is a particularly conspicuous act of consumption. However, to gain social prestige in the *qiaoxiang*, these emigrants have to make "cultural remittances," i.e., remittances for collective consumption (schools, roads, hospitals, libraries, orphanages, etc.). Min Zhou and Xiangyi Li (2014, 2018) find that the sending of remittances for collective consumption serves as a unique mechanism of social-status compensation. To elucidate the cause-effect relationship between *qiaoxiang* migration and the rite of passage, the following figure is elaborated (Figure 2 below).

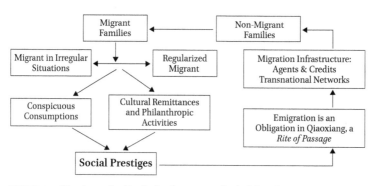

FIGURE 2   Qiaoxiang migration & rite of passage, author's elaboration

In sum, transnational migrations contribute to *qiaoxiang* development while reinforcing the existing social structures of inequality and uneven development in the homeland, stimulating more migrations. Xia (2020) discovered that, in Qingtian, village people are divided into two categories – those who have emigrant family members and those who have no emigrant family members. The category "have emigrant family members" is further divided into two subcategories, one represented by the rich emigrant, who travels frequently between China and the host countries and participates intensely in transnational activities, and the other by the poor emigrant (usually irregular migrants), who cannot afford frequent international trips and participate little or not at all in transnational activities.

The dissimilation created by transnational migration strengthens *qiaoxiang* people's belief in the power of emigration to change family fortunes. In these places, emigration is a social aspiration. Being an emigrant, in this case, bestows certain kinds of social prestige, in the form of an imprimatur of cosmopolitanism. Local labeling of some people as *huaqiao* (overseas Chinese) hints at the status that they may enjoy elsewhere, even if they do not enjoy such status in a given host society. On the issue of diasporic social capital, Julie Chu (2010) emphasizes the displacement experienced by those who are forever "stuck" at home, while others circulate across the world. Far from being pitied as exiles, diasporans are envied in their hometowns. In Longyan, the village of her fieldwork, half the population lives abroad, and their community is viewed as privileged. It is felt that those who stay behind, through their very stasis, are "exiled" – exiled, that is, from what has become the typical situation of diasporic crossings of distant horizons. Chu writes: "For my Fuzhounese subjects, the ultimate form of displacement was seen and experienced as the result of immobility rather than physical departure from a 'home'" (Chu 2010: 34). Chu is attentive to how the very ideas of "dwelling," "home," and "mobility" are in radical flux (Chu 2010: 7–8).

Xia (2021) discovered that in a *qiaoxiang* in Qingtian, having a son who is idle and unwilling to emigrate is embarrassing for the parents and causes them to "lose face" (*diu mianzi*) in the village. This is because, in *qiaoxiang* villages, only old folks and children are left behind. Any young adult who is unwilling to go abroad is stigmatized as being "mentally ill" (*naozi you maobing*). In other words, for *qiaoxiang* youth, emigration is a moral obligation. "In Qingtian, young people have to go abroad for the rest of their lives. Anyway, none of them stay in China. Who would like to leave a familiar environment? But we have no choice. Qingtianese must go abroad to *eat the bitterness* …" (Xia 2021: 59).

In an informal interview, my Cantonese friend Ms Guan told me that "in my hometown in Guangdong, young people are expected to emigrate. I would have emigrated to the USA by an arranged marriage, but my auntie told me that Brazil was going to give an amnesty to irregular immigrants in 1998. So I decided to emigrate to Brazil. I was very lucky that three months after my arrival, I received an amnesty" (interview held on 15 January 2021).

In sum, migration is part of the *qiaoxiang* social and cultural landscape, and for village youth, it is a way of life. This emigration-oriented culture is carried on as part of the rite of passage. In spite of the general rise in living standards in rural areas and increased employment opportunities, young adults still have to go abroad and there is no indication that transnational migration flows may come to an end. For many young men and women, out-migration gives them the opportunity to broaden their social networks beyond narrow kinship and neighborhood ties. In the case of the young men, we may conceive it as a necessary stage in their existence, a rite of passage to adulthood and a step toward manhood (Monsutti 2007). It is through emigration that the rural youth of the *qiaoxiang* persuade their village elders to believe in their entrepreneurial capacity and that they are worthy of respect. They will keep commuting between Brazil and China for part of their life. Through these mobilities, the social boundaries are transposed and *qiaoxiang* migration is renovated and perpetuated.

5   The Rite of Passage: A *Bitterness* That Is Hard to Swallow

The notion of rite of passage was proposed at the beginning of the twentieth century by Arnold van Gennep (1960), referring to rituals and ceremonies performed at major junctures of social life, such as birth, marriage or death. Each rite generally involves three stages: separation, transition (or liminality), and incorporation. Gennep's theory was reframed by Victor W. Turner (1969) and Pierre Bourdieu (1982). Bourdieu considers these rituals as *actes d'institution*, i.e., "institutionalized acts" (Bourdieu 1982).

The first to apply the concept of rite of passage to migration studies was the American scholar Joshua Reichert. In a paper in 1982, he posited that, at the community level, "migration becomes deeply ingrained into the repertoire of people's behaviors, and values associated with migration become part of the community's values." For young men, and in many settings for young women too, "migration becomes a rite of passage, and those who do not attempt to elevate their status through international movement are considered lazy, unenterprising, and undesirable" (Reichert 1982, apud Massey et al. 1993). Alessandro Monsutti argued that in the Afghan-Iran border regions, migration to Iran had become a rite of passage for young Afghans, in achieving masculinity and reaching adulthood (Monsutti 2007).

Between the 1980s and the 1990s, very few migrants entered Brazil legally, sponsored by their parents under the "family union" visa. Many had to enter Brazil irregularly, or to enter regularly but overstay the time limit. If the emigration broker (i.e., snakehead) is involved, a sum of 100,000 yuan (15,000 US dollars) may be charged if the passage is successful (Ouyang and Shen 2016). Depending on his financial resources, an emigrant may choose the most comfortable and expensive route, which means that he arrives at destination in two or three days, or he may choose a less smooth and riskier route, by crossing into Brazil from Bolivia or Surinam. The route via Bolivia or Surinam can cost US $15,000 (my interview with a Cantonese immigrant in August 2014). In some cases, the employer in Brazil would pay the sum to the snakeheads, but the smuggled migrant has to pay the debt by working for 3 years without wages. After paying all the emigration debts, he is free to work for any employer. This *guanxi* (social relations)-based arrangement sounds "reasonable" and works well in most cases, since both the employers and employees know each other from their native villages. They are either relatives or friends, and there is no reason for anything to go wrong. But accidents do happen: employing illegal migrant is also risky for employers. If detected by the police, the employers can receive a heavy fine or might have their business licenses suspended, and their illegal employees could be deported.

In spite of this risk, driven by social, economic and cultural forces, *qiaoxiang* youth are eager to emigrate. For most of these young adults, emigration is a social ritual, a rite of passage that they must go through. The migratory passages generally undergo the following stages: first, the separation period. The migrants (young adult) cross the international borders (usually smuggled abroad), and successfully "hide-down" in the host country (working illegally without being detected by the local police). This period may last for 3 to 6 years depending on individual situations.

Second, the transition period (liminality). Emigration means separation, both spatially and socially, from hometown, parents, relatives, friends, wife and children, etc. Although temporary, it may last several years. During this period, the newcomers have no legal status and have to depend on their *guanxi* for survival. Lacking legal documents, they are reduced to what Susan Coutin (2013) called "social space of non-existence" where the migrant is physically present but legally absent: "This space excludes people, limits rights, restricts services, and erases personhood. The space of non-existence is largely a space of subjugation" (Coutin 2013:172). In the case of Chinese undocumented immigrants, they are supposed to "eat" all sorts of bitterness, i.e., endure all the associated difficulties and survive all the socio-economic pressures and exploitative conditions imposed by the local society as well as by their own co-ethnics (Hiah and Staring 2016; Liu and Olivos 2020).

During this transition period (liminality), the newcomers have no legal status and have to depend on their *guanxi* for survival. Lacking legal documents, they live in irregular situations, which can be deadly. It can mean working for low wages in a sweatshop, or being unemployed. It can mean the denial of medical care, food, social services, education, and public housing. In this irregular situation, recent arrivals often live with relatives, friends, or coworkers, with many individuals living together in a one-bedroom apartment. Since Brazilian law does not protect illegal workers, their fate depends entirely on the good-will of their employers. These undocumented migrants may benefit from expressions of ethnic solidarity on the part of friends, relatives, temples and churches, but being irregular in legal status, they live at the bottom of the diasporic social ladder.

Also in this period, the migrant has to legalize himself or herself by resorting to amnesty as arranged by the Brazilian government (1988, 1998, 2009), by marrying a legalized co-ethnic Chinese (or, in rare cases, a Brazilian citizen) or by having Brazil-born children (Shu 2021). By having a child, both the mother and the father will receive a Brazilian "green card," in accordance with the legal principle of *jus soli* ("right of the soil") – that is, being born on Brazilian soil. After regularizing their legal status, they may visit their hometown in China and leave their baby in the care of grandparents or relatives.

Third, incorporation. Having legalized themselves, the couple may invest in a *pastelaria* or restaurant, or rent a commercial room to sell low-priced daily-use products imported from Yiwu. After earning enough money, he/she would participate in the diasporic associations and engage in charity activities on behalf of the host society and donate money for *qiaoxiang* philanthropic activities, and finally, getting incorporated in both *qiaoxiang* and host society, as a successful entrepreneur and qualified "Huaqiao" (Table 1 below).

Many *qiaoxiang* emigrants are unskilled rural peasants, but they were willing to endure hardship or "eat bitterness" (*chi ku*, 吃苦), i.e., to pass through the ordeal of social non-existence in a foreign country. This bitterness includes: the tortuous (sometimes perilous) passage into the host country, by means of trafficking; a heavy work load; long working hours; underpaid extra hours; substandard living and working conditions; psychological pressures and social isolation, etc. Under these various stresses, the employer-employee relation can go wrong.

As a matter of fact, there have been frequent reports in Brazilian newspapers about the ill-treatment of irregular immigrant workers by their co-ethnic employers (not only Chinese, but also Bolivians, Peruvians, etc.). On 4 April 2013, the police in Rio de Janeiro rescued an irregular Chinese immigrant who was a victim of his irregular situation:

TABLE 1   Rite of passage in *qiaoxiang* migration model (author's elaboration)

Rite of Passage in Qiaoxiang Migration Model

Category 1	Stage 1: Separation	Stage 2: Transition	Stage 3: Incorporation	Category 2
Initial category: *Qiaoxiang* Rural youth	Borderline Traverses	"Eating all bitterness" in host society; Struggling for survival while waiting for legalization	Legalization and opening one's own business	New category: *Huaqiao* (overseas Chinese)
Preparing for emigration: a, Make contacts with co-villagers abroad; b, Negotiate with emigration agents (snakeheads); c, Fund-raising Funds (borrow money or debt for work arrangements). Borderline passage	Two modes of Emigration: A, Regular emigration; B, Irregular emigration (a, Legal leave but illegal entry; b, legal entry but overstay; c, Illegal entry but legal stay; d, illegal leave and illegal stay).	Life in irregular situation (a, no legal status and no formal employments; b, no social and economic rights; c, local police harassments; d, co-ethnic exploitations; e, economic pressures & psychological isolations); Pay back the emigration debts if exist.	Legalization (a, wedding with legalized co-ethnics or with local Brazilians; b, having a Brazilian child; c, government amnesty every 10 years); Make remittances (private & public consumption)	Visits to hometown: a, Show one's success by ostensive consumptions and by donations to philanthropic activities; b, Enjoying the favorable treatment of the homeland governments; Practicing Transnationalism.

Yin Qiang Quan, 23 years, who was smuggled to Brazil in May 2012. His cousin Yan Ruihong, 28 years, owner of a *pastelaria*, paid the emigration debts of circa 30,000 Brazilian Reals (approx. $15,000 US dollars at that time), and received Yin in his *pastelaria*. According to the news reports, Yin had to work for Yan for three years without salary in order to pay back the emigration debts. Yan offered free food and lodging as well as 200 Reals per month for Yin's personal use. After 3 years of "debt by work," Yin would receive the salary of 1,500 Reals a month. It seemed a reasonable arrangement. But after one year of work, Yan complained that his employee (his cousin) was "lazy" and "unwilling to eat bitterness." The two started to quarrel and one attacked the other. Yin got seriously injured and a Brazilian neighbor denounced them to the police after hearing the quarrels and beatings (Figueira et al. 2013). Yan Ruilong was arrested by the police. Based on the Brazilian Penal Code, he was accused of "reducing the victim to a condition analogous to that of slavery" (art. 149); "violation of labor rights" (art. 203); and "failure to provide first-aid" (art. 135). In addition, Yan was accused of "beating and torture" according to law 9.455/97. The end of the story was: Yan stayed in prison for a year, and was then released. He still lives in Rio de Janeiro with his family. His cousin Yin, being a victim, received Brazilian legal protection and was not deported (Martins 2013).

This is a typical case of the failure of the *qiaoxiang* migration model: through the *qiaoxiang* migration network, the newly arrived migrant is received and made to "eat bitterness" in a totally new country without any legal protection. Within the migratory network, the receiver/employer is able to exploit his undocumented employees (Hiah and Starling 2016; Liu and Olivos 2020). Under such stresses, the *qiaoxiang* model is liable to go wrong.

6 The Chinese Popular Trade in Brazil

The term "popular" in Portuguese has a connotation that is not entirely conveyed by literal translation into English. It refers to the lower classes and emphasizes class inequality. The notion of "popular markets" emphasizes the working-class background of most vendors and consumers, who seek to dissociate themselves from the stigma of irregularity and illegality. The denomination "popular markets" refers to low-income individuals' activities, and although it can be derogatory, it typically celebrates the communitarian ties that knit together a wider fabric of social cooperation and solidarity. Precisely in this sense, contemporary scholars have approached these markets as what Peruvian scholars José Matos Mar and later Aníbal Quijano call "popular economies," broadly understood as non-hegemonic modes of production, distribution, and consumption, which give form to a vibrant system of local and transnational socio-economic relations (Piza 2021).

The livelihood of the migrant has never been easy. When migrants arrive in Brazil, they need to survive by peddling goods on the streets, an occupation considered by Brazilian authorities to be informal and illicit, and thus subject to action by the police (Coletto 2010). In the years 1995–2005, some such migrants engaged in "contraband" – bringing imported products from the Ciudad Del Este of Paraguay, a free-trade area (located strategically near the triple frontier between Argentina, Brazil and Paraguay), where imported consumer goods from East and Southeast Asia were exempt of taxes. These individual *contrabandists* (known in Brazil as *sacoleiros*) brought perfume, watches, Walkmans, cameras, and video-cameras produced in Japan, Korea, Taiwan, and Hong Kong from Paraguay into São Paulo and Rio de Janeiro. Such items were in high demand among Brazilian consumers. Brazil at the time still charged very high import taxes, and for this reason, contraband activities became highly profitable. "If you make one or two successful trips, bringing two or three *sacolas* (big plastic bags) of these imported products to São Paulo or Rio de Janeiro, you can live for six months without working" (Li and Guo 2020).

Because these smuggling activities were quite profitable, they became risky. Bandit attacks, official blockades, police extortion, robbery, etc., all contributed to make such trips hazardous and eventually infeasible. Before 2010, most Chinese migrants involved in smuggling had quit these activities. Such activities started to decline in Brazil around 2010, as the Brazilian government further intensified its campaign against smugglers (Pinheiro-Machado 2017: 19).

From the 2000s through to the 2010s, Chinese migrants had a big impact on the development of popular markets (Piza 2021) in the center of São Paulo, which they supplied with all sorts of low-price products made in China. Every year, they imported thousands of containers of day-use products directly from Yiwu and sold them to Brazilian clients of all categories, from street vendors, shopkeepers, and supermarkets to shopping centers. While big wholesalers operated in their exclusive offices and warehouses, small traders worked in the commercial galleries on the Rua 25 de Março and adjacent neighborhoods, selling their products to Brazilian consumers, street vendors and shop-owners from all over Brazil. Chinese businesspersons from other Brazilian cities and states also made regular trips to São Paulo to purchase the imported products and resell them in their host cities (Silva 2018).

Trading activities in commercial galleries had multiplied in the period between 2000 and 2015. These galleries were usually subdivided into a large number of small booths (or stalls) of no more than 4 m², each stall constituting an individual store. For the gallery owners, it is more advantageous to divide such commercial spaces into dozens of stalls and lease the stalls than to lease the whole space. In São Paulo, thousands of Chinese stallholders are spread across commercial buildings and warehouses on Rua 25 de Março, and the nearby Brás district where the Early Morning Fair (*feira de madrugada*) was located (and which operated from 2 AM to 6 AM, Silva 2018). There were around 4,500 stallholders in these two commercial areas, roughly half were Chinese migrants (São Paulo Department of Sub-prefectures 2013, apud Piza 2021). Many Chinese merchants rented these stalls to sale cheap products "made in China," such as handbags, suitcases, shoes, jeans, toys, clothes, etc. (Silva 2018; Piza 2021).

Around 2010, São Paulo had displaced the Ciudad del Este of Paraguay as the regional center of importation. Smuggling from Ciudad del Este to São Paulo had been greatly reduced in scale, and mainly concerned special products such as cigarettes and electronic items. Since 2012, São Paulo has become a new Mecca for the retail and wholesale trade in cheap China-made daily-use products.

With São Paulo saturated, other centers of popular commerce have emerged in the inland of São Paulo and other Brazilian states and cities. They include Shopping Oiapoque in Belo Horizonte (MG) and Feira dos Importados in Brasília (DF). Chinese transnational business networks have been established in all Brazil's big cities, and through these networks, they import cheap Chinese popular products from Guangzhou and Yiwu, and distribute them throughout the whole Brazil.

7 The Current Economic Crisis and the Perspectives of *Qiaoxiang* Migration: A Tentative Conclusion

After the Soccer World Cup in 2014, the Brazilian economy started to slow down and Chinese migrants began to lose money. Before 2014, the profit of import companies of Chinese immigrants was between 20 to 30 percent. At the end of 2015, the Brazilian currency (the Real) depreciated by 46 percent against the US dollar. Coupled with rising inflation and declining local consumption, Chinese popular commerce faced serious challenges. Many import companies were forced to shut down. The Qingtianese trade in popular consumer products low in price and quality had declined rapidly. Since the beginning of 2020, the exchange rate of Brazilian Real to US dollar has fallen below 5:1, as against 4:1 in 2019. The Brazilian currency had depreciated by more than 20 percent over 2019. As a result, most Chinese ethnic enterprises became unprofitable (Li and Guo 2020).

The *pastelarias* also suffered from the economic recessions that happened after the 2016 Olympic Games in Rio. With high unemployment, social order deteriorated and businesses receded day by day. A Cantonese immigrant named Azhu told me her story:

> Business was good until 2016. After 2016, the Brazilian economy entered into recession. The number of customers diminished and the social order went from bad to worse, as a result of which bandit attacks became frequent. We had been attacked many times. One day, when I was in the *pastelaria*, one boy from the *favela* [slum] came to my shop, and snatched a gold necklace from a customer sitting at a table easting pastels. This was the last straw. It killed off my pastel business. We shut down our *pastelaria* in 2017. My husband decided to go to the United States, where his family had restaurants. My eldest son, now 18, was sent to China to study at Jinan University. I have to stay in Rio de Janeiro with my two younger kids. I opened an online store selling cell phone cases and accessories. The business was not good. I hope my husband will be able to establish himself quickly, so that we may join him soon in the US
>
> MY CONVERSATION WITH AZHU, held on 15 February 2019

In 2020, due to the COVID-19 pandemic, restaurants and bars in Brazil suffered big losses as a result of the lockdowns and social distancing required by the war on the pandemic. According to a journalist, 300,000 restaurants and bars of Brazil closed in 2020 (Grandi 2021). There is no statistical data about the number of shutdowns of Chinese business establishments (restaurants, *pastelarias*, low-price stores, etc.), but we can be sure that many have closed their doors or survive only by running delivery services or by e-commerce (Li and Guo 2020). What to do? Quit Brazil? For many, it is almost impossible to leave Brazil and restart a business in China. One Qingtian migrant in Rio de Janeiro said: "I came to Brazil at the age of 18. In the course of 20 years, I made a lot of Brazilian friends. All my business contacts, relationships and clients are here in Brazil, and there is no chance to restart if I return to my hometown in China. I have travelled around the world and finally settled here. Brazil is my second home" (Li and Guo 2020).

So what will become of the *qiaoxiang* migration model?

Godfried Engbersen (2013) proposed diminutive causation as the counterpart of the cumulative causation (Massey 1990; Massey et al. 1993). Based on his analysis of the role of migrant networks in reducing immigration from Morocco to the Netherlands, Engbersen argues that it is crucial to move beyond examinations of migrant networks, not only by taking into account macro institutional factors (labor markets, state policies) but also by analyzing the relevance of other feedback channels.

Based on Engbersen's idea, we find that three macro-level institutional changes have taken place in Brazil since 2007. First, Brazilian migration law became more and more restrictive. In the Amnesty of 1998, most irregular Chinese immigrants were amnestied; but in 2009, only sixty-eight percent were. In 2018, the Amnesty law was approved by congress but was vetoed by President Michel Temer. This was a deadly blow to a large number of Chinese irregular migrants – probably more than five thousand of them – who have in many cases been waiting for amnesty for several years (Shu and Qiao 2021: 34–55, 47). Second, job opportunities for immigrants have decreased due to the successive financial crises of 2008, 2015, 2016 and the pandemic of 2020–2022. Third, anti-immigration discourses – particularly anti-Chinese rhetoric – is on the rise. Innumerable official and non-official campaigns have been launched against Chinese businesses and trading companies accused of "tax evasion," "dealing in contraband" and "selling counterfeit products." Meanwhile, social order has deteriorated on a daily basis in Brazil. Bandit attacks, robbery and murders have became commonplace. These changes have negatively affected the beliefs and desires of settled Chinese immigrants to help bringing more migrants to Brazil.

Last but not the least important is the question of left-behind children. Chinese migration to Brazil has produced a large number of "left-behind children" (*liushou ertong* 留守儿童). We have no official data on Brazil-born "left-behinds," so we don't know the real dimension of the problem. During their struggle to climb the social ladder in a foreign society, many migrants left behind their China-born children, and many migrant couples sent their foreign-born children back to be cared for by relatives in the home village. According to statistics issued by the Qingtian Municipal Bureau of Education, in 2015, 34.91 percent of Qingtian school students have parents or a single parent abroad; and 88.66 percent have expatriate relatives (Kong 2018). These "left-behind children" (born overseas or born in China) can operate as push or pull forces in the case of expatriate parents. If the situation in the migrant-receiving country worsens, these left-behind children may resist the idea of emigration, and if it improves, the opposite happens. If China's economy prospers, some expatriate parents may find that their left-behinds are pulling them back. Also, as China is becoming an aging society, fewer people are available for emigration.

At present, we find that the outlook for the *qiaoxiang* migration model is not very bright, and one might even say that it is gloomy – at least in the case in Brazil. The bleak economic prospects, the extremely volatile exchange rates and the lack of everyday safety mean that these immigrants are reluctant to fetch their left-behind-children to Brazil. Instead, they become even more evidently a floating population between Brazil and China, always thinking of returning to China. What is certain is that, for those who are determined to migrate to Brazil, their passages will be easier than before, less perilous and more comfortable because they have financial resources at their disposal.

References

Brainard, Lawrence and John Welch. 2012, 21 January. "Brazil and China: Clouds on the Horizon." https://www.americasquarterly.org/article/brazil-and-china-clouds-on-the-horizon/. Accessed on 28 July 2022.

Bourdieu, Pierre. 1982. "Les rites comme actes d'institution" (The Rites as Institutionalized Acts). *Actes de la recherche en sciences sociales* 43: 58–63.

Chu, Julie Y. 2010. *Cosmologies of Credit: Transnational Mobility and the Politics of Destination in China*. Durham, NC: Duke University Press.

Coletto, Diego. 2010. *The Informal Economy and Employment in Brazil: Latin America, Modernization, and Social Changes*. Palgrave Macmillan.

Coutin, Susan Bibler. 2003. "Illegality, Borderlands and the Space of Nonexistence." In *Globalization under Construction: Governmentality, law, and Identity*, eds., Richard Warren Perry and Bill Maurer, pp. 171–202. Minneapolis, MN: University of Minnesota Press.

Engbersen, Godfried. 2013. "Networks and Beyond: Feedback Channels and the Diminutive Causation of International Migration." Paper presented at the THEMIS International Migration Conference, Oxford, UK, 24–26 September.

Figueira, Ricardo Rezende, Sudano, Suliane and Edna Galvão. 2013. "Os Chineses no Rio: a Escravidão Urbana" (The Chinese in Rio de Janeiro: An Urban Slavery). *Brasiliana: Journal for Brazilian Studies* 2(2): 90–112.

FitzGerald, David. 2012. "A Comparativist Manifesto for International Migration Studies." *Ethnic and Racial Studies* 35: 1725–1740.

Gennep, Arnold van. 1960. The Rites of Passage. Monika Vizdon, trans. Chicago: University of Chicago Press.

Grandi, Guilherme. 2021, 5 April. "Cerca de 300 mil restaurantes fecharam as portas no Brasil em 2020" (About 300 Thousand Restaurants Closed Their Doors in Brazil in

2020). Gazeta do Povo. https://www.gazetadopovo.com.br/bomgourmet/mercado-e-setor/restaurantes-brasileiros-fecharam-portas-brasil. Accessed on 10 December, 2021.

Guo, Bingqiang. 2005. *Baxi Qingtian Huqiao Jishi 1910–1994* 巴西青田华侨纪实 1910–1994 (Factual Records of the Qingtianese Immigrants in Brazil 1910–1994). Qingtian, Zhejiang Province, China: Qingtian xian zhengfu.

Hiah, Jing and Richard Staring. 2016. "'But the Dutch Would Call it Exploitation': Crimmigration and the Moral Economy of the Chinese Catering Industry in the Netherlands." *Crime, Law and Social Change* 66(1): 83–100.

Kong, Lingjun. 2018. Qingtian Huaqiao da 33 wan, *Yang liushou* ertong jinnianlai que yuelai yueshao 青田县华侨达 33 万 "洋留守" 儿童近年却越来越少 (Qingtian Has 330,000 emigrants, But Left-over Children Are Less and Less). http://biz.zjol.com.cn/zjjjbd/gdxw/201808/t20180830_8144921.shtml. Accessed on 15 October, 2020.

Li, Chao and Yifei Guo. 2020, 14 April. Bainian haiwai mousheng shi, 30 wan qingtian huasheng rujin mianlin quliu jueze 百年海外谋生史, 30 万青田华商如今面临去留抉择 (One Hundred Years History of Out-migration and Struggle Abroad, 30 Thousand Qingtianese Businessmen and Women Face the Choice of Quit or Stay), 2020. https://36kr.com/p/664538328805254. Accessed on 15 October, 2020.

Li, Minghuan and Diana Wong. 2017. "Moving the Migration Frontier: A Chinese Qiaoxiang Migration Model?" *International Migration* 56(1): 63–77.

Liang, Zai, Miao David Chunyu, Guotu Zhuang and Wenzhen Ye. 2008. "Cumulative Causation, Market Transition, and Emigration from China." *American Journal of Sociology* 114(3): 706–737.

Liu, Minghui and Francisco Olivos. 2020. "Co-ethnic Exploitation among Chinese Migrants within an Ethic Economy." *Asian and Pacific migration journal: APMJ* https://doi.org/10.1177/0117196819899243. Accessed on 10 January 2022.

Martins, Felipe. 2013, 5 April. "Chinês dono de pastelaria é preso por manter primo como escravo no Rio" (Chinese Owner of Pastelaria Arrested for Keeping His Cousin as Slave in Rio). https://noticias.uol.com.br/cotidiano/ultimas-noticias/2013/04/05/chines-dono-de-pastelaria-e-preso-por-manter-primo-como-escravo-no-rio.html. Accessed on 10 October, 2021.

Massey, Douglas. 1990. "The Social and Economic Origins of Immigration." *The ANNALS of the American Academy of Political and Social Science* 510(1):60–72.

Massey, Douglas, Arango, Joaquin, Hugo, Graeme, Kouaouci, Ali, Pellegrino, Adela and J. Edward Taylor. 1993. "Theories of International Migration: A Review and Appraisal." *Population and Development Review* 19(3): 431–466.

Monsutti, Alessandro. 2007. "Migration as a Rite of Passage: Young Afghans Building Masculinity and Adulthood in Iran." *Iranian Studies* 40(2):167–185.

Ouyang, Yunwei and Peng Shen. 2016, 14 August. "Taishan ren liyue da Maoxian" 台山人里约大冒险 (The Adventures of Taishanese in Rio de Janeiro). https://kknews.cc/entertainment/b63e99.html. Accessed on 15 October, 2020.

Pinheiro-Machado, Rosana. 2017. *Counterfeit Itineraries in the Global South: the Human Consequences of Piracy in China and Brazil*. London/New York: Routledge.

Piza, Douglas. 2021. "Legibility in Mobility and Emplacement: Chinese Vendors in São Paulo Popular Market." In *Studies on Chinese migration: Brazil, China and Mozambique*, Bueno, André and Veras, Daniel, eds., pp. 223–264 Rio de Janeiro: Projeto Orientalismo/UERJ.

Reichert, Joshua. 1982. "Social stratification in a Mexican Sending Community: The Effect of Migration to the United States." *Social Problems* 29: 422–433.

Qingtian Huaqiao Shi Editors' Committee. 2011. *Qingtian Huaqiao Shi* 青田华侨史 (The History of Overseas Qingtianese). Hangzhou, China: Zhejiang Renmin Chubanshe.

Santos, Enestor dos and, Soledad Zignago. 2010, 1 September. "The Impact of the Emergence of China on Brazilian International Trade," (Working Papers, Number 1022). BBVA Bank, Economic Research Department.

Shen, Weihong and Lina Huang. 2016, 7 August. Guangdong Taishan youpian Baxi Cun, Lüju Baxi Xiangqin bi Cunli renkou Haiduo 广东台山有片「巴西村」旅居巴西乡亲比村里人口还多 (Brazilian Villages in Taishan, Guangdong, Where the Number of Emigrants Surpasses the Number of Hometown Residents). https://kknews.cc/zh-hk/news/8x8rbn.html. Accessed on 15 October, 2020.

Shi, Xueqin. 2000. Gaige Kaifang Yilai Fuqing Qiaoxiang de Xinyimin-Jiantan Feifa Yimin Wenti 改革开放以来福清侨乡的新移民—兼谈非法移民问题 (New Emigrants from Fuqing County after Reform and Open-door Policy and the Question of the Illegal Migrants) *Huaqiao huaren Lishi Yanjiu* 4: 26–31.

Shu, Chang-sheng. 2009. "Chineses no Rio de Janeiro." *Revista Leituras da História*. Ano II17: 44–53.

Shu, Changsheng 束长生. 2018. Baxi Huaqiao Huaren Yanjiu Wenxian Zongshu yu Renkou Tongji 巴西华侨华人研究文献综述与人口统计 (The Studies of Chinese Migration to Brazil: Literature Review and Statistical Estimations) *Huaqiao Huaren Lishi Yanjiu* 1: 30–40.

Shu, Changsheng and Jianzhen Qiao. 2021. Cong Kuli dao Touzi Yimin – *baxi Huaqiao huaren gaishu* 从苦力到投资移民—巴西华侨华人概述 (From Coolies to Investors – an Overview on the Chinese Migration to Brazil). In *Zhongba Hezuo yu Baxi Wenti Yanjiu* 中巴合作与巴西问题研究 (Sino-Brazilian Cooperation and the Studies on Brazil). Jatoba, Julio Reis, Sun, Yuqi, and Chunhui Lu, eds., pp. 34–55. Macao: University of Macau Press. https://library2.um.edu.mo/ebooks/991010061949406306.pdf.

Silva, Carlos Freire da. 2018. "Conexões Brasil-China: a Migração Chinesa no Centro de São Paulo" (Brazil-China Connections: the Chinese Migration in Downtown São Paulo). *Cadernos Metropolitanos*, São Paulo 20 (41): 223–243.

Turner, Victor W. 1995. *The Ritual Process: Structure and Anti-Structure*. New York: Routledge.

Woon Yuen-fong. 1996. "The Re-emergence of the Guan Community of South China in the Post-Mao Era: The Significance of Ideological Factors." *China Information* 11(1): 14–38.

Xia, Cuijun. 2021. *"Liudong" Shijiaoxia Qiaoxiang Qingnian Shehui Quge Yanjiu – yi Zhejiang Qingtian xinchun weili* "流动"视角下侨乡青年社会区隔研究 – 以浙江青田幸村为例 (Youth M and Social Distinction in *Qiaoxiang* – The Case of Xingcun Village in Qingtian, Zhejiang Province). *Huaqiao Huaren Lishi Yanjiu* 1: 54–60.

Zhou, Min and Xiangyi Li. 2014. "Social Status Compensation: Variations on the Sending of Cultural Remittances among Chinese Overseas." UCLA: International Institute.

Zhou, Min and Xiangyi Li. 2018. "Remittances for Collective Consumption and Social Status Compensation: Variations on Transnational Practices among Chinese International Migrants." *International Migration Review* 52(1): 1–39.

© 2025 Singapore Chinese Cultural Centre and Chinese Heritage Centre, Nanyang Technological University
https://doi.org/10.1142/9789811279218_0004

Homeland, Host Country, and Beyond: Identity Transformation among Chinese Migrants in Singapore

祖国、移居国或其他：在新加坡的中国移民身份认同的转变

Shaohua Zhan (占少华)[1] | ORCID: 0000-0002-9996-8833
Sociology Programme, School of Social Sciences, Nanyang Technological University, Singapore
shzhan@ntu.edu.sg

Abstract

This paper examines identity transformation among Chinese migrants in Singapore in the context of transnationalism and widespread use of ICTs (Information and Communication Technologies). Based on how strongly migrants identify with the homeland and the host country, the paper constructs four ideal types of identity: transnational, assimilatory, sojourning, and cosmopolitan. The study finds that the most common identity is the transnational sort, characterized by the migrant identifying strongly with both homeland and host country. Nevertheless, migrants also hold other identities including those beyond the four ideal types, demonstrating the diversity and fluidity of migrants' identity transformation. The paper also examines the factors that affect migrants' identity transformation.

---

1 Shaohua Zhan is an associate professor and deputy head of Sociology Programme at Nanyang Technological University in Singapore. His research interests include international migration, land politics, and food security, with a focus on China, Singapore, and other Asian nations. He is the author of China and Global Food Security (Cambridge University Press, forthcoming) and The Land Question in China: Agrarian Capitalism, Industrious Revolution, and East Asian Development (Routledge, 2019). His work has appeared in *Ethnic and Racial Studies*, *New Left Review*, *The Journal of Peasant Studies*, *World Development*, *The China Quarterly*, and *The China Journal*, among others.

© KONINKLIJKE BRILL NV, LEIDEN, 2022 | DOI:10.1163/17932548-12341467

---

* This chapter was originally published as: Zhan, S. (2022). Homeland, Host Country, and Beyond: Identity Transformation among Chinese Migrants in Singapore. *Journal of Chinese Overseas*, 18(2), 265–286. Reprinted with kind permission from Brill.

This is an Open Access chapter published by World Scientific Publishing Company. It is distributed under the terms of the Creative Commons Attribution-NonCommercial-NoDerivatives 4.0 (CC BY-NC-ND) License which permits use, distribution and reproduction, provided that the original work is properly cited, the use is non-commercial and no modifications or adaptations are made.

Keywords

identity transformation – transnationalism – ICT use – Chinese migrants – Singapore

摘要

本文研究了在跨国主义和信息技术普遍运用背景下在新加坡的中国移民身份认同的转变。根据移民对祖国和移居国的认同程度，文章构建了四种身份认同的理想类型：跨国认同、同化认同、旅居认同和普世认同。本文通过研究发现最为普遍的是跨国认同，即移民对祖国和移居国同时保持高度的认同。然而，在新加坡的中国移民也发展出其他类型的认同，而且相当比例移民的认同类型在四种理想型之外，这证明了移民身份认同的多样性与易变性。文章还探讨了影响移民身份认同的主要因素。

关键词

认同转变 – 跨国主义 – 信息技术运用 – 中国移民 – 新加坡

1 Introduction

The transformation of identity after migration has received wide attention in migration and diaspora studies. It was once believed that migrants would gradually forgo their attachment to the home country while aligning their identity with the host country (Gordon 1964). Since the 1990s, the transnational turn in migration research has challenged this notion of linear identity change. Research shows that migrants have not severed the links to their home country after migration, but "maintain, forge, and sustain multi-stranded social relations that link together their societies of origin and settlement" (Basch, Schiller and Blanc 1994: 6). Many migrants are involved in cross-border social, economic or political activities and maintain social relations with family members and communities in the home country. In recent two decades, the proliferation of Information and Communication Technologies (ICTs) has further stimulated transnational activities, as it enables migrants to sustain transnational families and communities across distance, form new social spaces, fields or habitus, and engage in homeland economic and political activities (Baldassar Nedelcu, Merla and Wilding 2016; Nedelcu 2012; Vertovec 2009; Zhou and Liu 2016).

The shift of focus to transnationalism has had a big impact on studies of overseas Chinese. Scholars have revised assimilationist theories and examined overseas Chinese in transnational perspective, with an emphasis on extraterritorial nationalism and multi-local and multi-ethnic identities (Barabantseva 2005; Christiansen 2005; Guo 2022; Ma 2003; Yan, Wong and Lai 2019). A major factor behind transnationalism among overseas Chinese is the rise of China since the 1980s. The market reform and the open-door policy have strengthened economic connections between the homeland and Chinese diaspora. The post-reform emigrants not only originated from coastal provinces, which were traditionally sending areas, but also from inland provinces across China, adding much diversity to the group (Liu 2005). The Chinese migrants who emigrated in recent decades have often maintained a high level of transnationalism, due to their living experience in and economic linkages with China (Ren and Liu 2015; Zhou and Liu 2016).

This paper examines identity transformation of Chinese migrants in Singapore in the context of transnationalism and widespread ICT use. Singapore as a British colony received large numbers of migrants from China, India, and Southeast Asia. After independence in 1965, Singapore became a nation with four main races: Chinese, Malays, Indians, and Others, with Chinese being the majority and accounting for three quarters of the population. Immigration from China nearly stalled in the 1960s–80s, it started to rise after China and Singapore established diplomatic relations in 1992. In the past three decades, China has become a major source of immigration to Singapore. In 2015, China accounted for 18 percent of the foreign-born population in Singapore, ranking only behind Malaysia (Yang, Yang and Zhan 2017).

Identity transformation is not only related to migrants' self-perception and subjectivity but is also shaped by structural forces such as the job market, immigration policy, and social discrimination and isolation (Levitt 2003). Chinese migrants in Singapore, and migrants in general, must navigate the choices of identity between home and host countries and confront the challenges of detachment from the homeland while facing difficulties in integrating into the host society. This article aims to understand this process by capturing different patterns of migrants' engagements with home and host countries and various identities arising from these engagements.

The paper shows that Chinese migrants in Singapore report a diverse range of identities, which can be classified into four ideal types. The first ideal type is the assimilatory identity, in which case migrants have largely forgone their homeland identity while identifying strongly with Singapore. The second is the transnational identity, in which case migrants identify strongly with both China and Singapore. The third is the sojourning identity, in which case migrants identify strongly with the homeland, but weakly with the host society. The last category is the cosmopolitan identity, in which case migrants do not have a strong attachment to either the homeland or the host country. I will also examine how the transformation to these identities has been shaped by social and political factors.

The data is drawn from a study on immigration and integration in Singapore between September 2017 and June 2019. This includes a survey of 240 Chinese migrants and 43 in-depth interviews. About half of the survey respondents were randomly selected from the online panel data of a commercial survey company, and the other half were surveyed by the research team through a snowballing method. To reduce the bias in data collection, the research team diversified the interviewees (23 males and 20 females) in terms of age, occupation, immigration status, and duration of stay. In addition to survey and interview data, the study collected policy documents and statistical data on Chinese migrants in Singapore.

The remainder of the paper is organized as follows. Section 2 reviews the literature on migrant identity. Section 3 briefly describes Chinese migration to Singapore in recent decades. Section 4 analyzes the survey data and reports quantitative findings on identity transformation. Section 5 examines the factors affecting identity transformation based on in-depth interviews. Section 6 concludes.

2   From Transnationalism to Diverse Patterns of Identity Transformation

The literature on transnationalism calls attention to migrants' simultaneous attachments to both home and host countries. This has challenged theories of immigrant assimilation. Research finds that transnational practices have strongly shaped migrants' identity formation, giving rise to multi-national or multi-local identities (Vertovec 2001). Migrants have constructed transnational identities through a range of homeland-related social, cultural, political, and economic activities (Cui 2017; Ehrkamp 2005; Erol 2012; Somerville 2008).

Although the literature on transnationalism has shed new light on the complex processes of identity transformation among migrants, it raises the question of whether the literature has overlooked other patterns of migrant identity change. It is found that frequent and institutionalized transnational practices have only existed in the case of a small proportion of migrants, while the majority maintain limited interactions with the home country (Waldinger and Fitzgerald 2004). After settling in the host country, some migrants would gradually be assimilated into the host country and have a waning sense of attachment to the home country (Vermeulen 2010; Vertovec 2009).

Rather than viewing transnationalism as desired or inevitable outcomes or as a sign of weakening national boundaries, Waldinger argues that the existence of transnationalism paradoxically highlights the importance of the territorial boundary. Migrants' transnational practices underscore "the social and political separation of immigrants from the people they have left behind" and "the ways in which alien status and alien origins at once impede immigrant acceptance" (Waldinger 2017: 5). The problematization of transnationalism by Waldinger suggests that identity transformation among migrants has been a process fraught with challenges and uncertainties as migrants navigate the separation from the home country and confront the challenges of adaptation in the host society. Migrants' identity transformation also depends a great deal on acceptance by the host society. A study of the Indian diaspora in the United States finds that the hostile environment after the 9/11 incident shook their sense of belonging and forced them to re-examine their identity (Bhatia and Ram 2009).

The literature on transnationalism has paid insufficient attention to temporary migrants as it often focuses on permanent immigrants who have acquired the right of permanent residency or citizenship in the host country. Temporary migrants are usually low-wage migrants who engage in low-skill occupations, such as construction, care work, and manufacturing. However, it has become increasingly common for some highly skilled migrants to work on a temporary basis. Singapore is a case in point. Most highly skilled migrants in the country need to renew their work passes periodically and only have a very limited chance to acquire permanent residency or citizenship (Zhan and Zhou 2020). With little to no chance of permanent settlement in the host country, how these migrants navigate the pathways of identity transformation remains an important issue of academic inquiry.

The scholarship on transnationalism focuses on the attachments to home and host countries, but many migrants have migrated to more than one country. This experience of multinational migration or stepwise migration has started to receive scholars' attention. Multinational migrants have engaged in activities in multiple countries and might form an identity that falls outside the binary of home and host countries (Paul and Yeoh 2021; Zhan, Aricat, and Zhou 2020). The literature on global citizen or cosmopolitan identity also suggests that some migrants would develop an identity that is not limited to any one nation (Beck 2017).

Building on the literature on migrant identity, transnationalism, and multinational migration, this paper proposes a framework to capture diverse

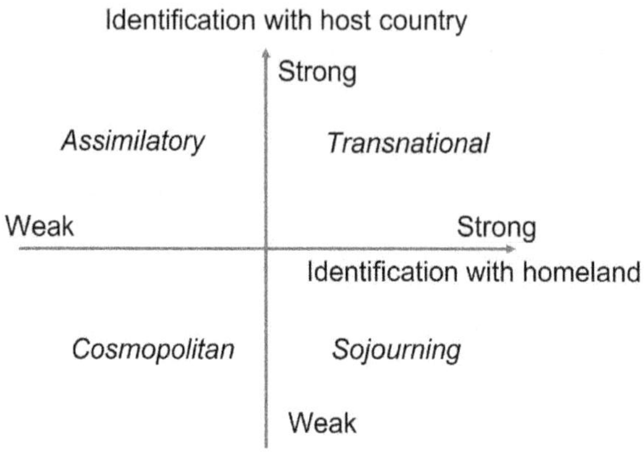

```
                    Identification with host country
                              |
                              | Strong
          Assimilatory        |  Transnational
                              |
  Weak                        |              Strong
  ────────────────────────────┼──────────────────────
                              |  Identification with homeland
                              |
          Cosmopolitan        |  Sojourning
                              |
                              | Weak
```

FIGURE 1   Patterns of identity transformation after migration

patterns of identity transformation among Chinese migrants in Singapore. The framework identifies four ideal types of identity based on how strongly migrants identify with home or host countries (Figure 1). When a migrant identifies strongly with both home and host countries, the migrant has developed a transnational identity. If the identification is weak with the home country but strong with the host country, the migrant has developed an assimilatory identity. If the attachment to the homeland is strong and that to the host country weak, the migrant has a sojourning identity. The last category is that a migrant identifies weakly with both home and host countries. In this case, the migrant may take a cosmopolitan identity. The migrant does not have a clear plan to settle in the host country or return to the home country, and he or she also remains open to migrate to another country when the opportunity presents itself. These are ideal types, and there will be a continuum along the spectrum between weak and strong attachments to both home and host countries (Figure 1).

3   Chinese Migration to Singapore

Singapore has recruited low-skilled foreign workers to fill job vacancies since the 1970s. As a regional financial and investment center, the city-state has also drawn many foreign expatriates due to the concentration of multinational companies there. After the 1990s, the city-state strove to build a knowledge economy and actively recruited highly skilled migrants from China, India, and other countries. In the meantime, declining fertility prompted the Singapore state to selectively offer permanent residency and citizenship to highly skilled migrants to replenish the population (Yang, Yang and Zhan 2017). The Singapore state intends to maintain the racial composition of its resident population (including citizens and permanent residents), which consists of 74 percent Chinese, 14 percent Malays, 9 percent Indians, and 3 percent other races (SDS 2021). It has granted permanent residency or citizenship to hundreds of thousands of migrants of Chinese ethnicity, from China, Malaysia, and other countries.

Singapore admits both low-skilled and highly skilled migrants from China, and a significant number of highly skilled migrants have become permanent residents or naturalized citizens. By 2015, migrants from China totaled approximately 450,000 and accounted for 18 percent of the foreign-born population (Yang, Yang and Zhan 2017). Low-skilled Chinese migrants usually work in construction, public transportation, manufacturing, and retail services. These migrants hold work permits and are ineligible to apply for permanent residency or citizenship. This paper focuses on highly skilled Chinese migrants. Highly skilled migrants hold an employment pass (EP) or an S pass (SP). EP holders are highly skilled professionals who occupy managerial, professional, or specialized positions, whereas SP is approved for middle-skilled workers and technicians. In 2021 a migrant had to earn a monthly salary of at least 4,500 Singapore dollars (SGD) to qualify for EP and 2,500 SGD for SP (Seow 2020). EP and SP holders are eligible to apply for permanent residency (PR) and then citizenship, but only about 30,000 of skilled migrants were granted PR every year in the course of the past decade, accounting for five percent of all eligible migrants (Zhan, Huang and Zhou 2022).

The influx of migrants, highly skilled migrants in particular, has caused a backlash against immigration in Singapore. Native Singaporeans accuse migrants of stealing jobs and increasing the strain on public resources (Gomes 2014; Yeoh and Lam 2016). Highly skilled Chinese migrants have also borne the blunt of the backlash. Although these migrants share a common ethnicity with the majority race in the host society, they have been perceived by native Chinese Singaporeans as a different race and are discriminated against by them (Ortiga 2015; Liu 2014). In response to the backlash, in the recent decade the Singapore state has tightened immigration and made it more difficult for migrants to acquire PR or citizenship. In addition, an array of policies has been implemented to prioritize native Singaporeans over PRs and pass holders in terms of employment and access to public resources (Zhan, Huang and Zhou 2022). The research for this paper took place in this context.

4 Patterns of Identity Transformation

The study surveyed 240 highly skilled Chinese migrants who had been in Singapore for at least a year. Table 2 below shows the demographics of the survey respondents. Male respondents are slightly more numerous than females. The respondents are relatively young, with an average of 35 years, compared with a median age of 42.5 years for the citizen population in Singapore in 2021 (Strategy Group 2021). Most of the respondents are highly educated, with 78.3 percent in possession of a university degree or above. More than two thirds have been in Singapore for 7 years or more. About 57 percent of the respondents have obtained permanent residency or been naturalized, whereas the rest have worked in Singapore on a temporary visa (Table 1). The characteristics of the survey respondents reflect the selectivity of Singapore's immigration policy, which prefers young, educated and highly skilled professionals. Of the respondents, most are engineers, technology specialists, professionals (legal, financial or medical), managers, executives, researchers, and educators, accounting for nearly 70 percent.

TABLE 1 Demographics of the survey respondents (N = 240)

	Frequency	Percentage
Gender		
Male	126	52.5
Female	114	47.5
Average age	35	N.A.
Marriage status		
Single	78	32.5
Married	156	65.0
Widowed or divorced	6	3.5
Duration of stay		
1–3 years	30	12.5
4–6 years	47	19.6
7–10 years	67	27.9
More than 10 years	96	40.0
Education		
High school and below	31	12.9
Associate degree	21	8.8
University degree	109	45.4
Master's degree	59	24.6
PhD or above	20	8.3

TABLE 1   Demographics of the survey respondents (N = 240) (cont.)

	Frequency	Percentage
Immigration status		
Temporary visas	104	43.3
Permanent residency	45	18.8
Naturalized citizen	91	37.9

TABLE 2   Identification with the homeland and host country (N = 240)

	Homeland		Host country	
	Frequency	Percentage	Frequency	Percentage
Very weakly	3	1.3	12	5
Weakly	8	3.3	32	13.3
Neutral	47	19.6	83	34.6
Strongly	115	47.9	87	36.3
Very strongly	67	27.9	26	10.8

The survey asked the respondents how strongly they identify with homeland and host country, that is, China and Singapore. Large proportions of the respondents identify strongly with homeland and host country, with more identifying strongly with homeland. Table 2 shows that more than 75 percent identified strongly or very strongly with homeland while 47 percent identified strongly with host country. This is probably because the respondents are all first-generation migrants, and most still have a strong attachment to China. Nevertheless, the proportion with a strong Singapore identity is also high, close to 50 percent. This suggests that integration into the host country is already happening quickly among these migrants.

The strength of host country identity is positively associated with migrants' duration of stay in Singapore (gamma = 0.25; ASE = 0.075). Of the respondents who have been in Singapore for more than 10 years, 59.4 percent identify strongly or very strongly with Singapore, higher than the proportion of all respondents, 47.1 percent. Immigration status also has a strong influence on one's identity with the host country. Of naturalized citizens, the proportion of those who identify strongly or very strongly with it is as high as 68.1 percent, as against only 34.2 percent of non-citizens who feel strongly as Singaporean residents. This demonstrates that immigration policy has a significant impact on identity transformation among migrants. Migrants on a temporary visa are much less likely to identify with the host country. In addition, the difference between temporary migrants and PRs is not significant, which suggests that the transformation of identity toward the host country is more likely after naturalization.

Homeland identity is also affected by one's duration of stay and immigration status, but to a lesser extent. Of the respondents who had been in Singapore for 1 to 3 years, 86.7 percent had a strong homeland identity. The proportion decreases in line with the increase in the duration of stay. Of those who have been in Singapore for more than 10 years, two thirds (66.7 percent) identify strongly or very strongly with China. Of naturalized citizens, 63.7 percent identify strongly or very strongly with China, whereas 83.2 percent of non-citizens reported a strong homeland identity.

Most respondents use WeChat, WhatsApp, and Facebook, while smaller proportions also use Instagram and Twitter (Table 3). The proportions of the respondents who use WeChat, WhatsApp, and Facebook daily or several times a day are 80.0 percent, 85.9 percent, and 47.5 percent respectively. WhatsApp and Facebook are the most frequently used social media tools in Singapore, and the high proportions of users among the respondents suggest that Chinese migrants have actively participated in the host society in terms of online communication. In addition, these migrants use WeChat, which is mostly used by people in China and overseas Chinese. The use of social media tools is not exclusive, and a migrant can use multiple social media sites or messaging apps. For instance, 161 respondents, or 67.1 percent of the total, use both WhatsApp and WeChat daily or several times a day. The application of social media tools correlates with Chinese migrants' self-reported identities. The use of WeChat is more prevalent among those who identify strongly or very strongly with the homeland. Of the respondents who use WeChat several times a day, 83.8 percent reported a strong homeland identity, higher than the proportion

TABLE 3 Use of social media tools (N = 240, percentage)

	WeChat	WhatsApp	Facebook	Instagram	Twitter
Never or rarely	7.9	2.1	23.8	47.5	68.3
Occasionally	12.1	12.1	28.8	12.9	16.2
Daily	15.8	24.2	20.8	13.3	9.6
Several times a day	64.2	61.7	26.7	16.3	5.8

of all respondents, 75.8 percent. The use of WhatsApp, however, correlates with neither homeland identity nor host country identity, probably because of the nearly ubiquitous use of the tool among Chinese migrants. The frequent use of Facebook is positively associated with host country identity. Of the respondents who use Facebook several times a day, 71.8 percent report a strong host country identity, higher than the proportion of all respondents, 47.1 percent.

The data shows that most migrants have been actively using social media tools to communicate with their contacts in China and Singapore and that they adopt a pragmatic approach toward ICT use. Nearly 86 percent of respondents are frequent users of WhatsApp. This is probably because WhatsApp is the most popular social media tool in Singapore, and many companies use it for work purposes. Furthermore, the use of social media correlates with one's identity. Those who use WeChat most frequently tend to have a strong homeland identity, whereas those who use Facebook most frequently tend to identify strongly or very strongly with the host country.

Other connections with the homeland also have a positive effect on one's homeland identity. Respondents who travel more frequently back to China tend to report a strong homeland identity. Of those who visit China more than once a year, 86.7 percent report a strong homeland identity. A total of 78 respondents, 32.5 percent, made economic transactions in China. The proportion of these respondents who reported a strong homeland identity is 82.1 percent, higher than the proportion of those who do not carry out economic transactions in China, 72.8 percent.

The homeland and host-country identities are not exclusive, as demonstrated by the literature on transnationalism. Table 4 cross-tabulates the two identities. The most common identity is the transnational identity, that is, migrants identify strongly with both homeland and host country. Of 240 respondents, 83 can be considered to have a transnational identity, accounting for 34.6 percent. This is followed by the sojourning identity, 42 respondents and 17.5 percent. There are 57 respondents situated between these two identities, as they hold a strong or very strong homeland identity but a moderate host country identity. As duration of their stay in Singapore extends or they are successfully naturalized, they are likely to move toward a transnational identity. However, if their attempt at naturalization is unsuccessful, they are likely to adopt a sojourning identity and even return to China. Of all respondents, those who hold an assimilatory identity or cosmopolitan identity are relatively few. Only 7 respondents can be regarded as having an assimilatory identity, and only one respondent as having a cosmopolitan identity. However, 23 respondents have a moderate homeland identity but a strong or very strong host country identity. As their duration of stay in Singapore extends, it is possible

TABLE 4 Cross-tabulation of Chinese migrants' identities in Singapore

TABLE 4A

		Host country identity					
		Very weakly	Weakly	Moderate	Strongly	Very strongly	Total
Homeland identity	Very weakly	0	0	0	2	1	3
	Weakly	0	1	3	1	3	8
	Moderate	0	1	23	20	3	47
	Strongly	3	12	38	50	12	115
	Very strongly	9	18	19	14	7	67
	Total	12	32	83	87	26	240

TABLE 4B

		Host country identity				
		Very weakly	Weakly	Moderate	Strongly	Very strongly
Homeland identity	Very weakly	Cosmopolitan (1, 0.4%)		0	Assimilatory (7, 2.9%)	
	Weakly			3		
	Moderate	0	1	23	20	3
	Strongly	Sojourning (42, 17.5%)		38	Transnational (83, 34.6%)	
	Very strongly			19		

that they will eventually adopt an assimilatory identity as their homeland identity weakens over time. In addition, another 23 respondents reported that they identified moderately with China and Singapore. These respondents would transition either to an assimilatory or to a cosmopolitan identity, depending on whether they are able to build a strong identity with the host country.

In summary, the findings reveal that Chinese migrants in Singapore have experienced diverse patterns of identity transformation. In line with the literature on transnationalism, this study finds that a significant proportion of these migrants has a transnational identity, as they identify strongly with both China and Singapore. A smaller but also significant percentage of respondents have a sojourning identity, and they identify strongly with China while living and working in Singapore. This partly has to do with Singapore's immigration policy, as most of them hold temporary visas. Migrants who have assimilatory and cosmopolitan identities are relatively few. However, a large number of respondents are situated between these ideal types, and they identify moderately with either China or Singapore. This indicates that migrants' identity transformation is a fluid and dynamic process, which produces a range of diverse outcomes. The next section, based on the in-depth interviews, examines the factors that have shaped identity transformation.

5 Factors behind Identity Transformation

Based on the analysis of data from the 43 in-depth interviews, this section identifies four factors that have shaped the identify transformation of Chinese migrants in Singapore: immigration policy, social and family networks, social discrimination, and culture and language.

5.1 *Immigration Policy*

In the context of Singapore, immigration policy has a strong influence on identity transformation among Chinese migrants, particularly those who have desired but failed to obtain permanent residency or citizenship. Of 43 interviewees, 17 were on temporary visas, either Employment Passes or S-Passes, and 12 of them said that they could not identify strongly with Singapore because their application for permanent residency had been rejected. They would be forced to leave the city-state if they failed to renew their work pass.

Singapore's immigration system allows highly skilled migrants who hold either an employment pass or an S-pass to apply for permanent residency and then citizenship. Before 2008, it was relatively easy for these pass holders to obtain permanent residency. Since 2009, the path to permanent residency has been significantly narrowed. The Singapore state reduced the number of newly granted PRs from 79,167 in 2008 to 29,265 in 2010 and the number remained around 29,000 thereafter (Strategy Group 2021). In the recent decade, it is common for one's application for permanent residency to be repeatedly rejected. This causes a high level of uncertainty for Chinese migrants in Singapore who are on temporary visas. Paul Xue, 38, migrated to Singapore in 2012 and worked as a medical technology specialist and earned a relatively high salary. He stayed in Singapore together with his wife and 6-year-old daughter. The family had a plan to settle down permanently in Singapore. However, their application for PR had been rejected three times. This had become a significant factor influencing Paul's identity transformation. Although he felt that he was integrated into Singapore socially and culturally, he did not feel like a full Singaporean. He remarked,

> I don't feel a full Singaporean because I want to join this family, I want this home, but this family kick me out. That is why I cannot feel at home. My desire to integrated is not reciprocated by the Singapore society. To me only a PR or citizen can call this place their home.

5.2 *Social and Family Networks*

Social and family networks play a critical role in "anchoring" migrant identity (Grzymala-Kazlowska 2016). Nearly all interviewees linked their identities to family members, friends, and social contacts. As first-generation migrants, Chinese in Singapore often have family members, relatives, and friends in China, and strong bonds between them lead migrants to identify with the homeland. In the meantime, these migrants have built social networks in Singapore, with both locals and other migrants. Some of them have brought family members to or formed a family in Singapore. The expansion of social and family networks in Singapore has also shaped their identity transformation, with the effect of moving toward the host society. The networks in the homeland and host country are not exclusive, and the co-existence of the two networks has laid the foundation for Chinese migrants to develop a transnational identity, that is, they have strong attachments to both home and host countries (You and Zhou 2019). The use of social media platforms has enhanced this trend, as it enables migrants to interact with people in the two societies at the same time.

Michael Liu, 56, came to Singapore in 1995 and worked in a construction company as a manager. He and his family (his wife and daughter) were naturalized several years after arriving in Singapore. Having spent 23 years in Singapore, he had built social networks and participated in various social activities. For instance, he often spent time with the locals at community centers. As a Red Cross member, he regularly gave blood. Michael also received help from many native-born Singaporeans in terms of work and leisure and felt that most Singaporeans were quite compassionate. However, he still felt that he and native-born Singaporeans were not connected at a deeper level due to different mindsets. His parents were still living in China, and he travelled back to China to visit them at least once a year. He was a frequent user of WeChat, by means of which he connected with friends and university alumni in China and Chinese migrants in Singapore. He identified very strongly with Singapore and only moderately with China, as he had been away from China for more than two decades. When asked about his identity, he said,

> I think of Singapore as my home because my family is here. When I go back to China, it's just for my parents, there isn't much more to it.... I'm used to things here, whereas when I go back to China, there's a bit of a cultural shock. In terms of weather, transport, culture, things here are familiar. My hometown has all four seasons so when I go back in winter, I'm not used to the climate at all. And the roads that I was familiar with when I was young are all gone now.... The lifestyles [of people in China] are completely different from mine.

Michael Liu's narratives demonstrate the importance of social and family networks in shaping one's identity. As he and his family settled down and fully adapted to life in Singapore, his attachment to the homeland had declined over time. Nevertheless, he still identified moderately with China after more than two decades living overseas and was proud of the economic progress that his home country had made. He purchased properties in China and invested in a company run by one of his relatives, which also connected him to the motherland.

It should be noted that migrants' social networks are not limited to ties with people in the homeland or those with local-born residents in the host society. Social networks are also formed among migrants, which may also affect migrants' identity transformation. Singapore is a global city, where Chinese migrants frequently interact with counterparts from other countries. In such contexts, some Chinese migrants have developed a cosmopolitan identity that extends beyond homeland and the host society. Caitlin Zhang, 41, migrated to Singapore in 2000 and was naturalized in 2007. She got married and settled down in Singapore and had three children. She first worked as a nurse for a few years and then as an accountant, for a large international investment bank in Singapore. At the bank, only 10 percent of employees were native-born Singaporeans whereas the rest were migrants from various countries. She and her family once lived in the Holland Village, an upscale neighborhood where high-income expatriates, particularly those from Western countries, choose to live. Although she regarded herself as Chinese culturally and was well adapted to life in Singapore, she tended to perceive herself as a global citizen with a cosmopolitan identity.

I think I'm a global citizen…. Actually when I say I'm Chinese, it's not really Chinese national but rather I'm a Chinese from an ethnic group perspective, not nationality perspective. So I don't really feel very strongly tied to any country, but I felt like the Chinese culture and the value are still most important to me…. I myself is an immigrant from another country so I have an open mind toward people from different cultures and backgrounds and the people that I usually hang out with, are all from all different background … so I don't feel any differences. I feel very comfortable here.

5.3   *Social Discrimination*

Chinese migrants share a common ethnicity with the majority in Singapore. However, as newcomers, they are perceived as a different race and often discriminated against by the host society (Liu 2014; Ortiga 2015; Yeoh and Lam 2016). Although blatant discrimination is rare, a significant proportion of Chinese migrants feel that they are sometimes on the receiving end of discrimination. The perceived discrimination is exacerbated by the immigration backlash and tight immigration policy of the last decade. Figure 2 shows that the proportion of respondents who felt frequent discrimination is low, but those who felt discrimination occasionally account for a significant percentage. A total of 60 percent of respondents felt discrimination by the general public, 33.8 percent by law and institutions, 44.2 percent by work colleagues, and 38.3 percent by neighbors.

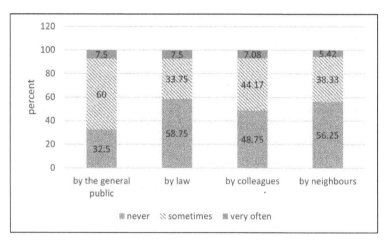

FIGURE 2   Perceived discrimination among Chinese migrants in Singapore

Social discrimination makes migrants less likely to identify with the host country, even though they have adapted to culture and social life there. Audrey Huang, 32, migrated to Singapore in 2012 and worked as an English teacher at a private tuition center. She came to Singapore to study as a master's student and got married to a native-born Singaporean after graduation. We interviewed her in August 2018, when she had a one-year-old daughter and was living with her in-laws. She was granted permanent residency after her marriage. She indicated that she was well integrated into Singapore society as she got along well with her native-born colleagues, husband, and in-laws. Nevertheless, she experienced discrimination at the workplace in the sense that her salary was lower than that of her native-born colleagues, even though she held a higher education degree. She grew sensitive to news and information how Chinese migrants were discriminated against. Although she regards Singapore as home, at the national level she identifies strongly with China. She remarked,

> Whenever I landed in Changi Airport [in Singapore], it's so nice ... I feel this is my home because my family, my husband, my daughter and my husband's family are here and I can feel the warmth that a family can provide ... so I find this home.... But whenever, I don't know, whenever they [general public] raised the issue Singaporeans and Chinese, you find that sometimes they attack those China Chinese.... Then I would identify myself as a Chinese.

5.4 Culture and Language

Acculturation is an inherent process in migrant integration into the host society. It is argued that the identity of migrants would be transformed in relation to the host society after they acculturate, that is, they adopt similar cultural behaviors and speak the same language as members of the host society (Berry, Phinney, Sam and Vedder 2006). However, not every migrant can successfully acculturate to the host society. Those who face difficulty in overcoming cultural differences and language barriers would be less likely to identify strongly with the host country. In general, younger migrants would be more successful at acculturation as they are more open to new cultural practices. The outcome of acculturation also has to do with one's occupation, social context, and personal efforts.

Although Singapore is an immigrant country where the majority race is comprised of people of Chinese descent, the city-state has developed a unique culture incorporating cultural elements from India and from Malaysia and other Southeast Asian countries, in addition to Chinese culture. The earlier Chinese migrants to Singapore were mainly from coastal provinces such as

Guangdong and Fujian, whereas recent Chinese migrants in Singapore came from a wider spread of places in China, where the local culture is different from that in coastal provinces. Judith Gao, 55, migrated to Singapore in 1997 with her husband and daughter. She had been working as an accountant for various companies in Singapore. She was a permanent resident as this made traveling back to China to visit her parents more convenient. Judith had largely adapted to culture and life in Singapore, but she admitted that she was not fully integrated due to cultural and linguistic differences. This led her to strongly identify with China and to identify only moderately with Singapore, despite living and working in Singapore for two decades.

> I think it is very hard for first-generation immigrants like us to fully integrate into Singapore society, it is easier for the second generation…. I feel that it is because of cultural difference. For instance, when chatting with Singaporeans, they tend to incorporate various languages such as Malay, Tamil and dialects here and there. To us, especially [I am] from the northern part [of China], it is hard to understand…. Sometimes they will also mix Hokkien dialect or Cantonese in English.

6 Conclusion

This paper introduces a new framework for capturing identity transformation among Chinese migrants in Singapore based on how strongly they identify with the homeland and the host country. The framework includes four ideal types of identity: transnational, assimilatory, sojourning, and cosmopolitan. The most common identity is the transnational identity, which accounts for slightly more than one third of respondents. In other words, nearly two thirds of respondents have other identities. This demonstrates diverse patterns of identity transformation among these migrants, which extend beyond the scope of transnationalism. Furthermore, identity transformation is a dynamic and fluid process. Forty five percent of respondents reported identities beyond the four ideal types, and their identities would undergo further transformations due to changing circumstances, such as the extension of the duration of their stay in Singapore and changes in immigration policy. The paper identifies four factors that have affected Chinese migrants' identity transformation in Singapore. Strict immigration policy leads to a high proportion of migrants living in Singapore on a temporary basis, which weakens their host country identity. Family and social networks across borders, networks that have been strengthened by the use of ICTs, give rise to the prevalence of a transitional identity among the migrants. Social discrimination pushes migrants' identity away from the host country, whereas the process of acculturation strengthens migrants' attachment to the host country.

This paper has its limitations. The sample size of the survey is relatively small. The paper only carried out a descriptive analysis of survey data, whose results should be verified by further statistical analysis. Future research should increase the sample size and conduct a more rigorous regression analysis. This would show how migrants' identity transformation is caused by multiple factors such as immigration status, duration of stay, demographic factors, socio-economic status factors, and the use of ICTs. In addition, the paper bases its analysis only on Chinese migrants in Singapore. Future research should compare Chinese migrants in Singapore with those in other countries or other migrant groups. For instance, the effects of the unique immigration policy of Singapore on identity transformation might not be applicable to the countries that have a more liberal immigration regime, such as the United States and Canada. A cross-national comparative study can further examine the applicability of the analytical framework for different migrant groups and in various contexts.

Acknowledgements

The research for this paper was supported by the Ministry of Education, Singapore, under its Academic Research Fund Tier 2 (MOE2015-T2-2-027). The paper was presented at the conference on "Boundaries and Bonds: An International Conference on Chinese Diaspora" (2–3 October 2021), organized by the Singapore Chinese Cultural Centre and Chinese Heritage Centre.

References

Baldassar, Loretta, Nedelcu, Mihaela, Merla, Laura and Raelene Wilding. 2016. "ICT-based Co-presence in Transnational Families and Communities: Challenging the Premise of Face-to-face Proximity in Sustaining Relationships." *Global Networks* 16(2): 133–44.

Barabantseva, Elena. 2005. "Trans-nationalising Chineseness: Overseas Chinese Policies of the PRC's Central Government." *Asien* 96: 7–28.

Basch, Linda, Schiller, Nina Glick and Christina Szanton Blanc. 1994. *Nations Unbound: Transnational Projects, Postcolonial Predicaments, and Deterritorialized Nation-states*. Langhorne, PA: Gordon and Breach.

Beck, Ulrich. 2017. "Mobility and the Cosmopolitan Perspective." In *Exploring Networked Urban Mobilities: Theories, Concepts, Ideas*, eds., M. Freudendal-Pedersen and S. Kesselring, pp. 140–152. Abingdon, UK: Routledge.

Berry, John W., Phinney, Jean S., Sam, David L. and Paul Ed Vedder. 2006. *Immigrant Youth in Cultural Transition: Acculturation, Identity, and Adaptation across National Contexts*. Mahwah, NJ: Lawrence Erlbaum Associates Publishers.

Bhatia, Sunil and Anjali Ram. 2009. "Theorizing Identity in Transnational and Diaspora Cultures: A Critical Approach to Acculturation." *International Journal of Intercultural Relations* 33(2): 140–49.

Christiansen, Flemming. 2005. *Chinatown, Europe: An Exploration of Overseas Chinese Identity in the 1990s*. New York: Routledge.

Cui, Dan. 2017. "Transnationalism and Identification among Chinese Immigrant Youth: a Canadian Study." *International Journal of Chinese Education* 6(2): 158–75.

Ehrkamp, Patricia. 2005. "Placing Identities: Transnational practices and Local Attachments of Turkish Immigrants in Germany." *Journal of Ethnic and Migration Studies* 31(2): 345–64.

Erol, Ayhan. 2012. "Identity, Migration and Transnationalism: Expressive Cultural Practices of the Toronto Alevi Community." *Journal of Ethnic and Migration Studies* 38(5): 833–49.

Gomes, Catherine. 2014. "Xenophobia Online: Unmasking Singaporean Attitudes Toward 'Foreign Talent' migrants." *Asian Ethnicity* 15(1): 21–40.

Gordon, Milton M. 1964. *Assimilation in American Life: The Role of Race, Religion, and National Origins*. Oxford: Oxford University Press.

Grzymala-Kazlowska, Aleksandra. 2016. "Social Anchoring: Immigrant Identity, Security and Integration Reconnected?" *Sociology* 50(6): 1123–39.

Guo, Shibao. 2022. "Reimagining Chinese Diasporas in A Transnational World: Toward a New Research Agenda." *Journal of Ethnic and Migration Studies* 48(4): 847–72.

Levitt, Peggy. 2003. "Keeping Feet in Both Worlds: Transnational Practices and Immigrant Incorporation in the United States." In *Toward Assimilation and Citizenship: Immigrants in Liberal Nation-states*, eds., C. Joppke and E. Morawska, pp. 177–94. New York: Palgrave Macmillan.

Lin, En-Yi. 2008. "Family and Social Influences on Identity Conflict in Overseas Chinese." *International Journal of Intercultural Relations* 32(2): 130–41.

Liu, Hong. 2005. "New Migrants and the Revival of Overseas Chinese Nationalism." *Journal of Contemporary China* 14(43): 291–316.

Liu, Hong. 2014. "Beyond Co-ethnicity: The Politics of Differentiating and Integrating New Immigrants in Singapore." *Ethnic and Racial Studies* 37(7): 1225–38.

Nedelcu, Mihaela. 2012. "Migrants' New Transnational Habitus: Rethinking Migration through a Cosmopolitan Lens in the Digital Age." *Journal of Ethnic and Migration Studies* 38(9): 1339–56.

Ortiga, Yasmin Y. 2015. "Multiculturalism on its Head: Unexpected Boundaries and New Migration in Singapore." *Journal of International Migration and Integration* 16(4): 947–63.

Paul, Anju Mary and Brenda S.A. Yeoh. 2021. "Studying Multinational Migrations, Speaking Back to Migration Theory." *Global Networks* 21(1): 3–17.

Ren, Na and Hong Liu. 2015. "Traversing between Transnationalism and Integration: Dual Embeddedness of New Chinese Immigrant Entrepreneurs in Singapore" *Asian and Pacific Migration Journal* 24(3): 298–326.

SDS (Singapore Department of Statistics). 2021. *Population Trends 2021*. Singapore: The Government of Singapore.

Seow, Joanna. 2020, 27 August. "Minimum salary for Employment Pass to rise to $4,500." *The Straits Times*, https://www.straitstimes.com/singapore/manpower/minimum-salary-for-employment-pass-to-rise-to-4500-from-3900-even-higher. Accessed on 21 May 2022.

Somerville, Kara. 2008. "Transnational Belonging among Second Generation Youth: Identity in a Globalized World." *Journal of Social Sciences* 10(1): 23–33.

Strategy Group. 2021. *Population in Brief 2021*. Singapore: Government of Singapore.

Vermeulen, Hans. 2010. "Segmented Assimilation and Cross-national Comparative Research on the Integration of Immigrants and Their Children." *Ethnic and Racial Studies* 33(7): 1214–30.

Vertovec, Steven. 2001. "Transnationalism and Identity." *Journal of Ethnic and Migration Studies* 27(4): 573–82.

Vertovec, Steven. 2009. *Transnationalism*. London and New York: Routledge.

Waldinger, Roger. 2017. "A Cross-border Perspective on Migration: Beyond the Assimilation/Transnationalism Debate." *Journal of Ethnic and Migration Studies* 43(1): 3–17.

Waldinger, Roger and David Fitzgerald. 2004. "Transnationalism in Question." *American Journal of Sociology* 109(5): 1177–95.

Yan, Miu Chung, Wong, Karen Lok Yi and Daniel Lai. 2019. "Subethnic Interpersonal Dynamic in Diasporic Community: A Study on Chinese Immigrants in Vancouver." *Asian Ethnicity* 20(4): 451–68.

Yang, Hui, Yang, Peidong and Shaohua Zhan. 2017. "Immigration, Population, and Foreign Workforce in Singapore: An Overview of Trends, Policies, and Issues." *HSSE Online* 6(1): 10–25.

Yeoh, Brenda S.A. and Theodora Lam. 2016. "Immigration and Its (Dis) contents: The Challenges of Highly Skilled Migration in Globalizing Singapore." *American Behavioral Scientist* 60(5–6): 637–58.

You, Tianlong and Min Zhou. 2019. "Simultaneous Embeddedness in Immigrant Entrepreneurship: Global Forces behind Chinese-owned Nail Salons in New York City." *American Behavioral Scientist* 63(2): 166–85.

Zhan, Shaohua, Aricat, Rajiv and Min Zhou. 2020. "New Dynamics of Multinational Migration: Chinese and Indian Migrants in Singapore and Los Angeles." *Geographical Research* 58(4): 365–76.

Zhan, Shaohua and Min Zhou. 2020. "Precarious Talent: Highly Skilled Chinese and Indian Immigrants in Singapore." *Ethnic and Racial Studies* 43(9): 1654–72.

Zhan, Shaohua, Huang, Lingli and Min Zhou. 2022. "Differentiation from Above and Below: Evolving Immigration Policy and the Integration Dilemma in Singapore. *Asian and Pacific Migration Journal* 31(1): 3–25.

Zhou, Min, and Hong Liu. 2016. "Homeland Engagement and Host-society Integration: A Comparative Study of New Chinese Immigrants in the United States and Singapore." *International Journal of Comparative Sociology* 57(1–2): 30–52.

"Finding the Distant Homeland Here": Contemporary Indonesian Poetry in Chinese

"在这里找到了遥遥的祖籍" – 印度尼西亚华文当代诗歌

Josh Stenberg 石峻山 | ORCID: 0000-0002-6832-2909
The University of Sydney, Sydney, Australia
josh.stenberg@sydney.edu.au

Abstract

This article focuses on three themes in contemporary Chinese-language verse from Indonesia: nationhood, language use, and the trauma of history. Through these themes, Chinese-language poets in Indonesia work through the many ways of being a speaker of Chinese in Indonesia, sometimes as an excluded alien, sometimes as a valued ally, and sometimes as an integrated minority. Such work provides unusual perspectives and tones to contribute to the much-discussed questions of Chinese-Indonesian identity, and functions as a reminder that literary corpora diverge within the "same" ethnic minority by linguistic expression. Borrowing a line from one of the most active poets, Sha Ping, this article suggests that Indonesians writing in Chinese are engaged on a quest to "find the distant homeland here" in Indonesia, even as they honor the trauma of history, the achievements of China, and the language of their ancestors.

Keywords

Chinese Indonesians – Sinophone literature – Indonesian literature – Chinese poetry

摘要

本文关注印度尼西亚当代华语诗歌的三大主题：国家认同、语言使用和历史创伤。通过这些主题，印尼华语诗人处理了各个层面的身份问题并探索了作为华语使用者

---

* This chapter was originally published as: Stenberg, J. (2022). "Finding the Distant Homeland Here": Contemporary Indonesian Poetry in Chinese. *Journal of Chinese Overseas*, 18(2), 312–334. Reprinted with kind permission from Brill.

This is an Open Access chapter published by World Scientific Publishing Company. It is distributed under the terms of the Creative Commons Attribution-NonCommercial-NoDerivatives 4.0 (CC BY-NC-ND) License which permits use, distribution and reproduction, provided that the original work is properly cited, the use is non-commercial and no modifications or adaptations are made.

的多种方式 – 有时作为被排斥的侨民，有时作为有价值的盟友，有时则作为被吸纳的少数民族。这些作品所提供的不寻常的视角和声音为备受讨论的印尼华人身份认同问题做出了贡献。它们提醒人们，即便在"同一个"少数群体中，文学的样貌也因语言表达而存在不同。借用最活跃的诗人之一莎萍的说法，本文认为用中文写作的印尼华人在印度尼西亚"找到了遥遥的祖籍"，即使他们同时也尊重历史的创伤、中国的成就和祖先的语言。

关键词

印尼华人 – 华文文学 – 印尼文学 – 华语诗歌

1   Introduction

Perhaps the most compelling of the Indonesian poets currently writing in Chinese is Sha Ping 莎萍 (b. 1936), also a central figure in the institutions of writing and publication in Chinese in the archipelago. It is therefore fitting to begin with lines from his 2009 poem "Pancoran" 班芝兰, about Jakarta's historic Chinatown. Addressed to the place itself, the poem begins "Because there were Chinese, there was a you" 有了华人 才有你, going on to praise Chinese Indonesians for extracting a livelihood through diligent labour in the face of adversity before it shifts to a description of the sights and sounds of festival time in Pancoran's Chinatown (Sha Ping 2010e [2009]: 12).[1] It is these festivities, a common source of ethnic symbolism and accounts of belonging, that cause the speaker to come to the realization that he has "found the distant homeland here" 在这里找到了遥遥的祖籍 (2010e [2009]: 12). A narrative of hard work structures the legitimation of community and the creation of an emotional homeland which is geographically Indonesian without severing ties to an ancestral land.

---

1 It is of course necessary to look past the poem's representation of cultural stereotypes of successful capitalism due to ethnic virtues of industry (and the shadowy contrast with the stereotype of an impulsive or lazy native). The problematic nature of such stereotypes is lucidly expressed by Ariel Heryanto, who noted that positive Chinese stereotype traits "include being industrious, rational, reliable, skilled, thrifty, and efficient" which are "the reverse of the stereotypical descriptions of the 'indigenous': lazy, irrational, corrupt, unskilled, hedonistic. However, contemporary ethnic Chinese are more frequently identified in negative terms: unpatriotic, selfish, materialistic, stingy, cunning, opportunistic, philistine, and, worst of all, 'communist'" (Heryanto 1997: 29).

In this poem the discovery of the homeland within the authorial self constitutes a happy fusion, and represents perhaps a notably optimistic formulation of Chinese-Indonesian identity expressed in a Chinese-language text. This sense of having earned a place in Indonesia through the labour of place-making while also bearing "the homeland" within oneself and expressing it publicly as a community encapsulates what this article attempts to explore: Chinese-language Indonesian literature (in this article, specifically free verse)'s intertwined struggles with nationhood, the assertion of language, and the trauma of history. Through these themes, Chinese-language poets in Indonesia work through the various facets of identity, the many ways of being a speaker of Chinese in Indonesia, sometimes as an excluded alien, sometimes as a valued ally, and sometimes as an integrated minority.

Circulating in the small and rather elderly Chinese-speaking literary community in Indonesia, such work provides unusual perspectives and tones to contribute to the much-discussed questions of Chinese-Indonesian identity. Despite its usefulness for illuminating seldom-considered elements of minority identity, contemporary Chinese-language literature from Indonesia has received little academic attention, and poetry almost none.[2] Considered in terms of academic field, the work occurs on three margins – the increasing bracketing of literature (and poetry even more so) to the contemporary study of ethnicity and identity, by no means exclusively but perhaps especially in Indonesia; the marginal position of Indonesia in Chinese-language/Sinophone literary studies; and the peripheral position of writing in Chinese, a putatively non-indigenous language, to Indonesian literary studies. Each of these marginal positions creates a challenge to summarize and instantiate this body of work without falling into overgeneralization or essentialism.

An article such as this, concerned with a little-known corpus, must also seek to strike a balance between analysis and summary, exhibition and argument, wider integration into scholarly debates and the need to sketch the foundations. The three themes focused on here – nationhood, language use, and the trauma of history – are by no means quantitatively dominant in the corpus of poetry in Chinese from Indonesia, but they are themes that are specifically local. While connected to concerns about all three elsewhere in the Chinese-speaking world, as well as from poets working in Indonesia, it is these

---

2 For Western-language surveys of other areas of this corpus, see Christine Winkelmann's *Kulturelle Identitätskonstruktionen in der Post-Suharto Zeit* (2008) and Stenberg (2017). The Chinese-language work of Sun Yat-sen University's Ma Feng 馬峰 has also brought the corpus to broader attention in the PRC, but otherwise most secondary literature consists of appreciations and explications from within the community, often by the same small group of authors and in the same publications.

identarian questions that allow this work to be framed as a meaningful corpus in need of consideration in Chinese-Indonesian and Chinese (or Sinophone) literary studies.

2 Historical Sketch

Verse output in the literary journals of the 1950s, such as *Spark* 火花 or *Coconut Isle* 椰岛, remains poorly known and little researched, and much of the corpus is likely lost.³ Contemporary poetry, which can practically defined as dating from the resumption of anthologization in the late 1990s, gathered speed after the fall of Suharto in 1998 and the greater possibilities of organising, publishing, and celebrating work in Chinese. This occurred at first through the Huoyi 获益 publishing house in Hong Kong and then in Indonesia itself. The last verse cited here dates from 2012, which is partly a reflection of when the materials were gathered for this work in Indonesia, mostly through the generosity of members of literary associations, often including the authors themselves; unfortunately, the corpus remains difficult to access in substantial numbers except through fieldwork collection. Both modern free verse and classical meter have been produced and are visible in the newspaper output, but since the latter is less anthologized, and perhaps also less concerned with identity-based framings, it is not treated here. Today writing in Chinese in Indonesia is in general decline, as the generation educated in Chinese-medium schools before 1965 dies out, with newer learners of Chinese little engaged with literature or committed to writing as a form of diasporic self-expression.

The corpus therefore occupies something of an academic blind spot as far as research is currently parceled up. On the one hand, there is the focus in PRC academia on the production of Overseas Chinese literature in Western nations and the more prominent corpus of literary work in Singapore and Malaysia. Indonesian output, small and relatively conservative in form and theme, has not elicited a widespread secondary literature. The modest return to publishing of Chinese-language literature in and from Indonesia has often first made its appearance in the literary supplements of the local Chinese-language press, as well as in dedicated small journals such as *Sino-Indonesian Literati* 印华文友

---

3 The literary production of this period is even more difficult to access than the more recent poems dealt with in this article. Besides occasional reprints of individual works in anthologies, the works are only known to me through secondary accounts such as the Master's theses of Maharani (2004) and An (2018). Since much of what was published was part of literary supplements, digitization projects of Chinese-language newspapers, such as that at Xiamen University, may increasingly capture some of this material.

(founded in 1999 in Hong Kong, before moving the following year to Jakarta), *The Call* 呼声, and *Cultivation* 耕耘. These journals circulate mostly in small cultural circles within Indonesia and are little-collected abroad. Selections from these outlets have then been formed or elaborated into dedicated anthologies and small collections with a limited domestic circulation; occasionally, publishers elsewhere (Xiamen, Singapore, or Hong Kong, for instance) publish Indonesia or Southeast Asia anthologies that include poetry.[4]

As with prose forms, the fact that much poetry is originally printed in the daily press is conducive to expression in shorter forms; that may simultaneously be a function of the relatively limited linguistic resources of poets and readers. Since education in Chinese ground abruptly to a halt in 1965, the education in Chinese of many writers and readers was interrupted before they could complete secondary school, and few had access to post-secondary education. Furthermore, the prohibition of Chinese texts entering the country and the possible danger of keeping Chinese libraries in the home meant that many authors went decades with only limited access to Chinese literary heritage or contemporary developments outside the country.

The formal conservatism of the writing and the politeness of tone is conspicuous, even where the verse considered is all "modern" (the smaller corpus of poems in classical forms is not being considered here). Aesthetically, the result of a primarily identarian motivation for publication and the framework of publication venue and readership is a poetic production that privileges short and simple forms of free verse for the direct expression of sentiment and opinion. Poets largely avoid both political controversy and formal experimentation.

The poems dealt with below were published in a modest number of anthologies, with the publication history of the corpus revealing the small and overlapping institutional networks of Chinese-language literary writing in Indonesia. For instance, anthologies were generally developed or compiled from verse published in the Chinese-language press in Indonesian. One of the latter, for

---

4   At the time of writing, WorldCat reports copies of *Two Hundred Modern Chinese Indonesian Poems* in the Singapore National Library, the Capital Library in Beijing, the Library of Congress, and four US university libraries. *Written for the Future* is held only in five US university libraries and the Library of Congress. To be sure, WorldCat is often incomplete as concerns Asian library holdings, and irregular or inaccurate Romanizations can produce problems, but it is clear that the books are not widely distributed. A wider range is reached by the Hong Kong and Xiamen publications, mostly single-author collections or national anthologies, in some cases as part of a nation-by-nation series of Chinese-language writing from Southeast Asia. Those interested in acquiring may find that PRC second-hand book retail sites as well as direct-from-author provide the easiest access.

instance, is a 2011 collection, *Two Hundred Modern Chinese Indonesian Poems* 印华新诗二百首, which was built around the ten year anniversary of the literary supplement *Cultivation* 耕耘, a publication attached to *Guoji ribao* 国际日报 and published by the Chinese Indonesian writers' association 印华作协 (PPTI), both the principal Indonesia-based publisher and the main web presence for this corpus. The editor of *Two Hundred Modern Chinese Indonesian Poems*, Sha Ping, was also for many years the vice-president of PPTI, and has tirelessly devoted himself to Chinese-language literature in Indonesia over the last two decades, sometimes sharing editing responsibilities with his wife, who publishes as Xiaoxin 小心. His projects have also been tightly interwoven with the work of the Indonesia-born, Hong Kong-based Dongrui 东瑞, who, through the Hong Kong publisher Huoyi, has been instrumental in reestablishing Chinese-language literary production in Indonesia by publishing anthologies and appreciations. As Dongrui wrote in his introduction to Sha Ping and Xiaoxin's 2010 *Written for the Future* 写给未来, the pair of them "have written a book every two years, and published five books in ten years; and, enjoying their trust, I have written five prefaces for them" 以两年一本书的速度写作，十年内出了五本书；我也蒙他俩的信任，写了五次序 (Dongrui 2010: 1). The readers and writers of this work are a small and transnational group of people in Indonesia or with Indonesian associations, belonging to the same organizations and circulating their work to one another.

3   Chinese Indonesian Poetry and the (Question of) Nation

In English, the Chinese-language poets who have most attracted attention are those who also write in Indonesian, such as Tangerang-based Wilson Tjandinegara 陈冬龙 (1946–2018) and Bandung author Soeria Disastra 卜汝亮 (b. 1943). Their work is noteworthy for their rejection of hard cultural or linguistic boundaries and their intercultural activities, including translation, self-translation, and literary cooperation. An example, in a poem about a local kind of tofu, is Disastra's "metonymic insertion of local food to represent local people as a way of neutralizing or disarming the question of alien as opposed to local provenance" (Stenberg 2017: 648). Tjandinegara's tireless cross-cultural interlocution earned him the admiration of Indonesian intellectuals, with Taufiq Ismail hailing him as "an advocate of intercultural contact, a translator of literature from Indonesian to Mandarin and vice versa, and a poet" (Allen 2003: 387). These are important voices, but it is also specifically because they reflect a pluralist view of Indonesianness and because they work in Indonesian that they are those that have most attracted attention in English. Other engagements with the nation reveal different imaginations of the Chinese Indonesian condition, and are not always as consonant with Western anglophone hopes for liberal multiculturalism.

Sha Ping, one of whose imaginations of that identity began this article, is today unusual among Chinese Indonesians, having been born in China rather than in Indonesia. Having grown up in Palembang, he returned to China in his early twenties, graduating from Xiamen University in 1961 before returning to Indonesia and making his life in Jakarta. Relative to his literary peers, he stands out for having direct lived experience of life in China. The rupture between China and Indonesia in the mid-1960s thus abruptly closed off his transnational life between his two homes. The poignancy of a poem such as "Returning Home" 回乡 is thus available for autobiographical reading – a 74-year-old man, living between two homelands, mourning a place that has grown unrecognizable due to dramatic developments in both economic and political spheres:

Returning Home	回乡
Shadows remain in the mind	脑海里还留有影子
While the retina is estranged	视网膜却感到陌生
The familiar sounds are vanished	熟悉的声音没有了
And who knows where the faces have gone	人面不知何处
A dry well is what remains	留下一口古井
Silently, mossily, waiting	伴着藓苔默默地等

SHA PING 2010a: 49

Moreover, Sha Ping was born on the island of Jinmen (Quemoy) – controlled since 1949 by the Taipei ROC government but situated off the Fujian coast and historically (and at Sha Ping's birth, still) a part of that province. The poem is concerned thus not only with the Cold War estrangement between the PRC and Indonesia but also with the enduring hostility across the Taiwan Strait. Thus, in "The Island" 岛, Sha Ping, who in a paratextual explanation identifies the poem as being about Taiwan, notes that the island "was once part of the mainland" 本是大陆的一块 and that it is still "attached by an umbilical cord" 连着脐带 (Sha Ping 2012a: 149). Sha Ping is not alone in expressing hope for what the PRC terms the Reunification of Taiwan, a preoccupation for many diasporic Chinese. Another instance can be found in a poem by Binjai (Sumatra) author Xiaoxing 晓星 celebrating the 2005 visit of KMT chairman Lien Chan to the PRC, where he met Hu Jintao, with Xiaoxing hoping that eventual unification will allow the Chinese nation to "build a dragon pagoda for the twenty-first century" 矗立二十一世纪龙塔 (Xiaoxing 2012a: 207). Equally enthusiastic, Ge Feng 戈峰's poem (2012a: 39), titled "Climbing the Great Wall" 登长城, recalls Mao Zedong's exhortation "One who fails to reach the Great Wall is not a hero" 不到长城非好汉 while ending "I came – I saw – I climbed/as for that visible but unattainable vantage point/it's alright not to get there" 我来过 仰望过 攀登过/那可望而不可及的眺望台/达不到也无妨, thus reaffirming both belonging to a political Chineseness despite diaspora and Mao's appeal to vigorous Chinese masculinity. At the same time, the poem seems to apply a deficiency model to diaspora, acknowledging and accepting that full Chineseness is obscurely out of reach for author and reader.

The rise of the PRC has generated a poetic resonance, usually highly positive and sometimes built around major international events, such as in the 2008 poems published celebrating the Olympics in Beijing, with Solo poet Yu Erfan 于而凡 hailing the Games as "not a sporting event/but the century-old dream/of a strong people and a rich nation" 这不是运动盛会/这是百年来/强民富国的梦想 (Yu 2009) and Bandung poet Xiao Zhang 肖章 proclaiming that "the overseas children of the dragon/without exception/are excited, proud/of the ancestral nation" 海外龙的后代/无不为有/崛起的祖籍国/而兴奋、自豪 (Xiao 2009).[5]

Sympathy or identification with the PRC can also appear vis-à-vis tensions with the West: in another poem, as when Xiaoxing laments what he considers attacks on China by the West during the 2009 Copenhagen climate conference: "big brother are you really trying to loosen our buttons/or are you just waving a big stick/forcing everyone else to cry uncle" 老大哥是真的要替我解扣/还是要挥舞大棍/逼子民众俯首称臣 (Xiaoxing 2012b: 222).

These poems, committed to iterations of Chinese political nationalism, are balanced by work, sometimes by the same authors, that clearly shows the authors' identification with the Indonesian nation. On occasions this identification is in a lyrical vein and transfers only indistinctly from aesthetic appreciation of a particular place to identarian questions, but at other times it is political, with close attention paid to the lives of non-Chinese Indonesians. One such poem is Alian 阿里安's 2011 "New Moon in a Foreign Land" 异域月缺 about Indonesian foreign workers abroad, in which he laments how workers' "Youth ravaged by foreign exchange/No one to tell about the wounds of rift" 青春被外汇欺辱蹂躏/裂口的创伤却无法伸诉 (11). This taking up of the sensitive, painful, and political issue shows a concern that adopts as its starting point not Chinese minority identity but the welfare of fellow Indonesians. Indeed, given that many Indonesian foreign workers are in Singapore or Hong Kong, it could even be read as taking up a grievance against Chinese-majority societies (who can read Chinese texts) on behalf of Indonesian fellow citizens (who cannot).

---

5 A rare English-language article on a Chinese-language Indonesian writer concerns Xiao Zhang's life and work (Mayo and Millie 2010).

The most interesting poems on the theme of the nation are not explicitly geopolitical. An enduring theme of Chinese-Indonesian poetry is distance from a motherland, and the consequences of that estrangement. The usual symptoms as presented in literary production are: rootlessness, homesickness, loss.[6] Chinese literature, of course, provides numerous tropes for such sentiments of exile, from the patriotic beauty, Wang Zhaojun, who was exiled in marriage to the Xiongnu, to Su Wu, who became a herdsman rather than be disloyal to the Han people. Indeed, Su Wu is perhaps dimly referred to in the title of a poem by Di Ou 狄欧, born 1959 in Jambi, titled "Homesickness" 望乡:

Born in foreign lands	生在异国
Roots in someone else's country	根在他乡
Homesickness persists	乡愁悠悠
For the vast home soil	乡土茫茫
Wanting to go back home for a visit	想回家看看
Yet unable to find the way back home	却找不到回家的路

DI 2011: 29

This sense of homelessness, of lost routes back to an origin, is also expressed in poems featuring rootlessness as a major feature of the overseas condition, as in these lines from Sha Ping's 1996 poem "Floating Weeds" 浮萍:

Roots, but no land.	有根，没有地。
Night and day floating, searching everywhere.	日夜飘泊到处寻觅。
Floating however many months and years;	漂泊了多少年月；
Searching the evasive centuries.	寻觅了躲闪世纪。

SHA PING 2011a [1996]: 111

This anxiety of rootlessness is repeated in the opening of the poem "Homesickness" 乡愁:

Roots in the northern land	home in the archipelago
To make a living	roaming, floating, migrating
Many layers of homesickness,	misery and grieving
let's not pass it on to the next generation	

SHA PING 2010b [2009]: 30

---

6 One scholar write of Philippines Chinese writers similarly, that they have a "self perception as rootless wanderers" (Lin 1997: 263). See also Stenberg 2021, for an attempt to deal with Philippines and Indonesian Chinese-language literary cultures comparatively.

根在北国	家住千岛
为了生存	流浪漂泊迁徙
多层的乡愁	酸楚的苦凄
不要再向下一代传继	

Later in the poem he describes homesickness as "the lonely one's unquenchable memory" 孤独者不灭的记忆 (2010b [2009]: 30). Another poem stages the betrayed hope of full acceptance of the Chinese in Indonesia after the fall of Suharto. Using, as he often does, tropes from classical poetry, Sha Ping asks the migrating wild goose: "Why go to the trouble of flying south/instead of finding a place to perch in the north?" 为什么每年要辛苦南飞/不在北方找一块地栖息? After all, the "south is not as beautiful as you imagined" 南方不如想象中美丽 and "the dry grasses everywhere/present the fear of conflagration" 到处是干巴巴的草堆/时刻有被火绕的恐惧 (Sha Ping 2012b: 152).

Similarly, the speaker in Yiruxiang's poem "The Child of the Ocean" 海洋的儿子 is spoken by a narrator who is confused that

everyone says	都说
my mother	我的母亲
is in the distant north	在那遥远的北方
YIRUXIANG 2012a: 88	

while in fact "child of the ocean/ your birth mother is the archipelago" 海洋的儿子/千岛是亲娘 (2012: 88), resonating with the mixed cultural and genetic heritage of many Chinese Indonesians. On the following page the same poet laments the many ethnic Chinese who died in Southeast Asia without being able to visit China again.

On the other hand, the title poem of a 2008 collection by Sha Ping, "Poem for the Future," seems explicitly to deny "rootless floating", "homesickness" or the "feeling that homeland has become strange land," opting instead for a universalism ("though skin colour is different the blood is just as scarlet" 肤色各异 血同样鲜红) and specifically what appears to be a plea for tolerance in a pluralistic Indonesia ("living harmonious together, selflessly contributing, respecting one another" 和谐共存无私无私奉献互相尊重 2010c [2008]: 7).[7] The exhortation not to pass racism or ethnic antagonism forward seems to foreshadow in the voice of someone born and rooted in "the northern land"

---

7 It is also worth noting surrounding the use of words such as "harmonious" that 2008 is the height of the Wen-Jia "harmony" discourse in the PRC. Perhaps the vocabulary of the PRC is being deployed to envisage a pluralistic future?

(i.e. China) and (though he cannot resolve such an identity himself) the "end of diaspora" mooted by Shu-mei Shih.[8]

The corpus offers a wide range of readings of the nation, from passionate identification with the Indonesian nation to a long-distance nationalism deeply encouraged by the increasing strength of and international respect bestowed upon the PRC. Among other things, this spread of identarian visions, sometimes within the same author's corpus, is a reminder both of the fungibility and contingency of this identity and the fact that Chinese-Indonesian writings in Indonesian (which usually do not offer any identification with the PRC) do not represent the views of those writing in Chinese, who are mostly older and had their initial education in Chinese.

4   The Trauma of History

While a recurrent theme is the longing for the unattainable return (e.g. Sha Ping's "Returning Home") – both to youth and to home – Ge Feng's "The Beach" 海滩 provides a different experience of going back in memory and geography, and directly addresses the community's historical trauma. In Ge Feng's case, however, the lost home invoked is not a remote or idealized ancestral China but rather his birthplace Lhokseumawe, in Aceh. This circumstance immediately signals trauma: perhaps nowhere in the archipelago was the Chinese community more thoroughly persecuted and removed in the 1960s than in Aceh (Melvin 2013). Ge Feng was himself forced into a camp, before settling in Medan. In this poem, he wonders, not without bitterness, whether "the beach remembers those vicissitudes" 沙滩是否记住这段沧桑 of 1966, when the local Chinese experienced "the pathos of standing under the hot sun, our souls being burned" 那站在烈日下被灼伤心灵的悲戚, a torment and a humiliation before being forced to leave Aceh. Seemingly returned to visit Aceh "now" (somewhere around the turn of the millennium) to stand on the beach, the speaker decides that these stinging memories "have turned into regret, have turned into an elegy" 成为遗憾 成为哀曲 (Ge 2012b: 31).

Chinese-Indonesian traumas of history are also sometimes folded into traumas of the wider national community. Where Ge Feng's poem is a sombre recollection of personal and community trauma in Aceh, "Aceh Calls for Peace"

---

8   In the Indonesian context, of course, this stance is also uncomfortably close (though approached from an unexpected angle) to the discourse of assimilation that New Order forced upon the "Chinese problem," with the proposed and legislated solution to the Chinese Other being its dissolution in the indigenous majority.

亚齐呼唤和平 by the north Sumatra poet Bai Yu stages the trauma of the 2004 Indian Ocean tsunami as only the most recent calamity of Aceh's violent past:

The tide ebbs and flows	潮来潮去
Rinsing the sand	浪洗沙粒
Rubbing out the traces	清除污迹
Taking the rubbish away	带去垃圾
Leaving behind a stretch of	留下了一段
Painful memory	惨痛的回忆

BAI 2011 [2007]: 20

The grief over the tsunami overlaps and embraces a wider grief over the Aceh Civil War and probably also the violence of the 1960s. Bandung poet Ming Fang is one of the few poets who has addressed historical violence directly, for instance in her 2012 poem "A History of Blood and Tears," in which she describes

screams still echoing in our ears wells of blood	惨叫声还在耳边回响
still rippling in front of our eyes	血井 还在眼前荡漾
how they have rushed by sixty-two years.	匆匆已过 六十二年

MING 2009[9]

The trauma of the historical violence is, however, as it also is in Indonesian-language literature, somewhat muted by the long double ban – ban on writing in Chinese, and ban on writing on the subject. Instead, it is the riots of 1998 that most clearly feature in the poetry of Chinese Indonesians and indeed create some of the best work in the whole corpus. It was Ming Fang also who authored a moving poem about 1998, within a month of the massacres, titled "After the Fiery Plunder" 火劫之后, which begins

At the end of May	五月底
I arrived in Jakarta, gaping with wounds	我来到了千疮百孔的椰加达
What used to be Chinatown	昔日的唐人街
Was still smoking	还在冒烟

MING 2011 [1998]: 92

She sees only "old Indonesian-born Chinese women in sarongs/trembling/passing through with bowed heads" 穿着纱笼的老侨生婆/战战兢兢/低头匆匆而过 as the community seeks to present itself as pribumi Indonesian while

---

9 Full translation in Stenberg 2017, 650–51.

concealing its young people (2011 [1998]: 92). The poem finishes with a young Chinese man

black hands, black feet	手黑脚黑
rifling through the rubble and cinders	在焦土与灰烬中
in the collapsed walls where he used to do business	在往日做生意的断墙内
trying to find	企图在寻找
after the fiery plunder	火劫之后的
some little hope	渺渺希望
MING 2011 [1998]: 92	

Fitted with an epigram indicating that the poem is written for the fifth anniversary of the violence is a poem by Qipa 奇葩, titled "An Umbrella" 一把伞. Here the historical moment's violence is metaphorically transmuted into the elements, finishing "Oh wind, oh rain, no more/no more may you trouble us/let us keep a spot of peace in this world" 风啊，雨啊，别再/别再闹了/留住人间一片的安宁吧 (Qipa 2011: 99). The narrator who is "hiding under the umbrella/ helplessly peering around" 躲在伞下/无助地张望 is at the mercy of the "cruel gusts of wind" 风舞情地吹刮 and the "wanton waves of rain/seeming about to crush everything" 雨肆意地飘泼/似乎要冲垮万物 (Qipa 2011: 99).

Other expressions of grief are less overt, such as Jakarta author Yuan Ni's 1998 lines:

You cannot see a battlefield	看不到战场
But there is a war	却有战争
You cannot hear the gunfire	听不到枪声
But blood is pouring	却有血流
YUAN 2011 [1998]: 200	

The collection in which that poem appears ends with a series of poems by Sha Ping about May 1998, each one on the anniversary of the violence. The copy I own, a 2017 gift from the editor, includes three more poems for 2012–2014 which were pasted into the back as a continuation of the series. The effect in my copy is touching and saddening, as these editorial pastings remind me of the physicality and fragility of the word as well as the depth and urgency of the author's writing, his annual compulsion to meditate on and commemorate ethnic violence. For me the most poignant is perhaps his 2009 anniversary poem, titled "The Wounds of May" 五月的伤口:

> The wounds of May   open and are not closed
> Time is the needle   years are the thread
> Passing through   slowly stitching
> Once healed   a scar remains for remembrance
> On rainy days   it will ache a little
> Fearful that splitting open   it may bleed again
> 　　　　SHA PING 2011b [2009]: 243

> 五月的伤口　　张着未闭
> 用时间作针　　以岁月为线
> 穿过　　　　　慢慢缝合
> 愈后　　　　　会结痂留下印记
> 雨天　　　　　会隐隐作痛
> 最怕震裂　　　再流血滴

In Zhang Ying's 1998 poem 黑色的网, the smoke from the burning buildings during the May riots covers the whole sky and blocks out the sun, while the narrator

> Hopes to escape this black net
> The pitch-black road is so long
> When will the glorious sun be seen again?
> 　　　　ZHANG 2011 [1998]: 224

> 希望快些冲出这黑色的网
> 黑黑的路啊这么遥长
> 几时才能见到灿烂的阳光？

Here violence has once again become a supernatural force, one that can swallow up hope itself, and leave the Chinese-Indonesian narrator doubtful that a road back to normality can be found again.

Other works go further back into imperial history, citing the violent origins of much Chinese-Indonesian migration. Thus, among Sumatran writers, the brutal history of Chinese coolie labour (peaking in the second half of the 19th century) features, for instance in poems such as "Piglets" 猪仔 ("Mentioning you is blood/ talking about you is tears" 提你是血　说你是泪 Sha Ping 2010d [2009]: 31), piglets being the term by which the coolies were abusively known. Going from early origins to very recent times, the trauma of violence constitutes a red thread through this literature. In this corpus, the traumas of history can operate as a brake on integration into a plural Indonesia, a reminder that difference may descend into violence. However, they can also achieve a cathartic effect, by facing and grieving the violence of history and, at some points, such as in Bai Yu's poem, folding it also into the national griefs of Indonesia.

5   Language Politics

In situations where a language is in some way marginalized or under threat, as has certainly been and still is the case with Chinese in Indonesia, the insistence on writing in Chinese as a political and cultural act can become a feature of the corpus. In the New Order years, Chinese in both written and spoken forms was widely suppressed in Indonesia. There was only one regular print outlet within Indonesia – the *Harian Indonesia* 印度尼西亚日报, and that was under close government control (Hoon 2006: 97). The effacement of the Chinese script went so far that Western travelers to Indonesia remember having their luggage checked for works in Chinese, since "printed matter in Chinese characters [fell] under the same category as pornography, arms, and narcotics in the short list of items visitors are prohibited from bringing into this, the world's fourth largest country" (Heryanto 1997: 27). Suppression was, however, uneven over genre, space, and time – Chinese singing and Hong Kong movies, for instance, continued to circulate – but Chinese Indonesians had to be perpetually wary of public expression (Dawis 2009).

Thus, for a certain circle of Chinese Indonesians, the resumption of writing and the reestablishment of publication outlets in Chinese has itself been a political statement – a reinscription of an erased community into the world Chinese-language community as well as a way to stake a claim as an element of multiethnic Indonesian society. As the inaugural editorial statement of one Sino-Indonesian publication said in 1999, "Chinese-language Indonesian writing is an inalienable constituent of global Chinese-language writing" ([phrase omitted]), while also carefully noting that such writing was "'rooted in Indonesia,' an inalienable and organic part of Indonesian literature as a whole" (*Yinhua wenyou* 1999). Thus, Tee Kim Tong's observation that Malaysian Chinese-language authors "write (or choose to write) in Chinese because such an act helps manifest their self and cultural identities as well as community consciousness" (Tee 2010: 84) is equally apt for those writing in Chinese in Indonesia.

The anxiety and loneliness of literary production in Chinese in evident in work such as that of Zhang Hanying 张汉英, whose "Street Lamp on a Cold

Night" 寒夜里的路灯 is subtitled "for Chinese Indonesian authors" 献给印华写作者 and begins

> You stand lonely at the side of the road
> Body draped in dust, torso ground down by the years
> Trembling slightly in the dense mists of evening
> I'm delighted to hear the faint sound of your heartbeat
> ZHANG 1997 [1992]: 298

> 你孤独地伫立路旁
> 披一身风尘，岁月磨伤了躯干
> 在朦胧的夜雾里微微地颤抖
> 惊喜依稀听见你心跳的声音

With its evocation of signs of life continuing despite hardship and its explicit address to writers, the ability to continue literary production in Chinese is in this poem cast as an absolute question of survival.

This praise of literary survival, combined with an assertion of the necessity of writing, is equally apparent in lines such as these by Yiruxiang: "You can't make a living from literature/but literature can bring people back to life" 文学养活不了人/但能复活人的心 (Yiruxiang 2012b: 107). These lines contain a commitment to literature in the abstract, but when written in Chinese in Indonesia, where writing in Chinese has never been lucrative but remains for these writers spiritually urgent, it necessarily evokes the period when Chinese literature was prohibited. Another aspect of the anxiety around language politics is personal names, since the New Order-era legislated suppression of Chinese names in favor of *pribumi* Indonesian names was for many Chinese a troubling manipulation of identity (Lie and Bailey 2017). That trauma has a shadowy presence in poems of his like "Name" 名字, in which he writes: "Some people are still living/Their names are dead/Some people are dead/But their names are still alive" 有的人活着/名字已死了/有的人死了/名字还活着 (Yiruxiang 2012c: 100). Although the more universal question of legacy, posterity and the desire to lead a meaningful life may be the primary meaning of these lines, the forced erasure of Chinese names in Indonesia provides an uneasy resonance, as the poets shift between pen names, Chinese names, and legal Indonesian names.

The Riau poet Fu Huiping 符慧平 (b. 1976), one of the youngest members of this writing community, is also concerned with the political power of language. "Language" 语言, she proclaims, is "no longer a bridge/the hypocritical blows/have collapsed you to rubbish/lying in silence," 不再是桥梁/经过虚伪的撞击/你坍塌成一座垃圾/躺在沉默里, going on to insist that they have "shipped you away/smelted, processed, refined you/into an elegant decoration" 他们把你运走/熔化，加工，提炼/便成精美饰品 (Fu 2011: 35). This could be read as a critique of the debasement of language through commercialization, but the image of the language attacked and shipped away and done to death, coming from a Chinese-language poet in Indonesia, must also carry a resonance of identity assimilated, excluded, othered. This reading is accentuated when one remembers that it comes from a poet of the generation where the ancestral language was subject to ban.

Taking another tack is Medan poet Hu'er 胡儿, who penned a "Pleading Roar of the Indonesian Language" 印度尼西亚语发出央求的吼声 which reads as a vociferous demand for the preservation of the integrity of Indonesian expression, specifically invoking the *Sumpah Pemuda* (which defined Indonesian as the national language of a projected independent Indonesia). The poem seeks to define Indonesian as both a proletarian and a logical language:

> I have come from the field of labouring production 　　我从劳动生产的领域中走过来
> I have come from the field of scientific experiment 　　我从科学实验的领域中走过来
> I have come from the field of social struggle 　　我从社会斗争的领域中走过来
> 　　HU'ER 2011 [2005]: 49

Later, however, the poem contains a defense of Chinese, framed in terms of the mid-century anti-colonial struggle:

> Actually my status is no different from the languages named below:
> Chinese, which participated in the expulsion of foreign powers
> Malay, which participated in the expulsion of British power
> 　　HU'ER 2011 [2005]: 50

> 其实我的角色与下列与语言一摸一样：
> 曾参与驱逐外国势力的汉语
> 曾参与驱逐英国势力的马来语

This strategy, linking Chinese and Indonesia in the spirit of earlier Bandung anti-imperialist internationalism (and the Peking-Jakarta alliance of the early post-war), is a reminder of the vintage of the education these poets received during the Sukarno period. The poet's pen name, too, draws attention, since it

"FINDING THE DISTANT HOMELAND HERE" 329

can be interpreted as meaning "Son of the barbarian" and may impishly suggest the marginal position of a corpus written beyond the borders, in a minority community.

Yueying 月影, who started teaching Chinese in a primarily Indonesian school in 1995, offers an explicitly transethnic view of Mandarin, setting one poem ("A Chinese Newspaper" 一份中文报纸) in the classroom. In that poem, his rambunctious Indonesian pupils are fascinated by "the dense blockish characters" 密密麻麻的方块字 of *Harian Indonesia*, the only permitted newspaper of the period. The teacher ruminates:

Chinese writing is profound, hard to learn	汉字很深奥，很难学
It's like dissecting the innermost feelings of Chinese culture	正如解剖中国人文化心语
Although they can't understand the paper, the kids	即使看不懂，大伙儿
They tell me "xiexie", which they have just learnt	说了一声刚学好的"谢谢"
And I answer them with "tidak apa-apa"	我也回了一句："抵达阿爸阿爸"

YUEYING 1997: 271

The insertion of the Indonesian for "you're welcome" in the final line presumes the bilingualism of the readership and enacts a Chinese-language class as a site of transethnic understanding. As with the poem by Sha Ping that began this article, poets seek to reconcile their writing in Chinese with the loyalties of and aspirations for their lives in Indonesia, for an identity that is at once ethnic Chinese and politically Indonesian, even if the terms that this corpus takes are notably different from either Anglophone academic discourse or from approaches taken in writing in Indonesian.

6   Conclusions

According to a definition offered by Deleuze and Guattari, "A minor literature is not the literature of a minor language but the literature a minority makes in a major language," and that "minor no longer characterizes certain literatures but describes the revolutionary conditions of any literature within what we call the great (or established)" (Deleuze and Guattari 1983: 18). Since the characteristics of a minority literature contain "the deterritorialization of the language, the connection of the individual and the political, [and] the collective arrangement of utterance" (Deleuze and Guattari 1983: 18), a writing community among historic, long-standing minorities such as the Chinese in Indonesia faces two dominant forces: the exclusionary state, which often defines mainstream identity (and canonical literature) against the Chinese; and the Chinese homeland, which defines belonging through ethnic essentialism but considers legitimacy by means of tests of political loyalty.

Since "[t]he transnational … is not bound by the binary of the local and the global and can occur in national, local, or global spaces across different and multiple spatialities and temporalities" (Shih and Lionnet 2005: 6), Chinese Indonesian verse can be placed on the outer reaches of a literary language with multiple complex power dynamics (Indonesian vs Mahua [Malaysian-Chinese] literature, Mahua vs Taiwan literature, Taiwan vs PRC literature). This makes it a fruitful site for those interested in "examin[ing] the relationships among different margins" (2), not least because it is a marginal form of expression also within the Chinese-Indonesian community, most of whose members do not speak any Chinese language. It therefore functions also as a reminder that literary corpora diverge within the "same" ethnic minority by language of expression, and that Sinophone work presumes a readership with a set of presuppositions and sympathies different from work in Indonesian (or Sundanese, or English, or Dutch) does. At the same time the corpus' expressive simplicity and the recurrence to themes of diasporic unease, language use, and traumatic events of recent Sino-Indonesian history gives this verse a distinctive place in Chinese-language or Sinophone letters.

Acknowledgements

The author would like to thank the editors and the anonymous reviewers for their feedback, as well as the colleagues and audience members at the "Boundaries and Bonds: An International Conference on Chinese Diaspora" jointly organised by Nanyang Technological University and the Singapore Chinese Cultural Centre (over Zoom, on 2–3 October, 2021). Research for this article was conducted with the support of the Discovery Early Career Research Award of the Australian Research Council.

References

Alian 阿里安. 2011. "Yiyu yue que" 异域月缺 (New Moon in a Foreign Land). In *Yinhua xinshi erbaishou* 印华新诗二百首 (Two Hundred Modern Chinese Indonesian Poems), ed., Sha Ping, p. 11. Jakarta Utara: Yinhua zuoxie.

Allen, Pamela. 2003. "Contemporary Literature from the Chinese 'Diaspora' in Indonesia." *Asian Ethnicity* 4 (3): 383–399.

An, Kang 安康. 2018. "Zhanhou Yinni Huawen wenxue bentuhua de shuxie (1945–2000)" 战后印尼华文文学本土化的书写 (1945–2000) (The Narrative of Localization of Sino-Indonesian Literature after World War II). M.A. dissertation, Xiamen University.

Bai Yu 白羽. 1997. "Guxiang ganzhe tian" 故乡甘蔗甜 (The Sugarcane of Home is Sweet). In *Feicui daishang* 翡翠带上 (In the Emerald Band), ed., Yan Weizhen, p. 30. Hong Kong: Holdery Publishing Enterprises Limited.

Bai Yu 白羽. 2011 [2007]. "Yaqi huhuan heping" 亚齐呼唤和平 (Aceh Calls for Peace). In *Yinhua xinshi erbaishou* 印华新诗二百首 (Two Hundred Modern Chinese Indonesian Poems), ed., Dongrui, p. 20. Jakarta Utara: Yinhua zuoxie.

Dawis, Aimee. 2009. *The Chinese of Indonesia and their Search for Identity: The Relationship between Collective Memory and the Media*. Amherst: Cambria Press.

Deleuze, Gilles, and Félix Guattari. 1983. "What is a Minor Literature?" *Mississippi Review* 11(3): 13–33.

Di Ou 狄欧. 2011. "Wang xiang" 望乡 (Gazing Toward Home). In *Yinhua xinshi erbaishou* 印华新诗二百首 (Two Hundred Modern Chinese Indonesian Poems), ed., Dongrui, p. 29. Jakarta Utara: Yinhua zuoxie.

Dongrui 东瑞. 2010. "Guang zheng bocai xinqin ru feng – xu Sha Ping, Xiaoxin 'Xie gei weilai'" 广征博采 辛勤如蜂 – 序沙萍，小心《写给未来》 (Recruiting Broadly, Diligent as Bees – A Preface for Sha Ping and Xiaoxin's *Written for the Future*). In *Xie gei weilai* 写给未来 (Written for the Future), eds., Sha Ping and Xiaoxin, pp. 1–4. Jakarta Utara: Yinhua zuoxie.

Fu, Huiping 符慧平. 2011. "Yuyan" 语言 (Language). In *Yinhua xinshi erbaishou* 印华新诗二百首 (Two Hundred Modern Chinese Indonesian Poems), ed., Dongrui, p. 35. Jakarta Utara: Yinhua zuoxie.

Ge Feng 戈峰. 2012a. "Deng Changcheng" 登长城 (Climbing the Great Wall). In *Yinhua xiaoshi senlin* 印华小诗森林 (A Forest of Short Chinese Indonesian Poems), ed., Sha Ping, p. 39. Jakarta Utara: Yinhua zuoxie.

Ge Feng 戈峰. 2012b. "Haitan" 海滩 (The Beach). In *Yinhua xiaoshi senlin* 印华小诗森林 (A Forest of Short Chinese Indonesian Poems), ed., Sha Ping, p. 31. Jakarta Utara: Yinhua zuoxie.

Heryanto, Ariel. 1997. "Silence in Indonesian Literary Discourse: The Case of the Indonesian Chinese." *Sojourn: Journal of Social Issues in Southeast Asia* 12(1): 26–45.

Hoon, Chang Yau. 2006. "'A Hundred Flowers Bloom': The Re-Emergence of the Chinese Press in Post-Suharto Indonesia." In *Media and the Chinese Diaspora: Community, Communications and Commerce*, edited by Sun Wanning, 91–118. London: Routledge.

Hu'er 胡儿. 2011 [2005]. "Yinniyu fachu yangqiu de housheng" 印度尼西亚语发出央求的吼声 (The Pleading Roar of the Indonesian Language). In *Yinhua xinshi erbaishou* 印华新诗二百首 (Two Hundred Modern Chinese Indonesian Poems), ed., Dongrui, pp. 49–50. Jakarta Utara: Yinhua zuoxie.

Lie, Sunny and Benjamin Bailey. 2017. "The Power of Names in a Chinese Indonesian Family's Negotiations of Politics, Culture, and Identities." *Journal of International and Intercultural Communication* 10.1: 80–95.

Lin, Ting Ting. 1997. "Sampaguita, Calamansi, and Halo-Halo: An Overview of Filipino-Chinese Literature." In *East Asian Cultural and Historical Perspectives*, eds., S.T. De Zepetnek and J. Jay, pp. 255–278. Edmonton: Research Institute for Comparative Literature and Cross-Cultural Studies, University of Alberta, 1997.

Lionnet, Françoise, and Shu-mei Shih. 2005. "Introduction: Thinking through the Minor, Transnationally." In *Minor Transnationalism*, eds., Françoise Lionnet and Shu-mei Shih, pp. 1–23. Durham, NC: Duke University Press.

Maharani 陈玉兰. 2004. "Buqu de jingjun – 20 shiji Yinni Huawen wenxue jianlun" 不屈的惊魂 – 20 世纪印度尼西亚华文文学简论 (Unbending Spirit – A Precis of 20th Century Chinese-Language Indonesian Literature). M.A. dissertation, Huaqiao University.

Mayo, Lewis and Julian Millie. 2010. "Driving Under the New Order." *Inside Indonesia*. https://www.insideindonesia.org/driving-under-the-new-order. Accessed 4 July 2022.

Melvin, Jess. 2013. "Why Not Genocide? Anti-Chinese Violence in Aceh, 1965–1966." *Journal of Current Southeast Asian Affairs* 32.3: 63–91.

Ming Fang 明芳. 2009. "Xuelei shi" 血泪史 (A History of Blood and Tears). *Yinhua zuoxie*. http://www.yinhuazuoxie.com/xinshi/xueleishi.html. Accessed 4 July 2022.

Ming Fang 明芳. 2011 [1998]. "Huo jie zhihou" 火劫之后 (After the Fiery Plunder). In *Yinhua xinshi erbaishou* 印华新诗二百首 (Two Hundred Modern Chinese Indonesian Poems), ed., Dongrui, p. 92. Jakarta Utara: Yinhua zuoxie.

Qipa 奇葩. 2011. "Yi ba san" 一把伞 (An Umbrella). In *Yinhua xinshi erbaishou* 印华新诗二百首 (Two Hundred Modern Chinese Indonesian Poems), ed., Dongrui, p. 99. Jakarta Utara: Yinhua zuoxie.

Sha Ping 莎萍. 2010a. "Hui xiang" 回乡 (Returning Home). In *Xie gei weilai* 写给未来 (Written for the Future), eds., Sha Ping and Xiaoxin, p. 49. Jakarta Utara: Yinhua zuoxie.

Sha Ping 莎萍. 2010b [2009]. "Xiangchou" 乡愁 (Homesickness). In *Xie gei weilai* 写给未来 (Written for the Future), eds., Sha Ping and Xiaoxin, p. 30. Jakarta Utara: Yinhua zuoxie.

Sha Ping 莎萍. 2010c [2008]. "Xie gei weilai" 写给未来 (Poem for the Future). In *Xie gei weilai* 写给未来 (Written for the Future), eds., Sha Ping and Xiaoxin, p. 7. Jakarta Utara: Yinhua zuoxie.

Sha Ping 莎萍. 2010d [2009]. "Zhuzai" 猪仔 (Piglets). In *Xie gei weilai* 写给未来 (Written for the Future), eds., Sha Ping and Xiaoxin, p. 31. Jakarta Utara: Yinhua zuoxie.

Sha Ping 莎萍. 2010e [2009]. "Banzhilan" 班芝兰 (Pancoran). In *Xie gei weilai* 写给未来 (Written for the Future), eds., Sha Ping and Xiaoxin, p. 12. Jakarta Utara: Yinhua zuoxie.

Sha Ping 莎萍 and Xiaoxin 小心. 2010. *Xie gei weilai* 写给未来 (Written for the Future). Jakarta Utara: Yinhua zuoxie.

Sha Ping 莎萍, ed. 2011. *Yinhua xinshi erbaishou* 印华新诗二百首 (Two Hundred Modern Chinese Indonesian Poems). Jakarta Utara: Yinhua zuoxie.

Sha Ping 莎萍. 2011a [1996]. "Fu ping" 浮萍 (Floating Weeds). In *Yinhua xinshi erbaishou* 印华新诗二百首 (Two Hundred Modern Chinese Indonesian Poems), ed., Sha Ping, p. 111. Jakarta Utara: Yinhua zuoxie.

Sha Ping 莎萍. 2011b [2009]. "Wuyue de shangkou" 五月的伤口 (The Wounds of May). In *Yinhua xinshi erbaishou* 印华新诗二百首 (Two Hundred Modern Chinese Indonesian Poems), ed., Sha Ping, p. 243. Jakarta Utara: Yinhua zuoxie.

Sha Ping 莎萍, ed. 2012. *Yinhua xiaoshi senlin* 印华小诗森林 (A Forest of Short Chinese Indonesian Poems). Jakarta Utara: Yinhua zuoxie.

Sha Ping 莎萍. 2012a. "Dao" 岛 (The Island). In *Yinhua xiaoshi senlin* 印华小诗森林 (A Forest of Short Chinese Indonesian Poems), ed., Sha Ping, p. 149. Jakarta Utara: Yinhua zuoxie.

Sha Ping 莎萍. 2012b. "Wen yan" 问雁 (Ask the Wild Goose). In *Yinhua xiaoshi senlin* 印华小诗森林 (A Forest of Short Chinese Indonesian Poems), ed., Sha Ping, p. 152. Jakarta Utara: Yinhua zuoxie.

Stenberg, Josh. 2017. "The Lost Keychain? Contemporary Chinese-language Writing in Indonesia." *Sojourn: Journal of Social Issues in Southeast Asia* 32(3): 634–668.

Stenberg, Josh. 2018. "Crossing the Finish Line." *Inside Indonesia*. https://www.insideindonesia.org/crossing-the-finish-line.

Stenberg, Josh. 2021. "Diverse Fragility, Fragile Diversity: Sinophone Writing in the Philippines and Indonesia." *Asian Ethnicity*: 1–19 (online first).

Tee, Kim Tong. 2010. "(Re)mapping Sinophone Literature." In *Global Chinese Literature: Critical Essays*, eds., Jing Tsu and David Der-wei Wang, pp. 77–91. Leiden: Brill.

Winkelmann, Christine. 2008. *Kulturelle Identitätskonstruktionen in der post-Suharto Zeit: chinesischstämmige Indonesier zwischen Assimilation und Besinnung auf ihre Wurzeln* (Cultural identity constructions in the post-Suharto period: Indonesians of Chinese origin between assimilation and reflections on their roots). Wiesbaden: Harrassowitz Verlag.

Xiaoxing 晓星. 2012a. "Pobing zhi lü" 破冰之旅 (Icebreaking Voyage). In *Yinhua xiaoshi senlin* 印华小诗森林 (A Forest of Short Chinese Indonesian Poems), ed., Sha Ping, p. 207. Jakarta Utara: Yinhua zuoxie.

Xiaoxing 晓星. 2012b. "Jianpai dahui" 减排大会 (Emission Reductions Conference). In *Yinhua xiaoshi senlin* 印华小诗森林 (A Forest of Short Chinese Indonesian Poems), ed., Sha Ping, p. 222. Jakarta Utara: Yinhua zuoxie.

Xiao, Zhang 肖章. 2009. "Cong dianshi yingmu shang kan Zhongguo guoqing dianli" 从电视荧幕看中国国庆典礼 (Watching the Chinese National Day Celebrations on a Television Screen). *Yinhua zuoxie*. Accessed on 24 June, 2020. http://www.yinhuazuoxie.com/xinshi/xiaozhangzhongguoguoqing.html.

Yan, Weizhen 严唯真. 1997. *Feicui daishang* 翡翠带上 (In the Emerald Band). Hong Kong: Holdery Publishing Enterprises Limited.

Yinhua Wenyou 印华文友, ed. 1999. "Fakan ci" 发刊词 (On Founding the Journal). *Yinhua wenyou*, 1: 1.

Yiruxiang 意如香. 2012a. "Haiyang de erzi" 海洋的儿子 (The Child of the Ocean). In *Yinhua xiaoshi senlin* 印华小诗森林 (A Forest of Short Chinese Indonesian Poems), ed., Sha Ping, p. 88. Jakarta Utara: Yinhua zuoxie.

Yiruxiang 意如香. 2012b. "Wenxue" 文学 (Literature). In *Yinhua xiaoshi senlin* 印华小诗森林 (A Forest of Short Chinese Indonesian Poems), ed., Sha Ping, p. 107. Jakarta Utara: Yinhua zuoxie.

Yiruxiang 意如香. 2012c. "Mingzi" 名字 (Name). In *Yinhua xiaoshi senlin* 印华小诗森林 (A Forest of Short Chinese Indonesian Poems), ed., Sha Ping, p. 100. Jakarta Utara: Yinhua zuoxie.

Yu, Erfan 于而凡. 2009. "Aoyun" 奥运 (The Olympics). *Yinhua zuoxie*. Accessed on 24 June 2020. http://www.yinhuazuoxie.com/xinshi/aoyunxinshiyuerfan.html.

Yuan Ni 袁霓. 2011 [1998]. "Qifen" 气氛 (Atmosphere). In *Yinhua xinshi erbaishou* 印华新诗二百首 (Two Hundred Modern Chinese Indonesian Poems), ed., Dongrui, p. 200. Jakarta Utara: Yinhua zuoxie.

Yueying 月影. 1997a [1995]. "Sixiang qu" 思乡曲 (Song about Missing Home). In *Feicui daishang* 翡翠带上 (In the Emerald Band), ed., Yan Weizhen, pp. 274–275. Hong Kong: Holdery Publishing Enterprises Limited.

Yueying 月影. 1997b. "Yifen zhongwen baozhi" 一份中文报纸 (A Chinese Newspaper). In *Feicui daishang* 翡翠带上 (In the Emerald Band), ed., Yan Weizhen, pp. 270–271. Hong Kong: Holdery Publishing Enterprises Limited.

Zhang, Hanying 张汉英. 1997 [1992]. "Han ye li de ludeng – xian gei Yinhua xiezuo zhe" 寒夜里的路灯 – 献给印华写作者 (Street Lamp on a Cold Night: For Chinese Indonesian Authors). In *Feicui daishang* 翡翠带上 (In the Emerald Band), ed., Yan Weizhen, p. 298. Hong Kong: Holdery Publishing Enterprises Limited.

Zhang, Ying 张颖. 2011 [1998]. "Heise de wang" 黑色的网 (The Black Net). In *Yinhua xinshi erbaishou* 印华新诗二百首 (Two Hundred Modern Chinese Indonesian Poems), ed., Dongrui, p. 224. Jakarta Utara: Yinhua zuoxie.

The Participation of Malaysian Chinese Women in the Workforce: Traditional Values and Choices

马来西亚华裔妇女劳动力参与：传统价值观与抉择

Jee Yin Chin (陈子莹) | ORCID: 0000-0003-3782-1112
Tun Tan Cheng Lock, Centre for Social and Policies Studies,
University of Tunku Abdul Rahman, Sungai Long, Malaysia
chinjy@utar.edu.my

Yee Mun Chin (陈亿文) | ORCID: 0000-0001-6073-7205
Tun Tan Cheng Lock, Centre for Social and Policies Studies,
University of Tunku Abdul Rahman, Sungai Long, Malaysia
chinym@utar.edu.my

Hooi San Noew (梁傸珊) | ORCID: 0000-0002-5614-4746
College of Liberal Arts, Wenzhou-Kean University, Wenzhou, China
hnoew@kean.edu

Abstract

The rate at which women participate in Malaysia's labor force is one of the lowest in the ASEAN region. Within the female workforce, Malaysian Chinese women participate more than women of other ethnic groups in Malaysia. Although this may indicate that the Malaysian Chinese are adapting to social changes that demand female participation in the workforce, a more in-depth study is needed to understand this phenomenon. In most circumstances, traditional Chinese values are omnipresent and affect women's decision to join the workforce. The question is to what extent and in what circumstances are Malaysian Chinese women bound by traditional values. This paper attempts to provide some insights into this question by providing an overview of Malaysian Chinese women's participation in the Malaysian workforce and the influences of Chinese traditional values on their decision to join the workforce. It is hoped that through this discussion, issues surrounding the participation of Malaysian Chinese women in the workforce can be highlighted, thereby opening up new avenues of research.

© KONINKLIJKE BRILL NV, LEIDEN, 2022 | DOI:10.1163/17932548-12341470

---

* This chapter was originally published as: Chin, J. Y., Chin, Y. M., and Noew, H. S. (2022). The Participation of Malaysian Chinese Women in the Workforce: Traditional Values and Choices. *Journal of Chinese Overseas*, 18(2), 335–357. Reprinted with kind permission from Brill.

This is an Open Access chapter published by World Scientific Publishing Company. It is distributed under the terms of the Creative Commons Attribution-NonCommercial-NoDerivatives 4.0 (CC BY-NC-ND) License which permits use, distribution and reproduction, provided that the original work is properly cited, the use is non-commercial and no modifications or adaptations are made.

Keywords

gender roles – Malaysian Chinese women – women participation in workforce

摘要

马来西亚的女性劳动力参与率为本区域最低，然而其华裔妇女的劳动力参与率却比马来西亚其他族群来得高。尽管这可能是马来西亚华裔跟随社会变迁的迹象，也就是需要更多的妇女参与劳动力；然而却仍还需深入探究。华人的传统价值观在华人社群里无所不在，也无时无刻都在影响华人妇女工作与否的抉择。现今的问题是，马来西亚华裔妇女在什么情况下，还被传统价值有所束缚？而其影响到底有多深？这项研究将以马来西亚华裔妇女劳动力参与率以及华人传统价值观如何影响她们进入职场的抉择为背景，深入探视这个问题。此项研究更希望通过此次讨论，马来西亚华裔妇女参与职场所面对的问题能够受到正视，并且为将来的研究铺路。

关键词

性别角色 – 马来西亚华裔妇女 – 女性劳动力参与

1 Introduction

Women have traditionally been deemed to be caretakers of the family. Such a role has discouraged them, especially those who are married and with children, from joining the workforce, particularly during their childbearing years. Statistics shows that in Malaysia, the rate of female participation in the workforce reaches its peak at the age of 20–24, and starts going down after that (see Figure 3). This reflects a trend – Malaysian women retreat from the workforce at childbearing age.

Nonetheless, the proportion of Malaysian Chinese women in the workforce is significantly higher than that of women of other ethnicities. This creates the impression that Chinese women diverge from the overall trend, one that suggests that Malaysian women leave the workforce as and when they are expected to perform their maternal and home-caretaker roles. Malaysian Chinese women, in contrast, presumably choose to remain active and continue to participate in the workforce. Such a phenomenon suggests that Chinese women are breaking away from tradition and exercising their autonomy by choosing to join or remain in the workforce instead of meeting their gendered expectations of taking care of family and children.

This paper intends to provide some insights into the above assumptions by providing an overview of the issues affecting women's participation in the workforce before delving into the issues faced by Malaysian Chinese women in the past and in recent times. By doing so, this paper aspires to contribute to a better understanding of issues that affect Malaysian Chinese women's participation in the workforce. Past research focused mainly on the participation of women in employment and directed little attention to understanding Malaysian Chinese women in the workforce.

1.1 *Women in the Workforce: An Overview*

Traditionally, women have always been responsible for a large portion of housework and for taking care of their children, tasks that consume most of their energy and time. Therefore, when they decide to join the workforce, they tend to choose flexible jobs with lighter workloads so that they can work and take care of their family at the same time. Such scenarios have been used to explain gender inequalities in the job market (Becker et al. 1985).

Becker (1985) also discussed the issue from the perspective of effort allocation between husband and wife. Housework is effort-intensive and wives (married women) are usually tasked with handling the bulk of it. This imbalance not only impacts on the choice of their occupation, but also their wage in the market. In other words, their limited contribution to the labor market mean that they earn less than men in general (Grimshaw, Damian and Rubery 2015). Scholars refer to this phenomenon as earning penalties for motherhood (Grimshaw et al 2015). This phenomenon will continue unless housework can be equally shared. While it is acknowledged that men have increasingly taken up a share of the housework, it is still a fact that women devote more time to domestic and child care work. On the other hand, an equal distribution of house work might have negative implications. According to Becker (1985), equal distribution of housework would have major implications for marriage, fertility, divorce, and many other family matters. Given these consequences, women (particularly married women) would rather choose not to work.

However, the rationale behind women's decision with regard to the matter is perhaps more nuanced than the explanation by Becker (1985) suggests. The notion that women must bear more responsibility for housework is an outcome of traditional values and norms. Thus, women's decision to forgo their career or choose a job with a lighter workload reflects an adherence to a tradition that has largely been seen as unfair to them. The notion that traditional values hinder women from working persists into the 21st century. Radical feminists would claim that the adherence to such a tradition is an outcome of the bias created by an overrepresentation of males in the economy that eventually causes the economy to be dominated by them (Cohen 2019). Nevertheless, attributing the unfairness solely to the overrepresentation of males in the economy might be too simplistic. In many modern economies, more women are participating in the workforce. For instance, there is an increase of women's participation in the workforce in Vietnam (Banerji et al. 2018), Just like many other Asian societies, males used to dominate the Vietnamese economy. However, their domination is declining. In this context, the proposition that the overrepresentation of males in the economy inhibits women's participation in the workforce does not hold true, as can be seen in the growing presence of women in the labor market, indicating that women have to some extent broken away from their traditional gender roles. They are making their own decisions, breaking from tradition and responding to the needs of a developing economy. Is there a similar trend in Malaysia, particularly among the Chinese female population?

2   Chinese Women in a Changing World

While women have been subjugated extensively under patriarchy, the world is changing. The source of the pressures exerted on women's career choices is shifting from tradition to coping with everyday needs.

In Hong Kong, Tong and Chiu (2017) found that many highly-educated married women who share common Chinese values choose to stay at home and not participate in the workforce. This trend contradicts the view that women are forced to stay out of the workforce. It is non-obligatory for these women but mostly voluntary after considering real-life needs. Highly-educated women will most likely marry highly-educated men who also have a high income. While their condition would have allowed them to stay in the workforce, the overtime working culture in Hong Kong causes married women to leave because they can no longer afford to work long hours. Given that academic performance is highly emphasized in Hong Kong, women there are under constant pressure to educate their children accordingly. Hence, the decision of whether to join the workforce or not is determined by real-life needs and finding a win-win solution that is agreeable to women. A similar trend can be observed among Singaporean Chinese women. Due to the rising cost of living, dual-earner families have been increasing too. Women there choose to enter the labor force due to economic concerns rather than to tradition (Chew 2005).

According to statistics from the early 2000s, 82 percent of women in Taiwan (which is of course Chinese in majority) joined the labor force but 30 percent of them quit after marriage (Peng and Wang 2005). Of those who quit, only 31 percent of them rejoined the labor force, and most of them had previously worked at the supervisory level. The most common reasons cited for leaving were "preparing to give birth" and "the distance between worksite and home.". Those who rejoin the workforce are those who are more competitive, have a higher education level, and earn an income that allows them to pay for childcare (Peng and Wang 2005). For these career-minded women, their values have changed over the generations, showing a stronger interest in developing their career when they mature (Peng and Wang 2005). Taiwanese women know what they want and what solutions are needed when they come across challenges in life. Nowadays, they are more confident, autonomous and competent in the workplace (Peng and Wang 2005).

More recent studies show that the public's general perception of the gender division of labor in Taiwan has improved a lot, with the traditional model of man as breadwinner and woman as housekeeper declining in recent years (Cheng and Loichinger 2017).

The case of Singapore has also confirmed this finding. Singapore consisted of 74.3 percent of Chinese in 2020, and its female labor force participation rate has been on an upward trend: from 56.5 percent in 2010 to 61.2 percent in 2020 (Department of Statistic Singapore 2021; Ministry of Manpower Singapore 2021). The Singapore government has implemented a family-friendly work policy to assist mothers to develop their careers while taking care of their families (Chew 2005). Though Singaporean women still face pressure to retain their traditional gender roles, the assistance provided by the Singapore government, for example providing childcare subsidy and encouraging the private sector to implement flexi working hours and flexible provisions for applying leave from work, etc., have lightened the burden on working mothers (Chew 2005). At the same time, Chew (2005) reiterated that the living cost in Singapore is rising and that fact has driven up the number of dual – income families. This phenomenon shows that real-life needs are more important than tradition. Eventually, it is the women who decide. The increase in the number of dual-income family would seem to confirm that this is so (Chew 2005).

The above examples in different countries are evidence of an upward trend in the participation of Chinese women in the workforce globally. Real-life needs, such as earning money to meet family expenses, rather than tradition are causing Chinese women to decide what is best for them. This trend also reflects the fact that the Chinese are adapting culturally to the social changes. Alongside these changes, more avenues are opening up for Chinese women to make their own choices. Adherence to tradition is non-obligatory. The question now is: do Malaysian Chinese married women also follow the changing trend of Chinese women in the world more generally?

3   Women's Participation in the Malaysian Workforce

In 2020, Malaysia had a population of 32.4 million, with 23.2 percent of Chinese ethnicity (6.9 million) (Department of Statistics Malaysia 2022). This makes Malaysian Chinese the second largest ethnic group in Malaysia as well as one of the largest Chinese populations outside China, Taiwan and Hong Kong (Ng et al. 2009). Noor and Mahudin (2016) point out that Malaysians, as a multi-ethnic nation, differ in their worldview and, unsurprisingly, that their differences include their perception of women's participation in the work force.

The overall labor force participation rate in Malaysia was 68.6 percent in 2021, with 80.9 percent male participation and 55.5 percent female participation (Department of Statistic 2021) (See Figure 1). This makes Malaysia's rate of participation in the labor force one of the lowest in the region (See Figure 2). Only half of women of working-age entered the labor force. From an economic point of view, to keep such a large number of possibly educated and experienced women out of the workforce is a loss for the productivity of the country.

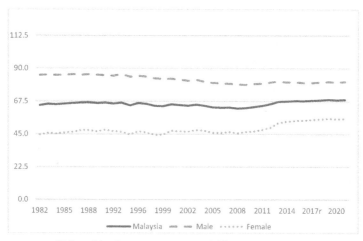

FIGURE 1   Malaysia labor force participation rate (%) by sex, year 1982–2021
SOURCE: DEPARTMENT OF STATISTICS 2022

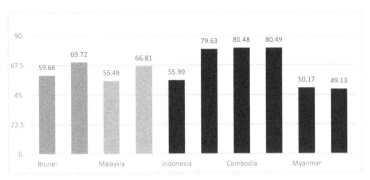

FIGURE 2   Female labor force participation rate in ASEAN countries in year 2019
SOURCE: WORLD BANK, 2020

3.1 *The Patterns of Malaysian Female Participation in the Labor Force*

Like women in many other countries, Malaysian women participate in the workforce after completing their education but the rate of their participation falls when they reach childbearing age. In 2021, their participation peaked in the age group 25–29 (a participation rate of 78.2 percent) but declined thereafter. Women leave the workforce at the age of 30–34 (a participation rate of 66.8 percent) (Figure 3). This trend suggests that Malaysian women tend to leave the workforce because of marriage and childbearing (Subramaniam, 2011; Noor and Mahudin, 2016).

With regard to unemployment, females have always had a higher rate than males (3.9 percent compared to 3.0 percent in quarter 2, 2018). This phenomenon is congruent with the finding that females are more likely to exit and re-enter the workforce but at the re-entry stage, many women are not able to look for a job (Ministry of Finance 2018).

Another explanation for higher female unemployment would be the general preference of employers for males over females because the former have a higher commitment to working long hours. This is confirmed by a comparison of the statistics for male and female working hours. The average for females in Malaysia is 43.9 hours per week compared to 46.5 hours for males. This trend distorts employers' perception in choosing their employees, since employer no longer judge men and women job seekers equally (Ministry of Finance 2018).

In order to attract women, particularly those of childbearing age, the Malaysian government has come up with several measures in the past few years: extending the duration of maternity leave, building more childcare centers, allowing tax deduction for parents sending young children to a registered

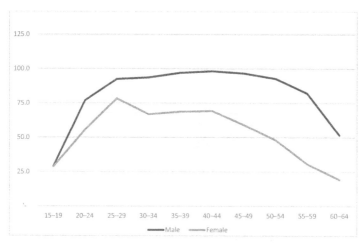

FIGURE 3   Malaysia labor participation rate, male and female in the year 2021
SOURCE: DEPARTMENT OF STATISTICS, 2022

childcare center, etc. (Khazanah Research Institute 2019a; Khazanah Research Institute 2019b).

However, as indicated in the data collected in 2021, the positive effects of these measures have yet to be seen. In other words, there are other factors causing Malaysian women to withdraw from the workforce apart from traditional perceptions of gender roles.

3.2   Factors Affecting Malaysian Women's Participation in the Workforce

The return of experienced working women to the workforce will be able to fill the gap of knowledge workers, especially in the service sector. The service sector is the preferred sector among women, especially those with tertiary education. Almost half of women outside the workforce had worked previously and the service sector is the biggest employer for women in Malaysia (Subramaniam, Ali and Overton 2010).

Abu Bakar, Nor'Aznin and Abdulla's (2010)'s findings are consistent with the theory that work experience and years of education will raise the probability of women joining the labor force. Meanwhile, husband's income and having children under 6 years old has a negative effect on female participation in the Malaysian workforce. The cost of childcare has also been included in the research.

The authors added that there is a higher chance that urban women will participate in the labor force as job opportunities are more abundant in urban than in rural areas. Besides locality, marriage age and fertility will also affect Malaysian women's decision to join or return to the workforce. Older marriage age and lower fertility rate have a positive effect on women's participation in Malaysia. The average marriage age of Malaysian women increased from 23.5 years in 1980 to 24.7 years in 1991. This rise would delay reproduction, meaning that women and can stay longer in the labor force (Abu Bakar, Nor'Aznin and Abdulla 2010).

Education is one of the reasons for the rise in the age at which Malaysian women marry. With education becoming more common, women tend to pursue higher education. Consequently, their fertility and the size of families are expected to drop (Abu Bakar et al. 2010). This explains the highest participation of women between 20–24 years old in the workforce – it is a point in time when they have just completed tertiary education and are not yet married. Having said that, there are multiple factors that influence Malaysian women's decision-making. It varies for every individual and generation. Malaysian Chinese women as a subgroup of Malaysian women are following the general trend of workforce participation on the part of Malaysian women, but in their own unique way.

4 Chinese Women in the Malaysian Labor Force

4.1 *A Brief History of Chinese Women's Migration*

Malaysian Chinese are the descendants of Chinese immigrants. Their ancestors migrated from China *en masse* in the 19th century, mainly as a result of the labor trade or by family arrangement. Most of them were men (Lee 1989; Ariffin 1992; Fan 2019). A large number of them landed in Malaya, now Malaysia.[1]

In the early 19th century, there were not many Chinese women in Malaya. One of the reasons was that the Chinese men who came to Malaya did not intend to reside in Malaya permanently (Lee 1989). As a result, they did not arrange for their families to relocate to Malaya and patriarchal Chinese tradition required women to stay with the family. At the same time, there was an official prohibition on women leaving China (Lee 1989). The patriarchal Chinese tradition of requiring women to stay with the family also contributed to this pattern.

---

1 Malaysia was founded on 16 September 1963. Malaya, Sabah and Sarawak were the founding states. In this paper, the discussion of Malaysian Chinese women's history relates mainly to Chinese women in Malaya, since the record of Chinese women's migration and participation in the workforce in Sabah and Sarawak on Borneo is thin.

The situation changed in the late-nineteenth century. The British colonial government allowed the large-scale immigration of Chinese women. This change was intended to bring the sex ratio into balance, thereby reducing sex crimes and increasing the labor supply. Meanwhile, Mainland China was facing an economic depression and many factories had closed down, leading to severe unemployment. The combination of push and pull factors resulted in a tremendous increase in Chinese women's migration (Ariffin 1992; Fan 2019). The number of Chinese women in Malaya in 1903 was 15,331 but by 1911 it had increased to 35,539 (Ariffin 1992).

After the British colonial government enforced the Aliens Ordinance of 1933, more Chinese women migrated to Malaya, since the law restricted only immigration by Chinese men (Ariffin 1992).

4.2 *The Education of Chinese Women in Malaya*

In the early 20th century, there were English-language schools and Christian-mission schools, as well as Chinese vernacular schools set up by the Chinese community. The Chinese schools were mainly funded by Chinese philanthropists. As the Chinese community has always valued literacy and education, there were quite a number of Chinese women who attended Chinese vernacular schools (Ariffin 1992). The first Chinese girls' school in Malaya – Kuen Cheng Chinese girls' school – was set-up in 1908 (Fan 2019).

The government under the Chinese Qing dynasty created guidelines for the setting up of girls' schools in 1907. The Chinese community responded swiftly and set up the first Chinese girls' school in Malaya – Kuen Cheng Chinese girls school – in 1908 (Fan 2019). This school became the pride of the Malayan Chinese (Zheng 1998). Nevertheless, it should be noted that even before the Qing dynasty began promoting education for women, Chinese society in Malaya had already learned its importance as a result of the formation of girls' schools by missionary groups (Zheng 1998). This development had led to an increase in the literacy rate among Chinese women in Malaya. According to Fan (2019), the literacy ratio of Chinese men to women in Malaysia in 1921 was 487:120. After World War Two, the ratio was 497:188 – a significant increase among women.

As the literacy rate among Chinese women increased, the types of occupation in which they were involved transited from traditional job types such as domestic maids and farmers to clerical jobs, teachers and even smallholders. Teaching was the most popular occupation among educated Chinese women during the 1930s (Fan 2019).

Chinese education for women in those years increased the attention given to gender equality by the Chinese community in Malaya and promoted the participation of women in society. During the Japanese occupation, Chinese girls' schools had actively participated in anti-Japanese activities (Fan 2019).

4.3 The Participation of Chinese Women in the Malaysian (Malayan) Workforce

From 1929 to 1933, the unemployment rate in Malaya was high due to the world economic depression. Many female workers lost their jobs while some women entered the workforce because of financial distress in the family. However, the types of job available to them were severely limited. Most worked as maids, hawkers and prostitutes before Chinese girls' schools were developed more extensively (Fan 2019).

Nevertheless, the economic depression had significantly increased the ratio of women in the workforce. From 1930 to 1940, the ratio of females in various sectors increased. The top three industries in which women participated were plantations (mostly rubber), services, and finance. Fan (2019) listed the factors that caused the changes:

i) Malaya was still suffering from the economic downturn in 1930. Some employers turned to employing women instead of men due to the lower pay women received. Apart from that, many women joined the workforce as hawkers and maids. The economic downturn made it easier for women to enter the labor force and to start earning and supporting their families.

ii) The structure of Malayan Chinese entrepreneurship had also shifted from tin mining and rubber plantation to commerce and manufacturing. This shift caused Chinese men to change their jobs and Chinese women had the opportunity to fill the vacancies left by men.

iii) The world economic crisis caused more Chinese women to migrate from China to Malaya. This provided plenty of cheap labor for Malaya and the opportunity for women to participate in the workforce.

iv) The education level of Chinese women in Malaya had risen, especially between 1910 and 1930. Girls' schools operating in various language mediums (English, Chinese, and Sino-English) gave women in Malaya a greater opportunity to receive an education. Education elevated Chinese women's ability to participate in the workforce.

Nevertheless, Fan (2019) also pointed out that even though working women had become more numerous, marriage was still an obstacle in the years 1929–1941 in the way of women continuing to work. Generally, Chinese women are domestic caretakers, particularly after they have given birth. Thus, most working women had to leave the workforce after marriage or after giving birth. Given this context, employers at that time preferred not to hire married women, even in female-dominated sectors such as education.

4.4 *The Values Held by Chinese Females in Malaysia*

Confucianism has been deeply embedded in Chinese culture for more than two thousand years. To a large extent, Chinese women were affected by Confucianism. Through Confucianism, women were given a subordinate role in the family as well as in society. As a daughter, women must obey their father. After they are married, they must listen to their husband and bear responsibility for reproducing the next generation, especially male offspring, to ensure lineage continuity. Even after their husbands die, women (wives who are also mothers) have to obey their son (Chia 1984; Loh Ludher 2003; Granrose 2006).

Men are always seen as the main family earners, while women or wives are seen as secondary earners in the family. The career of married women is thus "subordinated" to that of men. Whatever their personal wishes, many Chinese women suppress their hearts' desire for employment if their husbands prevent them from taking a job (Loh Ludher 2003; Ministry of Women, Family and Community Development 2014). Most of the time, women will have to abide by the traditional expectation – to stay at home and handle household chores.

In the patriarchal Chinese family model, women are required to give up their opportunity for education. Women were also taught in school the importance of "feminine" features, such as gracefulness and gentleness. Women were bound to feminine hobbies, activities, school subjects, and occupations (Chia 1984).

Loh Ludher(2003) demonstrated that even in the 1990s, the Chinese women in Malaysia were still adhering to traditional family roles. Her research found that most of them were still complying with the traditional ideology that women were supposed to be the family caretaker for children and the elderly. Some interviewees in the study admitted that they were expected to pay for the caregivers or their in-laws for taking care of their children in return for being able to go back to work (Loh Ludher 2003). In instances where caregiving was not cost-efficient, they would be the ones to sacrifice their careers and stay at home to take responsibility. Chinese women were also still subscribing to the practice of having men or in this case their husbands as patriarchs (*yi jia zhi zhu*, 一家之主) who made the major decisions in the family. In some cases, even husbands who failed to be the major earner got to maintain their "patriarchal" status in the family.

Such traditional values are often quoted as the main reason that Chinese women leave the workforce. Overall, traditional values have assigned to women the "reproductive" role, bearing the responsibility for ensuring that the family is taken care of while they themselves continue to reproduce the next generation, biologically and socially. They are not expected to be the breadwinner, a role that is assigned to men. Consequently, Chinese women's participation in the workforce is generally not encouraged. Even if they do participate, they are expected to play subordinate roles. In this context, the radical feminist explanation may hold some truth. Chinese beliefs and values are encapsulated patriarchy – a system created and dominated by men. However, such arrangements are probably a reaction to the limitations presented by the social and physical environments of human societies. Such environments require the segregation of male and female duties, a working formula to preserve society. Unfortunately, exploitation and unfair treatment are its by-products and women have had to bear the brunt due to their subordinate roles.

Given the passage of time, are Chinese women in Malaysia still bound by the same beliefs? Chia (1984) highlighted the fact that women in Malaysia enjoy more flexibility in adhering to those principles. Unlike in China, Malaysian law gives women the right to inherit and hold property. Women in Malaysia are also allowed to intervene in family matters. Given their job opportunities, women in Malaysia can earn extra income for the household, making them more economically independent. Chia also mentioned that Chinese parents in Malaysia have more open minds due to their exposure to mass–media and to modern ideas such as gender equality.

Chinese women in Malaysia are also progressive, in the sense that many demand that their rights be recognized. Fan's (2019) research, which focused on Malayan Chinese women between 1929 and 1941, found that they started organizing or participating in labor strikes and union activities to demand for higher salary and speak out against sexual harassment. These activities had slowly increased their self-confidence, belief in the right to autonomy, and financial independence. Fan (2019) mentioned that economic and social development in China and Malaya during the 1900s had allowed Chinese women to enjoy most rights, i.e., education, property inheritance and participation in economic activities.

Traditionally, as Chia (1984) showed, Chinese women are considered responsible in the family for the continuation of the lineage. Women will be put under pressure if they fail to reproduce a male offspring. Such a failure is seen as a dereliction of duty under Confucianism. As a result, the husband of a woman unable to perform that role will be allowed to marry another woman. However, this tradition is in the course of changing. Data from the Malaysia Family Life Survey conducted in 1976/1977 and 1988/1989 indicate that in Malaysian Chinese families, the wife is the one who decides on fertility outcome (Rasul 2008). This reflects the change in Chinese women's status in the family.

4.5 Tertiary Educated Chinese Women in Urban Areas

Most Malaysian Chinese reside in urban areas and usually work in the trading sector (Arrifin, Horton and Guilherme 1996; Amin 2004; Ng et al., 2009). Generally, the rate of female participation in the labor force in rural areas has been decreasing over time, while in urban areas it has increased. A high rate of urbanization and job diversification in the case of Malaysian Chinese could be one of the reasons for the fact that female labor force participation is higher among Chinese women than among other ethnic groups. This has been the case even since the years 1957–1970 (Hirschman 1980). Ariffin et al. (1996) highlighted that the female participation rate in urban area had exceeded that in the rural area in the years 1970 to 1985.

The Chinese population in urban areas continued to grow after the implementation of the New Economic Policy (NEP). This development has opened up more job opportunities for Malaysian Chinese women. According to Abu Bakar et al. (2010), urban women have a higher chance of participating in the labor force, given that job opportunities are greater in urban than in rural areas. The participation of Chinese women in the labor force also increased significantly after the implementation of NEP. A possible reason could be that the effects of NEP are more beneficial in urban areas (Amin 2004). Chinese who mostly reside in urban areas felt the effect more than Malays and Indians (Amin 2004). Moreover, dual-income families are common in urban areas due to the high cost of living, which drives Chinese women to go out to work (Ng et al. 2009).

Statistics also shows that large numbers of tertiary educated Malaysian Chinese women in the labor force live in urban areas (see Figure 4).

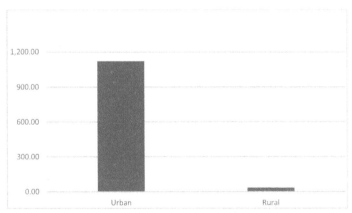

FIGURE 4   Tertiary Educated Malaysian Chinese female in labor force by strata, 2020
SOURCE: DEPARTMENT OF STATISTICS, 2020

4.6 Malaysian Chinese Women's Participation in the Labor Force in Today's Society

The historical background and social and economic development have shaped the trend of the workforce from the point of view of Malaysian Chinese women today. Loo's (2014) interviewee (interview conducted in 2010s) – a married Chinese woman with tertiary education – mentioned that she had many female friends who are highly educated and worked as professionals. However, they decided to quit their jobs and dedicated themselves to childbearing. Their main concern was the quality of childcare and their child's education. Such an observation shows that highly educated Chinese women are able to make their own decisions about whether to focus on their career or not, and to gradually disregard pressures generated by Chinese traditions.

On the other hand, Chong (2016), through her in-depth interviews, found that the higher educated married Chinese women in Malaysia are still restricted by the patriarchal values of other parties (husband, original family, husband's family or social perception). However, they are able to fight for their own decisions and choices in the matter of their career.

Although they need to give in at a certain level, they are able to pursue their post-graduate study and continue their careers (Chong 2016). One of the interviewees (married with two children, a PhD graduate) said that she felt lost (insecure) when she quit her full-time job for child-bearing (Chong 2016). She later decided to pursue a PhD and participated in research work (Chong 2016).

Both Chong's (2016) postgraduate interviewees tried to quit their careers in order to bear children, but they never gave up on their professions. They slowly made a "come-back" after their children had grown up, and they discovered a working style that allowed them to work while at the same time coping with their families (Chong 2016).

Chong (2016) reiterated that highly educated Chinese women built their professions by pursuing their education and developing their self-consciousness, autonomy and sense of gender equality. At the same time, these Chinese women have been awarded the gender role of wife, mother or daughter-in-law. Despite being modern women, they still need to continue in the traditional role, while at the same time they need to adapt to their existing environments in order to live happily.

Amin (2004) examined the employment of married women of different ethnicities and their reactions to the New Economic Policy (NEP) and New Population Policy (NPP). He found that the rate of participation in the labor force on the part of Chinese women in Malaysia increased to a significantly greater extent between the implementation of NEP in 1971 and of NPP in 1982 than that of Malay women. He explained that NEP has greater effects on urban areas, whose inhabitants are mostly Chinese.

Amin's (2004) research also found that women responded positively to the increment of their wages and increased their participation in the workforce, whereas their husband's wages had a negligible economic impact on their decision to do so. Chinese women showed the most significant result in terms of these two effects. In short, as suggested by Amin (2004), married women's decision regarding employment is dependent on their own preferences and wishes, even though social values and culture are also likely to have an impact. This phenomenon is obvious among Chinese women. Statistics show that Malaysian Chinese women have a higher rate of participation in the labor force (within their own ethnic group) between the ages of 20–49 than other major ethnic groups – the Malays and the Indians. (See Figure 5)

Noor and Mahudin (2016) found that although most women hope to enter full-time employment, the intention is stronger among Chinese women than among Malay women. They also have more support from their husbands than do Malay women.

Compared to other ethnic groups in Malaysia, Chinese females educated at the tertiary level have the highest rate of participation in the labor force (Refer Table 1). The trend from 2016–2019 also shows that Chinese graduates' participation rate is the highest (Refer Figure 6). This indicates the unique position of Malaysian Chinese women in deciding on whether or not to join the workforce.

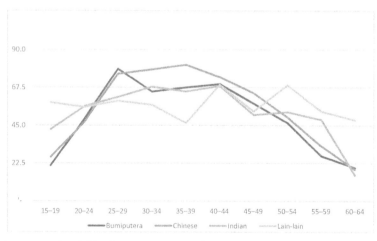

FIGURE 5   Female labor force participation rate by age group and ethnic group, Malaysia, 2021
SOURCE: DEPARTMENT OF STATISTICS, 2022

TABLE 1   Labor force participation rate by educational attainment, ethnic group and sex, Malaysia, 2021

Educational attainment	Total (%)	Malaysian citizens					Non-Malaysian citizen
		Total	Bumiputera	Chinese	Indians	Others	
No formal education	64.4	40.7	41.0	37.1	34.6	70.2	84.4
Primary	68.8	55.5	57.9	48.3	55.3	80.1	89.6
Secondary	67.4	66.0	64.4	69.7	69.3	71.2	86.1
Tertiary	71.2	71.9	71.0	75.5	68.4	74.7	52.0

SOURCE: DEPARTMENT OF STATISTICS, 2022

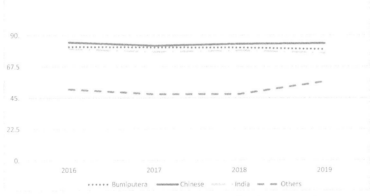

FIGURE 6   Female graduates labor force participation rate by ethnic group and sex, 2016–2019
SOURCE: DEPARTMENT OF STATISTIC, 2020

Meanwhile, other statistics show that the number of Chinese female graduates outside the labor force remains constant, at around 100,000 people (Refer Figure 7). The number of people outside the labor force indicates people not looking for jobs and intent on staying outside the workforce. This indicates that many Chinese females have a tertiary education but have chosen to stay outside the workforce. The reasons for their staying outside the workforce have mainly to do with housework/family responsibilities and children's schooling (see Table 2).

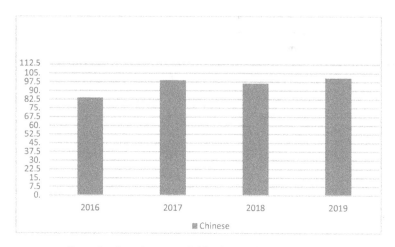

FIGURE 7 Chinese female graduates outside labor force, Malaysia, 2016–2019
SOURCE: DEPARTMENT OF STATISTICS, 2020

TABLE 2 Graduates outside labor force by the reasons for not seeking work, Malaysia, 2016–2019

('000)	2016	2017	2018	2019
Female	412.1	475	507.6	562.2
Schooling/training programme	129.9	143.2	130.1	125.9
Housework/family responsibilities	208.5	240.4	270.7	311.8
Going for further studies	7.5	7	10	6.3
Disabled	2.6*	3.4	3.2	3.5
Not interested, just completed study	11.2	12.4	15.9	20.1
Retired	52.5	68.6	77.7	94.7

*Data to be used with caution due to high relative standard error
SOURCE: DEPARTMENT OF STATISTICS, 2020

While Chinese women with a tertiary-education actively participate in the workforce, some among them choose to stay outside the workforce. This shows that there is room for them to choose between career and family.

5 Preference Theory – Women in the Modern World Can Choose Their Own Preferred Lifestyle

The question remains: are Malaysian Chinese women free to make their own decisions on matters related to their career? Hakim (2002) argued that nowadays, women's position has changed. She developed the Preference Theory, which posits that economic and social changes have given women genuine choices. The theory was developed empirically based on the 1999 British Survey.

Hakim (2002) came to such conclusions due to the fact that the contraceptive revolution had given women the chance to control their own fertility. Furthermore, she believed that women had been given equal rights to access all positions, occupations and careers in the labor market for the first time in history by the equal opportunities revolution. Although gender discrimination still happens, she believed that women can get any paid employment they want.

The expansion of white-collar occupations provides plenty of job opportunities for women. Jobs for secondary earners also expanded; these jobs normally come with flexihours and job shares and are themselves part – time (Hakim 2002).

More importantly, Hakim (2002) pointed out that with accumulated wealth, one can make personal preferences regarding jobs. One's preferences have become more important than financial necessity. Hakim further elaborated that many women can afford to work part-time or even not work at all because their husbands are earning enough for the whole family.

Malaysian Chinese women who have access to higher education mostly live in urban areas and find it easier to access job opportunities and are able to decide on family fertility plan. They are better able to make their own choices.

From the literature we covered, it is clear that Malaysian Chinese women nowadays are doing their best to fulfil their own lifestyle preferences despite pressure from traditional gender roles.

6 Conclusion

From the first wave of feminism to postmodern feminism, women have slowly gained in equality and autonomy. However, women are still struggling to make their own decisions with regard to joining the workforce, especially after marriage and having children. The decision is informed by women's gender roles, the family's financial status and the availability of job opportunities.

Based on the above discussion, Chinese women in Malaysia are changing and their participation in the labor force is higher than that of women in other ethnic groups. This could be due to their historical background, education level, degree of urbanization and awareness of autonomy.

The higher participation rate of Malaysian Chinese women in the workforce is an indication that the Chinese community in Malaysia and probably other parts of the world prioritizes pragmatic needs. Traditional values and gender roles are gradually losing their grip as women struggle to make ends meet. The Chinese women in Malaysia may have achieved Hakim's description of what it means to be a modern woman – a person possessed of the capacity to make genuine choices based on that person's lifestyle preferences. However, this conclusion is still hypothetical. It should be noted that even the change itself remains volatile, for the Chinese community is still adjusting so as to allow women to make their own decisions in matters related to their career. Multiple rounds of social adjustment might be required, both cognitive and social. A more conclusive empirical research regarding Malaysian Chinese women's reactions to the social changes and their career choices will be necessary before any further discussion of this matter is possible.

References

Abu Bakar, Nor'Aznin and Abdulla Norehan. 2010. "Labor Force Participation of Women in Malaysia." *Journal of Pembangunan Sosial* 13(Jun):115–130.

Amin, Shahina. 2004. "Ethnic Differences and Married Women's Employment in Malaysia: Do Government Policies Matter?" *Journal of Socio – Economics* 33(3): 291–306.

Ariffin, Jamilah. 1992. *Women and Development in Malaysia*. Ariffin Jamilah, ed. Petaling Jaya: Pelanduk Publications.

Banerji, Angana, Gjonbalaj, Albe, Hlatshwayo, Sandile and Anh Van Le. 2018. "Asian Women at Work." In *Finance and Development*, pp. 13–17. International Monetary Fund.

Becker, Gary Stanley. 1985. "Human Capital, Effort, and the Sexual Division of Labor." *Journal of Labor Economics* 3(1, Part 2): S33–S58.

Cheng, Yen-Hsin Alice and Elke Loichinger. 2017. "The Future Labor Force of an Aging Taiwan: The Importance of Education and Female Labor Supply." *Population Research and Policy Review* 36(3):441–466.

Chew, Irene K.H. and Naresh Khatri. 2005. "The Impact of Government and Family Responsibilities on the Career Development of Working Women in Singapore." In *Employment of Women in Chinese Cultures*, ed., Granrose Cherlyn Skromme, pp. 128–145. Cheltenham: Edward Elgar.

Chia, Oaipeng. 1984. "Traces of Confucianst Influence On Malaysian Chinese Women and Its Implications." In *Women in Malaysia*, eds., Aiyun Hing, Nik Safiah Karim and Rokiah Talib, pp. 174–186. Kuala Lumpur: Pelanduk Publications.

Chong, Boonfong (Zhang Wenfang). 2016. Malaixiya Huayi yihun nüxing duochong juese yu nüxing ziwo zhi tanjiu 马来西亚华裔已婚女性多重角色与女性自我之探究 (The Study of Multiple Roles and Women Self of Malaysian Chinese Married Women). Master Thesis, National Chi Nan University.

Department of Statistics. 2020. *Labor Force Survey Report 2019*. Putrajaya: Department of Statistics Malaysia.

Department of Statistics. 2021. *Labor Force Survey Report 2020*. Putrajaya: Department of Statistics Malaysia.

Department of Statistics Singapore. 2021. *"Census of Population 2020 Statistical Release 1 – Key Findings, Department of Statistic, Singapore."* Department of Statistics Singapore. doi: 10.1007/978-3-030-82844-8_5. Accessed on 8 June 2022.

Department of Statistics. 2022. *Labor Force Survey Report 2021*. Putrajaya: Department of Statistics Malaysia.

Department of Statistics. 2020. *Graduates Statistic 2019*. Putrajaya: Department of Statistics Malaysia.

Department of Statistics Malaysia. 2022. *Launching of Report on the Key Findings Population and Housing Census of Malaysia 2020*. Putrajaya: Department of Statistics Malaysia.

Fan, Ruolan. 2019. *Immigration, Gender and Overseas Chinese Society: Studies on Chinese Women in Malaya 1929–1941*. Guangzhou: Jinan University Press.

Grimshaw, Damian and Jill Rubery. 2015. *The Motherhood Pay Gap: A Review of the Issues, Theory and International Evidence*. Geneva: International Labor Office.

Hakim, Catherine. 2002. "Lifestyle Preference as Determinants of Women's Differentiated Labor Market Careers." *Work and Occupations* 29(4): 428–459.

Hirschman, Charles and Akbar Aghajanian. 1980. "Women's Labor Force Participation and Socioeconomic Development: The Case of Peninsular Malaysia, 1957–1970." *Journal of Southeast Asian Studies* 11(1): 30–49.

Jamilah, Arrifin, Horton, Susan and Guilherme Sedlacek. 1996. "Women in the Labor Market in Malaysia." In *Women and Industrialization in Asia*, ed., Susan Horton, pp. 207–243. London: Routledge.

Khazanah Research Institute. 2019a. *Time to Care: Gender Inequality, Unpaid Care Work and Time Use Survey*. Kuala Lumpur: Khazanah Research Institute.

Khazanah Research Institute. 2019b. *Gender Role Values: What Do Women Want?* Kuala Lumpu: Khazanah Research Institute.

Loh Ludher, Lee Lee. 2003. "Chinese Women in Industrial Home-based Sub-contracting in the Garment Industry in Kuala Lumpur: Neither Valued nor Costed." *Akademika* 63(July):11–30.

Lee, Sharon M. 1989. "Female Immigrants and Labor in Colonial Malaya: 1860–1947." *International Migration Review* 23(2):309–331.

Loo, Yit Mei. 2014. Nation and Gender in Malaysia's Childcare Policy Discourses, 1980–2014. Master Thesis, National Chi Nan University.

Ministry of Finance. 2018. *Economic Outlook 2019*. Putrajaya: Ministry of Finance Malaysia.

Ministry of Manpower Singapore. 2021. *A Gender-Inclusive Workforce*. Ministry of Manpower Singapore. https://stats.mom.gov.sg/Pages/a-gender-inclusive-workforce.aspx. Accessed on 12 October 2021.

Ministry of Women, Family And Community Development. 2014. *Study to Support the Development of National Policies and Programmes to Increase and Retain the Participation of Women in the Malaysian Labor Force: Key Findings and Recommendations*. Kuala Lumpur: Ministry of Women, Family and Community Development.

Ng, Kokmun, Loy, Johnben Teik-Cheok, Gudmunson, Clinton G. and Winnee Cheong. 2009. "Gender Differences in Marital and Life Satisfaction Among Chinese Malaysians." *Sex Roles* 60(1–2):33–43.

Noor, Noraini M and Nor Diana Mohd Mahudin. 2016. "Work, Family and Women's Well-Being in Malaysia." In *Handbook on Well-Being of Working Women*, eds., Marry L. Connerley and Jiyun Wu, pp. 717–734. Dordrecht: Springer.

Peng, T.K. and Tsai-Wei Wang. 2005. "*Women in Taiwan: Social Status, Education and Employment*." In *Employment of Women in Chinese Cultures*, ed., Cherlyn Skromme Granrose, pp. 84–106. Cheltenham: Edward Elgar.

Rasul, Imran. 2008. "Household Bargaining Over Fertility: Theory and Evidence from Malaysia." *Journal of Development Economics* 86(2):215–241.

Subramaniam, Geetha. 2011. Flexible Working Arrangements in Malaysia and the Participation of Women in the Labour Force. PhD. Thesis, Victoria University of Wellington.

Subramaniam, Geetha, Ershad, Ali and John Overton. 2010. "Are Malaysian Women Interested in Flexible Working Arrangements At Workplace?" *Business Studies Journal* 2(2):83–98.

Tong, Yuying and Stephen Wing-kai Chiu. 2017. "Women's Labor Force Participation in Hong Kong: 1991–2011." *Chinese Sociological Review* 49(1):35–64.

Zheng, Liangshu 郑良树. 1998. Malaixiya Huawen jiaoyu fazhan shi 马来西亚华文教育发展史 (History of the Development of Malaysian Chinese Education). Kuala Lumpur: The United Chinese School Teacher's Association of Malaysia.

Revolutionary Cosmopolitanism and its Limits
The Chinese Communist Party and the Chinese in Singapore, Medan and Jakarta Compared (1945–1949)

革命的民族多元性与其局限:
中国共产党与新加坡、棉兰、雅加达华侨华人关系之对比 (1945-1949)

Guo-Quan Seng (成国泉)
National University of Singapore
hissgq@nus.edu.sg

Abstract

This article analyzes the extent and limits of the Chinese Communist Party's (CCP) revolutionary cosmopolitanism in Southeast Asia. Between 1945 and 1949, the CCP intellectuals Hu Yuzhi and Wang Renshu operated a network of leftwing newspapers in Southeast Asia's major urban centers. They championed the revolution in the homeland, while supporting anti-colonial nationalist movements in the region. Taking a comparative approach, I argue that the CCP's revolutionary cosmopolitanism developed and diverged on the ground according to the diasporic community's social structure, the contingency of events in the process of decolonization and initiatives taken by local CCP leaders. While the CCP in Jakarta turned neutral in the face of republican atrocities against Chinese, Singapore and Medan went on to mobilize merchants and youths to take part in local anti-colonial movements. The CCP stood for a moderate, anti-colonial Malayan nationalism in Singapore, in comparison with a more radical, non-assimilationist position in solidarity with Indonesia's independence struggle in Medan.

Keywords

Chinese Communist Party – Singapore – Medan – Jakarta

---

* This chapter was originally published as: Seng, G.-Q. (2020). Revolutionary Cosmopolitanism and its Limits: The Chinese Communist Party and the Chinese in Singapore, Medan and Jakarta compared (1945–1949). *Journal of Chinese Overseas*, 16(1), 1–30. Reprinted with kind permission from Brill.

This is an Open Access chapter published by World Scientific Publishing Company. It is distributed under the terms of the Creative Commons Attribution-NonCommercial-NoDerivatives 4.0 (CC BY-NC-ND) License which permits use, distribution and reproduction, provided that the original work is properly cited, the use is non-commercial and no modifications or adaptations are made.

摘要

此文针对中国共产党在东南亚的民族多元性革命与其局限加以分析。从1945至1949年,分布在东南亚的重要城市的中共知识分子胡愈之与王任叔等人经营着一个左翼的报业网络。他们呼吁在地华侨华人拥护国内的革命并同时支持区域的反殖民运动。通过对比的视角,此文论述中共在东南亚执行的多元民族性革命,如何因为华侨社会结构、去殖民运动的偶然性以及在地领导等因素而发展出相似与不同的历史轨迹。受排华事件的影响,中共在雅加达采取了中立的姿态。相对而言,中共在新加坡和棉兰都进一步推动商人与青年加入反殖民运动。中共在新加坡主张华侨融入温和、反殖的马来亚民族主义运动,相较于在棉兰倡导激进而不入籍印尼的亲印度尼西亚独立抗争。

关键词

中国共产党 – 新加坡 – 棉兰 – 雅加达

On at least two separate occasions, in January and April 1946, Hu Yuzhi 胡愈之 published an almost identical essay, "On the double mission of the Overseas Chinese," in Jakarta and Singapore respectively. The first appeared in *Shenghuo Bao* (*Seng Hwo Pao*, Life Daily, 5.1.1946) in Jakarta, followed by *Fengxia* (Below the Wind, 6.4.1946) in Singapore—leftist journals run by an underground Chinese communist network in Southeast Asia. *Minzhu Ribao* (Democracy Daily News)—another important node—in Medan, northeastern Sumatra, would most likely have carried the same editorial. One of the most famous interwar Shanghai writer-editors, Hu Yuzhi had relocated to Singapore, from where he coordinated the party's region-wide propaganda campaign. On this occasion, Hu declared that the Overseas Chinese had a dual mission (*liangchong renwu*) in post-war Southeast Asia. They had to help the local nations achieve freedom and independence, but at the same time they should contribute to China's postwar recovery and revival.

Singapore, Jakarta and Medan were key nodes in the regional British and Dutch colonial projects, to which Chinese migrants from the provinces of Guangdong and Fujian had flocked starting in the nineteenth century. In Singapore, the Chinese immigrants and their descendants formed an outright majority (75% in 1931). In both Batavia/Jakarta (16.5% in 1930) and Medan (35.6% in 1930), they were significant minorities (Saw 2007: 29; Volkstelling VII 1933–6: 183, 186). However, the Overseas Chinese were not a homogenous group. They were split by class, and culturally along the lines of degree of assimilation (e.g. the local-born Peranakans versus the more recently arrived Totoks in Java), native-place origins, and educational streams. Ever since the turn of the twentieth century, nationalists from the homeland generally found it difficult to mobilize and unite diasporic communities in Southeast Asia until after the start of the Sino-Japanese and Pacific Wars (1937–1945), when China's very existence was under threat (Wang 1976: 405–23). In the late 1930s, the Singapore-based Hokkien tycoon Tan Kah Kee 陈嘉庚 became the public face of this diasporic nationalist unity, when he was nominated as Chair of the Federation of the China Relief Fund of the South Seas (henceforth, China Relief Fund). His visits to Chongqing and Yan'an, the capitals of the Guomindang and the Chinese Communist Party, partners at the time in a United Front alliance, in early 1940 put him in direct contact with both Chiang Kai-shek and Mao Zedong.

In 1940, at the request of Tan Kah Kee, the CCP dispatched a score or so of high-profile Shanghai and Hong Kong-based writers, editors and social activists to Singapore to counter Guomindang propaganda. After the three colonial cities fell to the invading Japanese army in early 1942, Hu Yuzhi and his comrades took refuge for three years in Northeast Sumatra. They re-emerged in August 1945 in a region fired up by nationalist struggles to resist the recolonizing Dutch and British empires. Out of this rapidly changing world order, the CCP's political vision of a dual-revolutionary movement was born. The CCP had sent its intellectual cadres to Southeast Asia as propagandists for its own domestic revolution, but in the process they became champions of a second revolution on the ground.

To be sure, this was not the first time Chinese communist revolutionaries overseas had worked for more than one nation-based revolution at a time. Conceived at first as the Nanyang branch of the CCP, the party itself and the Soviet-led Communist International (Comintern) had tried ever since 1927 to localize the movement and to attract Malay and ethnic or migrant Indian followers. As Caroline Hau (2014: Chapter 4) and Anna Belogurova (2019) show, ideas of the nation (*minzu*) were fluid in the eyes of these "cosmopolitan revolutionaries," who moved between China and Malaya/Nanyang and were committed to both. In a departure from the practice of previous generations of cosmopolitan CCP revolutionaries, the high-profile cadres in the dual revolutionary phase (1945–9) did not themselves become Malayan, Nanyang or Indonesian *communists*. Not restricted to collaborating with local communists, they worked with a broad range of anti-colonial actors, and sought to cultivate a localized anti-colonial sensibility among their Overseas Chinese audiences.

This article examines the extent and limits of CCP's revolutionary cosmopolitanism in three Southeast Asian cities—Singapore, Jakarta and Medan (northeastern Sumatra)—in the immediate aftermath of the Pacific War. Taking a comparative approach, it argues that revolutionary cosmopolitanism developed and diverged on the ground according to the diasporic community's social structure, the contingency of decolonization events and initiatives taken by local CCP leaders. While the CCP in Jakarta turned neutral in the face of republican atrocities against Chinese, Singapore and Medan went on to mobilize merchants and young people to support local anti-colonial movements. Under Hu Yuzhi and Wang Renshu respectively, they stood for a moderate, anti-colonial Malayan nationalism in Singapore, in comparison with a more radical, non-assimilationist path in solidarity with Indonesia's independence struggle in Medan.

1 Cosmopolitan Revolutionaries, Provincial Connections

While prior waves of exiled CCP members came from its provincial Fujian and Guangdong rank and file, the propagandists of dual-revolution were highly prominent public figures who had already made their names in the literary and publishing sphere in cosmopolitan Shanghai society.[1] At the forefront of the May Fourth Movement either in Shanghai or in their respective provinces, they drifted towards Lu Xun, the League of Left-Wing Writers, and the communist party in the 1920s and 1930s. As the radical authors of a cosmopolitan Shanghai modernity, they were part of a broader leftwing movement that Vera Schwarcz argued put forth a second May Fourth enlightenment campaign for China in the 1930s (Lee 1999; Schwarcz 1986). To extend this cosmopolitan enlightenment vision to Southeast Asia, the writers and their sponsors turned to wartime resistance networks and their own provincial connections.

The CCP sent two batches of high-profile underground party authors, editors and journalists to fight the propaganda war with Guomindang in Singapore. In November 1940, Zhou Enlai, as secretary of the party's Southern Bureau, in charge of China's unoccupied territory, dispatched Hu Yuzhi and Wang Jiyuan to work in Tan Kah Kee's daily newspaper *Nanyang Siang Pau* in Singapore. Both would edit the CCP's flagship newspapers in Southeast Asia—*Nanqiao Ribao* (*Nan Chiau Jit Pao*, Overseas Chinese Southern Daily) in Singapore and *Shenghuo Bao* in Jakarta—after the war. A Shaoxing co-native of Lu Xun, Hu

---

[1] At its peak, the Chinese Malayan communist movement counted between 10,000 and 15,000 members, with about 1,500 banished by the British colonial authorities back to China every year from across the whole of British Malaya. Banishment figures are for the years 1928–31. See Yong 1997, 101, 105.

Yuzhi was best known for editing *Dongfang Zazhi* (*Eastern Miscellany*), a flagship intellectual journal of the Commercial Press in Shanghai, and *Impressions of Moscow* (1931), and for publishing the translation of Edgar Snow's *Red Star Over China* (1936) and the *Complete Works of Lu Xun* (1938). He became an underground communist party member in Shanghai in September 1933. Likewise a Zhejiang native, and party youth league member since his student days, Wang Jiyuan was a reporter in Shanghai with *Shen Bao* (Shanghai News) and the leftwing *Shenghuo Ribao* (Life Daily), before he worked for the communist-owned International News Agency in Chongqing and Hong Kong. In Singapore, Hu became the chief editor of *Nanyang Siang Pau* (South Seas Commercial News), while Wang served as its literary supplement editor (Hu 1996: 347).

In June 1941, the party sent a second batch of party and party-affiliated writers and editors to Singapore: Wang Renshu 王任叔, Shen Zijiu 沈兹九, and Zheng Chuyun 郑楚云 among others to Singapore; and Shao Zonghan 邵宗汉 to Penang's *Xiandai Ribao* (Modern Daily).[2] (Li 2009: 125–6; Yang 2003) One of the most radical members of this group was Wang Renshu. A co-native of Chiang Kai-shek of Fenghua, Zhejiang, a novelist, literary theorist, journal editor, and student leader in his hometown, he was inducted into the CCP in 1926 when the party sent him to Guangzhou as a secretary in Chiang's chief of staff office. Steeped in Marxist-Leninist theory, Wang was also a charismatic organizer on the ground. He would emerge as a leader of the CCP group in Indonesia after the war. On 4 February 1942, less than two weeks before the fall of Singapore, the CCP intellectuals, together with close to one hundred members of Tan Kah Kee's China Relief Fund, fled Singapore by boat for northeastern Sumatra (Hu 1996: 391; Zhang 2018). Together with Wang, Shao Zonghan and this group would stay behind in Medan to edit *Minzhu Ribao* (Democracy Daily News) after the war.

The CCP's wartime resistance network afterwards became the organizational basis for the founding of *Minzhu Ribao*. In Medan, a handful of young local born and sojourning Chinese youths and schoolteachers had taken the initiative to make contact with the MCP and CCP in Malaya and China in the late 1930s (Huang 2003: 166–182). After the Japanese took Sumatra in March 1942,

---

2 Shen Zijiu was a native of Deqing county in Zhejiang. She studied in Japan in the 1920s, and edited feminist journals in the 1930s in Shanghai, where she entered the CCP. In Singapore, she married Hu Yuzhi, and became the editor of *Xin Funü* (New Women), under the *Nanqiao Ribao* umbrella of publications. Zheng Chuyun was a native of Fuan county in Fujian. He entered the CCP in the late 1920s while studying in Beijing; Shao Zonghan was a native Wujin county in Jiangsu. He was an editor of newspapers in the 1930s in Shanghai, where he became active in the leftist anti-Japanese movement. He did not enter the CCP until returning to China in 1950.

perhaps no more than twenty or thirty of them, with a left-wing bookstore in Medan as their base, organized two cell groups to continue their resistance underground. Their resistance took the form of recording Allied news broadcasts from a transistor radio for circulation in the cyclostyle-printed samizdat newspaper, *Qianjin Bao* (Onwards News) (La 2003). In October or November 1942, Wang Renshu made contact, and persuaded both groups to form a joint anti-Fascist league, so as to make a broader appeal to indigenous Indonesians (Zhou 2019: 39–41). Forced to remain dormant after a major Japanese suppression campaign in September 1943, the surviving members of this young underground resistance force formed the backbone of the editorial and reporters' team for *Minzhu Ribao* (Lin et. al. 2003, 262–5). In late August 1945, Hu Yuzhi and Wang Renshu held a three-day conference in Medan, where they convened the wartime resistance network and China Relief Fund refugee merchants. The dual-revolutionary mission was determined at this meeting: they set out to "democratize" Overseas Chinese society, and to mobilize Overseas Chinese support for Indonesia's independence struggle (Lin et. al. 2003: 262–3). The CCP Central Committee, through its Southern Bureau in Hong Kong, was quick to endorse this political line (Hu 1996: 394).

In Medan, however, the CCP intellectuals had neither provincial connections nor ideologically committed merchant allies among Chinese business leaders. Funding quickly ended in March 1946 once fighting between the Indonesian revolutionaries and the re-colonizing Dutch forces erupted. Initially, *Minzhu Ribao* had taken over the premises and printing presses of a pre-war, Guomindang leftist newspaper, operated by the three Ye brothers (Ye Yichang 叶贻昌, Yifang 贻芳, and Yidong 贻东) along with their major shareholder, Hiu Ngi Fen 丘毅衡, the Hakka owner of a local pharmacy chain, who had agreed to lend *Minzhu Ribao* their premises and printing press. With the exception of Ye Yidong, all the shareholders withdrew their capital in March 1946 (Zhu 2003: 284–5). The withdrawal of Hiu Ngi Fen, a Hakka pre-war President of the East Sumatra Chinese Chamber of Commerce and an ally of Tan Kah Kee, was particularly symbolic (Buiskool 2009: 122). His turn to a pro-Dutch and pro-Guomindang position signaled the isolation of the CCP intellectuals and their youthful followers in the business-driven Chinese community.

In comparison, Hu Yuzhi continued to rely on Tan Kah Kee and his Hokkien allies' financial support to build his newspaper networks. Within a year, he had started the youth weekly journal *Fengxia* (*Below the Wind*, December 1945), the monthly journal *New Women* (founded January 1946), the daily newspaper *Nanqiao Ribao* (founded November 1946), and its evening edition (founded a few months later). Almost two-thirds of the known investments for *Nanqiao Ribao* came from Tan Kah Kee, his relatives, his former employees, or prominent members of the Hokkien community.³ Beyond the Hokkiens, however, the only major investor was Chen Yueshu 陈岳书, a Zhejiang co-provincial of Hu. Himself a pro-CCP bookseller, Chen had settled in Singapore in the 1920s to escape political persecution. His Shanghai Book Company was one of the big four Chinese book publishers in Singapore. As the only Shanghainese (or Waijiang) representative on the Chinese Chamber of Commerce, Chen's hosting of Hu Yuzhi and his wife throughout their sojourn in Singapore indicates the continued salience of native-place origins to revolutionary connections (Hu 2016; Chen 2012).

In Jakarta, Wang Jiyuan turned to an existing network of CCP-aligned Hokkien *Totoks*⁴ to set up the *Shenghuo Bao* (*Life Daily*) in October 1945. Huang Zhougui 黄周规 and Weng Fulin 翁福林 organized and funded the paper. Hailing from different parts of Fujian, both had sought refuge in the Dutch East Indies in the late 1920s and early 1930s via kinship-native place connections overseas. Huang, a Nan'an district compatriot of Tan Kah Kee, had entered the CCP while studying at a teachers' training college back in the hometown. Active in the regional China Relief Fund before the war, he afterwards actively contributed to reviving Chinese schools and communal associations in Jakarta. As founding director of *Shenghuo Bao*, Huang remained in his position until he left Indonesia for good in 1965 (Qian 2013). A native of Longyan in western Fujian, Weng Fulin went into exile through his family in Medan in 1929. Moving to Batavia in 1931, he got rich by producing film posters for the thriving cinema chains in the Dutch colony. After the war, Weng became one of the biggest cinema chain operators in Java. He donated the premises of *Shenghuo Bao* at Mangga Besar no. 79, and remained one of its biggest shareholder until he was forced to leave Indonesia in 1965–66 (Weng 2013).

During the first phase of mobilization (1945–6), the CCP intellectuals tapped into the existing wartime resistance and sub-ethnic China Relief Fund networks across the three cities to found pro-CCP newspapers and journals. From these urban centers, they would serve as mouthpieces for the CCP in its

---

3 Zhang Chukun 张楚琨 (1996) revealed that the newspaper company issued 400,000 yuan of shares. He recounted the major shareholders who owned about 300,000 yuan. Among the 300,000-yuan major shareholders were Tan Kah Kee (110,000 yuan), while Tan's son-in-law Lee Kong Chian 李光前, and one of his protégés Liu Yushui 刘玉水 each contributed 10,000 yuan. Tan's eldest son and eldest nephew were also mentioned as major contributors. Wang Yuanxin (Ong Goan Heng 王源兴), a self-made rubber tycoon from Palembang, contributed 10,000. Two of the journalists, Zhang Chukun and Gao Yunlan 高云览, both from Fujian, went into business and contributed 90,000 yuan from their enterprise. Chen Jingqing 陈镜清 also appears to be a Hokkien. See Zhang 1996.

4 Indonesian term for new arrivals as opposed to *Peranakan*, the local-born creoles.

ensuing civil war against the Guomindang in China. Conceiving its revolution as part of a bigger global wave of anti-colonial and anti-capitalist revolutions, the CCP championed not only the cause of its own revolution in China but also those of local anti-colonial nationalist movements in Malaya and Indonesia.

2   Imagining Malayan and Indonesian Political Identities

One of the political missions of the CCP's newspapermen and women in Southeast Asia was to help the diaspora identify with the local nations and their struggle against Western colonialism. These local nationalist identities began to be *imaginable* for the Overseas Chinese through the intellectuals' articulation of a postwar Mao Zedong-inflected socialist universalism—"New Democracy," which encompassed the newly rising nations of Southeast Asia under socialist revolutionary leadership. According to this vision, far from standing as an obstacle to assimilation, Chinese-ness gave the Overseas Chinese unique access to the vanguard socialist and revolutionary theory. It was this vanguard socialist identity *in Chinese*, I argue, that made the adoption of local nationalisms both imaginable and attractive to their Overseas Chinese readers.

The opening issue of *Fengxia* in Singapore set the tone for the CCP propagandists' anti-colonial, pro-Southeast Asian stance for its Overseas Chinese readers. *Fengxia* or *Negri di Bawah Angin*, Hu Yuzhi explained, was the name the Malay-speaking peoples on the coasts of the region called their homeland in response to "those *angmoh*'s [Hokkien: red-haired people]," who first came to the Straits of Malacca 450 years ago, "and used their hands to point to the West, to show that they were blown here by the seasonal monsoon" (*Fengxia* no. 1, 1.12.1945). Since then, "the people of Nanyang [have become] colonial subjects who lost their independence and freedom, but after the war, all minzu, even the most backward hill tribe minzu, are trying to recover their lost independence and freedom" (*Fengxia* no. 1 & 3, 1.12.1945 & 17.12.1945). Looking toward the prospect of the end of Western colonialism, Hu declared that "the future of war and peace will be decided in the lands below the winds." The Overseas Chinese, Hu urged, should no longer be satisfied with demanding equal status with all nations (i.e. Europeans) but should demand to be one of the masters of Nanyang (*Fengxia* no. 1, 1.12.1945). To achieve that, the task of *Fengxia* and its writers was to help "reform the mind (*xinli de gaizao*) and build the spirit (*jingshen de jianshe*)" (*Fengxia* no. 1 & 3, 1.12.1945 & 17.12.1945).

If the name "Below the Wind" signified an attempt at seeing the region from an indigenous perspective, Hu Yuzhi and his comrades looked to Indonesia and its anti-colonial struggle for a model local nationalist movement. It is telling that *Fengxia* editors passed over Sukarno and Hatta, the proclaimers of Indonesian independence, and chose instead the then premier Sutan Syahrir to feature in its maiden issue. Unlike Sukarno and Hatta, Syahrir had gone into hiding when the Japanese occupied Java, only to reappear after the war to struggle for independence while reserving "very sharp criticism for those who had collaborated with Japanese fascism during the war." Syahrir was chosen not only for his politics but also for his intellectualism and his socialistic concern for culture and the proletariat. Translating Syahrir's essay "*Budaya dan massa*" (*Wenyi yu dazhong*, or Literary arts and the masses) from *Pudjangga Baroe* (The New Poets) from the 1930s, Wang Jinding introduced him as a leader who not only "possesse(d) many valuable views on literature and the arts but has also written many exquisite political and social scientific theses, one of which is 'Engels and us'" (*Fengxia* no. 1, 1.12.1945). Syahrir argued in this essay for Indonesian translations of Emile Zola and Gorky, and for the indigenization of Zola's naturalism and Gorky's proletarianism. Here, socialist literary theory served as a bridge between Overseas Chinese identity and Indonesian nationalism.

Across Southeast Asia, *Fengxia* gave precedence to communist-led over nationalist anti-colonial movements. For Burma, the journal translated an article from the Australian Communist newspaper *Tribune* that foregrounded one of the Burmese Communist Party's founders Thakin Soe's anti-Fascism over the nationalist Aung San's momentary lapse in the sense of his collaboration with the Japanese. In the same way, it was the Hukbalahap in the Philippines, and the MCP's Malayan People's Anti-Japanese Army in Malaya, that featured over ethno-nationalists. Non-communist nationalists like Aung San, Sukarno, Shahrir and Hatta were subordinated by ideology although their broader mass appeal and following were acknowledged (*Fengxia* no. 1 & 2, 1.12.1945 & 10.12.1945).

Yet as Wang Renshu would point out, whether communist or anti-colonial nationalist, a social-scientific analysis of history showed that the time was ripe for people everywhere in the post-war world to launch New Democratic revolutions to move beyond capitalism and imperialism towards socialism. In his two-part essay, "The historical development of New Democracy," Wang tried to dispel doubts that the "New Democracy" championed by Mao and the CCP was a cover for communism, an extension of old democracy, or just another name for socialism (*Fengxia*, no. 5 & 6, 31.12.1945 & 7.1.1946). Quoting from Mao's *On New Democracy*, he distinguished it as "a republic ruled by the dictatorship of a few classes," as opposed to the dictatorships of the proletariat (socialism) and bourgeoisie (old democracy). Wang attributed New Democracy to

Lenin's revolutionary leadership and social-scientific study and theorization of the Russian revolutionary experience. Workers and peasants could unite with the bourgeoisie, as had happened in the February Revolution, to overthrow the Tsarist feudal regime and form "New Democracies" as a transitory stage towards the socialist (October) revolution. In fact, in both Europe and the colonized and semi-colonized parts of the rest of world, fascist domination everywhere ensured that there would no longer be any direct transition, as previously thought, from capitalist democracies to socialism. Instead, Wang argued that fascism and imperialism had enslaved peoples, proletariat and bourgeoisie alike, and destroyed the bourgeois ownership of the means of production. The immediate task was for all conquered and colonized peoples to fight in solidarity across class divisions for their freedom and sovereignty from fascism and imperialism to build New Democracies. Wang's articulation of a universal New Democracy utopia made Malayan and Indonesian nationalism accessible to its China-oriented readers as an inherent part of a new Chinese communist-led regional and global movement.

In Malaya (including Singapore), the CCP intellectuals championed the MCP as not only as the most progressive party but also the party that could best safeguard and elevate the standing of Chinese in Malaya. A female soldier of its Anti-Japanese Army was featured in the second issue of *Fengxia*'s cover, immediately after its first had covered the founding of the United Nations (*Fengxia* no. 2, 10.12.1945). The MPAJA, the journal argued, "had made the five million people of Malaya of various nations (*minzu*) and classes come together and organize themselves, producing a self-consciousness of the nation and democracy" (*Fengxia* no. 1, 1.12.1945).[5] Despite their support for embracing local nationalisms, the CCP editors at this point did not have a concept for Chinese outside China other than "Overseas Chinese" (*huaqiao*), even for members of the "Malayan" communist party. "Although the people's anti-Japanese army consisted of three minzu (Chinese, Malay, Indian)," the editor pointed out that, "its cadres were mostly Overseas Chinese, so the honor [of serving in] the Anti-Japanese Association belongs to the Overseas Chinese" (*Fengxia* no. 1, 1.12.1945).

The *Fengxia* editors also paid special attention to the newly formed Malay Nationalist Party (MNP), a united-front ally of the MCP. *Fengxia* kept track

---

5 To cover the demobilization of the MPAJA on 1 December 1945, Fengxia had sent a crew to Kuala Lumpur. A by-product of the expedition to Kuala Lumpur was Wang Jinding's reportage, *Under the Three-starred Flag* (1945/6), which recorded observations of and interviews with MPAJA squadron leaders stationed in and still maintaining order in the smaller towns of Johor, Negri Sembilan, and Malacca.

of the birth of the Malay Nationalist Party (*Persatuan Kebangsaan Melayu Malaya*), and sought to dispel the perception among Chinese that Malays were politically backward. Present at the founding of the party in Ipoh in November 1945, the *Fengxia* journalist compared the formation of the MNP to that of India's Congress Party, China's Guomindang, and Indonesia's Partai Nasional (*Fengxia* no. 3, 17.12.1945). Although later than these other Asian nationalist parties, *Fengxia* attributed the lateness of its formation to "centuries of colonial rule" rather than "any fault of the Malays themselves." Despite the MNP's professed goal of claiming "Malaya for Malays," the journal had good reason to be positive in the eyes of its Chinese readers, for the MNP declared its readiness to work with other racial groups in the country. At its inauguration congress, the MNP noted the urgent need to prevent further racial clashes between Malays and Chinese in Batu Pahat in Johor.

In Jakarta, *Shenghuo Bao*, a twice-weekly paper at this point, called on the Chinese to support the Indonesian nation during the early days of its independence war. "It is very clear," exclaimed Wang Jiyuan, "on whose side the sympathies of the Chinese people (*Zhongguo ren*) lie" (*Shenghuo Bao*, henceforth SHB, 31.10.1945). In the midst of the colonial war in mid-November, Wang castigated the Chinese in Jakarta for "standing by as other Overseas Chinese were being robbed and killed, and as the Indonesian nation fought bitterly for its independence and freedom." Calling for a public figure like "Singapore and Malaya's Tan Kah Kee" to emerge and lead the Chinese in Java, Wang tried to rally the community to "unleash the revolutionary Overseas Chinese spirit, and to dare to speak and act in solidarity" (SHB, 14.11.1945). Even as some Chinese were looted or injured by Indonesian forces during the fighting, he pointed out that they had to understand that the "Indonesian nation is in the midst of exchanging flesh and blood for its independence and freedom." The Overseas Chinese should "by all means avoid provoking the feelings of the Indonesian nation," for "[w]hat we have done to help the Indonesian nation is really far from enough" (SHB, 15.12.1945). A guest editorial written by Hu Yuzhi set out the official CCP line on "the dual duty of Overseas Chinese"—"first for the liberation of the local nation, and second for the renaissance of the home nation" (SHB, 5.1.1946). As I will explain below, however, the editorial policy of *Shenghuo Bao* turned pro-Dutch soon after Jakarta was re-taken by Allied forces led by the British in late 1945.[6]

In Medan, *Minzhu Ribao* (*Democratic Daily News*) remained resolutely anticolonial throughout the Indonesian struggle for independence. I have not examined extant copies of the *Minzhu Ribao*, but its editors have recalled that the

---

6 For a social-spatial history of the Dutch retaking of Jakarta in late 1945, see Cribb 1991, 66–73.

paper allocated equal page space to Chinese, Nanyang and Indonesian news, with its Indonesian page devoted to the latest "developments in the Indonesian war of independence, and introducing Indonesian history, culture and customs" to its Chinese readers (Lin et al. 2015: 400).[7] It maintained a "propaganda line that argued that the Overseas Chinese community and Indonesian nation had suffered the same fate under colonial rule, such that the Overseas Chinese should sympathize with and support the Indonesian people's independence struggle." When clashes occurred between Indonesians and Chinese in Siantar and Bagan Siapi-api, the paper's "Indonesia Research Society" issued a statement "declaring Overseas Chinese empathy for the Indonesian independence struggle, and advocating friendly relations between the two races" (Lin et al. 2015: 402).

For important sections of Chinese diasporic communities in Singapore (Malaya), Jakarta and Medan, these CCP-run newspapers were the first broadsheets to introduce the Malayan and Indonesian nationalist movements to their Chinese diasporic readers. Their circulation figures ranked them consistently between second and third among more established Chinese-language newspapers in their cities.[8] In all three cities, they were the most important left-wing alternative to the established commercial or pro-Guomindang daily newspapers. They contained not only news about local nationalist movements but a new way of seeing local society and the world from the standpoint of Indonesian and Malayan nationalists. Yet the newspapers remained at the same time resolutely diasporic—at key moments, it was political developments in the homeland that dominated the headlines. As the civil war in China, and the anti-colonial struggles in Southeast Asia, intensified between 1946 and 1948, CCP operatives moved out of the newsrooms and onto the public square, to mobilize revolutions for China and Southeast Asia.

---

7 Xiamen University and the Beijing National Library have collections of Medan's *Minzhu Ribao*.

8 *Nanqiao Ribao* attained a Malaya-wide circulation of 10,000 compared to *Nanyang Shangbao's* and *Xingzhou Ribao's*—the more established Chinese daily newspapers—roughly 30,000 copies each. See The National Archives (henceforth TNA, United Kingdom), FCO141-15954, Malayan Political Intelligence Journal (henceforth MPIJ) no. 6, 30.4.1947, "Supplement on Chinese press"; *Minzhu Ribao* and *Shenghuo Bao* were commonly referred to as the Big Two or Big Three Chinese-language newspapers in Medan and Jakarta. See Lin et al. 2015; and Liang 2013, 1–4.

3 Mobilizing Youth and Merchants

Up until early 1946, CCP diasporic mobilization was limited to raising capital for newspapers and influencing political opinion in Chinese communities in all three cities. By varying degrees, as can be seen from the mission of *Fengxia*, youth mobilization had always been a central plank in the intellectuals' arsenal of weapons. However, rising tension between warring sides in China and Indonesia made it more imperative for political parties to mobilize the Chinese for contributions for, if not physical participation in, the wars. In early 1946, the CCP directed its Nanyang network to set up branches of the pro-Communist liberal-democratic party China Democratic League (henceforth CDL) in cities with significant Chinese communities. As political contests escalated, the CDL's CCP leaders mobilized merchant-community leaders to form new CDL branches and raise funds, while they themselves organized Overseas Chinese youth for local anti-colonial movements. Stuck in a re-colonized and Guomindang-dominated city, the CCP intellectuals in Jakarta (Batavia) were much less active than their counterparts in Medan and Singapore.

The two-revolution agenda proved hardest to execute in Jakarta. Under both Dutch colonial and Indonesian republican pressure, the underground CCP in Jakarta/Batavia quickly withdrew from local politics and stuck strictly to a homeland-oriented leftist editorial line. In January 1946, the Republic of China Consul-General Jiang Jiadong arrived in Jakarta/Batavia, visited Sukarno in Yogyakarta, the Republican capital, and took a strictly neutral position in the ongoing hostilities (Heidhues 2012: 394). As the pro-Republican Peranakan Chinese leader Ang Jan Goan 洪渊源 (2009) noted in his memoirs, "those who became leaders of the *Chung Hua Tsung Hui* (Chinese General Association)" in the city "were Guomindang members, and those who became administrators of other [Chinese organizations] were also mostly Guomindang people." As early as February 1946, Wang Jiyuan's *Shenghuo Bao* turned its back on its anti-colonial stance and remained neutral, or even pro-Dutch. *Shenghuo Bao* appeared apprehensive about the loss of China's diasporic citizens to the Indonesian and Dutch courting of the local Chinese. By February 1946, its editors leaned closer to the Dutch vision of a multi-national federal "East India" state as opposed to the Indonesian proposal for a unitary state. In Wang Jiyuan's words:

> Indonesia in the future will not be an Indonesian-chauvinistic Indonesia. In the future, if East India can construct an independent and autonomous state, it has to adopt the spirit of federalism. On the principles of

solidarity and none-invasion, every nation (minzu) should enjoy the opportunity to develop, free and equal.
SHB, 6.2.1946

This apparently neutral but actually pro-Dutch position became solidified in June 1946 after the Tangerang crisis. After the Dutch retook the town of Tangerang, irregular Indonesian militia in the countryside attacked the rural Chinese, killed about 1,000 of them, and caused about 15,000 flee to Jakarta as refugees (Heidhues 2012: 387). As Mary Somers Heidhues (2012) notes, the intensity of the revolutionary war on Java meant that the Chinese there were more exposed than elsewhere in Indonesia to extortion, physical acts of violence and the scorched-earth tactics of retreating Indonesian forces. "We the overseas Chinese," protested Wang, "have always maintained our neutrality in the ebbs and flows of the Indonesian independence movement." "If wanton massacres are carried out over small misunderstandings," he warned, "this will anger the entire Overseas Chinese (community), and cause fissures between both nations (minzu)" (SHB, 21.6.1946). *Shenghuo Bao* would maintain this neutral posture until early August 1949, when the Roundtable Conference set Indonesia on a clear path toward independence (SHB, 4.8.1949).

Outside of Jakarta, CCP intellectuals mobilized fellow members of the publishing and journalistic circles and merchants to form overseas branches of the China Democratic League (CDL) in Medan and in Singapore, and other peninsular Malayan cities. Founded by left-wing intellectuals in 1941 as a front for the CCP, the CDL consistently served up a liberal-democratic critique of the dictatorial tendencies of Chiang Kai-shek and the Guomindang. With the support of Tan Kah Kee and his China Relief Fund network, Hu Yuzhi and Hu Shouyu 胡守愚, a CDL representative from Hong Kong, founded the Malayan headquarters of the CDL in Singapore in April 1946. Together with Tan Kah Kee, they rallied left-leaning intellectuals and merchants in Penang, Kuala Lumpur, Seremban (Negri Sembilan) and Ipoh to form sub-branches (TNA: FCO141-15954, MPIJ 2, 15.5.1946, Supplement 1; FCO141-15955, MPIJ 12, 31.7.1947, MPIJ 13, 15.8.1947). In June 1946, Chinese educators and intellectuals in Medan accepted the Singapore CDL's invitation to set up a branch and sub-branches in the city and elsewhere in the East Sumatra province.[9] The CDL's

---

9   Sub-branches were formed in towns across the province: sub-branches were set up in Brastagi, Bindjei, Pematang Siantar, Serbalawan, Batoe Bahra, Perlanaan, Kisaran and Asahan. See Nationaal Archief: 2.10.14 3970, "Nefis Publicatie 23, September 1946," 9–10. I thank Anne van de Veer for sharing this Dutch archival source with me.

politics were professedly homeland-oriented. CDL leaders repeatedly stressed that there would be "no interference in Malayan politics" (TNA: FCO141–15954, MPIJ 2, 15.5.1946, Supplement 1, 8). On the surface, the CDL in Southeast Asia operated as a party of intellectuals and community leaders concerned primarily with the democratic development of the homeland. Its modus operandi consisted of mass meetings to generate public opinion against Guomindang actions in China. One such event was a Tan Kah Kee-initiated mass meeting in the Singapore Chinese Chamber of Commerce. Attendees heard speeches protesting the Guomindang's political assassination of the pro-CCP intellectuals Li Gongpu and Wen Yiduo in Kunming, and petitioned President Truman against intervention in China's civil war (*Fengxia*, no. 33, 20.7.1946; no. 43, 28.9.1946; TNA: FCO141–15954, MPIJ 11, 30.9.1946, 2).

The economic proximity of Singapore to Medan also facilitated the transnational anti-colonial solidarity of Chinese merchants in both places. At the initiative of Hu Yuzhi, Lau Bo Tan 刘牡丹, a construction magnate, and a right-hand man of Tan Kah Kee, established and served as President of the Singapore-based "Friends of Indonesia" in the early 1946. The association brought together members of the MCP, the MNP and the Malayan Democratic Union alongside the CCP intellectuals and merchants allied with the group (Yong 1988: 40–2; *Fengxia* no. 8 & 9, 21 & 28.1.1946). According to Dutch intelligence, Lau ran a shipping line between Singapore and Medan and smuggled weapons to the Indonesian republican forces in Asahan (Nefis Publicatie 23, September 1946). Chinese merchants based in Singapore Malaya donated to local revolutionary movements as long as they did not upset their business operations.

Politically, not to mention financially, it was difficult for Overseas Chinese merchants to commit their resources to two revolutions at the same time. The core financial supporters of the CCP propaganda efforts discussed in the previous section hailed either from Tan Kah Kee's personal native-place or from Hokkien and China Relief Fund networks or were individual revolutionary exiles who had made money in Southeast Asia and reconnected with the CCP overseas. Motivated by some form of progressive diasporic nationalism, the Tan Kah Kee clique supported the CDL and its propaganda campaigns overseas but they were not prepared to sacrifice their local business interests. By mid-1947, the CDL and *Nanqiao Ribao* began to feel the financial strains of operating the newspaper as scores of new CCP exiles joined the network from Shanghai and Hong Kong (TNA: FCO141–15955, MPIJ 13, 15.8.1947). Only revolutionaries-turned-merchants like Huang Zhougui and Weng Fulin in Jakarta and Zhao Hongpin in Medan were prepared to go all the way with the CCP, often with the intention of returning to China once the mission had been completed (Ping 2003). Both groups were primarily loyal to China or China's communist revolution.

In the final analysis, Chinese mercantile participation in the local leg of the CCP's dual revolution was ultimately restrained by the very logic of the anti-capitalist socialist revolution itself. No other case better illustrates this fundamental tension than Tan Kah Kee's famous renunciation of the Malayan communist armed struggle. It is well-known that when the British outlawed the MCP in a state of emergency declared in June 1948, Tan publicly renounced the MCP as a terrorist movement, citing the communist extortion of his and his close associates' rubber factories in Malaya as evidence of their criminal tendencies (Chui 2007: 159–160). In fact, tensions between the CDL and MCP had been brewing for some time. In late 1947, in a meeting at Tan Kah Kee's invitation between Tan, Hu Yuzhi and the MCP representative in Singapore, Zhang Mingjin 张明今, Tan urged the MCP to learn from the CCP example of uniting the "national bourgeoisie." Hu Yuzhi reprimanded the MCP leadership for "committing the ultra-left (*guozuo*) error of leading workers' strikes that failed to unite all forces that could be united, and for scaring off the national bourgeoisie." In response, the MCP's Central Committee, when informed of this exchange, described "Tan Kah Kee and Lee Kong Chian 李光前 as reactionaries, and Hu Yuzhi as a coward."[10]

Unlike in these efforts to mobilize merchants, CCP intellectuals in the three cities had a lot more success with young local Chinese. Medan and Jakarta again represented two opposite modes of post-war diasporic Chinese youth mobilization. In Medan and East Sumatra, under the leadership of Wang Renshu, CCP intellectuals turned the young wartime underground resistance movement into a vibrant youth wing of the East Sumatra branch of the CDL. As the Marx-Lenin-Maoist theoretician of the group, it is interesting to note Wang's changing positions on the nationalist orientation of the young Chinese in his charge. During the war, as a good internationalist—this was before the dissolution of the Comintern in 1943—Wang had initially proposed that young Chinese seek out the direction and leadership of the local Communist Party of Indonesia (henceforth, PKI) rather than the CCP (Zhou 2019: 40). Afterwards, the anti-Chinese tendencies of Indonesia's revolution notwithstanding, Wang's low assessment of the PKI's organizational discipline contributed to his decision to keep the underground CCP cell network among the young leaders intact, while they worked to expand on youth mobilization across the region

---

10   The direct quote is from Guo 1999, 307–8. Although unattributed, the quote came most likely from Zhang Mingjin himself, whose identity was kept anonymous among the few oral-history interviews historian Guo Rende did with MCP veterans in the late 1990s.

(Wang 2001: 300–1). By late January 1946, the younger underground CCP members had managed to amalgamate the more politically-oriented "youth corps" and "youth unions," with sports and alumni associations from Pangakalan Brandan (Huoshui Shan), Tebingtinggi, Kisaran, Bindjei, Asahan, Belawan, Simpang, Batangkoei and Rantau to Medan, to form a 34-group-strong Youth Federation of East Sumatra (Nefis Publicatie 23, September 1946, Bijlage 5). Although they did not merge with any Indonesian organization, Zhou Taomo (2019: 44–51) shows that Wang Renshu and the CCP intellectuals were instrumental in East Sumatra in promoting Indonesian nationalism and inter-ethnic solidarity among these Totok Chinese youths through their journalism and cultural activities. On Java, in contrast, the CCP in Dutch-occupied Jakarta failed to mobilize any Chinese youth for either revolution. It was in Republican-held Yogyakarta—the revolutionary capital—that Indonesian revolutionaries managed to mobilize Peranakan Chinese for their nationalist revolution (Zhou 2019: 23–9).

In Singapore, while the underground CCP followed a clear youth agenda during its propaganda campaign, Hu Yuzhi left the actual mobilization of young people to the MCP's youth corps—the New Democratic Youth League (henceforth, NDYL). In comparison with Wang Renshu's doubts about sending young Chinese into the PKI, Hu Yuzhi trusted the MCP and left it to mobilize local young Chinese. This mutual understanding reflected the CCP's differing political visions for young and old in Malaya: while they recruited the more senior Overseas Chinese into the China-oriented CDL, they encouraged members of the younger generation to identify with and become part of the local revolutionary movement.[11] As discussed above, *Fengxia* helped by cultivating among its young readers a scientific-Marxist worldview in politics, and a social-realist taste in literature and culture. The furthest it went in youth mobilization was to organize a correspondence course for unemployed and undereducated youth. The *Self-Learning Youth Society Guide* (青年自学辅导社) organized weekly readings, quizzes and writing exercises for young people through the pages of *Fengxia* (*Fengxia*, no. 69, 5.4.1947). From April 1947 until the journal shut down in June 1948, 1,061 youths actively corresponded with and became subscribing members of the society (*Fengxia*, no. 132, 26.6.1948). The division of labor with the MCP on the youth front was most obvious from the prominence *Fengxia* gave to Chen Tian, the MCP-appointed leader of the NDYL. He featured in a

---

11   NDYL and CDL members regularly attended each other's assemblies. See for instance the British intelligence reports on the pan-Malayan NDYL annual congress in Kuala Lumpur (24.9.1946), FCO141–15954, MPIJ 12, 15.10.1946; on the banning of CDL in China reportedly affected the membership of the NDYL in Penang, see FCO141–15955: MPIJ 20, 31.11.1947.

special weekly column as a result of his journey to Prague to attend the World Festival of Youth and Students on behalf of Malaya (*Fengxia* no. 86, 92, 94, 95, 96, 98, 104, 105, 1947–1948).

Engaged as it was in the civil war at home, the CCP understood the importance of mobilizing public opinion, merchant-community leaders and youth in the diaspora. Unlike the Guomindang, however, the CCP's dual revolutionary mission made it sensitive to local nationalist movements in a way that the former was not.[12] Its mobilization strategies on the ground were thus sensitive to the opinions of the local anti-colonial nationalists, with a radical bias in favour of local leftwing movements. Largely ineffective in Jakarta/Batavia during the revolutionary war, the CCP was able to mobilize important segments of merchant leaders and youth in Singapore and Medan. While merchants stayed on board the diasporic revolutionary platform as long as it did not affect their local businesses, the CCP had more success with cultivating a generation of young people, ideologically committed to revolutions in both their adoptive and original homelands.

4   From Huaqiao to Huazu in Singapore (Malaya)

At the heart of the CCP's dual revolutionary agenda stood the question of dual nationality. Implicit in this vision was the assumption that Overseas Chinese should regard themselves as citizens not only of China but also of the emerging nations of Southeast Asia. As the new nations demanded the undivided loyalties of local-born and resident Chinese subjects, however, it soon became clear that not only were many Chinese unwilling to give up their *de facto* Chinese nationality but that the CCP itself was not prepared to forgo the allegiance of the Overseas Chinese. On the question of nationality, the CCP underground in Singapore, Medan and Jakarta found itself having to react to both demands from local nationalist movements and the wishes of the local Chinese themselves. It was not until late 1947, and only in Singapore, as part of the political contestation over "Malayan" citizenship in the impending Federation constitution, that the CCP leaders on the ground refashioned the "Chinese sojourner" (*huaqiao*) citizen of China into a new "Chinese racial" (*huazu*) citizen of Malaya.

When the question of nationality was first raised by the Indonesian Republic and the British and Dutch colonial governments in April and May 1946, the

---

12   For the Guomindang's insensitivity to localization, see Zhou 2019, chapters 1 and 3; Yong 1990.

CCP in Southeast Asia prevaricated. Unwilling to let the Overseas Chinese give up their Chinese nationality, the CCP took cover behind a radical but clearly inconsistent critique of colonial citizenship. In an important essay outlining the group's position on Chinese diasporic nationality, Cai Gaogang 蔡高岗, who was based in Medan, actually affirmed the Sino-Dutch friendship treaty of 1944 while completely ignoring the recently promulgated citizenship law of the Indonesian Republic (*Fengxia*, no. 23, 11.5.1946).[13] Cai called the treaty's recognition of Chinese nationality law within Dutch East Indies jurisdiction a "very important improvement" from the previous Sino-Dutch agreement (1911), which had defined all Chinese subjects in the colony as Dutch subjects. Turning to Malaya, he criticized the citizenship rules in the colonial Malayan Union constitution (which came into effect on 1 April 1946) for "only specifying the qualifications required for citizenship without mentioning the rights that [should] come with citizenship." Although the British government had clarified that the Chinese in Malaya could enjoy dual nationality status, for Cai, "colonial citizenship itself was a very hollow term." He argued that "there would be no need to retain Chinese nationality" only when the "territories of Nanyang have all become independent and democratic." This argument was self-serving since Cai presented no criticism of the Sino-Dutch treaty on the one hand and conveniently left unmentioned the Indonesian Republic's citizenship offer to foreign residents on the other.

This inconsistent stance on diasporic nationality status stemmed from a late-Qing era epistemological framing of the Chinese overseas as by definition "sojourners" (*Huaqiao*). The historian Wang Gungwu has shown how Qing China's pioneering, proto-national scholar-diplomats coined the term in the 1880s when they conjoined communities of "Chinese" people (*huamin*, *huaren*) they encountered abroad with the concept of sojourning (*qiao*) (Wang 1976). The twentieth-century Chinese nation-state further strengthened this citizen-sojourner identity among Chinese overseas by adopting a nationality law based on the principle of patrilineal blood-line, and by conveniently rendering the diasporic homeland as "the land of the ancestors" (*zuguo*). (Shao 2009; Chan 2018: 17–47).

Hu Yuzhi's early post-war writings show how he struggled within this sojourner-citizen epistemological framework, even as he began to make sociological and political claims to point beyond it. In his essay "On new understandings of *huaqiao* status 关于华侨地位的新认识," Hu deconstructed the nationalist sojourner-citizen by identifying four sociological types of *huaqiao*:

---

13   Cai Gaogang, a.k.a. Cai Fusheng 蔡馥生, was a native of Jieyang county in Guangdong. Trained in economics, he joined the CCP in the early 1930s.

1) the temporary sojourner—"the only true type of sojourning people," 2) permanent settlers in Nanyang, 3) the local-born "*baba*", and 4) the local-born person of "mixed blood," who is "no longer pure Chinese (*huaren*)" (*Fengxia*, no. 3, 17.12.1945). Hu claimed that all four types of Chinese identified politically with the Republic of China not only because of China's nationality law but because "every country in Nanyang had been a foreign colony (Siam being a proto-colony) [...] wherein the local peoples could not speak of the rights of democracy and freedom, whereas China the ancestral land at least was nominally independent and autonomous." With the same stroke, he chipped away at the myth of the sojourner-citizen—three out of the four types were in fact permanent settlers—as he turned the "sojourner-citizen" into a move toward local struggles for freedom and democracy. While he urged the *huaqiao* to become one of the new constituent peoples (*minzu*) of the Nanyang nations, Hu neither called for an end to the term *huaqiao* nor addressed how a Chinese *minzu* might become part of the new Malaya or Indonesia.

It was left to Qu Zhefu 屈哲夫, a journalist for *Fengxia* with no CCP affiliations, to bring Hu Yuzhi's deconstruction of the sojourner citizen to its logical conclusion.[14] Three weeks after Hu's essay appeared, Qu proposed "using the two characters *huazu* to replace *huaqiao*." In "The Chinese Nation in Nanyang and Politics 南洋华族与政治," Qu mostly repeated what Hu had pointed out—that the majority of Chinese overseas were permanent settlers with no intention of returning China—to explain why the sojourner-citizen name had become a misnomer (*Fengxia*, no. 6, 7.1.1946). Unlike Hu, however, Qu did come up with an alternative name for the Chinese overseas—(*haiwai*) *huazu*—his translation of the term from English. While "this is how foreigners call us," it also had the benefit, Qu argued, "of showing that we are not 'guests'." It is not clear if by *zu* he meant Chinese race or nation, but in the essay he referred to the Chinese in Southeast Asia as "this branch of the Chinese nation (*Zhonghua minzu*) in Nanyang." Qu's call for the Chinese in Southeast Asia to call themselves *huazu* rather than *huaqiao* would be forgotten for nearly two years, until it was revived in late 1947.

It was in the debates over citizenship options for and political orientation of the Chinese under the impending Federation of Malaya constitution that Qu's deconstructed "*huazu*" would be adopted and conceptually clarified. As part of a broader left-wing coalition campaign to oppose the British and

---

14 Not much is known about Qu. He stopped reporting for *Fengxia* in March 1946 and worked for the pro-Guomindang *Zhongxing Ribao* before leaving Singapore in 1948 for further studies in London University. See Lian 1948.

conservative Malay proposals for the Federation constitution, Hu Yuzhi and his papers urged the Overseas Chinese to take part in local politics and adopt local citizenship. Shen Zijiu, his wife and a feminist activist, criticized the apolitical mindset of the Overseas Chinese merchants, who had traditionally insisted that "businessmen should only talk business" (*zaishang yanshang*). Instead, she urged them to "not be afraid of politics" (*Fengxia* no. 79, 4.6.1947). Commenting on the White Paper for the Federation of Malaya constitution, another writer asked whether it was "the metropole's plan to increase the authority of the native ruling class on the surface, but to use this power in reality to control colonial interests from the rear?" (*Fengxia* no. 86, 2.8.1947). In August and September 1947, Hu Yuzhi adopted Qu's concept of *huazu* but gave it a stronger conceptual grounding in Chinese ways of understanding the home and homelands.

Hu's new *huazu* disconnected the concept of ancestry from the Chinese nation—usually rendered as an "ancestral state" (*zuguo*) in Chinese. He did this by first defining the state in social-scientific or Hegelian-Marxist terms. "Humans made the state," he argued, "because there was a need for it" at that given stage in the development of human history. Every state was made up of its own territory, people and sovereignty. In the contemporary period, there were "states [ranging] from the proto-state tribes of the Sakai's, [an aboriginal group in Malaya] to the [the most advanced state-form in the] United States of America or the United Socialist Soviet Republics" (*Fengxia* no. 91, 6.9.1947). Having given a scientific definition of the state, he returned to deconstructing the etymology of the "ancestral" by a reference to "western languages, [in which] 'state' (*guo*) and 'nation' (*minzu*) are often denoted interchangeably by the word 'Nation' (original in English)." Historically speaking, he argued, it is

> not correct if *zuguo* is seen only as the land where our ancestors lived. Most Americans have ancestors who come from Europe, the Indians' ancestors are Aryans, but Americans won't treat Britain as their *zuguo*, and neither will Indians treat Europe as their *zuguo*.
>
> FENGXIA no. 92, 13.9.1947

To dissociate the nation from a strictly racially defined meaning, Hu added: "Nation is not race. A state (*guojia*) may encompass many different races, but it can only be one *minzu*." This definition of Malaya as a multi-racial unitary nation-state, which differed from the MCP's three-*minzu* Malayan nationalism, set Hu on a collision course with the MCP.

Further disaggregating racial from national identity, Hu made a clear distinction between the Chinese notions of hometown, homeland (ancestral land) and nation-state in Chinese.¹⁵ It was already a Chinese customary practice, he pointed out, to see "the hometown (*jiaxiang*) and ancestral land (*zuguo*) as different things. The hometown (*jiaxiang*) refers to our permanent place of residence, but *zuguo* refers to the place that holds our ancestral tombs, our place of birth and the source of our race (*zhongzu*)." In other words, having ancestral graves, or being born to Chinese ancestors, simply gave one a Chinese racial identity, it was rather the person's chosen place of residence that should determine one's nationality. Malaya's citizenship law, as advocated whether by the Left or the Right, required all citizens to treat Malaya as their permanent residence. This was, in Hu's view, a more "progressive" way to determine citizenship than China's "backward" nationality law, which recognized Chinese-ness by paternal bloodline. "When China implements democratic politics in the future," Hu argued, "there would be a real need to change such a backward and inappropriate nationality law" (*Fengxia* no. 94, 27.9.1947). As reiterated by another writer, rather than remain as citizens of China, the Chinese in Malaya should form a distinct race (*zhongzu*) in relation to the local state (*Fengxia* no. 95-6, 9.10.1947).

The championing of a Chinese-Malayan national identity for the diasporic sojourner-citizen community in Malaya gave the MCP and CCP a common political cause up to late 1947. That common cause, however, began to unravel as soon as it became clear that their constitutional protests against the Anglo-Malay Federation constitution failed to stop its implementation. I have mentioned the clash between Tan Kah Kee, Hu Yuzhi and the MCP over MCP-organized labor strikes on the estates and factories of Chinese enterprises in Malaya. These underlying tensions spilled over into the public sphere in the early months of 1948 in the form a debate over the meaning of "nation" and "state."¹⁶ In particular, an MCP-affiliated writer criticized Hu's championing of a multi-racial Malayan nation, which contradicted the MCP's multi-national state vision. The writer raised the counter-examples of multi-national states like the Soviet Union and Switzerland.¹⁷ Hu Yuzhi was most likely ordered by

---

15 For an analysis of how discourses of home and origins intersected among the Chinese in West Kalimantan, see Hui 2011, 31–106.

16 Another related and better known polemical debate about the correct "form" (*xingshi*) and "content" (*neirong*) of Malayan Chinese literature and arts broke out between MCP and CCP-aligned intellectuals in late December 1947 and lasted till mid-March 1948. Hu Yuzhi was also the target of that attack. The literary historian Fang Xiu has designated the period 1945–1948 as a time when the proponents of "the specificity of Malayan Chinese literature and arts" (马华文艺的独特性) managed to "correct the [China-centric] creative inclination of 'sojourner literature and arts.'" See Fang 1978, 29.

17 Zhui Zhen's essay in *Combatants' Friends* no. 81 and 82, cited in Hu Yuzhi's letter to the editorial, *Fengxia*, no. 117, 13.3.1948.

the CCP in Hong Kong to retract his earlier line, just as he was advised to leave Singapore for Hong Kong:

> I declare that what I said in the headline editorial of *Fengxia*, no. 92, that "within a state [...] there can only be one nation (*minzu*), was wrong." [...] I took "state" and "nation" to be synonyms, when I really meant the latter. The state that the colonized peoples aspire to build should be seen as a tool to protect the interests of the nation, and not as a tool for class exploitation against the interests of the nation. I said it that way so that the masses would find it easier to understand, yet I contributed to the misgiving that I had plagiarized from "bourgeois scholars." From this I cannot absolve myself, so I am willing to accept the criticism of Mr. Seeking the Truth. I acknowledge that the state and the nation should be (analyzed) separately.
>
> *FENGXIA*, no. 117, 13.3.1948

Both parties agreed to put an end to the sojourner-citizen mindset of the Chinese in Malaya.[18] While there was a real difference on paper between the MCP's multi-national state and Hu Yuzhi and his bourgeois allies' multi-racial nationalism, it was unclear how the MCP planned to set up a multi-national state with autonomous republics or districts for the "three great nations" (三大民族)—Chinese, Malays and Indians. That was never a priority. It was perhaps not so much substantive differences over national identity but difference over united front strategies, and Hu's continued support for Tan Kah Kee and Tan Cheng Lock, that triggered the attack. Hu refused to support the escalation of a class struggle-based vision of the Malayan revolution. At about the same time, the MCP consulted regional fraternal parties, including the CCP's Zhou Enlai, and received advice that it would be appropriate to launch an anticolonial armed struggle to win Malaya's independence (Chin 2003, 201–6).

5   Conclusion

By March 1948, both Hu Yuzhi and Wang Renshu had left Southeast Asia to return to a China still riven by civil war. Wang had been expelled by the Dutch in July 1947 in the first "police action" against Indonesian-controlled territory. Hu's differences with Malaya's communist party led to his withdrawal from Singapore. But the pro-CCP newspapers did not last for much longer in

---

18   For the MCP line on adopting Malayan nationality, see Ma Hua, "马来亚华侨与政治斗争," in *Combatants' Friend*, 26.12.1947.

Singapore after Hu's departure. *Fengxia* closed in June 1948 at the start of the Malayan Emergency, whereas *Nanqiao Ribao*, under Tan Kah Kee's endorsement, remained in print, but only until 1950. The CCP's newspapers in post-independence Indonesia lasted longer. They received a new lease of life in 1949, when the CCP assumed power in China, but eventually wound down with all other Chinese newspapers under the assimilationist and increasingly conservative politics of the 1960s. In contrast to the Malayanization of Chinese political identity by 1959 (Chui 2007), both the CCP's and the Guomindang's newspapers in Indonesia continued to address their Chinese readers as presumed nationals of China into the 1950s and 1960s (Zhou 2019: 80–1).

The CCP, or to be more precise its intellectuals, had a brief but very deep engagement with diasporic Chinese societies in the Southeast Asia during the 1940s. This brief dual-revolutionary phase of their encounter with Southeast Asia has until recently been obscured for a variety of reasons, the chief of which was the great efforts they themselves made to keep their CCP identity underground. Fear of anti-communist suppression notwithstanding, this was also an attempt at abiding by the internationalist socialist ethic of subsuming overseas revolutionary organizations into the local national parties. In this sense, the dual-revolutionary mission was their response to the Overseas Chinese in Southeast Asia as constituents to be mobilized for the diasporic homeland and diasporic subjects to be assimilated into their adopted new nations. This was a tricky dual mission in the context of escalating political tensions between nationalists and returning colonial powers and of increasing pressure on the Chinese to demonstrate their political loyalty.

Although these factors had a huge influence, the outcome, as I have tried to show, was neither entirely determined by place (the size of the Chinese population) nor by the pace of decolonization (revolution or gradual devolution). At all three sites, at the same time as they rooted for the CCP in the homeland, the intellectuals tried to identify their readers with the local revolutionary nationalist movements in the early months of the post-war period. Jakarta, recolonized as Batavia in late 1945, was the earliest to surrender its local assimilationist mission, as the Guomindang moved in to take overwhelming control of Overseas Chinese associations. It was in Medan and Singapore that the intellectuals pursued comparable strategies of mobilizing merchants and youths. They were a minority and, more importantly, the exigencies of the violent anti-colonial revolution in Medan meant that in as much as Wang Renshu wished to amalgamate the sympathetic merchants and radical youth into the fold of an Indonesian-led revolution, that form of anti-colonial mobilization was closed off from as early as the days of the anti-Japanese resistance.

In Singapore (including Malaya), the fact that there was a bigger Chinese population and the Chinese dominance of the Malayan communist movement gave Hu Yuzhi far more leeway to articulate a radical Chinese-Malayan nationalist identity for his readership. Unlike in Indonesia, the gradual pace of decolonization gave Hu Yuzhi more time and space to entrench and develop institutions and political idioms for his dual mission. Despite the declining influence of Tan Kah Kee after the war, his inner Hokkien clique remained intensely loyal to him and his pro-CCP political project. While Hu focused on nurturing the youth through his publications, the strength of the MCP meant that he could leave their mobilization to the local party's youth wing. Only in Singapore did the CCP intellectuals come round to campaigning for local citizenship instead of diasporic Chinese nationality. Yet ironically, the more Hu Yuzhi worked with the broad anti-colonial but non-revolutionary coalition fronted by Tan Cheng Lock, the more moderate his politics for Malaya became. Even if Hu Yuzhi came to disagree with the MCP's revolutionary vision, he left in his wake a generation of young Chinese eager to stake their claims for a radical new Malayan homeland in the decolonizing world of the 1950s and 1960s.

New research into China's foreign ministry archives shows that socialist China studiously avoided exploiting the ethnic Chinese in Southeast Asia to spread communist revolution in the region during the 1950s and early 1960s. Beijing understood the predicaments of the ethnic Chinese minorities, whose loyalty to their new nationalist governments was under suspicion within the broader context of the Cold War. Historian Zhou Taomo argues that Beijing's strategic aim in Southeast Asia was not so much to promote communist revolution as "to see the continuation of a stable alliance between the two [countries] that would lead Indonesia along the lines of [Sukarno's] militant anti-imperialism" (Zhou 2019: 154). For Singapore and, by extension, Malay(si)a, Beijing prioritized its endorsement of the anti-colonial Lee Kuan Yew's incumbent democratic-socialist government in Singapore over his more radical and pro-communist left-wing opposition (Liu n.d.).

The CCP's dual-revolutionary phase (1945–49) in its relations with Southeast Asia was a forerunner of the kind of finesse with which socialist China handled the region's Chinese minority problem in the 1950s. Key personalities involved like Hu Yuzhi and Wang Renshu 王任叔 were led directly by Zhou Enlai, who would go on to shape socialist China's foreign relations and Overseas Chinese policy in the 1950s. Scholars unaware of this earlier high-profile underground connection tend to misread China's Dual Nationality Treaty with Indonesia in 1955 as an anomaly.[19] In fact, the broad directions of socialist China's post-1949 Overseas Chinese policy in Southeast Asia were forged on the ground,

---

19 For instance, James To writes that "[i]n 1955, Beijing appeared to have temporarily brushed the OC [Overseas Chinese] aside in an effort to address the issue of dual nationality" (To 2019, 59).

through the underground revolutionaries' difficult encounters with diasporic communities, communist parties, and local nationalist movements. With the dissolution of the Comintern in 1943, these experiences became all the more important in view of the fact that the CCP emerged as its own arbiter in its relations with communist parties and ethnic Chinese in the region.

Acknowledgements

I would like to thank Zhou Taomo for sharing an advanced copy of her book manuscript (2019) for my reference. I would also like to thank Hui Yew-Foong, Kung Chien-wen and two anonymous reviewers for reading earlier versions of this article. Their comments have helped to improve it.

References

Belogurova, Anna. 2017. "Networks, Parties, and the 'Oppressed Nations': The Comintern and Chinese Communists Overseas, 1926–1935." *Cross-Currents: East Asian History and Culture Review* 6(2): 558–582.

Belogurova, Anna. 2019. *The Nanyang Revolution: The Comintern and Chinese Networks in Southeast Asia, 1890–1957*. Cambridge: Cambridge University Press.

Buiskool, Dirk. 2009. "The Chinese Commercial Elite of Medan, 1890–1942: The Penang Connection." *Journal of the Malaysian Branch of the Royal Asiatic Society* 82(2): 113–129.

Chan, Shelly. 2018. *Diaspora's Homeland, Modern China in the Age of Global Migration*. Durham: Duke University Press.

Chen, Mengzhi 陈蒙志. 2012. *Shanghai shuju lishi zhong de shidai yinji* 上海书局历史中的时代印记 (Imprints of History in the History of the Shanghai Book Company). Kajang, Selangor: Chong Fah Hing.

Chin, Peng. 2003. *My Side of History*. Singapore: Media Masters Pte. Ltd.

Cribb, Robert. 1992. *Gangsters and Revolutionaries: The Jakarta People's Militia and the Indonesian Revolution*. Sydney: Allen and Unwin.

Cribb, Robert. 2013 *Shelun quanji* 社论全集 (The Complete Collection of Editorials), Volumes 1 and 2 (1945–50), ed., Yinni Shenghuo Bao Jinian Congshu bianwei hui. Guangzhou Beijing: World Affairs Press.

Fang, Xiu 方修. 1978. *Zhanhou Mahua wenxue shi chugao* 战后马华文学史初稿 (A Preliminary Outline of Post-War Chinese Malaysian Literary History). Singapore: T K Goh.

Fengxia 风下 (Below the Winds) (December 1945–June 1948) Accessed via Chinese periodical full-text database 民国时期期刊全文数据库 1911–1949. http://www.cnbksy.com/.

Guo, Rende 郭仁德. 1999. *Maxin kang Ri shiliao: Shenmi Laite* 马新抗日史料：神秘莱特 (Sources on the Anti-Japanese Resistance Movement in Singapore and Malaya: The Mysterious Lai Teck). Johor Baru: Rainbow Publishing Company.

Harper, Tim. 1999. *End of Empire and the Making of Malaya*. Cambridge: Cambridge University Press.

Hau, Caroline. 2014. *The Chinese Question: Ethnicity, Nation, and Region in and Beyond the Philippines*. Singapore: National University of Singapore Press.

Heidhues, Mary Somers. 2012. "Anti-Chinese Violence in Java during the Indonesian Revolution, 1945–49." *Journal of Genocide Research*, 14(3–4): 381–401.

Hu, Xuwei 胡序威. 2016. "Gen shushu Hu Yuzhi dao Xinjiapo 跟叔叔胡愈之到新加坡 (Following My Paternal Uncle to Singapore)." Lianhe Zaobao, 26 March 2016.

Hu, Yuzhi. 1996. "Wode Huiyi 我的回忆 (My Recollections)." In *Hu Yuzhi wenji* 胡愈之文集 (The collected works of Hu Yuzhi). Volume 6. pp. 321–407. Beijing: Sanlian shudian.

Hui, Yew-Foong. 2011. *Strangers at Home: History and Subjectivity Among the Chinese Communities of West Kalimantan, Indonesia*. Leiden, Boston: Brill.

La, Gu 拉古. 2003. "Dadi shudian de chuangban yu jieshu 大地书店的创办于结束 (The Founding and Closure of Dadi Bookstore)." In *Wangbuliao de suiyue: Yinni sudao huaqiao kangri douzheng "jiu-erling" shijian liushi zhounian ji huaqiao aiguo minzhu yundong jinian teji* 忘不了的岁月：印尼苏岛华侨抗日斗争 "九.二〇" 事件六十周年暨华侨爱国民主运动纪念特辑 (The Unforgettable Days: Commemorative Volume on the Sixtieth Anniversary of the 'September Twentieth' Incident in the Anti-Japanese Struggle of the Overseas Chinese and the Democratic and Patriotic Movement of the Overseas Chinese on the Sumatran Island of Indonesia), eds., Huang Shuhai 黄书海, pp. 55–59. Beijing: World Affairs Press.

Lee, Leo Ou-fan. 2001. *Shanghai modern: the Flowering of a New Urban Culture in China, 1930–1945*. Cambridge, Mass: Harvard Univ. Press.

Lian, Shisheng 连士升. 1948. "Wandering Records of a European Tour 欧洲漫记." Nanyang Siangpau 南洋商报, 19 October 1948, p. 3.

Liang, Yingming 梁英明. 2013. "Zongxu 总序 (General Preface)." In *Shenghuo Bao de Huiyi* 生活报的回忆 (Memories of Shenghuo Bao) eds., Qian Ren 千仞 & Liang Junxiang 梁俊祥, pp. 1–4. Guangdong: World Book Publishing Company.

Lin, Kesheng 林克胜, Chen Wenying 陈文营 and Zhang Ailin 张爱麟. 2003. "Mianlan Minzhu Ribao chuban qianhou 棉兰《民主日报》出版前后 (Events Surrounding the Publication of Medan's Democracy Daily News)" In *Shenghuo Bao de Huiyi* 生活报的回忆 (Memories of Shenghuo Bao), eds., Qian Ren 千仞 & Liang Junxiang 梁俊祥, pp. 260–274. Guangdong: World Book Publishing Company.

Lin, Kesheng 林克胜, Chen Wenying 陈文营 and Zhang Ailin 张爱麟. 2015. "Minzhu Ribao 民主日报 Democracy Daily News." In *Yinni Subei Huaqiao Huaren Cangsang Suiyue* 印尼苏北华侨华人沧桑岁月 *Tumultuous Age for the Chinese of Northern Sumatra, Indonesia*. pp. 398-404. Indonesia: North Sumatra Chinese Community Social and Education Association.

Liu, Philip Hsiao-pong (n.d.), "Love the Tree, Love the Branch: Beijing's Friendship with Lee Kuan Yew, 1954–1965." *The China Quarterly*: 1–23.

Peng, Yaxin 彭亚新 ed. 2009. *Zhonggong zhongyang nanfangju de wenhua gongzuo* 中共中央南方局的文化工作 (The Southern Bureau of the Chinese Communist Party: Cultural Work.) Beijing: History of Chinese Communist Party Publishing House.

Ping, Fan 平凡. 2003. "Zhao Hongpin de geming rensheng 赵洪品的革命人生 (The Revolutionary Life of Zhao Hongpin)." In *Wangbuliao de suiyue: Yinni sudao huaqiao kangri douzheng "jiu-erling" shijian liushi zhounian ji huaqiao aiguo minzhu yundong jinian teji* 忘不了的岁月：印尼苏岛华侨抗日斗争"九.二O"事件六十周年暨华侨爱国民主运动纪念特辑 (The Unforgettable Days: Commemorative Volume on the Sixtieth Anniversary of the 'September Twentieth' Incident in the Anti-Japanese Struggle of the Overseas Chinese and the Democratic and Patriotic Movement of the Overseas Chinese on the Sumatran Island of Indonesia), ed., Huang Shuhai 黄书海, pp. 166–169. Beijing: World Affairs Press.

Qian, Ren 千仞 2003, "Huang Zhougui yu Shenghuo Bao rongwei yiti 黄周规与《生活报》融为一体 (Huang Zhougui and "Shenghuo Bao" Become One Entity.) In *Shenghuo Bao de huiyi* 生活报的回忆 (Memories of Shenghuo Bao), eds., Qian Ren 千仞 & Liang Junxiang 梁俊祥, pp. 175–180. Guangdong: World Book Publishing Company.

Reid, Anthony. 1979. *The Blood of the People: Revolution and the End of Traditional Rule in Northern Sumatra*. Kuala Lumpur: Oxford University Press.

Saw, Swee Hock. 2007. *The Population of Singapore*. Singapore: Institute of Southeast Asian Studies. Second edition.

Shao, Dan. 2009. "Chinese by Definition: Nationality Law, Jus Sanguinis, and State Succession, 1909–1980." *Twentieth Century China* 35(1): 4–28.

Schwarcz, Vera. 1986. *The Chinese Enlightenment: Intellectuals and the Legacy of the May Fourth Movement of 1919*. Berkeley: University of California Press.

The National Archives (TNA), United Kingdom, Foreign and Commonwealth Office (FCO) series.

To, James Jiann Hua. 2014. *Qiaowu: Extra-territorial Policies for the Overseas Chinese*. Leiden: Brill.

Volkstelling van Nederlandsch Indië 1930, 1933-6, [Census of 1930 in Netherlands India], Volume 7: Chinese and Other Foreign Orientals. Batavia: Departement van Landbouw, Nijverheid en Handel.

Wang, Gungwu. 1976. "A Note on the Origins of Hua Chiao." In *Community and Nation: Essays on Southeast Asia and the Chinese*. Wang Gungwu, pp. 118-127. Singapore: Heinemann Educational Books (Asia).

Wang, Gungwu. 1976. 1976, "The Limits of Nanyang Chinese Nationalism, 1912-1937." In *Southeast Asian History and Historiography: Essays presented to D.G.E. Hall*, eds., C.D. Cowan and O.W. Wolters, pp. 405-424. Ithaca: Cornell University Press.

Wang, Renshu 王任叔 2001 [1947], "Yindunixiya de geming guangan 印度尼西亚的革命观感 (Revolutionary Observations and Thoughts on Indonesia.)" In *Baren yu Yindunixiya—Jinian Baren (Wang Renshu) danchen 100 zhounian* 巴人与印度尼西亚—纪念巴人（王任叔）诞辰100周年 (Baren and Indonesia: Commemorating the Centennial of Baren's [Wang Renshu] Birth), pp. 251-329. Hong Kong: Nan Dao Publisher.

Weng, Xihui 翁锡辉. 2013. "印尼爱国侨领翁福林传记 (The Biography of the patriotic PIndonesian Overseas Chinese leader Weng Fulin.)" In *Shenghuo Bao de huiyi* 生活报的回忆 (Memories of Shenghuo Bao), eds., Qian Ren 千仞 & Liang Junxiang 梁俊祥, pp. 227-250. Guangdong: World Book Publishing Company.

Yang, Xuechun 杨学纯 2003, "Shao Zonghan tongzhi geming de yisheng 邵宗汉同志革命的一生 (The revolutionary life of comrade Shao Zonghan)." In *Wangbuliao de suiyue: Yinni sudao huaqiao kangri douzheng "jiu-erling" shijian liushi zhounian ji huaqiao aiguo minzhu yundong jinian teji* 忘不了的岁月：印尼苏岛华侨抗日斗争"九．二O"事件六十周年暨华侨爱国民主运动纪念特辑 (The unforgettable days: Commemorative Volume on the Sixtieth Anniversary of the 'September Twentieth' Incident in the Anti-Japanese Struggle of the Overseas Chinese and the Democratic and Patriotic Movement of the Overseas Chinese on the Sumatran Island of Indonesia), ed., Huang Shuhai 黄书海, pp. 439-441. Beijing: World Affairs Press.

Yong, Ching Fatt 杨进发 1988, *Chen Jiageng Yanjiu Wenji* 陈嘉庚研究文集 (The Collected Works of Tan Kah Kee.) Beijing: China Friendship Publishing House.

Yong, Ching Fatt 杨进发 1997, *The Origins of Malayan Communism*. Singapore: South Seas Society.

Yong, C.F. and McKenna, R.B. 1990, *The Kuomintang movement in British Malaya, 1912-1949*. Singapore: Singapore University Press.

Zhang, Chukun 张楚琨. 2014. "Chen Jiageng yu Nanqiao Ribao 陈嘉庚与《南侨日报》(Tan Kah Kee and Nanqiao Ribao)." In *Xiamen dangshi wang* 厦门党史网 (Xiamen Party History Web). Accessed 1.7.2019. http://xm.zgfjlsw.org.cn/contents/10593/27873.html.

Zhang, Xina 张曦娜. 2018. "Wang Yamei 70 nianhou de huaijiu zhi lü yu Yu Dafu fenghuo tongzhou 汪雅梅 70 年后的怀旧之旅 与郁达夫烽火同舟 (Wang Yamei's Nostalgic Tour 70 Years Later, Sharing the Same Wartime Refugee Boat as Yu Dafu)."

Lianhe Zaobao 联合早报, 12 March 2018. Accessed 1 June 2019. http://www.zaobao.com.sg.

Zheng, Yeying 郑椰影. 2013. "Zheng Chuyun shengping 郑楚云生平（节选）(The Life of Zheng Chuyun [Abridged])." In *Shenghuo Bao de huiyi* 生活报的回忆 (Memories of Shenghuo Bao), eds., Qian Ren 千仞 & Liang Junxiang 梁俊祥, pp. 257-269. Guangdong: World Book Publishing Company.

Zhou, Taomo 2019. *Migration in the Time of Revolution: China Indonesia, and the Cold War*. Ithaca: Cornell University Press.

Zhu, Peiguan 朱培琯 2003, "Sumendala minbao gaizu ji kuozhan neiqing zhuishu 《苏门答腊民报》改组及扩展内情追述 (Recalling an Insider's Understanding of the Reorganization and Expansion of Sumatra People's News)." In *Wangbuliao de suiyue: Yinni sudao huaqiao kangri douzheng "jiu-erling" shijian liushi zhounian ji huaqiao aiguo minzhu yundong jinian teji* 忘不了的岁月：印尼苏岛华侨抗日斗争 "九.二O" 事件六十周年暨华侨爱国民主运动纪念特辑 (The Unforgettable Days: Commemorative Volume on the Sixtieth Anniversary of the 'September Twentieth' Incident in the Anti-Japanese Struggle of the Overseas Chinese and the Democratic and Patriotic Movement of the Overseas Chinese on the Sumatran Island of Indonesia), ed., Huang Shuhai 黄书海, pp. 283-288. Beijing: World Affairs Press.

PROJECT MUSE®

The Patriarchy of Diaspora: Race Fantasy and Gender
Blindness in Chen Da's Studies of the Nanyang Chinese

Rachel Leow

Twentieth-Century China, Volume 47, Number 3, October 2022, pp.
243-265 (Article)

Published by Johns Hopkins University Press
DOI: https://doi.org/10.1353/tcc.2022.0030

For additional information about this article
https://muse.jhu.edu/article/864557

THE PATRIARCHY OF DIASPORA: RACE FANTASY AND GENDER BLINDNESS IN CHEN DA'S STUDIES OF THE NANYANG CHINESE

RACHEL LEOW

This study critically appraises the earliest sociological investigations of Nanyang (South Seas) Chinese communities by the sociologist Chen Da (1892–1975). By exploring Chen's corpus of work and highlighting systemic blind spots of race and gender, the study reveals the normative rather than empirical quality of his sociological elaboration of the *huaqiao* (overseas Chinese). Tracing the genesis of his research and his travels through Southeast Asia, it shows that, at each stage, Chen's investigations, academic networks, connections he made with his local informants, and even his collaborations with his principal translator offered an understanding of the world beyond a patriarchal, patriotic Chinese diaspora that he declined to fully explore. The paper thus offers an intimate window into the historically contingent conceptual work that went into constructing the Chinese "diaspora," and it highlights the need to exercise caution in making ahistorical use of social science studies of overseas Chinese.

KEYWORDS: diaspora, gender, *huaqiao*, knowledge production, Nanyang, race, sociology

Chen Da (陈达 1892–1975) was—and is still—considered an eminent sociologist of labor and population in China; he had a long and illustrious career association with the founding of sociology at Tsinghua University in Beijing.[1] He is the "Chen" of the pithy saying often trundled out in discussions of Chinese sociology: "*Bei Chen nan Sun*" (北陳南孫) or "In the north there is Chen, and in the south there is Sun," the latter a reference to Chen's equally famous contemporary Sun Benwen (孫本文 1891–1979) in Nanjing.[2] Both of them were part of a first generation of US-trained Chinese sociologists who called in various ways for the Sinicization of sociology and for the production of sociological work by Chinese social scientists based on

---

1 Biographical accounts include Wang Renze, "Chen Da," in *Minguo renwu zhuan* [Biographies of people in the Republic of China], vol. 9 (Beijing: Zhonghua shuju, 1997), 385–91; Wen Xiang, "Chen Da, Pan Guangdan yu shehuixue de 'Qinghua xuepai'" [Chen Da, Pan Guangdan, and the "Tsinghua school" of sociology, *Xueshu jiaoliu* 268, no. 7 (July 2016): 155–59. The banning of sociology in China after 1952 complicates this history somewhat.

2 Fang Yuan and Quan Weitian, "Shehui xuejia Chen Da" [Sociologist Chen Da], *Shehuixue yanjiu* 2 (1980): 128

Chinese realities.³ Both were also representatives of what Zheng Hangsheng identified as the "syncretic [综合 *zonghe*] school of sociology." Associates of this school were influenced by their American training and their association with contemporary sociologists like Robert E. Park at the University of Chicago and especially William Ogburn and Franklin Giddings at Columbia University, and they sought to look beyond Marxist materialism to emphasize cultural and psychological factors in their social analyses.⁴

Chen is perhaps best known in China for his monumental 1934 study, *Renkou wenti* (人口問題 Problems of population), a study of demography, labor, and overpopulation.⁵ Under a scholarship funded by the Boxer Indemnity, Chen made an educational sojourn in the United States between 1916 and 1923, during which time he took three degrees and witnessed from abroad China's entry into the First World War, the Russian Revolution, and the May Fourth movement. When he returned to China, he began to teach at Tsinghua University. Over the next 20 years, he moved between academia and government work, conducting both sociological research and practical work for the Nationalist government well into the wartime period, investigating problems of labor and administering population survey projects that then fed back into his academic work. Chen can thus be understood as part of a broader, global history of social scientists as "world-makers," embedded in passionate projects of collecting and inventing facts for national and imperial purposes.⁶

Renkou wenti, however, is bookended by two major studies of Chinese migration, one published in 1923 and a second published in 1938, which at least one of Chen's students has regarded as the more important of his works.⁷ These have been frequently used

---

3 Others include Fei Xiaotong and Pan Guangdan, the latter of whom was especially close to Chen Da and took over leadership of the Tsinghua University sociology department after Chen stepped down in 1943. Of all the pioneering sociologists of this generation, Chen was the only one who conducted research into the overseas Chinese.

4 Zheng Hangsheng, *Zhongguo shehuixue shi xinbian* [A new compilation of the history of Chinese sociology] (Beijing: Zhongguo renmin daxue chubanshe, 2000); Arif Dirlik, "*Zhongguohua*: Worlding China," in Arif Dirlik, ed., *Sociology and Anthropology in Twentieth-Century China: Between Universalism and Indigenism* (Hong Kong: Chinese University of Hong Kong Press, 2012), 1–39; Ana Maria Candela, "Sociology in Times of Crisis: Chen Da, National Salvation and the Indigenization of Knowledge," in "World-System Biographies," special issue, *Journal of World-Systems Research* 21, no. 2 (2015): 362–86; Yung-chen Chiang, *Social Engineering and the Social Sciences in China, 1919–1949* (Cambridge: Cambridge University Press, 2001). Contemporaries recognized Giddings's influence in particular on the early development of Chinese sociology; see, for example, Chih Meng, "The American Returned Students of China," *Pacific Affairs* 4, no. 1 (1931): 1–16.

5 Chen Da, *Renkou wenti* [Problems of population] (Shanghai: Shangwu yinshu guan, 1934).

6 Jeremy Adelman, ed., *Empire and the Social Sciences: Global Histories of Knowledge* (London: Bloomsbury Academic, 2019); Tong Lam, *A Passion for Facts: Social Surveys and the Construction of the Chinese Nation-State, 1900–1949* (Berkeley: University of California Press, 2011).

7 This student was Han Mingmo, whom Chen taught in Lianda during the wartime years and who later became a professor of sociology at Peking University. The works in question are Ta Chen [Chen Da], *Chinese Migrations, with Special Reference to Labor Conditions* (Washington, DC: United States Government Printing Office, 1923) and Chen Da, *Nanyang huaqiao yu minyue shehui* [South Seas Chinese and social conditions in Guangdong and Fujian] (Shanghai: Shangwu yinshu guan, 1938). The latter was translated into English in 1940 as Ta Chen [Chen Da], *Emigrant Communities in South China: A Study of Overseas Migration and Its Influence on the Standard of Living and Social Change*, ed. Bruno Lasker (New York: Institute of Pacific Relations, 1940).

as references ever since, principally mined for their rich empirical detail and the rarity of their scope as perhaps the only studies of prewar "emigrant districts" (華僑社區 *huaqiao shequ* or 僑鄉 *qiaoxiang*)—Guangdong and Fujian—in relation to Chinese communities in Southeast Asia. But they are not well understood as contingent products of particular personal, national, and global histories and circumstances. In this article, I take a critical approach to Chen Da's putatively empirical sociology of the Nanyang (南洋 South Seas) Chinese and show how the conditions of his social-scientific world-making have baked in deep racial and gendered assumptions about the *huaqiao* (華僑 overseas Chinese).[8] To do so, I draw not only on his corpus of sociological publications on emigrant Chinese communities but also on his little-used travel and fieldwork diaries from mid-1930s travels in the Nanyang, and I highlight some of the unexplored omissions and divergent interpretations of his data that emerge from field study to collaboration, publication, and translation. I show how, at each stage of his research into Chinese emigrant communities, his investigations, his academic networks, and the connections he made with his local informants offered an understanding of the world beyond a patriarchal, patriotic Chinese diaspora that he constantly declined to fully explore. The world that Chen moved in, carefully gathering social facts, was resolutely male and—in spite of the region's ethnic complexity—resolutely Chinese. The patriotism of the *huaqiao* concept has been relatively well established in the literature, and yet too little attention has been paid to the gender of this patriotism and to the struggle of Chinese racial theorizing in the ethnically heterogeneous South Seas.[9] Chen's sociology of the *huaqiao*, I argue, laid the foundations not only for a patriotic Sinocentrism of the diaspora but also for an unassailable patriarchalism of the concept of Chinese diaspora that, even today, largely goes unremarked.

Sociology and the Making of the *Huaqiao*

It is worth elaborating briefly here on Chen Da's use of the term *huaqiao*, which many studies have shown was under conceptual construction during the late Qing

---

[8] For a similar critical appraisal of sociology in the field of British history, see Jon Lawrence, "Social-Science Encounters and the Negotiation of Difference in Early 1960s England," *History Workshop Journal* 77, no. 1 (2014): 215–39. I am grateful to Lucy Delap for this suggestion.
    Following Wang Gungwu and others, I take *huaqiao* to be a category that emerged under specific historical conditions of rising Chinese nationalism during the late Qing and the early Republican era. Wang Gungwu, "A Note on the Origins of Hua-ch'iao," in *Community and Nation: Essays on Southeast Asia and the Chinese* (Singapore: Heinemann Educational Books, Asia, 1981), 118–27.

[9] For accounts that make clear the male domination of accounts of Chinese diasporic intellectuals and revolutionaries but lack critical reflection on this matter, see Soon Keong Ong, "'Chinese, but Not Quite': Huaqiao and the Marginalization of the Overseas Chinese," *Journal of Chinese Overseas* 9, no. 1 (2013): 1-32; Huang Jianli, "Umbilical Ties: The Framing of the Overseas Chinese as the Mother of the Revolution," *Frontiers of History in China* 6, no. 2 (2011): 183–228; Shelly Chan, *Diaspora's Homeland: Modern China in the Age of Global Migration* (Durham, NC: Duke University Press, 2018), chaps. 2 and 3. For examples of works that consider Chinese theorization about southern racial complexity from a literary perspective, see Cheow Thia Chan, "Indigeneity, Map-Mindedness, and World-Literary Cartography: The Poetics and Politics of Li Yongping's Transregional Chinese Literary Production," *Modern Chinese Literature and Culture* 30, no. 1 (2018): 63–86; Emma Teng, *Taiwan's Imagined Geography: Chinese Colonial Travel Writing and Pictures, 1683–1895* (Cambridge MA: Harvard University Asia Center, 2004).

and early Republic.¹⁰ Chen's studies were curiously untethered from the proliferation of studies of Nanyang *huaqiao* being conducted almost simultaneously by a circle of intellectuals surrounding Jinan University and its Department of Nanyang Cultural and Educational Affairs, including Liu Shimu (劉士木 1889–1952), Yao Nan (姚楠 1912–1996), Su Qianying (苏乾英 1910–1996), and especially Li Changfu (李長傅 1899–1966), who was perhaps the most prolific writer on the Nanyang Chinese in the Nanjing era.¹¹ Li Changfu's interest in the overseas Chinese was actually provoked by reading Harley Farnsworth MacNair's *Chinese Abroad*, as he laments in the introduction to his 1927 study, *Huaqiao*: "The study of *huaqiao* was not started by Chinese people but by foreigners; this is a great shame to Chinese academia." Li took *huaqiao* to mean "all *hua* people (short for *Zhonghua* [中華] people) who sojourn and live abroad" (華者，中華之簡稱，僑者，旅寓之意；凡我國人旅寓於國外者，皆可稱之曰華僑).¹² Li's educational sojourn was in Japan rather than America—he spent a short stint at Waseda University between 1929 and 1931—and his writings, perhaps influenced by Japanese ideas of colonization as "people planting" (植民 *shokumin*), exhibit an understanding of Chinese migration to the Nanyang as a form of developmental colonization or settler development (拓殖 *tuozhi*), along with the civilizational benefits that implied.¹³ He specifically viewed China's colonization (殖民 *zhimin*) of the Nanyang as a developmental process, of "leaving the motherland for a relatively undeveloped country" to settle permanently and participate in economic activities while maintaining political relations with the motherland, though he was careful to distinguish this from European colonialism, which he viewed as having greater state support.¹⁴ Like many northern Chinese intellectuals—Li was a

10 See, for example, Zhuang Guotu, *Huaqiao huaren yu Zhongguo de guanxi* [Overseas Chinese and their relationship with China] (Guangzhou: Guangdong gaodeng jiaoyu chubanshe, 2001); Wang Gungwu, "Southeast Asian Hua-Ch'iao in Chinese History-Writing," *Journal of Southeast Asian Studies* 12, no. 1 (1981): 1–14.

11 His works include early statements on the meaning of *huaqiao*: Li Changfu, "Shijie de huaqiao" [Overseas Chinese across the world], in Li Changfu, *Li Changfu xiansheng lunwen xuanji* [Anthology of the writings of Li Changfu] (Guangzhou: Jinan daxue chubanshe, 2001). Perhaps his most famous works are Li Changfu, *Zhongguo zhimin shi* [A history of Chinese colonialism] (Shanghai: Shangwu yinshuguan, 1937) and various studies of Nanyang history and geography, such as *Nanyang shi gangyao* [Outline of the history of the Nanyang] (Shanghai: Shanghai Commercial Press, 1936) and *Nanyang dili* [Nanyang geography] (Kunming: Zhonghua shuju, 1940). For an overview of studies of *huaqiao* published in the Guomindang period, see Li Anshan, "Zhonghua minguo shiqi Nanyang yanjiu shuping" [Overseas Chinese studies during the Chinese Republican era], *Jindaishi yanjiu* 4 (2002): 290–314.

12 Li Changfu, *Huaqiao* [Overseas Chinese] (Shanghai: Zhonghua shuju, 1927), 1. The work he refers to is Harley Farnsworth MacNair, *The Chinese Abroad* (Shanghai: Commercial Press, 1924).

13 Others associated with the Jinan school also expressed similar views; see, for example, Liu Jixuan and Shu Shicheng, *Zhonghua minzu tuozhi Nanyang shi* [The history of Chinese peoples' development of the Nanyang] (Zhengzhou: Henan renmin chubanshe, 2016). For more studies, see Zhao Canpeng, "Jinan daxue Nanyang wenhua shiye bu de lishi yange" [The historical development of the Nanyang Cultural Affairs Department at Jinan University], *Dongnanya yanjiu* 6 (2007): 5–12; Leander Seah, "Between East Asia and Southeast Asia: Nanyang Studies, Chinese Migration, and National Jinan University, 1927–1940," *Translocal Chinese: East Asian Perspectives* 11, no. 1 (2017): 30–56; Chan, *Diaspora's Homeland*, chap. 2.

14 Li Changfu, "Nanyang huaqiao yizhi shi niaokan" [A bird's-eye view of the Nanyang *huaqiao*], in *Li Changfu xiansheng lunwen xuanji*, 62. For an appraisal of *shokumin* particularly through the writings

Jiangsu native—he also subscribed to stereotypes about the nature of the southern peoples that would push them to do such un-Confucian things as traveling away from their family burial grounds. The southern coastal residents, he thought, were piratical by nature and "late bloomers" in the adoption of Confucian norms, and so—while they were no doubt bettering even less developed lands in the southern seas—they were themselves far less civilized than their northern counterparts, who would not have sojourned at all.

On this matter, Chen's approach to the *huaqiao* was diametrically opposed. He seems never to have cited works on the Nanyang by the Jinan scholars, nor did he engage with their usages of the term *huaqiao*, although his work was certainly known to some within the Jinan circle, at least later on,[15] and he did interact with Liu Shimu in conceptualizing his 1938 study, though I have not been able to ascertain the extent of this exchange.[16] Unlike the Jinan scholars, Chen made a distinction between two types of emigrant Chinese with "different natures and different outlooks on life": those who migrated out of China, *qianmin* (迁民 literally, people who moved), and those who grew up in the South Seas, *qiaomin* (僑民 literally, people who lived abroad). He considered *huaqiao* to be a "common name" (俗稱 *sucheng*) or an umbrella term for *haiwai Zhongguoren* (海外中國人), a category that for him included both *qianmin* and *qiaomin*.[17] And rather than regarding mainlanders as civilizing the less developed southern Nanyang lands, he came to express in his work the view, in effect, that emigrant Chinese constituted an "element of social change" (社會變遷的一個原素 *shehui bianqian de yige yuansu*) for the emigrant districts of Guangdong and Fujian. In other words, rather than China civilizing the barbaric Nanyang periphery, the *huaqiao* of the Nanyang were, in fact, sources of modernization for a more backward China. Emigrants, Chen concluded in *Nanyang huaqiao yu minyue shehui* (南洋華僑與閩粵社會), tend to stimulate social change in China: materially, they remitted money home and transformed the economic base of their home villages (侨乡 *qiaoxiang*); beyond the material, they also brought different practices and values back to the emigrant districts. Across the realms of livelihood and work, food, clothing and shelter, family structure, education, health habits, and religion, emigrants were a major stimulus of change and transformation. They had the cumulative effect of disintegrating the family structures of "traditional society" (傳統社 *chuantong shehui*) and of fundamentally

---

and teachings of Nitobe Inazō at Tokyo University, see Alexis Dudden, "Nitobe Inazō and the Diffusion of a Knowledgeable Empire," in Jeremy Adelman, ed., *Empire and the Social Sciences: Global Histories of Knowledge* (London: Bloomsbury Academic, 2019), 111–22.

15 He is mentioned, for example, by Yao Nan, one of the founding members of the Nanyang South Seas Society: Yao Nan, "Zhongguo dui dongnanya shi de yanjiu" [Chinese research on Southeast Asia], in Yao Nan, *Xingyun yeyu ji* [Stars, coconut trees, and rain: a Singaporean collection] (Singapore: Xinjiapo xinwen yu chuban youxian gongsi, 1984).

16 Liu is briefly mentioned as a project contact. Chen, *Nanyang huaqiao yu minyue shehui*, 11. Liu Shimu's understanding of *huaqiao* was also very different from Chen's; he thought that *huaqiao* was a simple abbreviation of *zhonghua qiaomin*, or Chinese people who lived in foreign countries, and he, like Li Changfu, tended toward a settler colonial conception of Chinese migration. See Liu Shimu and Xu Zhigui, *Huaqiao gaiguan* [Overseas Chinese survey] (Shanghai: Zhonghua shuju, 1935), 1–4.

17 On *sucheng*, see Zheng Jiancheng, "'Sucheng' yu 'huncheng': Chen Da lun 'huaqiao' gainian" ["Common name" and "mixed name": Chen Da on the concept of "overseas Chinese"], *Huaqiao huaren wenku xuekan*, 2017, 109–16.

changing and improving the "mode of living" (生活方式 *shenghuo fangshi*) or "standard of living" (生活程度 *shenghuo chengdu*) of families in emigrant districts.[18]

One of the reasons for Chen's discursive isolation from the Jinan circle may be the genesis of *Nanyang huaqiao yu minyue shehui* in a research agenda established by the American-based Institute for Pacific Relations (IPR), an international nongovernmental research organization with roots in missionary activism and Wilsonian internationalism. Though largely forgotten today, the IPR had a remarkable influence on public knowledge and on both elite and popular discourse about the Asia-Pacific region prior to the Second World War.[19] At a time when the US government was investing heavily in its domestic white middle classes through the New Deal, the IPR was uniquely committed to a broader mission of fostering transracial and international understanding and communication, beyond state politics and official government policies, regarding issues concerning China, Japan, and the broader Asia-Pacific region: China, in particular, consumed more of its research budget in the 1930s than all other countries combined. Owing no doubt to the networks he established in the United States while he was a student, Chen was invited to the IPR's inaugural conference in Honolulu in 1925 as an expert on Chinese migration, the subject of his PhD dissertation and first monograph publication.[20] What became his 1938 study was developed in conversation with a research agenda agreed upon at a major IPR conference in Banff in 1933, which resolved to "concentrate new research projects in the next biennial period to the subjects of Standards of Living and Cultural Relations."[21] In particular, it was intended to speak to a set of research questions about comparative standards of living between East and West, including a specific question about how far migration had affected standards of living in Pacific communities.[22]

Chen's initial research fieldwork plan, drafted in 1934, was sent for comment to a wide range of academics within the broad networks of the IPR, including Robert E. Park of the University of Chicago and Romanzo Adams of the University of Hawai'i, Tao Menghe (陶孟和 1887–1960) of Nanjing Academia Sinica and Wu Wenzao (吳文藻 1901–1985) of Yenching University, and Liu Shimu of the Nanyang Department at Jinan. Among those most directly involved in the project was undoubtedly Bruno Lasker (1880–1965), a research associate of the IPR and a social scientist with wide-ranging

---

18 In his writing, Chen explicitly comments that he regards his "mode of living" (*fangshi*) and "standard of living" (*chengdu*) to be roughly equivalent in meaning *if* one subscribed, as he did, to a broader understanding of "standard of living" than merely an economic one that encompassed solely the "cost of living." For his commentary on this, see Chen, *Nanyang huaqiao yu minyue shehui*, 8–10.

19 Studies of the IPR include: John N. Thomas, *The Institute of Pacific Relations: Asian Scholars and American Politics* (Seattle: University of Washington Press, 1974); Tomoko Akami, *Internationalizing the Pacific: The United States, Japan and the Institute of Pacific Relations, 1919–1945* (New York: Routledge, 2003). On the IPR's connection with the Rockefeller Foundation and its research into rural reconstruction, see Chiang, *Social Engineering*.

20 Chen, *Chinese Migrations*.

21 Bruno Lasker and W. L. Holland, *Problems of the Pacific: Proceedings of the Fifth Conference of the Institute of Pacific Relations, Banff, Canada, 14–26 August, 1933* (Chicago: University of Chicago Press, 1934), 476–77.

22 See the list of questions in Lasker and Holland, *Problems of the Pacific*, 476–77.

interests in unemployment, public health, social legislation, labor, and slavery.[23] Lasker was instrumental at the research-design stage, traveled part of the way to Southeast Asia with Chen in early 1935, and remained in close cooperation with him throughout. They arranged to travel in opposing directions around the Nanyang, Chen moving counterclockwise from Borneo through to Malaya and the Dutch East Indies and Lasker beginning in Manila and traveling onward, clockwise, to Singapore.[24] They also agreed on a division of labor between them: Chen would focus on making Chinese contacts, and Lasker would confine his inquiries to American and European government officials and representatives, whom, he explained, Chen had a harder time accessing.[25] In the planning stage, Lasker furnished Chen directly with notes and "literary excerpts" that Lasker himself had collected independently,[26] though he was disheartened by Chen's apparent reluctance to assimilate them into his research methodology: "I have compiled an enormous amount of information from the literature on Southern Chinese emigration for Ta Chen," Lasker wrote in a personal update to his IPR colleague William Holland, "and am only afraid that his methodical mind will not know what to do with it even if I carefully index these more than 150 pages for him."[27] Lasker was also responsible for overseeing and editing the 1940 English translation of Chen's 1938 study, and it is in the divergence between the two that a moment of contingent discourse formation can be discerned.

In comparing the original and the translation, it becomes clear that there was a kind of intellectual tussle at play, centered directly upon argumentation and the question of the extent and centrality of Nanyang *huaqiao* influence on Chinese emigrant districts. The structure of the English translation differed in small but critical ways from that of the Chinese original. Lasker's translation laid out an introduction and 10 chapters that more or less followed the sequence of Chen's chapters, though with the creation of a few extra chapter divisions. Chen's Chinese original, however, distributes all its chapters between just two major parts: Part I, "*Huaqiao* Districts: Traditional Lifestyle and Its Changes," and Part II, "An Element of Social Change: The Influence of Migrants [移民 yimin]." Lasker commented on this explicitly in his editorial foreword: "The Chinese author in the present case has enviable mastery of the English language; nevertheless certain passages of the text required further elucidation, or changes in phraseology to make clear their intended meaning. Moreover the order of the report had to be changed because it made too great a demand on Western students who are accustomed to a different sequence of statement in the presentation of a given body of social information."[28]

---

23 Lasker traveled with Chen to Xiamen to meet with Lim Boon Keng. Lim was at that time the president of Xiamen University, which formed the initial base for the assembling of Chen's research teams, with Wu Ruilin (Lingnan University), Fu Shanglin (Sun Yat-sen University) and Xu Shengjin (Xiamen University) in consultancy. Chen Da, *Langji shinian* (Beijing: Shangwu yinshuguan, 1946), chap. 1.

24 Bruno Lasker (Manila) to Charles Loomis, 23 November 1934, folder 26, box E23, Institute of Pacific Relations Records, Manuscript M004, University of Hawai'i at Mānoa, henceforth IPR Records.

25 Bruno Lasker (Amoy) to William Holland, 11 November 1934, folder 25, box E23, IPR Records.

26 As was acknowledged in Chen, *Emigrant Communities in South China*, 10, although not in Chen, *Nanyang huaqiao yu minyue shehui*.

27 Bruno Lasker (Hong Kong) to William Holland, 29 October 1934, folder 25, box E23, IPR Records.

28 Bruno Lasker, editorial foreword to Chen, *Emigrant Communities in South China*, vi.

The arrangement of Chen's chapters and parts makes clear his argumentative intention: of all the factors that were changing China at the time, he considered emigrants to be the *principal* one, and he says so explicitly in his introduction:

閩粵的華僑社區，有它的生活方式 如本書各章所敘述的。這種生活方式的形成與變遷，當然有許多原素，但南洋的遷民實是主要原動力之一。

The *huaqiao* districts in Guangdong and Fujian have their own specific modes of living, as the chapters of this book will elaborate. There are, of course, many elements [原素 *yuansu*] that contribute to the formation and transformation of their modes of living, but the Nanyang *qianmin* actually constitute one of the principal [主要 *zhuyao*] driving forces.

However, this section is translated by Lasker as:

The emigrant communities in East Guangdong and South Fujian have a mode of living—if here we may briefly anticipate the findings given in subsequent chapters—readily distinguishable from that of other rural areas in China. Among the forces motivating social change the influence of the overseas Chinese from the Nanyang is, of course, only one, but it is striking and unmistakable.[29]

Their intellectual tussle takes place in the argumentative gap between "one of the principal driving forces" and "only one, but striking and unmistakable." In fact, evidence from Lasker's correspondence with the IPR in 1934–1935 frequently reveals their mutual struggle; in conceptualizing the project, Chen apparently "again and again [came] out with the insane idea that perhaps he was engaged only to finish the fieldwork and that subsequently someone else will be engaged to write up the result."[30] It is also clear from the correspondence that the original study had not been intended to furnish arguments about the importance of the Nanyang *huaqiao* to China at all but rather to appraise standards of living in China: as Lasker wrote, "We [do] not set out to study Chinese emigration, nor the character of Chinese settlement and colonization in the south-sea countries.... Our concern, as I understand it, is 90 per cent with the home community."[31] In March 1935, Lasker circulated among a limited number of IPR members a separate interim report of his own on Chen's project that was intended to comment on Chen's project in view of its relevance to the broader IPR program of research into comparative standards of living.[32] On this point, Lasker's report demonstrated a definite divergence from Chen's arguments. In compiling this report, Lasker had access to the reams of letters and field reports that were being channeled to Chen from his platoon of research assistants stationed in the field sites under study between 1934 and 1935, and he was thus able to draw his own

29 Chen, *Nanyang huaqiao yu minyue shehui*, 8 (the direct translation is my own); Chen, *Emigrant Communities in South China*, 11.
30 Bruno Lasker (Amoy) to William Holland, 2 November 1934, folder 25, box E23, IPR Records.
31 Lasker to Holland, 11 November 1934.
32 Bruno Lasker, *Changing Standards of Living in South China as Affected by Overseas Migration* (Honolulu: Institute for Pacific Relations, 1935).

conclusions. Lasker frequently cited reports from Kenneth Chun (陈观胜 Chen Guansheng dates unknown), a former student at the University of Hawai'i and one of Chen's researchers, whom Chen had likely come to know while he was stationed in Honolulu as a visiting Carnegie Professor of International Relations in 1930 and whom Lasker likely also met at that time.[33] Contrary to Chen, Lasker thought that "remittances enlarge, but do not materially change the standard of living," and he cited Kenneth Chun's field reports:

> Change in food and clothing are usually in quantity and quality, but very seldom in kind or style. It is true, some of the returned emigrants have brought Western clothes back with them; but they wear these only on special occasions. We have not seen a single woman here wearing anything other than the Chinese styles. However, the gains in quantity and quality are considerable…. This is also true of food…. There are no visible changes in the eating habits of the returned emigrants. They still stick to Chinese bowls, chopsticks, and food. However, there are improvements to the quantity and quality of the food….
>
> The wasteful superstitious practices are still rampant…marriages are still concluded without the consent of those to be married. One young man who favored a "liberal" marriage, nevertheless went through the old-fashioned marriage ceremony and, when he was asked why he permitted it, said he could not fight against the combined opinion of home and community. Quite a few of the young returned emigrants have expressed themselves in the same vein—that it is futile to battle against the dead weight of traditional authority.
>
> The changes enumerated in previous paragraphs represent only a small portion of the emigrant families. Our experience in Zhanglin [樟林] has shown us that, in the great majority of them, the returned member does not exert any discernible influence at all.[34]

This direction of critique of Chen's conclusions can also be found in a subsequent review of the published book by Francis Hsu (许烺光 1909–1999), a Bronisław Malinowski–trained anthropologist and specialist on Yunnan magic and science. Hsu wrote critically of Chen's study, rejecting his conclusions and stating bluntly that, in his scrutiny of the very same facts that Chen made available in his study, he had nonetheless drawn completely opposite conclusions. "South Seas emigration has…not only had no effects opposed to the traditional ways of life, but has caused them to be expressed with greater clarity and force," he insisted, stating furthermore that "wealth acquired through emigration

---

33 Kenneth Chun is mentioned frequently in *Ka Leo o Hawaii* (Voice of Hawaii), the university's student newspaper between 1928 and 1932, presumably when Chun was enrolled as a student. For reports on Chen Da's semester course on international relations there, see "Dr. Chen to Give Course in China's Foreign Relations," *Voice of Hawaii*, December 13, 1929; "Prof. Ta Chen Is Recognized Labor Expert," *Voice of Hawaii*, February 14, 1930; "Chen Discusses Chinese Family of Present Day," *Voice of Hawaii*, February 28, 1930; "Ta Chen Talks to Int. Club on Labor Body," *Voice of Hawaii*, March 7, 1930; "Chinese Program," *Voice of Hawaii*, April 25, 1930. Bruno Lasker was also in Hawai'i at the time; see "Bruno Lasker Finds Hawaii Very Romantic," *Voice of Hawaii*, February 14, 1930.

34 Lasker, *Changing Standards of Living in South China*, 9, 23.

has in most cases merely added oil to the lamp of age-old tradition."[35] It is possible that this struggle was on the minds of IPR researchers after the war. Lasker's opinion of Chen was by no means fully negative, as he wrote to Holland's Chinese counterpart in the IPR, Wellington Liu (劉馭萬 Liu Yuwan 1897–1966): "It is a very pleasant experience to work with the professor. Though we always disagree a little on interpreting what we find...we nevertheless have a great deal of fun together...and I admire his thoroughness, his modesty—though this is excessive—and his scientific zeal for the truth and nothing but the truth."[36] But his frustrations, as expressed in a more candid remark to Holland that Chen "has not a very original mind," came to be echoed by other American IPR associates.[37] Having spent most of the wartime years in Kunming doing meticulous census work and labor research for the Nationalist government, Chen wrote to the IPR in 1947 to request funding for publishing something out of these investigations; one of the proposed studies was on the urbanization of Kunming through the modernizing efforts of migrants. His request was politely declined after some internal discussion: "I am [not sure]," one reviewer wrote privately to Holland, the IPR research secretary, "that he has enough flexibility to undertake work on the topic you suggest."[38] Chen's marshaling of social facts into an argumentative theory about the positive, modernizing influence of emigrants on China, part of a developmentalist drive that ran in an opposite direction from his Jinan contemporaries, seems to have been a patriotic interpretation from preexisting convictions about the value of emigrants to China. He had not, perhaps, heeded enough Lasker's comment in Honolulu in 1930: "A sociologist must be like a child. Otherwise he loses the significance of the facts. If one goes to a place with set theories, he is likely to gather only those facts which suit his theories."[39]

BETWEEN FACT AND THEORY: CHEN DA'S TRAVELS IN THE NANYANG

Although the bulk of the ground-level fieldwork for *Nanyang huaqiao yu minyue shehui* was done by his research teams,[40] Chen Da did visit the places that appear in his final study, and he recorded his travels in a book published a decade later and

---

35 Francis L. K. Hsu, "Influence of South-Seas Emigration on Certain Chinese Provinces," *Journal of Asian Studies* 5, no. 1 (1945): 48, 57.

36 Bruno Lasker (Hong Kong) to Wellington Liu, 11 November 1934, folder 25, box E23, IPR Records.

37 Lasker to Holland, 11 November 1934.

38 Frank W. Notestein to William Holland, 3 January 1947, file on Chen Da, box 315, Institute of Pacific Relations Records, 1927–1962, Rare Book and Manuscript Library, Butler Library, Columbia University. My thanks to Vanessa Lee at the Butler Library for her help in processing my digital scan request during the COVID-19 pandemic.

39 "Bruno Lasker Finds Hawaii Very Romantic."

40 Chen sought to compare two emigrant districts with one nonemigrant district in South China, along with the communities abroad with which the former were in contact. He designated three districts for specific investigation: one in northeastern Amoy, another in northwestern Amoy, and a third in northeastern Swatow. At each place, 4–7 investigators spent 4–10 weeks collecting general data from a total of 1,348 families who had either returned from or had members in the South Seas. Chen, *Nanyang huaqiao yu minyue shehui*, 3–7.

called *Notes from Ten Years of Roaming* (浪跡十年 *Langji shinian*; 1946). Part travelogue, part autobiography, and part research notebook, this volume was described by Chen as a kind of unsystematic aide-mémoire or what he called "casual writing" (隨便的文筆 *suibian de wenbi*) as part of the practice of empirical sociology (實證社會學 *shizheng shehuixue*).[41] He explained that he sought nothing more than to jot down noteworthy observations for the purposes of furnishing a basis for later argument. As he explained:

> A large part of human life is made up of trivial matters, such as food, clothing, shelter, and daily activities. For these events, we should observe [觀察 *guancha*] with all our five senses and seek to reduce errors when observing. Second, we should record our observations at the time of observation.… If [we do not do so], there are many things that will pass before our eyes like clouds, leaving no trace and no chance to study them in the future. If the memory is not detailed, there will be no reliable basis for narrative or argument. Third, we should seek to understand the meaning of these observations and be able to explain the observed phenomena and the recorded facts.

The places to which he traveled were determined by the areas of concentration of emigrants from the Southern Chinese districts at the center of his study, and thus for three months in early 1935 he traveled across the Dutch East Indies, British Malaya, Siam, and French Indochina. "The aim," he wrote, "was less that of securing data for comparison of living conditions at home and abroad as it was to study those factors in the overseas Chinese community which contribute to the *particular kind of influence* which it exerts on the mode of living in the home communities of its members in South China."[42] In the following sections, I elaborate first on the racially complex milieu of Chen's encounters and the way he persistently reconciled and resolved them into a fantasy of Chineseness that supported his emigrant theories and then on the persistent masculinity of the world in which he moved and how that shaped his theories about the role of women in emigrant societies.

Beyond Biology and Culture: Fantasies of Chineseness in the Malay World

As outlined earlier, Chen, unlike his Jinan contemporaries, distinguished clearly between *qianmin* and *qiaomin*, and in the course of his writing he did not often use the term *huaqiao* without this qualification.[43] For Chen, the principal distinction between them was racial and a secondary distinction was jurisdictional. *Qiaomin* were mostly mixed race, usually born of a father who had emigrated from China and a mother who was a native local woman (當地的土人女子 *dangdi de turen nüzi*). *Qianmin*

---

41 Preface to Chen, *Langji shinian*, 4.
42 Chen, *Emigrant Communities in South China*, 10; translation by Bruno Lasker; emphasis mine.
43 These distinctions were not made in Chen, *Emigrant Communities in South China*, the English-language version of Chen, *Nanyang huaqiao yu minyue shehui*.

were straightforwardly people of Chinese blood who sojourned. This, Chen thought, mapped onto a further jurisdictional difference: China's consulates would consider *qianmin* as falling within their sphere of interests and protection, while European colonial governments considered *qiaomin* to be under their jurisdiction. *Qiaomin*, Chen said, were "mostly mixed race [混血兒 *hunxue'er*]; they do not speak Chinese and do not know Chinese history or geography."[44]

Chen's ideas about race are discernible in development from his earliest work, in particular his master's degree research while a student at Columbia in 1920 and his subsequent 1923 monograph based on his doctoral dissertation on Chinese migration. His master's thesis in political science, on birth control, illustrates his early inculcation with the widespread ideas about biological race and evolution that marked so many Chinese intellectuals of that era.[45] Steeped in the eugenics discourses of the age, he developed an early conviction, which he would carry throughout his work during the Guomindang and Chinese Communist Party regimes, that birth control or "volitional limitation of the family" was the only possible check on the "inevitable evils of unlimited propagation" that he saw as the root cause of Chinese poverty.[46] For Chen, birth control was the only way to guarantee the constant improvement of the quality of the race, since having large families was incompatible with "leisure" and leisure time was crucial for self-cultivation and civilization.[47] He was greatly taken with Margaret Sanger's work and played a role in introducing her to other May Fourth intellectuals and arranging her visit to China in 1920.[48] In his direct contrasting of "volitional selection" as being more beneficial for racial improvement than "natural selection,"[49] his views were also exemplary of the attractiveness to intellectuals in this period of Spencerian "eugenic control-fantasies" rather than the impersonal and unmanipulable Darwinian laws of evolution.[50] Racial improvement, in short, could be managed through carefully chosen human action. In his personal life, Chen practiced what he preached: as an advocate of "equal replacement" of the population (对等更替 *duideng gengti*), he believed that a couple should have no more than two children; as far as I can tell, he had only two children himself, about whom very little information can be found, owing no doubt to his difficult trajectory through the Maoist era.[51]

---

44 Chen, *Langji shinian*, 8–9.

45 Ta Chen [Chen Da], "Practical Eugenics in the United States: Birth Control" (master's thesis, Columbia University, 1920).

46 Chen, "Practical Eugenics in the United States," 17, 51. Chen helped organize the Maternal and Child Health Association in Beiping in 1932 and also set up a guidance center and a periodical, *Renkou fukan* [Population supplement], to advocate birth control and late marriage. See Wang Renze, "Chen Da."

47 This idea appears in Chen, "Practical Eugenics in the United States" and is repeated in Chen, *Chinese Migrations*, 64.

48 See Ta Chen [Chen Da], "For a Birth Control League in China," *China Critic*, August 21, 1930.

49 Chen, "Practical Eugenics in the United States," 27–28.

50 Christian Geulen, "The Common Grounds of Conflict: Racial Visions of World Order 1880–1940," in Sebastian Conrad and Dominic Sachsenmaier, eds., *Competing Visions of World Order* (London: Palgrave Macmillan, 2007), 69. Chen had certainly read Herbert Spencer, and he referred to his work in Chen, *Chinese Migrations*, 29.

51 Chen's views on birth control and late marriage became fatefully politicized during the policy fluctuations between pronatalism and antinatalism over the course of the 1950s. His long-standing advocacy for population control, reaffirmed in an essay published during the Hundred Flowers campaign in spring 1957, placed him on the wrong side of Mao's view that "demographic power was strength" (*ren duo liliang da*):

There is little specifically about birth control in his study of Chinese migration published several years later, but he brought to this study his ideas about active racial improvement. Chen's 1923 study was based primarily on library research rather than fieldwork; he canvassed official documents of Chinese, European, and American governments, secondary literature of journals and periodicals, and Western (though not Chinese) studies of Chinese emigrants.[52] In this work he dealt for the first time with the issue of racial mixing and intermarriage and, perhaps surprisingly, was inclined to view miscegenation in a positive light as one of the active mechanisms by which a race might be improved. Though his conclusions remained tentative, chiefly held back by "the paucity of statistical material on racial amalgamation," one of the main overall conclusions of his study was that "there has been evidence to show the eugenic benefits of miscegenation between the Chinese and other nationals."[53] He cites not only various American and European studies that suggested that Chinese blood had an improving and permanent effect on non-Chinese peoples but also those that suggested that mixed Chinese races might be superior to "pure" ones. He drew, for example, on Ernest J. Reece's study of racial mixing in Hawai'i, which asserted that "the Chinese Hawaiian is far superior to both of the elements in his make-up" and was also superior to the Caucasian-Hawaiian,[54] and he elsewhere observed that "white blood does not persist in the mestizos...the Chinese is the only race that implants permanent characteristics upon mestizo offspring."[55] From James Brook's journal, he noted that "the mixed breed of the Chinese with the Malays or the Dyaks are a good looking and industrious race.... This mainly arises from education and early formed habits which are altogether Chinese; and in religion and customs they likewise follow, in a good measure, the paternal stock. The race is worthy of attention, as the future possessors of Borneo."[56] This early attention to mixed-race Chinese groups and his more extensive use of American and European sources may have been a stimulus to his *qiaomin/qianmin* distinction, disposing him to view miscegenation in a far more benign light than his Japan-influenced contemporaries.

In his field travels a decade later, however, Chen was presented with quite a different set of realities. Throughout his travels he met community leaders who had largely maintained connections with China or represented Chinese interests, which naturally had a self-selecting effect: those with whom he spoke regularly expressed the opinion that racial mixing between Chinese and non-Chinese would not have improving effects and that the mixing of non-Chinese with Chinese blood would result in the latter becoming

---

"The more people there are, the more, faster, better, and more thriftily we can build socialism." Along with many antinatalist social scientists such as the famous president of Beijing University Ma Yinchu (1882–1982), Chen was censured as a rightist during the anti-Rightist movement of 1957 and eventually deposed; unlike Ma, he was rehabilitated only posthumously. For Chen's offending essay, see Chen Da, "Jieyu, wanhun yu xin Zhongguo renkou wenti," *Xin jianshe* 5, no. 104 (1957): 1–15. For background on population debates of the 1950s, see Penny Kane, *The Second Billion: Population and Family Planning in China* (London: Penguin, 1987); Thomas Scharping, *Birth Control in China 1949–2000: Population Policy and Demographic Development* (London: Routledge, 2005).

52 See the chapter bibliographies in Chen, *Chinese Migrations*.
53 Chen, *Chinese Migrations*, 2–3.
54 Chen, *Chinese Migrations*, 126–27.
55 Chen, *Chinese Migrations*, 109.
56 Chen, *Chinese Migrations*, 77.

degraded. On February 4, 1935, he recorded a conversation with a Surabayan Chinese man named Lin Huiye (林徽業 dates unknown) who conveyed a typically troubling sentiment: "Mixed race people think that Chinese people are no good...but in the past hundred years, mixed race populations have been waning. The native people [土人 *turen*] have a simplistic culture and are famous for being lazy. They don't understand hygiene [衛生 *weisheng*], and when Chinese people mix with them, they degrade the quality of the race."[57] In Singapore, probably owing to the doors opened by letters from the Penang-born president of Xiamen University Lim Boon Keng (林文慶 1869–1957), he was able to meet with important community leaders of both Chinese and Straits Chinese, including Tan Kah Kee (陳嘉庚 1874–1961) and Tan Cheng Lock (陳禎祿 1883–1960), and he had a particularly extensive conversation with the former, who conveyed to him similar racially charged sentiments about the intrinsic laziness of Malay peoples. As Chen records Tan Kah Kee's words, "The reason *huaren* were able to open up Malaya is really because the *turen* lacked ambition and physical strength. Not a single one among Malaya's *turen* could have built up a 100-acre rubber plantation. But the laziest *huagong* [華工] can set up a rubber plantation four times that size."[58] Perhaps most disturbingly for him, the *qiaomin* he encountered in Java and Siam seemed to have vanished altogether from visible Chineseness: "It is sometimes difficult to identify whether *qiaomin* who have assimilated [同化 *tonghua*] with natives are Chinese [中國人 *Zhongguoren*] or not."[59]

These social facts presented Chen with an interpretive problem: how were emigrant communities meant to be an element of positive social change if intermarriage either "degraded" the Chinese race or caused them to become indistinguishable from the *turen*? His solution was to privilege the cultural over the material and biological, in a kind of wishful fantasy of racial thinking. For example, he observed of the mixed-race children he saw in Zhanglin, Shantou, that "while the physique [體質 *tizhi*] of mixed-race boys is sometimes distinguishable, the differences are not very significant" and that the most important of them lay in "language and living habits" (語言與生活習慣 *yuyan yu shenghuo xiguan*).[60] Of still greater significance, beyond culture, was what was in their hearts: despite their physical assimilation, "many [*qiaomin*] still love the motherland and express a strong sympathy for it."[61] From his conversation with H. H. Kan (1881–1951), he recorded an idea of Chinese *xinling* (心靈 mind, mentality, or perhaps soul or spirit), which transcended blood:

> On the surface, some habits of the *qiaomin* resemble those of natives, while others resemble those of Europeans—but when you investigate [偵察 *zhencha*, rather than 觀察 *guancha*] his heart, he is still a Chinese person. *Qiaomin* can take natives as wives, but all children born to them still have the *xinling* of Chinese children.[62]

---

57 See Chen's conversation with Lin Huiye in Chen, *Langji shinian*, 44–45.
58 See Chen's conversation with Chen Jiageng in Chen, *Langji shinian*, 91–94.
59 Chen, *Langji shinian*, 27.
60 Chen, *Langji shinian*, 12.
61 Chen, *Langji shinian*, 9.
62 Chen, *Langji shinian*, 32.

Chen's idea of *xinling* echoed the influence of his teacher Franklin Giddings, whose emphasis on culture and social psychology had produced the heuristic of the "social mind" to assess collective social phenomena.[63] Chen's conclusion—that even if Chineseness were to be biologically lost through racial mixing, it could nonetheless be transmitted through a metaphysical *xinling*—was also a contingent ideological formation, produced out of the creative adaptations of prevailing discourses of biological race with, as James Leibold put it, "the expectation that culture would gradually displace race as the dominant hermeneutic of national unity" in China.[64] Thus, while noting that in Siam "three-quarters of the Siamese Chinese have been 'Siamized' [暹化 *Xianhua*]"[65] and that "the degree of Siamization of the *qiaomin* is very high" there,[66] in Zhanglin, Shantou, he was able to recuperate his vanishing countrymen. He observed that the Siamese Chinese were the most likely to maintain close business and educational connections with their emigrant districts and that they were after all, despite their mixed backgrounds, retrievable into Chineseness: "After living in Zhanglin for a long time, [Siamese mixed-race boys] are all Sinicized [漢化 *Hanhua*], and, if no one specifically points them out, it is not possible to tell who is mixed."[67]

In Chen's travelogues and studies of emigrant Chinese, we catch a glimpse of the ways in which, as Frank Dikötter, James Leibold, and others have shown, Republican-era elites at the time were grappling with multiple meanings of racial Chineseness, as "Chinese elites negotiated their way through myriad indigenous categories as well as the globally circulating norms of Western modernity to fashion an authentic, meaningful and practical form of identity."[68] Republican intellectuals from Liang Qichao (梁啟超) and Gu Jiegang (顧頡剛) to Lin Huixiang (林惠祥) and Zhang Xuguang (張旭光), in addressing similar issues of how to historicize the political unity of China's current geobody with its racial heterogeneity, contemplated at least two competing paradigms. Some made use of Western racial theory to posit a homogenous single progenitor of the Han race and called for the maintenance of Han racial purity. Others argued that it was precisely China's lineage diversity that had served as an ancient source of strength throughout its long history of physical interactions between Central Plains Han peoples and the "nomadic, seminomadic and swidden communities of the periphery," and they called for the "infusion of fresh blood" (新血統的混入 *xin xuetong de hunru*) to continue to strengthen the Han core in the face of Japanese aggression and other threats to the Chinese geopolity.[69]

---

63 For an introductory appraisal, see James J. Chriss, "Giddings and the Social Mind," *Journal of Classical Sociology* 6, no. 1 (2006): 123–44.

64 On this point, see James Leibold, "Searching for Han: Early Twentieth-Century Narratives of Chinese Origins and Development," in Thomas S. Mullaney, James Leibold, Stéphane Gros, and Eric Vanden Bussche, eds., *Critical Han Studies: The History, Representation, and Identity of China's Majority* (Berkeley: University of California Press, 2012), 233.

65 Chen, *Langji shinian*, 30; see the notes on his visit to the Siamese Zhonghua zhongxue (Chung Hwa Middle School), 18 February 1935.

66 See Chen's conversation with Chen Daosheng in Chen, *Langji shinian*, 146.

67 Chen, *Langji shinian*, 12.

68 Leibold, "Searching for Han," 218; Frank Dikötter, *The Discourse of Race in Modern China* (Oxford: Oxford University Press, 2015).

69 Leibold, "Searching for Han," 233.

A genealogical appraisal of Chen's writings demonstrates how the problem became further complicated in considering the *huaqiao*, since it had to encompass populations living in "peripheries" beyond China's territorial geobody. As Chen observed, in the South Seas, unlike within China, intermarriage could (and historically did) result in the peripheral vanishing rather than the improvement of the Chinese racial center. Chen's theorizing of the persistence of Chinese characteristics among the *huaqiao* despite the facts he "observed" in his travels—their adoption of a great range of diverse cultural practices, their physical indistinguishability from *turen*, their ignorance of the Chinese language—enabled him to posit the continued benefits of emigrant Chinese for China by connecting their beneficial qualities to something beyond biology and even beyond culture. Though he theorized a category, *qiaomin*, that specifically differentiated these mixed-race communities from "pure" Chinese, he nonetheless drew them into a fantasy of Chineseness that was able to account for the attenuation of nearly every biological and cultural characteristic—"miscegenation," changes in food habits, clothing and shelter habits, and even the loss or rejection of Chinese culture and language—and still claim them as part of his central thesis, that they were "elements" of positive social change and improvement for the Chinese core. It is worth noting too, finally, that Chen's *qiaomin* category elides what would increasingly become a more salient distinction for Chinese emigrant communities in the South Seas, namely the distinction between, on the one hand, locally born "mixed-race" Chinese and, on the other hand, locally born "pure" Chinese, those who had not intermarried with *turen* but who nonetheless had, and wanted, little to do with China.[70]

Fact-Making and the Male Gaze

As an intellectual of the May Fourth generation, Chen was typically progressive in his views on women, and a significant proportion of his early research focused on women in the labor force and the social changes that were enabling their fuller participation.[71] During his time in government service for the Guomindang, he witnessed the promulgation of its new civil code (1929–1930), which promoted marriage reform and particularly emphasized the need for monogamy and free choice in marital partners for women; indeed Chen explicitly viewed the Nationalist government as a source of "modern influence" with regard to marriage.[72] In his 1938 study, one of the central components of his theory that emigrants were "elements of social change" was specifically gendered, namely that he regarded the social progress of women in emigrant districts as resulting from migrant influences. It was with regard to women that Chen made the distinction he did not with the *qiaomin* category, namely distinguishing between Chinese girls (中國婦人 *Zhongguo furen*) and foreign-born Chinese girls (南洋女子 *Nanyang nüzi*, 暹羅女子 *Xianluo nüzi*, or 僑生的中國女子

---

70 An insightful account of this transition is Fujio Hara, *Malayan Chinese and China: Conversion in Identity Consciousness, 1945–1957* (Singapore: Singapore University Press, 2003).

71 See Ta Chen [Chen Da], "Woman and Child Labor," *Monthly Labor Review* 15, no. 6: 142–49.

72 Chen, *Emigrant Communities in South China*, 140. On Republican developments in matters concerning marriage and divorce, see Susan Glosser, *Chinese Visions of Family and State, 1915–1953* (Berkeley: University of California Press, 2003).

qiaosheng de Zhongguo nüzi), who were, he suggested, more progressive in their outlook. Chen argued that these changes were largely due to "the attitude that the foreign-born Chinese daughter-in-law assumes toward her place in the household. She has either had a school education or has had experience of earning money as a girl. In either case, she has developed her personality in ways not accessible as a rule to girls in the Chinese village."[73] The "great majority" of rural women in China, Chen said, "have neither attended a modern school nor been overseas…socially, they are deemed inferior to men; and this inferiority is accepted by most women without protest."[74] Nanyang girls, he concluded, were more equal and free in their relations with Chinese men than the great majority of rural women in China, which gave them "a spirit of greater independence in the subsequent marriage relation."[75] This, Chen added, sometimes brought about crises within a family; he cited the case of a man introducing his foreign-born Chinese wife to the village family, who balked at her "clothes of a modern cut," the fact that she had been to school, and the fact that, perhaps most appallingly, she had persuaded her husband to divide up the family property in China against customary practice.[76]

One clear differentiating factor that went largely unstated by Chen was that he was, in effect, contrasting urban Nanyang women with women from rural South China.[77] This progressive, urban-biased view sits uneasily alongside what is perhaps the more lasting and influential aspect of his 1938 study, which is the principal exposition of the phenomenon of the *liangtoujia* (兩頭家 "dual-headed family" or "dual-headed household"). Chen's study outlines the *liangtoujia* system as a system of transnational polygamy in which a male emigrant keeps wives and families both in his village of origin and in his host society, with principal, predominantly rural wives in the former and either "foreign-born Chinese girls" (南洋僑生女子 *Nanyang qiaosheng nüzi*) or Nanyang native women (南洋土人女子 *Nanyang turen nüzi*), predominantly urban, in the latter.[78] This, Chen asserted, was a largely harmonious endeavor: "If the head of the family is staying abroad and intends to marry a concubine, his wife in the home village usually raises no objection"[79] as long as he satisfies his financial obligations to both households. Chen stated that, on the whole, "mothers and wives in China often express themselves as entirely satisfied with the son's or husband's second matrimonial venture in the Nanyang."[80] Yet, Chen himself recognized this tension with his sympathies toward modern monogamy, admitting in passing that "not all the influences in respect to marriage that come from the Nanyang are necessarily in the

---

73 Chen, *Langji shinian*, 146.
74 Chen, *Emigrant Communities in South China*, 129. The order of this and the above statements is different in the Chinese original.
75 Chen, *Emigrant Communities in South China*, 145.
76 Chen, *Emigrant Communities in South China*, 146.
77 I am grateful to both Penny Kane and Stephen Miles for, separately, pressing this point.
78 As famously elaborated in Chen, *Emigrant Communities in South China*, chap. 6, and Chen, *Nanyang huaqiao yu minyue shehui*, chap. 5. Lasker translated "Nanyang native" as "Malay," even though Chen clearly meant this category to include Siamese and other non-Chinese women; compare, for example, Chen, *Emigrant Communities in South China*, 141 and Chen, *Nanyang huaqiao yu minyue shehui*, 156.
79 Chen, *Emigrant Communities in South China*, 130.
80 Chen, *Emigrant Communities in South China*, 142.

direction of progress," since "the more influential emigrants tend to support concubinage and the dual marriage system."[81]

The dissonance between these two views was also highlighted in the critiques of Francis Hsu, who accused Chen of willfully reading facts against what they said. Hsu pointed out that, in his view and based on his own research in Yunnan, successful returning migrants tended in fact to be even more traditional in their reinforcing of gender norms and the roles of women. Even on the basis of Chen's own data, for all the distress that an overly modern foreign-born Chinese daughter-in-law might create when she went to (rural) China, such wives remained in a small minority—there were only 38 foreign-born wives among 846 marriage cases studied, which made his comments based on them little more than anecdotal.[82] Lasker's citation of Kenneth Chun's correspondence also suggests that Chen might have been overlooking data regarding the "harmoniousness" of the transnational polygamous relationship. As Chun wrote:

> All too often, it is the chief breadwinner who has gone abroad, and he does not remit a single cent home. In such circumstances, the wife and children have to slave to keep body and soul together. Sometimes the emigrant is gone for many years without sending a word. Worse than that, he sometimes leaves a newly married wife in the village and then marries a native girl in the South Seas. Only God knows what mental anguish, forlorn hope, increased hardship these women have to undergo. In a number of cases, the women we interviewed broke down and wept. One of them begged us with tears to find her son for her.[83]

These field notes from Kenneth Chun reveal a key feature of Chen Da's research, which is that by and large he did not conduct interviews himself. Indeed, as is clear from his field notes, Chen's travels did take him to the South Seas, but he seems to have engaged almost exclusively with men: Chinese consuls, community leaders, entrepreneurs, businessmen, and teachers, as well as European colonial officials and missionaries and at least one IPR contact, Victor Purcell (1896–1965). His interlocutors were also exclusively from nonlaboring backgrounds. From the questions and conversations he recorded, it is clear that he was extremely interested in marriage practices in the Nanyang and in polygamy among the *huaqiao*. He made careful notes on Chinese marriages to Siamese women and on the forms of polygamy practiced by the Siamese, in which women were also entitled to property.[84] From prominent Straits Chinese community members such as S. Q. Wong (1888–1980) and Lim Cheng Ean (1889–1987), he learned about the contemporary legal battles concerning monogamy and Chinese customary marriage. He recorded notes on the infamous Six Widows case decided in 1908 in the Supreme Court, in which it was ruled that, in the eyes of colonial law, polygamy was legal under Chinese "customary law" and thus Chinese could take concubines who might inherit property. He also noted a generational

---

81 Chen, *Emigrant Communities in South China*, 140.
82 Hsu, "Influence of South-Seas Emigration," 50.
83 As cited in Lasker, *Changing Standards of Living in South China*, 7.
84 As noted in Chen's conversations with Cai Xueyu, Chen Yiru, Chen Daosheng, and Zeng Dingsan in Chen, *Langji shinian*, 127–29, 143–44, 146, and 141–42, respectively.

shift in attitudes, namely that "the old acquiesced to this ruling, but the young opposed it," and furthermore that *qianmin* openly took concubines, while *qiaomin* might have them, but not openly.[85] In Penang and Singapore he noted the increase in "new-style marriages,"[86] in modern matchmaking practices,[87] and in the sociability of Chinese women, who even enjoyed going out dancing.[88] In Solo, he met a Peranakan Chinese writer, Tjan Tjee Som (曾珠森 1903–1968), who furnished him with a Malay-language article he had written on the challenges that modern, "individualistic" Chinese women faced in marrying and finding jobs; Tjan translated the gist of it for him. Chen copied all of it into his notebook and was so taken with Tjan that he sought him out again in London the following year while on his European sabbatical.[89] Thus, typically for Chinese intellectuals of the era, Chen appraised the question of women's advancement and liberation through overwhelmingly male eyes.

The reliance on male testimony is especially problematic given that Chen's travels coincided specifically with a time of escalating Chinese female labor migration, a phenomenon little touched upon in his empirical study. In 1931 Malaya's Chinese female population was about 580,000, or roughly 34% of the whole Chinese population there; the second-highest count in the region was in Indonesia, about 465,000.[90] In Siam in 1929, there were 131,500 women out of a total population of 445,000, a proportion of roughly 30%. W. L. Blythe estimated that the most intense period of Chinese female immigration to Malaya was from 1934, when the quota was imposed, to 1938, when a limit was placed on female immigrants—precisely the period when Chen was in the region.[91] A similar story can be told for Siam, where the number of Chinese women increased by nearly 70% between 1929 and 1937.[92] It should also be noted that the increase in Chinese female migrants was more than outweighed by the increase in locally born Chinese women. By 1921 locally born women already made up more than half the total number of Chinese females in Penang and Melaka, while in Kelantan they accounted for 90%. From 1931 onward, "the trend was clearly a steady increase in the number and proportion of locally born Chinese females until, by 1957, they constituted a majority in all states."[93]

---

85 See notes on S. Q. Wong in Chen, *Langji shinian*, 96–97.
86 See notes on He Baoren, Tan Cheng Lock, and Lim Cheng Ean in Chen, *Langji shinian*, 100–102, 103–5, and 114–15, respectively.
87 See notes on Huang Yankai in Chen, *Langji shinian*, 107–10.
88 See notes on A. L. Hoops in Chen, *Langji shinian*, 98–99.
89 See notes on Tjan Tjee Som in Chen, *Langji shinian*, 46–47.
90 Fan Ruolan, *Yimin, xingbie yu huaren shehui: Malaiya huaren funü yanjiu 1929–1941* [Migrants, gender, and Chinese society: research into Malayan Chinese women, 1929–1941] (Shanghai: Zhongguo huaqiao chubanshe, 2005), 4–5.
91 Wilfred Blythe, "Historical Sketch of Chinese Labour in Malaya," *Journal of the Malayan Branch of the Royal Asiatic Society* 20, no. 1 (1947): 65; Tan Liok Ee, "Locating Chinese Women in Malaysian History," in Tan Liok Ee and Abu Talib Ahmad, eds., *New Terrains in Southeast Asian History* (Athens: Ohio University Press, 2003), 361.
92 Bao Jiemin, "The Gendered Biopolitics of Marriage and Immigration: A Study of Pre-1949 Chinese Immigrants in Thailand," *Journal of Southeast Asian Studies* 34, no. 1 (2003): 139. In contrast, the population of Chinese women in the whole of the United States was just over 15,000, and in Australia it was fewer than 2,000. Fan, *Yimin, xingbie yu huaren shehui*, 4.
93 Tan, "Locating Chinese Women in Malaysian History," 363.

However, despite Chen's consistent and progressive attention to Chinese women's labor, Chinese laboring women appear almost nowhere in Chen's fieldwork diaries.[94] Instead, in addition to male testimony gathered from fieldwork, Chen's 1938 study (as well as his 1923 study) relied heavily on the use of district and prefectural gazetteers of Fujian and Guangdong as sources of information about Chinese family practices and norms concerning women, laboring or otherwise. Characteristic observations can be found in Chen's sections on "culture traits": in Quanzhou (泉州) "peasant women wear straw slippers and carry burdens…the gentlemen are seldom quick-witted"; in Chaozhou (潮州) "girls and women are chiefly engaged in embroidery" and are "seldom seen on the streets," while "the gentlemen are simple in appearance and intelligent in spirit."[95] As the historian Bao Jiemin has observed, gazetteers are best understood as morally didactic and deeply ideological texts, aimed at establishing norms of gendered behavior rather than accurately reflecting men and women's lives; an example is the way county gazetteers recorded cases of widow chastity and the filial piety displayed by "exemplary wives" (烈女 lienü) toward their mothers-in-law when their emigrant husbands died.[96] Chen's use of male fieldwork testimony might be understood as representing a modernized version of this practice, and in some respects he was just as embedded in a particular moral universe as the compilers of gazetteers were.

To take just one example, Chen's travel notes on Zhanglin and its women have a faint echo of the didactic, moralizing gazetteers:

The women in Zhanglin take care of housework at home and do all the physical labor outside, such as carrying burdens, removing grass, and cutting rice…. Women seem to work harder than men. One reason is because many of the men of working age are already in the Nanyang, and another is because of local habits [本地的習慣 bendi de xiguan]…. The local women are natural-footed [添足 tianzu]…. Huaqiao families often have women who take care of household duties and assume various responsibilities.

There are few men residing in Zhanglin, and those who are there are usually the old and the young. Among them are…depraved elements, the lazy and the unambitious; these useless youths depend on remittances from the Nanyang and have the bad habit of sitting in teahouses, gambling and smoking opium. These men do not work and are often lazy; passing the years in a trance, they are generally unpromising people. As for the more ambitious and risk-taking men, they have largely crossed

---

94 The lack of attention to women in Chen Da's emigrant studies has furnished the departure point for several useful studies since: see, for example, Ye Wencheng, "Minnan qiaoxiang chuantong hunsu yu funü diwei" [Traditional marriage customs and the position of women in traditional Fujianese qiaoxiang], in Ma Jianzhao, Qiao Jian, and Du Ruile, eds., *Huanan hunyin zhidu yu funü diwei* [Marriage systems and the position of women in South China] (Nanning: Guangxi minzu chubanshe, 1994); Li Minghuan, *Ouzhou huaqiao huaren shi* [History of overseas Chinese in Europe] (Beijing: Zhongguo huaqiao chubanshe, 2002), esp. 467–82; Huey Bin Teng, "Law, Gongqin and Transnational Polygamy: Family Matters in Fujian and British Malaya, 1855–1942," in Philip Huang and Kathryn Bernhardt, eds., *Research from Archival Case Records: Law, Society and Culture in China* (Leiden: Brill, 2014), 408–60.
95 Chen, *Emigrant Communities in South China*, 30–31.
96 Bao, "Gendered Biopolitics of Marriage and Immigration," 132–33.

the sea to become sojourners [番客 *fanke*; literally, "barbarian guests"]. Those who stay in the village are physically weak and mentally ill.[97]

These assertions updated China's moral universe according to Chen: exemplary emigrant families had strong, household-leading women who worked hard, while ambitious and risk-taking men went abroad and remitted money home. In addition, the new *lienü* were the exemplary women who stayed behind, the *fankeshen* (番客婶 left-behind wife), who would be "an intelligent younger woman [who] often fully appreciates why it is desirable or even necessary for her husband to have another wife overseas" or, more rarely, might maintain household harmony and live in complete accord with a foreign wife brought back to the village by the returning husband.[98] But in reality, the highly idealized viewpoint expressed here, and woven by Chen into empirical social fact, obscured ground-level realities of women's actual lives, as the handful of subsequent studies of women's much-less-than-harmonious experiences of the *liangtoujia* system have demonstrated. Instead, women's and girls' experiences of the *liangtoujia* system ranged widely across complex and layered forms of servitude, child betrothal, marriage, concubinage, abandonment, and estrangement, as well as a wide range of experiences of support and oppression within the larger in-law familial unit—all of which was enormously complicated by the inadequacy of the legal mechanisms that governed those relations to the task of transnational protection.[99] Even at the time, the divergence between empirical realities and Chen's ideological viewpoint could be discerned in the slippages between what he wrote and what he (or rather his researchers) saw. To return to Kenneth Chun's reports, as quoted by Lasker:

> Among those fortunate emigrants who have been able to accumulate sufficient savings for a new house, built and furnished partly in foreign style [洋楼 *yanglou*], the women have the work done for them by girl servants, while they themselves hobble around on their tiny feet.[100]

The layers of power relations within the familial unit, alluded to here by Chun, appear nowhere in Chen's study, and were, given Chen's methodology, likely either invisible to him during his travels among men or deemed by him to be irrelevant to his objective of assessing the influence emigrants had on their home villages. In this respect, Chen's ideas about modern emigrant women and the transformation of the traditional family unit were in the end—and much like the ideas of his gazetteer-writing predecessors—deeply patriarchal in their assumptions and more normative than empirical in their conclusions.

---

97 Chen, *Langji shinian*, 13–14.
98 Chen, *Emigrant Communities in South China*, 142–43.
99 See Shen Huifen, *China's Left-Behind Wives: Families of Migrants from Fujian to Southeast Asia, 1930s–1950s* (Singapore: NUS Press, 2012); Huey Bin Teng, "Law, Gongqin and Transnational Polygamy"; Rachel Leow, "'Do You Own Chinese Mui Tsai?' Re-examining Race and Female Servitude in Malaya and Hong Kong, 1919–1939," *Modern Asian Studies* 46, no. 6 (2012): 1736–63.
100 Lasker, *Changing Standards of Living in South China*, 9. This is in direct contrast to Chen's earlier assertion that Zhanglin women were "natural-footed."

Conclusion

Written from a mindset of what Ana Maria Candela has called the "habitus of crisis" common to late Qing and Republican intellectuals,[101] Chen Da, with his studies of emigrant communities in South China and the Nanyang, inscribed the *huaqiao* onto the Chinese geobody as elements of beneficial transformation, a contribution to the project of national salvation for a geopolitically beleaguered China. In doing so, Chen produced a gendered and racial formation that overlooked or theorized away differences in order to argue that, in the end:

> As one surveys the totality of the new culture contacts and importations produced by emigration and the return of so many of the emigrants, one can only come to the conclusion that the net result is revolutionary in its implications. Just as the Chinese in the Nanyang have been among the chief carriers of the Republic in its early days, they may be expected to be among the chief carriers of cultural reformation when the time for that is ripe.[102]

This was thus, at its core, a normative project. In inscribing emigrant communities into the Chinese geobody, Chen was sociologically embedding into Chinese scholarship a fantasy about Chineseness that still has enormous contemporary purchase both in its essentialist assumptions about Chinese communities outside China and in its reinforcement of gendered ideologies of the Chinese family. As I have shown in this essay, Chen's travels in the South Seas offered avenues for encounter with difference that he declined to fully pursue. Yet this is not to downplay his significant accomplishments as a social scientist and as a product of what was undoubtedly an era of spectacularly rapid transition: rather, like many intellectuals who inhabit accelerating times, Chen strained valiantly toward the most avant-garde values of the age but would eventually be left behind by them.[103] Still, his notebooks remain exemplary records of his scholarly curiosity as well as of his acuity and passion for research. In places, they contain observations that do more clearly reflect the complex world of social facts that he encountered in the South Seas, which, as my recovery of Lasker's, Hsu's, and other contemporary critiques suggest, Chen might have interpreted differently. One amusing encounter Chen had with French border officials while he was in Indochina is suggestive of the way travel exposed mismatches between his own mental frameworks and those he was encountering in his own short sojourn:

> When I was preparing to leave Saigon, I was required by the shipping company to visit the Asian Immigration Bureau to complete the necessary paperwork. At the bureau, I saw that the Chinese section was divided into five groups [幫 *bang*], namely Hainanese, Cantonese, Teochew, Hakka, and Hokkien. I handed in my

---

101 Candela, "Sociology in Times of Crisis," 363–64.
102 Chen, *Emigrant Communities in South China*, 257.
103 I am grateful to Andrew Hardy and one of the anonymous reviewers for encouraging me to push this point more clearly.

passport and asked the border official: "Which group does my China [我的中國 *wo de Zhongguo*] come under?"[104]

As a sociologist, Chen was frequently modest about what theories could be ascertained from facts and was said to have always insisted that "if you have one set of materials, you can make one set of statements; if you have two sets of materials, you can make two sets of statements; if you have ten sets of material, you can make nine sets of statements, but never eleven of them."[105] Bruno Lasker, in his editorial foreword to *Emigrant Communities in South China*, also says of Chen that "the author modestly abstains from building many theories on the facts he has collected, but he provides social theorists with new, significant data."[106] Yet as I have suggested above, Chen's empirical sociology, in the very act of fact-gathering and social survey, seems to have smuggled in a theory, even an ideational fantasy, of Chineseness from the South that went well beyond mere *guancha* (觀察 empirical observation). Rather, battening their mental hatches against more complex empirical realities, his studies disciplined the heterogeneity of the South Seas into a patriarchal project oriented toward the transformation, improvement, and modernization of the Chinese homeland.

Acknowledgments

I am grateful to Andrew Hardy, Penny Kane, and Saul Dubow for their critical readings of early drafts of this essay, as well as to the participants in conferences on the Chinese diaspora at Nanyang Technological University and Australian National University in 2021, to whose conveners I register my gratitude for the invitations, opportunities to present, and comments. All remaining errors are mine.

Notes on Contributor

Rachel Leow is an associate professor in modern East Asian history at the University of Cambridge. Her first book, *Taming Babel: Language in the Making of Malaysia* (Cambridge: Cambridge University Press, 2016), dwelt on issues of knowledge production, language, ethnicity, and race-making among Malay and Chinese communities in colonial and postcolonial Malaysia. Her new research seeks to outline a critical social and intellectual history of Chinese communities in Southeast Asia and highlights the inadequacy of Sinocentric and "diasporic" perspectives in understanding them.
    Correspondence to: Rachel Leow. Email: rl341@cam.ac.uk.

104 Chen, *Langji shinian*, 152.
105 As quoted in Yuan and Quan, "Shehui xuejia Chen Da," 131.
106 Lasker, editorial foreword to Chen, *Emigrant Communities in South China*, vi.

Part 2
(第二辑)

人力资本跨国流动及其融资网络*

龙登高[1]

摘要

本文考察三种移民及其融资网络：19世纪契约华工、17–18世纪欧洲到美利坚的契约白奴（indentured servants），重点则探讨1980–2010年的福州偷渡客、蛇头与跨国融资网络。三者相互印证，从特殊的移民现象形成一般性的认识。研究发现：跨越国界，移民通常经历了从农民到工人进而到企业主的转换，往往意味着人力资本的边际价值提升。跨洋迁移对普通人来说成本很高，但由于能够催生出特定群体的跨国融资网络创新，促成跨国移民及其人力资本的提升，因而利益相关方都能从中获得可观的回报。也就是说，鲜为人知的民间跨国融资网络，是通过出国移民过程中人力资本的未来收益变现而形成的。这些发现，澄清了以往有关契约华工、偷渡移民的认识误区，原创性地揭示了跨国的民间融资体系的形成及其特征，解释了围绕跨国移民所形成的信贷信用机制与跨国融资网络，也论证了人力资本的跨国实现路径，从而具有其理论贡献。

关键词：偷渡移民 契约华工 人力资本 跨国流动 融资网络

---

* 本文在新加坡南洋理工大学"跨界与连线"国际学术研讨会（2021）、清华大学"货殖论坛 商联天下"（2021）、江门五邑大学国际学术研讨会（2012）发表主旨演讲，中央研究院（台北，2007）发表专场演讲，感谢国内外同仁的交流与讨论。

[1] 龙登高，清华大学经济学研究所，长江学者特聘教授，15811043508，dglong@tsinghua.edu.cn。

Transnational Flows of Human Capital and the Financial Networks

LONG Denggao

Abstract

This paper examines three types of emigration and their financial networks: indentured Chinese from the 19th century and indentured servants from Europe to America in the 17th and 18th centuries, with a focus on undocumented migrants and smugglers from Fuzhou, and their international financial networks from 1980 to 2010s. The three confirm each other and form a general understanding of this particular immigration phenomenon. The study finds that as migrants cross national borders, they often experience a metamorphosis from farmer to worker and then to business owner, which usually entails an increase in the marginal value of human capital. International migration is costly to the average person. However, the costliness can also give rise to a special kind of international financial network for migration, leading to increased human capital and sizable capital gains. In other words, these little-known international financial networks are formed by cashing future earnings of human capital in emigration.

These findings have clarified previous misunderstandings about indentured Chinese and undocumented migrants, creatively revealed the formation and characteristics of international financial systems, explained the credit mechanism and international financial networks formed around transnational immigrants, and demonstrated the transnational realization path of human capital, thus making theoretical contributions.

Keywords: Undocumented Migrants; Indentured Chinese; Human Capital; Transnational Flows; Financial Networks

一、引言

（一）缘起

20世纪80年代至21世纪初，中国沿海福州、温州等地偷渡客不惜债台高筑，屡叩欧美国门，前赴后继，趋之若鹜。国内外媒体与宣传机构，以及很多研究人员，为偷渡客的悲惨遭遇而哀其不幸，怒其不争，为他们受骗上当的非理性选择而困惑不解。中国大陆的媒体，呼吁不要上当受骗；美国的媒体与学者则痛陈偷渡客在唐人街的悲惨生活，揭露他们所受的残酷剥削（邝彼得，2001）。偷渡是痛苦的，甚至不少人间惨剧发生。无论是偷渡过程中的惊心动魄与担惊受怕，还是偷渡成功后艰难困苦与种种非人遭遇[2]。非正规移民从偷渡到异国谋生，他们的悲惨遭遇，国内外媒体的报道不胜枚举。

无独有偶，19世纪投奔怒海，前往东南亚、拉美及美国的契约华工（indentured labor），在华南被称为"卖猪仔"，跨洋长途旅程时有可能葬身海底，在异国他乡工作饱受凌辱，也被认为是受拐骗甚至掳掠。1850–1875年契约华工的记载，都有触目惊心的大量中途死亡数字。1847–1873年中美洲苦力海上死亡率，输入古巴36.84%，秘鲁35.18%，圭亚那30%，巴拿马22.34%。[3] 哈瓦那契约华工，1857年10个国家65艘船，从中国装运23928人，途中死亡3342，平均高达14%。[4]

上当受骗的移民应该是存在的，可是，上当受骗是在信息不对称的情况下发生的，不可能延续数十年。他们对其间的苦难与风险，应该有所了解，也应该有所思想准备。既然如此，他们为什么仍然不畏艰难，前赴后继？在国际机构与美国基金资助下的欧美学者，通过实地调研取得了成果，如陈国霖（Ko-lin Chin. 1999, 2004），邝治中

---

[2] 非法移民历尽艰险，悲剧时有发生。INS（Immigration and Naturalization Service）统计，在美国南部亚利桑那沙漠等地，每年有数百名越境移民死亡，1999–2001年在此被抓获的华人移民达670人。2004年英国莫克姆湾23名捡贝壳人溺水而死，2000年英国多佛港惨剧，58人遇难，1993年美国纽约黄金探险号10人死亡，等等，无不骇人听闻。

[3] 彭家礼《十九世纪西方侵略者对中国劳工的掳掠》，载陈翰笙（1985）。

[4] "英国驻哈瓦那总领事J.T.克劳福致外交大臣文"1857年12月30. 陈翰笙（1985：第2辑160–170页。）

（即邝彼得，Peter Kwong, 1997, 2001），彭轲与朱梅（Frank Pieke and Mette Thuno, 2004; Frank Pieke, 2007）等，从社会学的角度做了一些学理解释，试图澄清媒体的感性认识。不过，由于偷渡客、蛇头及其资金往来，都是地下运作的，缺乏可靠的记载，更没有统计数据，因此其研究成果是有限的。

本文根据美国警方与法院发布的案例、美国政府如国土安全局与报刊公布的调查材料，结合笔者在美国的几次（2003, 2005-2006, 2010, 2018）与福州的实地调研，将偷渡客、契约华工与17-18世纪欧洲的契约白奴（indentured servants）三种移民群体相互印证，用经济学理论分析其通过跨国流动实现人力资本价值的逻辑关系，以及围绕移民形成的跨国融资网络。

（二）人力资本与偷渡客

人力资本与偷渡客、契约奴似乎风马牛不相及。然而，从经济学视角来看，任何人都是一种人力资本载体；人力资本价值的提升，通常是通过教育、培训来实现，但也可以通过跨国流动来实现，而后者往往是被人所忽视的。

一是劳动力或人力资源，通过跨国流动，其边际价值得到改变，多数得到提高。就像一盆水，在江南水乡的边际价值几乎是零，甚至有可能是负数，但在沙漠里，就可能贵如黄金了。中国农民为数甚巨，在农村囿于一亩三分地，其价值几乎趋于零。但跨国流动后就不一样，通常得到大幅度提升。中国城市化率，1978年不足18%，1990年26%，2000年也不过36%，因此农村劳动力总的来说人满为患，国内消化能力有限。新世纪后城市化快速发展，2010年为50%，2020年已高达63%，农民大量转变成市民，农民的边际价值提升，偷渡现象越来越少了。

二是跨国移民后，其能量得到充分释放，人力资本价值得到实现。一个简单的事实是，中国农民的劳动力通常大量闲置，[5] 而在美国唐人街的偷渡客，在中餐馆每天紧张工作12小时。如果说农民到美国后边

---

[5] 农民居家打麻将，买码赌博，非常普遍，农闲季节尤其无所事事。

际价值提升，与之相对照，中国的许多白领、金领移民到美国后，其边际价值多数被降低了，因为英雄无用武之地，其原有的才能在美国得不到发挥。

三是跨国移民的边际价值提升，通常来说，其障碍越大，成本越高，风险越大，其投资收益通常越高。本文所论移民群体，其障碍与风险，可能无出其右。

关于"偷渡"，官方文献中，清朝雍正十二年谕旨已明令打击"人民偷渡外洋"[6]。历代中国政府对人民出境都是严加管制的，至今仍是如此，而偷渡客更是被严厉打击的。[7] 偷渡客属于非正规移民的一种类型，指未经批准而进入他国的人员，也被称为非法的、秘密的、无证件的或非正常的移民（ILO 2004），即所谓非法移民（不被国际组织正式使用）、无证移民、未批准移民等。

20世纪90年代后期以来，美国未获许可的移民每年超过70万人，在绝对数量和增长速度上都超过合法移民。美国国土安全部2006年8月公布的报告显示，非正规移民总数达到1100万，而2000年的数字为850万人，每年增长40.8万。当年华人非正规移民23万，比2000年增加4万。在亚洲国家中，略高于韩国与菲律宾的21万，低于印度的28万[8]。美国非法移民的洪流主要来自墨西哥与中美洲，中国无证移民居于第五位。在美国华人无证移民中，被抓获而后释放的有7.2万名，被明令递解出境而仍留在美国者逾3.9万名（Brian Friel 2006）。在欧盟，2002年提出难民申请的中国人有3675人，在10多万申请者中占不到4%。[9] 2005年

---

[6] 官兵拿获者有赏，"倘不卖力稽查，致疏纵"，则罚。（《光绪大清会典事例》卷623，页2）

[7] 中国出入境边防检查机关对本国公民出境除了要检查护照外，还要仔细检查前往目的国的签证，严格管制本国人员出境，这也是中国不同于其他国家的一个独特的做法。

[8] 专门的移民研究机构Pew Hispanic Center的估计略高，2006年美国的非正规移民高达1200万，其中约12.5%即150万人来自亚洲。华裔占亚裔的23%，约有34.5万人，占全美总数的2.9%。较之1990年的7万人，占总数的2%，都有所增长。

[9] 欧洲时报2004年4月3—5日。

国际劳工组织估计滞留在法国的中国偷渡客人数约为5万。英国边境拦截的非法移民数量，2000–2003年来自中国者居于第五位。[10]

中国虽然拥有世界1/5的人口，但移民与非法移民在世界总量中的比例不大。在非正规移民最盛、人数最多的美国，2000年来自中国者只占1.6%，2006年占2%，同期在欧洲的比例，法国的4%可能是最高的。因此，世纪之初中国非正规移民大约占世界总数的2–3%。2010年以后，源自中国大陆的非正规移民大幅度减少。

二、跨国实现人力资本价值

人力资本在跨国流动中实现其边际价值的提升，从而吸引投资从中获益。偷渡费用高昂，20世纪90年代达四五十万人民币，但这里的关键在于，多数移民并不是在走出去时就已经拥有了如此巨额资金。实际上，移民个体或家庭几乎是无法自我实现，无力支付跨洋船票或偷渡费用的，必须通过金融工具寻求未来收益的变现。他们以跨国移民作为申请理由，先进行借贷，到达目的地后通过在当地的辛勤工作获得此后的工资、收益，并以此分期付款，偿清债务。例如赊单工制度通过签订"卖身"契约，出卖自己4–8年的劳动力乃至人身自由，以还清移民贷款。移民者靠劳动和跨国流动中边际价值提升形成了足够的回报预期与信用保障，使利益相关方看到了其中的人力资本投资回报，于是不断吸引各方资源围绕跨国移民形成投资网络，并在融资网络内生成了信用、信贷机制，实现分期付款，从而发挥跨期调剂的金融功能。

（一）从农民到工人到企业主

"在福州放下锄头，到纽约拿起铲子"，形象反映了跨国流动实现从农民到工人的转变。其人力资本的边际价值，在农民人口众多的

---

[10] 其中申请庇护的人数，2000年4000名，2005年2365名。英国每日电讯报2006年1月3日。

中国，几乎趋近于零。到纽约变成工人，在低端劳动力稀缺的美国，其边际价值大幅提升，体现于其收入水平的强烈反差。

1993年部分移民工作量与收入，115个餐馆工人，每周工作72小时，月薪1520美元。制衣厂工人（通常是女工），每周工作70小时，月薪1252美元。其他工种更高一些。非法移民所获工资，高于联邦规定的最低工资线（陈国霖，1999：230）。相比较而言，当年福建省人均GDP低于全国平均水平，为3556元人民币，约为440美元。城镇居民可支配收入2922.93元，约当340美元；农村居民纯收入1210.51元，仅当约140美元。[11] 这意味着，福州农民如果能够在纽约就业，1993年其收入陡增数十倍，甚至接近百倍。[12]

另一方面，农民的人力资本在农村是闲置的，因为福州农民人均不足1亩地，无活可干，即使在地里绣花一样精耕细作，人力资本的天花板仍很无法突破。农民只有走向市民化，从事工业与服务业，其人力资本价值才能得到释放。但八九十年代中国城市化率还非常低，跨国移民却能实现从农民到工人的转变，实现人力资价值的提升。而美国经济对底层劳动力的需求很大，约1200万非正规移民，正是市场所需要的劳工。

并非被欺骗而偷渡。法国的非法移民受审时，法官总会问："遣送回国，或蹲监狱三个月，你可以选择"，回答都是千篇一律的，"我不愿意回国"（www.panoeu.com）。显然他们不是被蛇头骗来的。像黄金探险号[13]中99名被遣返的偷渡客，60人又通过非法途径返回美国，有的屡次三番偷渡。为了实现人力资本，不少偷渡客九死一生，锲而不舍。Li入狱两年后被遣返，回到中国被殴打、罚款、强迫结扎。他无力偿还偷渡费，因为欠钱被亲友看不起，1年后，他背负5万美金欠款，再次来到美国。他不断地在美国各地的中餐馆间流浪打工。长乐

---

[11] 2020年福州城镇非私营单位就业人员年平均工资为93513元，约当1.3万美元。与二三十年前可谓天壤之别。

[12] 相当一部分偷渡客，在福州是青年市民，但移民前后的收入差别，基本上也与农民类似。

[13] 同情黄金探险号非法移民的美国人专门制作了纪录片，开设了网站www.goldenventuremovie.com，本文所引材料皆出自此网站。

人Kaiqu Zheng，1990年他搭机偷渡来美，被海关怀疑是恐怖分子，原机遣返。1993年搭上黄金探险号，坐了两年牢后，面对遥遥无期的自由，他自愿被遣返。不久，他又搭飞机回来，但假护照被识破，第三度被遣返，可谓锲而不舍。

（二）获得自由后的未来预期收益

偷渡客的参照对象，不是美国人，而是祖籍地乡亲。相对于美国合法的华侨华人更不用说美国公民来说，4年非法打工期间的确可以说是悲惨的，但相对于在家乡的农民来说，一旦偷渡成功，他们获得的工资是很有吸引力的。更重要的是，4年后获得自由的生存与发展，其普遍性是家乡农民所不具备的。

1. 4年后偷渡客通常走出纽约唐人街，在外州开店，成为店主，有房有车。美国4万家中餐馆，无处不在，大多都是福州人所开设的。
2. 其下一代在美国接受良好的基础教育，进而多能在名校上大学。美国重视基础教育，即使是偷渡客的孩子，中小学都是一视同仁。在国内城市打工，他们的孩子却大多成为留守儿童，与父母分离。
3. 通过大赦、或不同州的规定，可能获得正式身份，从而能够带动亲属移民；这种连锁移民，使之能获得对人力资本投资的收益。农民如果在国内打工，即使一二十年，也不可能获得大城市户口。
4. 移民省吃俭用，回老家盖豪宅，光宗耀祖。有的甚至成为新一代爱国侨领，衣锦还乡。历经千辛万苦，此类移民反而比一般人更加怀念和家乡，具有强烈的中华情。

媒体总是大力宣传并苦口婆心地劝告人们不要上蛇头的当[14]，然而侨乡对美国同乡的信息其实有足够多的了解，在信息充分的条件下，通

---

[14] 主管官员说，各级政府结合多佛尔港惨案、金色冒险号事件等等例子，召开群众大会，开展偷渡人员家属座谈会，向不了解实情的群众揭露"蛇头"的骗术和罪行。

常能够做出理性的选择。否则不可能解释二十多年来福州前赴后继的偷渡热，不可能解释九死一生之后，仍然有那么多人屡次三番进行偷渡，不可能解释福州侨乡拔地而起的一座座豪宅，也不可能解释几十万福州人到了美国，福州人的餐馆逐渐遍布美国。

以偷渡英国为例，偷渡成功并找到工作后，一般每月省吃俭用可寄回家上万元。平潭村村都有不少人到国外打洋工、打黑工，大约有七成左右的人能够在国外赚到钱，多的一年十几万元，少的也有几万。大致而言，六七成的偷渡客能够赚钱是可信的，偷渡集中地长乐与福清等地兴起的豪宅与寄回的汇款可以说明。世纪之交，长乐人一年合计从境外汇回来的资金达到30多亿元人民币。[15]

在陈国霖（1999：249）的300个访谈对象中，有190人即64%的移民打算永久留在美国，85人即29%的人想赚到足够的钱后回到中国。一名长乐人说，"自我来这儿后，我的家就变得富有了。我的父母很幸福，因为受到别人的尊敬。"一名来自闽侯的移民说，在美国非常辛苦，但"为了成功，就必须忍受这一切。我相信来这儿的决定是对的"。一名21岁的长乐人说，"我想我来美国的决定没错，因为这儿有很多赚钱的机会。尽管要吃很多苦，但只需工作几年就能还清债务，还清后我就可以存钱。如果呆在中国，我这一辈子又能赚多少钱呢？我将根本没有翻身的机会。"

在美国的偷渡移民，假如偷渡费5万美元，借款2万，每年还款1万，4年还清债务。此后，他的选择空间更大，收入也会增加，他可以帮忙或担保，让自己的妻子或亲戚过来。一个受访对象就是这样，妻子到美国后，两个人打工，很快就小有积蓄，4年后从曼哈顿迁至康涅狄克州纽黑文市，买房子与车子，开餐馆。他们还有两个孩子，都在美国享受高质量的义务教育，摆脱了中国高考的激烈竞争，节省了许多中国孩子所需要的高昂留学费用。

"去拼搏赚钱"是他们压倒一切的动机，而不是去享受西方福利，他们对迁移过程中的成本与风险，都有足够的估计。正如彭轲与朱梅等

---

[15] 瞭望东方周刊2005-1-23。

的研究结论：他们是"一群希望靠自身的力量寻找就业机会、赚钱致富的移民。"（Frank Pieke and Mette Thuno, 2004）"翻身"的机会对留在原居地的农民来说不具备普遍性。著名的偷渡源地长乐的一个偏僻乡镇，有4个"先富裕起来"的朋友，到2003年笔者调研时，3个留在国内的都处境平常，没有进一步富起来，唯有这个偷渡美国者，经历几年艰辛之后，在美国有房有车，还开了一家餐馆，两个孩子在美国读书——被乡亲视为成功者。

（三）成本、机会成本与风险

偷渡客在家乡盖漂亮房子，每年有钱寄回家赡养老小，为此他可以忍受任何苦难。许多不久后在美国买房子买汽车，开餐馆，有可能在8–10年之内全家彻底翻身，如此，还有什么不能承受之苦？还有什么风险不能承担？

偷渡客的确付出了很高的机会成本。就工作压力、生活的安逸来说，其实通常比不上在家乡，在老家至少是温饱的，或者是小康的，个别甚至是优裕的生活。一些偷渡客表示失望，大多数怀念家乡生活，甚至后悔当初的决定。但现实给予的选择是有限的，无奈的，也是残酷的。他们不甘心于世世代代的贫穷，希望改变现状，不惜代价。已经度过了悲惨岁月的一个访谈对象，实现了美国梦，但仍不满。有些失落地说，"其实这么辛苦为了什么呢，整天工作，没有休息与娱乐，还不如在家呢"。当他们这么说的时候，既有一种无奈与不满，也包含着一种成功人士的困惑。许多在奋斗中有所失去的成功人士，就像许多华人专业人士，他们在美国成家立业，但也失去了在中国飞黄腾达的机会，也难免产生"好山好水好寂寞"的惆怅。

事实上，无论他身在何处，要实现其人力资本价值，哪一个农民不需要经历凤凰涅槃呢？即使出国留学——另一类人力资本投资者，哪一个学子不经过4–9年炼狱般的洗礼呢？有的要痛割机会成本，或者要忍受家庭分离，忍受文化孤寂。

关于风险，主要是来自于出境与入境。在中国，偷渡与非正规移民，被视为犯罪而严加打击的，不遗余力。当偷渡者在出国之时被截获，被遣返或被引渡回国，执法人员都视之为犯罪分子。

在美国及欧洲，偷渡客即使被抓获，仍可生存下去，极个别才被遣返。或者可以钻法律的空子，以各种理由在美国打三年官司，期间可名正言顺地打工，从而赚到足够的收益来还清债务并有所补偿。至于美国金色号惨剧、伦敦拾贝惨剧，在他们看来，其概率可能就像交通事故一样，那是天命之所属，几乎不能归入风险来考虑的。当记者充满同情地采访福州乡亲看到这些惨剧有何感想时，乡亲居然满不在乎地告诉他："以前都没有过，别人都没事。"面对这种小概率的大事件，人们通常都怀有侥幸心理。

黄金探险号的偷渡客中，目前总共220名在美国，在现存270人中，占81.5%。在拉美避难者与回到中国者只有38名，仅占14%。有171名通过各种途径获得释放、庇护或其他身份，占现存总数270人中的63%。如果再加上后来又返回美国的60人，则占总数的85.5%[16]。他们遍布美国各地，大多数人在自己的或他人的中餐馆工作。许多已经结婚，在美国生儿育女。只有少数人成为美国公民。大多数由于没有合法身份，他们14年没有见过家乡的家人了，包括配偶与孩子。因为没有身份，他们被雇佣而遭受虐待，工资远远低于政府规定的最低水平与社会平均水平（Jeffrey. S Passel. 2006），甚至被拖欠、扣留。他们没有福利与保险，一旦生病或工伤，则无所依靠[17]。但偷渡客通常是与老家的乡亲们比较，只有他们的下一代才与美国人进行比较。

但对于中国农民而言，只要有途径改变自身的命运，任何苦难都不畏惧，因为这种途径实在太少了。正如平潭县一名立志出国打工青年

---

[16] 死亡与失踪16名，占船上总数286名的5.6%。14人未成年而获释。2人得到艺术家签证，35人得到政治庇护，12人通过梵蒂冈在拉美获得政治避难。55人交保获释。53人得到特赦，非合法身份。当时遣返99名，60人重回美国。

[17] 他们长期与家庭分离，夫妻分离有的长达6-7年，家庭危机也在所难免。在美国华人网上论坛上，有一名曾漂泊唐人街的穷秀才，曾流落街头，被好心的制衣工移民接纳在他们合住的地下室里度过一夜，他发现，简陋的地下室里，充斥着三级片录像。

所说："人活一世，就得拼搏，男人可以去冒险，甚至是生命危险，但不能穷，只有最没本事的人才在家里受穷。"因此，"等筹到资金，我就马上去英国打工赚钱。"梦想有朝一日能出国挣大钱，从根本上改变自己的穷日子，无疑是许多平潭青年男子，乃至不少普通中国年轻人追求的人生目标。平潭一名干部说，"出国打工几乎是每一个普通平潭男子的梦想。"如能干的林斌，在家过得也不是很差。但林斌说他要赚大钱，盖新房子，还想做华侨成为富翁，让家里人在村里能抬起头来（瞭望东方周刊，2005-1-23）。问题不在于实现人力资本所付出的代价的高低，而在于是否存在实现人力资本的途径。

（四）市场需求与社会容忍：欧美如何对待偷渡客

市场对底层劳工的需求很大，因此美国很多时候在事实上默许偷渡客。这些非正规移民，只要不犯罪，基本上就可以在美国生存下去。遇到大赦，或通过各州不同的制度与政策，有可能获得美国身份。来自中国的偷渡客，不少以计划生育不让生孩子的理由，申请难民身份。在英国，对未成年偷渡客的宽容态度，连留学生翻译都羡慕其待遇。更重要的是，非正规移民在欧美有就业机会，可获得生存与发展机会。彭轲、朱梅（Frank Pieke, Mette Thuno. 2004）等的研究表明，非正规移民之所以屡禁不绝，根本原因在于欧洲存在就业机会。

偷渡客通常被冠以非法移民，欧美却不乏同情之声与辩解之言。David Kyle, Zai Liang (2001)认为，不能把偷渡进程各个阶段中的人物与行为一律视为犯罪或邪恶。Frank Pieke, Mette Thuno (2004)等认为作为商业操作过程的跨国迁移，不一定是犯罪性活动。无证移民国际合作平台（PICUM）对欧洲的情况做出了如下总结："居住在欧洲的无证移民被排除在社会以外，并且在面对边缘化的情况时极度脆弱。欧洲需要并正在使用无证移民，但同时又不愿对他们所做出的贡献给予任何奖励。无证移民在许多方面受到打击，包括在接受基本的社会服务方面受到阻挠。值得警惕的是，现已出现了一种趋势，即将无证移民本身视为罪犯并对公民和民间组织为他们提供社会和人道主义的援助进行惩处的趋势"（ILO 2004）。

在具有移民传统的美国，偷渡客与无证移民受到广泛的同情。1993年黄金探险号惨案，当时的纽约市长David Dinkins曾信誓旦旦："这些人来美国寻找自由，我一定会让他们成为公民。"3年后，当地的居民组成声援团体，每周在监狱外集会，藉歌声表示抗议。有人定期探视被羁押的偷渡客，由义务律师为其上诉，并派代表至华府游说。专门的黄金探险号网站，收集和整理了轮船上移民的文字与影视资料，为之鸣不平。各国无证移民，也大张旗鼓地走上街头，要求自己的利益。2006年4–5月，美国各州数百个城市数百万人游行，声援无证移民，要求修改移民法。仅4月10日，全美39个州约149个城市近200万民众举行了声势浩大的游行，要求为无证移民寻求出路，给予合法身份。2007年美国总统也力图通过新移民法解决身份问题，奥巴马实行大赦。2020年新冠疫情期间，来自拉美的非正规移民还在游行，争取其正当权益。

美国移民局的官员并不痛恨偷渡者，但他们憎恶蛇头，还有那些做假的律师。法国有的法官同情非法移民，在非法移民等待遣送的12天中，有的就被释放出来。只有20%的非法移民最终被驱逐，80%的人由于各种不同的原因留了下来（韦尔，2002）。美国联邦与各州的许多法律都在一定程度上保护无证移民。[18] 非正规移民因为没有证件，生活有许多不便，通常也不能享受美国的福利。《华尔街杂志》有一则报道，2002年上半年，纽约政府为911之后失业工人提供培训项目，前3个月约350人前往签到，其中300人因为无证件而不合格（Mei Fong，2002）。联邦与许多州为无证移民提供了一些便利和基本生存条件。如1996–2002年美国税务局累计给出的纳税号码高达680万个。这一号码可以在当地税务局拿到，有的地方甚至可以通过同税务局挂钩的教会和当地居民的社区活动中心申请这一号码。他们绝大多数都是无证移民。纳税对于无证移民转合法身份时有所帮助，还可以帮助这些人在一些州开设银行账户，考驾照等。税务资料是独立的，美国法律禁止税务当局同联邦移民官分享纳税人的资料，不会成为移民官遣返非法入境者的证据。

---

[18] 直到2006年7月，联邦法律才开始实施，医疗补助受益人需提供合法身份证明，以保证非法移民不能得到美国纳税人所资助的任何医疗好处。

20世纪60年代以前，美国基本上是一个自由移民的国家。在"国家"的名义下，保护既得利益者，反对自由选择，是对人权的违背。美国人、媒体、议会、政府，对非法移民的问题众说纷纭。墨西哥进入美国的非法移民如潮水一般，达七八百万。但当美国讨论移民法修改时，墨西哥政府表达自己的立场，不是如何加强对墨西哥本国进行人口流动的管制，而是旗帜鲜明地要求保护无证移民，甚至反对美国在边境修筑长城。

三、利益关联方与人力资本的跨国投资

不惜重金仍要冒险出国受洋罪，这里的关键是，偷渡客并非已经有40万人民币的资金，而是通过移民生成信贷创造出来的！或者说，各利益相关方围绕偷渡移民进行人力资本的投资，形成了跨国融资网络，形成了金融工具创新，福州农民获得了信贷渠道，能够将人力资本未来收益变现。相反，如果没有跨国移民，就不可能形成跨国融资网络，就不可能生成信用与信贷。

（一）融资方式：借贷与分期付款

1. 借钱首付

偷渡伊始，需先期支付给蛇头一笔钱，相当于首付。这笔钱只是移民总费用的一部分，但对八九十年代的福州农民来说，鲜有人能够通过存款积累，即使省吃俭用勒紧裤带存钱，那也将遥遥无期。通常以如下三种形式完成首付。一是亲友借贷，二是合会（Financial rotating association）[19]的形式筹集，[20] 三是民间放贷，其中不乏高利贷。

在八九十年代的福州，只要偷渡，通常就能获得借贷。求学或经商，则很难借到钱，因为经商的风险太高，求学的还款期太长，而且

---

[19] 合会是侨乡和海外华人社会普遍的融资模式，宋代就有明确记载（龙登高2007）。通过互助实现"跨期调剂"，如今却被视为所谓"非法集资"。

[20] 据福州大学苏文菁教授的调研。

二者也缺乏成熟的信用机制与融资体系。在长乐、连江等地，甚至获得民间借贷的途径，唯有偷渡。"借钱做生意没人肯借，如果是出国打工，只要你愿意去借钱，不愁借不到，当然要利息。"[21] 在福清一些"偷渡文化"高度成型的村落里，要做点小买卖，大家是不信任你、甚至不怎么瞧得起你的，你当然也借不到一分钱。而当你鼓起勇气要"出去"，即使你昨天还不名一文，背着一屁股烂债，也很快就会有人愿意资助（借）你十几万[22]。做生意有风险，一旦亏本，投资付之东流。放高利贷也是如此，如果不能确信你具有偿还能力，谁也不会放贷出去。由此可见，无论是借钱的亲友，还是放高利贷者，都对出国移民的投资回报具有信心。

借贷，实质上就是未来收益变现。也就借助第三方实现"跨期调剂"，这就是金融的本质。

2. 担保与分期付款

唐人街老板为偷渡客担保，首付之后，有此担保即可启动旅程。到达目的地之后，据说第二天就在中餐馆或车衣厂上班，通常就是担保人的店铺。老板群体有时分为总担保人与分担保人，几天内向蛇头交清偷渡款。偷渡客则通过为老板打工，每月从工资中扣款，分期付款偿清债务，包括唐人街老板的垫付资金和在家乡的欠款。

偷渡客通常由老板包食宿，加之极端节衣省食，因此他们几乎没有消费开支。如果第一年非熟练工月薪1000美元，第二年以后作为熟练工可达1500美元，几乎可全部用于分期付款还债，通常3-4年左右就可以还清债务。当然食宿条件是极差的，甚至唐人街地下室的一个床位三个人轮流睡，每人8小时。唐人街人满为患，卫生条件可称恶劣，污水横流，垃圾遍地。

---

[21] 瞭望东方周刊，2005-1-23。
[22] 《访福清偷渡现象：40岁以下的男子大多走光了》，http://cn.news.yahoo.com/2004-02-18

跨国网络内的人际信用（详后）是担保品，比如亲友借贷，唐人街老板担保，信贷的基础是信用与偿还能力，如此形成信贷与分期付款的融资方式。

3. 专业化的地下跨国金融机构

由于移民的增多，与国内联系的密切，也包括偷渡"业务"的扩大，跨国金融网络逐渐走向专业化，专门从事放贷的民间金融机构形成，为新移民与偷渡客提供跨国金融服务，从中获利。具体来说，蛇头群体中开始出现分工，有蛇头专营放贷，郑翠萍在曼哈顿的钱庄业务日益红火。一方面是因为其良好的信用，这是金融机构的生命线，另一方面，则是其经营跨国汇兑，是当时正规银行所做不到的服务。在纽约钱庄存入美元，第二天在福州的乡下亲友就可以取到人民币。

这种跨国金融业务，在闽粤侨乡源远流长，最初的侨批水客，到专业的侨信局，成为连接侨乡与海外乡亲的金融纽带。（Liu Hong, Gregor Benton, 2018）

（二）围绕偷渡客人力资本而形成利益共同体与投资网络

在这一跨国金融网络中，各利益相关方形成共同体，蛇头、唐人街老板、侨乡放贷客都获得投资机会，通过对偷渡客人力资本的投资而获益。

唐人街老板获得廉价的劳动力，中餐馆与车衣厂得到持续发展。其中的车衣厂，面临来自中国制造价廉物美的竞争仍能延续一时。它与珠三角的订单生产如出一辙，实际上是将中国廉价劳动力的优势，通过偷渡从东南沿海转移到美国唐人街，其优势是节省了跨洋运输费用。

蛇头是偷渡的组织者，通常是一个群体，来自国内和国外。在媒体上蛇头大多是面目狰狞的，事实上，他们就是地下的跨国移民中介，从中获取收益。平潭中介郑先生说，顾客送不到目的地，他就得赔付所有的费用，这个风险就得由他承担，风险这么高，他送走一个人也只能挣几千元。市场竞争所致，"因为做的人太多，赚高了你没地方赚。"[23] 在陈国霖（1999: 234）的访谈对象中，逾50%以上的移民都说他们没有借钱支付预押金，但90%的在美国开始找工作时身负债务。其中62%需要请求在中国的亲戚帮助，55.7%得到了美国亲戚的援助，20%是在美国和中国的朋友资助下来到美国的。在105名已经还清走私费的移民中，他们平均花了26个月，即2年多的时间。

蛇头在侨乡与唐人街多是具有信誉的"侨领"。郑翠萍长期经营跨境偷渡，供不应求，在家乡门庭若市，排起长队报名，据说有妇女从队列人群的胯下挤进去，希望为丈夫获得偷渡机会。蛇头往往是一个群体，高峰时租用轮船跨洋运输，其中金色探险号功亏一篑。郑翠萍被抓获，美国警方如获至宝，以为抓到一个贩卖人口的黑社会集团。然而，偷渡各方是一个市场联结的网络，金色探险号从中国沿海，到泰国经非洲肯尼亚，分别接上那里的偷渡客，远渡重洋到达纽约外海上。最后一环是高难度的接驳环节，由于承接者越南华人渔民发生内讧，失约不能前来，乘客无法从轮船转移到小船来上岸，以致发生惨案。郑翠萍与其他环节的蛇头都是交易关系，而不是指令关系，并非黑社会集团。郑翠萍在纽约唐人街与家乡都富有声誉，以致在纽约审判时，乡亲们纷纷向法院发来陈情书，声称她是一个好人，一个善良的人。[24]

投资回报的持续与增长，源于华人族群在美国经济中的扩展（详后）。有学者认为，老移民挤压新客，老板剥削非法移民，因此偷渡移民不可能成功，这种现象的确是存在的。但只是问题的一个方面，其假设前提之一，就是族群经济为一个固定函数，就像一块蛋糕，老板或老移民多切一点，新客与无证移民就会少一点。然而，问题的另一方面是，他们不仅在分蛋糕，更重要的是在制造更大的蛋糕。新移民来得多了，中餐馆就会增多。假设一个大厨先后担保了5个乡亲赴美，不久他们6个乡亲就能开一家新的中餐馆或外卖店，大厨成为老板，新移民成为大厨。以此类推，像滚雪球一样越来越大，遍布美国的福州人中餐馆就是如此形成的。亲友移民链越来越长，乡亲在美国的发展

---

[23] CCTV经济半小时 2004-4-21
[24] 被美国警方称之为"蛇头"之母的萍姐（Sister Ping, Cheung Chui Ping），在福州亭江与纽约唐人街都素有口碑（Patrick Radden Keefe, 2006）。

空间越来越大。因此，虽然老移民多切了一点，但新移民也能分得一份，也能逐渐增加，因为族群经济具有自我增生的机制。因为有了一定的资本积累，这些利益共同体能够创造更高的价值，获取更大的收益，也能应付更高的偷渡费。

老移民与新客，老板与无证移民，他们形成了一个利益共同体，从偷渡客的人力资本实现中获取各自的利益与价值增殖。邝教授自己也谈到，那些先来者利用后来者劳动力，在餐馆与车衣厂发了财。逻辑上正是如此，持续的新客，虽然会给先来者带来压力，却为还清债务开办新餐馆或走出唐人街的先来者提供了劳动力或合作伙伴。而先来者，通过提携后来者，自己也得利。十年或几年之后，后来者（新客）就会成为先来者，如此类推。

（三）信用与信贷的生成

在跨国金融网络的形成过程中，利益相关方的博弈下，同时逐渐生成了信用与信贷机制。对于偷渡客而言，在这一网络内获得信贷机会，即以第三方为担保的借款，或者说，将人力资本的未来收益变现获得融资。

由于这一跨国网络的特定性，第三方担保的特定性，这一信贷机制具有较高的门槛。在八九十年代的长乐农村等地，信用制度缺失，正规信贷机制尚未生成，这几乎成为普通人获得融资机会的"唯一"途径。就像最近20年，中国普通人获得信贷的机会，就一般意义而言，唯有信贷购房。简单来说，平常百姓只有信贷购房时才能从银行借到钱，除此之外，经商、投资、求学都不可能。这是因为，购房信贷机制已经较为成熟，自20世纪20年代从美国形成以来经过不断试错与改善，形成了银行、消费者、投资者、房利美与房地美、政府等各利益相关方之间的信贷机制。可见信贷工具的形成是非常不容易的。

这一地下跨国金融网络中所生成的信贷机制，其基础有二：

一是具备偿还能力。对偷渡客而言，以出国移民与打工为预期而筹集到资金，从而为自己创造获得更高收入的条件，这是一种人力资本变现。偷渡客人力资本的投资，不仅仅是其个人行为，因为他的投资来自于家人与国内外亲友。如果没有足够的回报预期与信用保障，乡亲们通常都不会借你几万、十几万，无论是做生意，还是读书，他们不会借钱给你。亲友关系并不能替代投资回报，主要作为信息纽带，也可成为信用纽带，但亲友信用是一柄双面刃[25]。只有在出国赚大钱的预期之下，他们才会借钱给你，你的人力资本才有机会得以变现。

二是网络内的人际信用。利益关联方形成的网络，具有约束机制（龙登高，2019），如果违约，就会受到惩罚。人际信用为纽带的网络，其边界是有限的，不具备拓展性。因此，蛇头与偷渡客网络，局限于福州地区，尤其是长乐、连江、福清等县。该地区之外，人际信用与网络约束机制就难以发挥作用。其他地区民众，无法利用这一人际信用基础上的金融网络来争取信贷。

（四）族群经济的扩展力

邝治中的一个有名的观点是，机会就像一个漏斗，越来越窄。主要是指族群经济发展前景有限，既不能容纳更多的移民，也不能给移民创造更好的前景。他说，如果移民一个月存1000美元，或许可以与他人合伙开一家快餐外卖店。但此时环顾周围，在曼哈顿，每个街区有两家福建人外卖店，他们正在彼此竞争相互残杀呢。中餐业因竞争激烈而彼此厮杀，给新移民留下的空间极小。如果囿于狭小的唐人街，的确是这样，中餐馆与制衣厂都趋于饱和，劳工饱和，市场饱和。但是，新移民以此为栖身跳板，而原来的非法移民合法化或赚钱之后大多选择离开唐人街，原有的餐馆业主可能改行，或抓住了新涌现出来的机会，转向其他行业或其他地区。唐人街与华人社会涌现出新的行业、新的需求、新的机会，会把移民由此引向更广阔的天地。（龙登高2007第四章）

---

[25] 宋人袁采《袁氏家训》就告诫子孙，亲友之间不可随便发生借贷关系，因为穷亲戚还钱不是一件容易的事。与其借一大笔，还不如干脆送一小笔钱作为礼物。把借贷关系与亲情区分开来，各有不同的分寸与应对之策。

另一方面，如果移民的前途除了所谓主流化之外别无他途，那当然在唐人街里也不可能有出路。但如果把美国视为一个多元化共同发展的经济体，就可以发现唐人街经济能够吸纳、消化移民，并有助于新移民在美国立足和发展。在这一点上，周敏（Zhou Min, 2005）的观点给人启发。如果把族群经济、劳动市场、就业市场视为固定不变的函数，那当然涌入的移民越多，机会就越少。然而，族群经济虽然在美国是作为边缘经济的存在，但仍具有自我扩张的能力。而且能够自我生成出新的市场机会，华人大巴就是华商抓住利基实现商业创新，形成城际直达大巴新行业的典型。（Long Denggao, 2014）

由此看来，可以把邝教授的"漏斗"倒过来，移民从一个狭小的漏斗口进入时，付出极高的代价，历尽艰辛，几年后从较大的漏斗口出来，他们会面临越来越宽广的机会与发展空间。事实上，这些移民的前辈，也是这么走过来的，所经历的苦难，有过之而无不及。没有百年前20世纪初华盛顿州州长家里的台山佣人，就没有骆加辉这位21世纪初的华盛顿州的华人州长。台山人马万昌（丁龙，1857–1936），就是19世纪后期的契约华工，获得自由后勤俭谋生，1901年将全部积蓄12000美元的巨款，捐给了哥伦比亚大学开设中国文化讲座。

四、历史上的契约华工与契约白奴

八九十年代的偷渡网络，主要集中于福州与温州两地。福州移民主要面向美国及日本等地，温州移民主要面向欧洲，及通过非洲移民欧洲。如今偷渡现象已经很少见了，这两个地区已经转型升级，成为经济发达地区，2020年福清成为中国工业百强县（市）第17位，长乐跻身中国工业百强区第55位。温州商人群体、福清商人群体已经形成国内外富有影响力的跨国商人网络，其中包括不少人由偷渡客转变为企业家。

如果回溯历史，19世纪中国沿海地区曾经形成跨国移民网络，而且与偷渡移民颇相类似的机制，只不过那时不需要偷渡，而是高昂的船票，那时跨洋航运的成本极高。这就是上百万的契约华工，尤以闽南地区、广东地区较为突出。

（一）19世纪的契约华工（Indentured labor）

偷渡客可以说签定的是一定期限的"卖身契约"，这与历史上的契约华工与契约白奴本质上是相通的。

19世纪的契约华工，类似的名称还有苦力（Coolie）、卖猪仔、及赊单工等。18世纪末，东印度公司开始在中国招募契约华工，1813年公司的垄断地位被打破，尤其是1857年东印度公司垄断特许权被取消后，不少洋行卷入其中。厦门德记行，1845年英国人德滴创建于厦门，渣打银行、大英火轮船公司等的代理。[26] 厦门契约劳工交易，主要由德记洋行、合记洋行包揽了厦门及附近地区的苦力买卖。

英国在1833年废除了加勒比海殖民地的奴隶制。1845年5月30日，第一艘满载印度契约劳工移民的船只从加尔各答抵达加勒比海上的特立尼达岛，[27] 契约华工也逐渐增多。但19世纪前期国内外都缺乏跨国劳工的法律和政策规范，因此乱象丛生，惨剧不断。1860年英法与清政府签订了北京《续增条约》，其中第五款："凡中国子民愿在英国各属或外洋别地承工者，大清国大皇帝准其按照两国议定之保工章程，与英民立约为凭……"。从此，中国民众可以跨国就业和移民，英法等国商人在中国沿海各城市设站开馆，公开招工。1800–1900年估计契约华工数达235万人，如表1所示。从18世纪到20世纪初，出国契约华工约300万人。[28]

契约华工之所以被称为"猪仔"，林则徐道出其缘由："当其在船时，皆以木盆盛饭，呼此等搭船者一同就食。其呼声与内陆呼猪相似，故人目此船为卖猪仔。"秘鲁和古巴形成了公开的"猪仔"拍卖市场。秘鲁和古巴拍卖华工的时候，剥光衣服排列成行，任凭顾主们看是否健

---

[26] 塞舌尔 包罗《厦门》）（刘瑞光 2020《由大德记引出的清末华工血泪史》鹭客社 2020-7

[27] Lucy Dow, Gale Review Blog 2021.12.02.

[28] 王启民，契约华工制的历史分期问题 [J]. 福建师大学报（哲学社会科学版），1982(01):95–101。

壮有力,担得起粗重劳动[29]。特立尼达岛和圭亚那有专为扣留到岸猪仔等待主顾选购的场所。20世纪初,锡矿和种植烟叶、橡胶事业的发展,东南亚吸收了大量的契约华工,马来亚是由买主在进口船上或岸上的猪仔行中挑选。1914年,马来亚禁止了契约工制度[30]。印尼金光集团创始人黄奕聪的父亲,就曾经是契约华工。[31]

表1:1800–1900年契约华工出国人数估计

	1800–1850		1850–1875		1875–1900	
	人数	年均	人数	年均	人数	年均
美洲	60000	1200	535000	21000	21000	840
美国	18000	360	160000	6400	12000	480
东南亚	200000	4000	645000	25800	700000	28000
澳洲	10000	200	60000	2400	8000	320
合计	320000	6400	1280000	51200	750000	30000

注:据陈泽宪《十九世纪盛行的契约华工制》估计表(历史研究1963年第1期)

1. 出国旅费资金垫付与分期付款

跨洋运输耗时长,成本高。1852年从厦门经好望角到西印度群岛,风帆船约100–130天,每人运费10英磅15先令6便士,折合银70元。[32] 如此昂贵的旅费,是一般民众所无力承担的,具有此财力的富人则不会冒险移民。

---

[29] 《古巴华工事务各节》第1册第7页"林阿榜等二人供,凡到夏湾拿上岸进卖人行,来买的人都要脱去周身衣服,看有无气力,与买牛马无异。
[30] 李长傅:《南洋华侨史》,第49页;P. C. Campbell《Chinese Coolie Emigration》第22–25页;H. F. MacNair <The Chinese Abroad> 第4章,第5节;J. W. Jenks《The Immigration Problem》第30–46页。
[31] 笔者对金光集团董事长黄志源的专访谈,2015,雅加达。
[32] 上海领事阿礼国致港督包令的报告,1852年9月1日,陈翰笙(1980,第2辑:页23–28)。

因此，通常由中介机构洋行先期垫付旅费，并预付华工约12元，以吸引移民。旅费很高，如1890年前往夏威夷的船票需要54美元。当然这些开销都需要移民工作之后，从工资中逐月扣除。所以垫付资金使华工的未来收益在移民前即可变现。

美国等地的"赊单工"制度以契约规定了华人与雇主之间的债权债务关系，华工须对移民中介负担服劳役的义务。[33] 1876年美国加利福尼亚州议会的调查报告 Chinese Immigration Testimony before the Committee of the Senate of California 记载了前美国驻华公使楼斐迪（F. L. Low）的发言"我们知道中央太平洋铁路公司，通过经纪人招雇成千苦力。他们预付一笔款子作为旅运费，以后再从工作中加利取偿。他们的合同内只简单地提到必须偿还垫付的船票，另加足够的红利，以抵补利息，按月5元或105角"。[34]

1890年夏威夷的华工契约规定：雇工"已在雇主所付旅费、衣食费共54美元的账单上签字"。"如果雇工勤勤恳恳工作3年，从中国赴夏威夷所欠旅费及其他用费共54元，即可一笔勾销。"如未满3年离职，54美元须偿还雇主。

除了旅费外，还有预付款，大约12元，部分留给移民的家属，部分作为移民必要的随身资金。咸丰5年林先前往夏华拿（哈瓦那），"立合同人林先"："今言明收到现银及衣服等共银十二元，到夏华拿照第7款交还。"这12元由"代办人"支付，工作后从工银逐月扣除。"代办人"类似于洋行的买办，收到分期付款，当然是从跨国银行、或洋行中获取。

跨国移民网络，各环节有不同国家与地区的中介机构。他们都是人力资本的投资方，各自获得投资回报。代办人付给猪仔12元，洋行付给客头20-30元，洋行从船主或受货人代表得60-75元（朱国宏，1994）。船主运抵后所获应该更高。

---

[33] 陈泽宪，十九世纪盛行的契约华工制[J]. 历史研究，1963(01):161-179。
[34] 见陈兰彬《使美纪略》，第3卷，59页；Otis Gibson《The Chinese in American》pp. 60-62.

2. 跨国移民网络与信用

离乡背井，跨洋移民，风险很大，不确定性很高，这对安土重迁的中国农民来说是一件不容易的决策。因此，洋行等中介及其代理、外国领事，都千方百计试图打动农民，消除其顾虑。除了天花乱坠，夸大其辞，甚至诱惑拐骗之外，也采取措施树立信用，以其长期吸引移民。

1852年上海领事阿礼国致港督包令的报告称："应由此地的洋行和英国领事当局向出洋工人郑重保证，契约是定会踏实照行的。把工人的工资的一部份在此地由洋行付给工人的家属，也是一个好办法。如果不这样办的话，是没有什么人愿意出洋做工的。"列为"第一"的是"中国人的信心将寄托在此地的洋行，或者和他们签订契约的人身上。出洋移民的信心将取决于洋行或外国签约人是否授权能够为安家费用、工人后来接眷出洋、和工满之后得到回国盘费等问题作出切实可信的担保。"[35]

同治三年（1862），法国领事致江西巡抚沈宝桢：法国商人"招募华民前往承工，所有现在大法国者，不但身享田园之乐，而且心悦见人之美。即有愿回本乡者，罔不饱其囊橐，公布其德政。"立约后，局商按名发给每工人洋钱8元衣服鞋袜被褥各一份。定限8年。"立约章程"第8条载明："雇主应拨给每工人田地，以为己业。其田亩数，由工人自谅其力，能种若干亩，即照数拨给。"礼拜日与每日歇息闲暇时，皆可耕种自己田地。这对中国农民来说，在国内是不可企及的。第4条，每日"腌肉半斤，或给腌鱼半斤"，这在中国连地主也难达到。[36]

自愿选择，是中外官方招工条约的必备条款。1860年1月"广州招工公所续增章程七款"第4款规定："每一出洋之人，均应亲至监查官员面前，由官员详细问明，是否本人自愿出洋，是否情愿接受契约内所列条款，是否情愿在契约上签字。如未经出洋之人本人完全情愿，无论

---

[35] 上海领事阿礼国致港督包令的报告，1852年9月1日，陈翰笙1980第2辑：页23–28。
[36] 总署清档。转引自陈翰笙《华工出国史料汇编》第1辑，页40–43。

如何不得令其签订契约。契约内如载明给予出洋之人以预支工资，此款应在签订契约之时如数点发。"[37] 携眷前往者，待遇提高。

3. 涉外契约

华工出国契约，应该是中国民间最早的涉外合同，在契约传统源远流长的中国（龙登高2018），具有独特的历史意义。

从几则华工合同，可以了解其移民融资机制概貌。现今所见合同是印制的，同一契约分别有中文版和英文版。可能以各中介公司、各移民点分别印制，说明其移民人数不少。因此合同的格式与规定略有不同，但主要内容差不多，年限、报酬与相关价格大体一致，估计市场竞争已形成了价格整合。

第一，合同期内无条件服从雇主，合同期常为8年。咸丰5年，18岁的林先远赴古巴，"立合同"云：

> 听从代办人指使，"或将合同转与别人，亦听从别人使令。当工以8年为期。"任何工种，"悉皆听从指使"；"本人身上无恙，踰八日起计工。若身上有病，不能当工，送入医院调理，俟病愈出院，亦踰八日起计工。""今言明虽知古巴岛工人及奴才工银不少，但将来受事主利益不少，祇依合同所定工银是实"；"恐口无凭，各立合同一纸交执为据"。

1890年前往夏威夷的华工契约写明："不论在田间干农活，还是在碾米厂、制糖厂当工人，还是在私人家庭中当家仆，均听从雇安排。""应遵从雇主、代理人或监工的一切命令。"[38]

第二，合同期8年之内也有相应的保障。咸丰五年，东莞县梁二，26岁远赴古巴。合同载明："每月工银4员，并无拖欠"；"凡

---

[37] 转引自陈翰笙1980，第2辑，页358。

[38] "雇工每月工作26天，工资为12美元5角。在前2年中，雇主从每月工资中扣除1美元5角，交付夏威夷政府由国库保存。扣满36美元为止"，为其回国支付旅费。如未满回国，则以此偿付雇主所持付的从中国来夏威夷的旅费。

有病送入医院，令医生看病施药，至愈为止"；垫付资金；"所有船脚、食用，均系代办人给足"；"今言明收到现银及衣服等共银十二元"，由代办人预先支给；"至夏华拿，将工银每月扣回1员，至扣足银数即止。事主不得藉端将工银扣除。"

广东茂名蔡瑞光，25岁，咸丰10年远赴古巴，于澳门在"工作合同"上画押，并签署"蔡瑞光收银拾式元"。从娴熟和较高水平的书法来看，应该是代签，蔡瑞光按手印。

契约具有可交易性。咸丰二年，中华福建人移民大吕宋国的"立约字"[39]说明，"惟凭有收画押字之人，就是东家"；"其水途日食以及船税，东家自出。今在厦门德记行先借出洋银……共折银11员半，"逐月扣银1员。移民中介机构"厦门德记行"，是厦门最早一家洋行，支付移民费用。可以看出，跨国中介，多方辗转，多层东家。

东莞梁二、广东林先、茂名蔡瑞光等都是由不同的中介机构与代办人经办前往古巴不同地点的契约华工。但他们行前所获得的卖身现银都是12元，昂贵的船票也获得垫付，价格统一应该是市场整合的结果。

4. 移民的收益

道光咸丰年间，社会动荡，大量五邑人出洋谋生，到光绪年间，一些积有余资的华侨纷纷回乡买田建房。光绪年间的新宁知县李平书评论说："宁邑地本瘠苦，风俗素崇俭朴。自同治初年以来，出洋之人日多，获赀回华。营建屋宇，焕然一新，服御饮食，专尚华美，婚嫁之事，尤斗糜夸奢，风气大变。"五邑现存的大量碉楼就是历史见证，甚至到广州等城市购房置业。移民的社会地位也有提高，所谓"有女要嫁金山客，打转船头百算百。"（刘进，2017）

在广东五邑，民众也自筹移民启动资金。咸丰六年（1856年）黄官奕"为因往金山获利，盘费不敷，恳求西龙社乡老黄玉涵、邓捷魁，值理黄会辉、黄达德、关瑞结等情愿发船位本银壹拾捌两正，言定以限

---

[39] 合同约定"或耕种，或牧羊，或作什事工夫，俱各听从东家使唤，不敢违逆"。"限八年为满以外，任从自主"。

一年为期,本息清还,每两要计息银壹两伍钱正。如至期无银还,仍要每两每年又加息银壹两算。……系伊父子家人填还抵足,毋得异言"。这份契据写明由黄官奕"合家担保",父亲黄元盛署名。(转引自刘进,2017)这18两当然不够全部旅费。

表2所示,1861–1866年11个移民点中,成年男性46695人,成年女性达2117人,儿童776人。女性和儿童的数量出乎意外,因为文字记载几乎没有谈及。主要集中于旧金山,英属、荷属西印度。这意味着约2000个夫妻与家庭移民,显示了移民的普遍性,在侨乡得到社会认可。1910年7月,梁芳荣的女婿恳请岳父将他带到金山谋生:"欲想发达,除外洋之外,再无他处。本不敢尽口,见亦属父子之亲,倘日后有发达,皆大人所赐也,然此恩此德,比于生身父母更大焉,当日夜焚香告祝大人之恩。"(转引自刘进2017)此时,跨国移民的谋生与发展机会,对侨乡民众产生了较强的吸引力。

表2:1861–1866年部分地点的移民构成

	成年		儿童	
	男	女	男	女
去旧金山	29091	893	511	15
去澳大利亚	7093		48	
去温哥华	1583		56	
英属西印度	3271	765	44	27
去孟买	2370			
去大溪地	1055			
荷属西印度	950	323	45	
去火奴鲁鲁	679	97	13	
去婆罗洲	62			
去纳闽岛	105	39	15	2
去爪哇	436			
合计	46695	2117	732	44

注:陈翰笙1980,第2辑,页378–379。

（二）契约白奴（17-18世纪）（Indentured Servant）

以上有关契约华工与偷渡客的论述在历史比较中可资印证。回顾美国历史可以发现，移民牺牲一段时期的自由来换取未来的发展，在17-18世纪的英国人与其他西欧人那里也普遍存在。白人契约奴（indentured servant），也译为契约奴、契约佣工、契约白奴等。1607年5月，伦敦公司遣送包括契约白奴在内的首批移民105人到北美洲，建立詹姆斯城。1620年五月花号上的100余名移民，除了朝圣者，也有30多名契约奴。早期在新大陆的生存死亡相当高。最早6000移民中，死于疾病、战争、饥饿者达4000多人。跨洋途中死亡率相当高，葬身大西洋者，也不计其数。

在美国的移民构成中，契约奴仆在17世纪达60%，18世纪仍有51%，德国亦被称为Redemptioner（Jeremy Atack, Peter Passell, 1994; David W. Galenson, 1984）。他们一无所有，只能以3-7年的人身自由与强制性劳役，来换取进入新大陆的机会及未来发展的空间。契约白奴和雇主有契约关系，只要契约还没到期，就不能拥有自由。

自愿卖身为奴的这些英国人、苏格兰人和爱尔兰人、德国人通过签立契约把自己卖掉，实现人力资本变现，把未来的收益变现，来支付船票。具体来说，就是船主或中介，或人贩子把他们用船运到美国去。17世纪，移民在欧洲与船主或代理人签署卖身契约，价格约为£5-6，这相当于英国农民一年的收入。如果活着抵达美国港口，这份契约由船主转手以£10-11卖出，获利100%。出价的种植园主或工厂主领走移民。在4-7年的契约期内，移民得无条件服从雇主，其工资抵偿£10-11，及期限之后的"自由费"（freedom dues）。雇主将会给予移民住房、土地、工具和一笔钱，契约移民转变为新的农场主。这是他在本国是很难实现的梦想，移民后只要付出四年的辛苦就可以成为独立农场主，可以看到契约白奴和偷渡客有着很大的相似性，也就是实现未来人力资本价值的变现。

五、结语

历史上几乎每一个移民都经历了常人无法忍受的艰辛奋斗,甚至血泪苦。克服常人难以想象的困难,排除各种障碍,极端忍气吞声,极端忍辱负重,甚至是非人的"卖身"时期,最终获得自由。他们也许没有受过很好的正规教育,但他们追求自由与发展的精神超出常人。自由之后,企业家精神得到充分释放。虽然大多数因为条件所限、能力所限,都在谋生层次,但都实现了从农民到市民、甚至企业主的华丽转身,特别是涌现了一批跨国企业家。

通过跨国流动,边际价值提升,人力资本获得较高边际收益的配置。由此,出国移民成为一种人力资本的投资行为,不仅是个体的、家庭的投资行为,而且是国内外家族与亲友的联合投资行为,甚至是海内外乡亲的共同投资行为。劳动力的跨国流动,包括所谓偷渡,是沿海农民的一种无奈的理性选择,也是经济全球化潮流中的大势所趋。

跨国融资网络围绕"卖身移民"而形成利益共同体,其中偷渡客利益相关方包括:蛇头、唐人街老板、借贷或民间放贷的亲友、偷渡客。在整个过程中,唐人街老板获得廉价的劳动力,其担保分散和降低了蛇头的风险。契约工只有到达新大陆才有可能实现其未来的人力资本,也才能吸引投资者。预支和出卖几年的劳动力,以此换取通往新大陆的船票。资金提供者是新大陆的农场主或工场主,获得投资的未来回报,而欧洲的船长或代理人获得当期回报。地下的跨国金融机构是提供放贷的民间机构,为偷渡客提供金融服务。各个利益共同体之间有分工,比如蛇头专营放贷。

不惜重金偷渡或卖身移民,是为寻求更好的谋生与发展机会,获得融资机会。追求自由与生存发展的强烈愿望,促成跨国移民,实现人力资本提升,创造了跨国融资网络金融工具的创新。非正规移民,突破更多的障碍与更大的困难,具有更原始的企业家精神,其成长过程亦充满荆棘与艰辛,成就了如今的美国中餐馆产业,创新了美国城际巴士行业等商业领域。(Long Denggao, 2011)

参考文献

陈国霖著，李滟波译《偷渡美国》，明镜出版社1999。

邝彼得《黑着：在美国的中国非法移民》，世界知识出版社

刘进(2017)：《追寻沉默的美国铁路华工——以中国近现代广东五邑侨乡文书为中心的探讨》，《美国研究》

龙登高(2007)：《跨越市场的障碍——海外华商在国家、制度与文化之间》，科学出版社

龙登高(2019)：《信用机制与跨国网络》，载龙登高、刘宏《商脉与商道：国际华商研究文集》浙江大学出版社

韦尔 P(2002)：走向共同发展的连贯一致的政策，《国际移民》（第40卷）

朱国宏(1994)：《中国海外贸易》，复旦大学出版社。

Brian Friel (2006): The Snakeheads' Secret Weapons. National Journal Group, Inc. 06-03.

David Kyle, Zai Liang (2001): Migration Merchants: Human Smuggling form Ecuador and China. The Center for Comparative Immigration Studies. UC San Diego.

David W. Galenson(1984): "The Rise and Fall of Indentured Servitude in the Americas: An Economic Analysis", *Journal of Economic History* 44, Mar., pp. 1–26.

Frank Pieke (2002): Recent Trends in Chinese Migration to Europe: Fujianese Migration in Perspective. IOM。

Frank Pieke, Mette Thuno (2004): Transnational Chinese: Fujianese Migrants in Europe. Stanford University Press.

Frank Pieke (2007)：五月在清华大学的学术演讲"欧洲的华人移民"。

ILO (2004)：在全球经济中为移民工人谋求公平待遇·国际劳工大会，第92届会议。

Jeffrey S. Passel, 2006a. Robert Suro. Rise, Peak and Decline: Trends in US Immigration 1992–2004. Pew Hispanic Center.

Jeffrey. S Passel. 2006b. Unauthorized immigrants: number and characteristics. Pew Hispanic center. 6.14

Jeremy Atack, Peter Passell (1994): A New Economic View of American History: From Colonial Times to 1940. W.W.Norton & Company. New York, London.

Ko-lin Chin (1999): Smuggled Chinese: Clandestine Immigration to the United States. Philadelphia: Temple University Press

Ko-lin Chin (2000): Quest for the "Good Life" Threatens Marriages of Illegal Aliens。An interview with author. July. http://usinfo.state.gov.

Liu Hong / Gregor Benton (2018): Dear China: Emigrant Letters and Remittances, 1820–1980. University of California Press

Long Denggao, et (2013): The Growth of Chinatown Bus: Beyond Ethnic Enclave Economy in America. Journal of Cambridge Studies 2013.1

Mei Fong (2002): Down and Out in Manhattan's Chinatown: Job Losses Caused by September 11 Traumatize Community, But Aid Is in Short Supply. By, The Wall Street Journal, April 4.

Peter Kwong (1997): Forbidden workers: illegal Chinese immigrants and American labor. New York: New Press.

Peter Kwong (2000): Few Chinese Illegals Find Wealth in the United States. Interview with author Peter Kwong, May. http://usinfo.state.gov

Peter Kwong (2001): "Impact of Chinese Human Smuggling on the American Labor Market". Global Human Smuggling: Comparative Perspectives. Edited by David Kyle and Koslowski. Baltimore: Johns Hopkins University Press.

Patrick Radden Keefe (2006): The snakehead: The Criminal Odyssey of Chinatown's Sister Ping. The New Yorker. 4.

Zhou Min (2005): "Ethnicity as Social Capital: Community-Based Institutions and Embedded Networks of Social Relations." Chapter 4 in Glenn Loury, Tariq Modood, and Steven Teles, eds., *Ethnicity, Social Mobility, and Public Policy in the United States and United Kingdom*. London: Cambridge University Press.

Benjamin N. Narváez. Abolition, Chinese Indentured Labor, and the State: Cuba, Peru, and the United States during the Mid Nineteenth Century. The Americas Volume 76, Issue 1. 2019. PP 5–40.

Tu T. Huynh. From Demand for Asiatic Labor to Importation of Indentured Chinese Labor: Race Identity in the Recruitment of Unskilled Labor for South Africa's Gold Mining Industry, 1903–1910 [J]. Journal of Chinese Overseas, 2008, 4(1): 51–68.

O. Nigel Bolland. Indentured Labor, Caribbean Sugar: Chinese and Indian Migrants to the British West Indies, 1838–1918 [J]. International Labor and Working-Class History, 1996, 49: 217–219.

Ginés Blasi Mònica. Exploiting Chinese Labour Emigration in Treaty Ports: The Role of Spanish Consulates in the "Coolie Trade" [J]. International Review of Social History, 2021, 66(1): 1–24.

GinésBlasi Mònica. A Philippine 'coolie trade': Trade and exploitation of Chinese labour in Spanish colonial Philippines, 1850–98 [J]. Journal of Southeast Asian Studies, 2020, 51(3): 457–483.

鄭榮九. Chinese Coolie Trade in the Latter Half of 19th Century [J]. Journal of Asian Historical Studies, 2018, 142: 171–204.

Fay Peter Ward. Robert L. Irick. Ch'ing Policy toward the Coolie Trade, 1847–1878. (Asian Library Series, number 18.) San Francisco: Chinese Materials Center. 1982. Pp. xviii, 452. $29.75 [J]. The American Historical Review, 1983, 88(3): 732–733.

Jane Kate Leonard. Ch'ing Policy toward the Coolie Trade, 1847–1878 [J]. The Journal of Asian Studies, 1983, 42(4): 923–925.

附表1 华人未获允许的移民在美国的数量(万人)

年份	1990	2000	2006	增长率
华人无证移民数量	7.0	11.5	23	228.6%
占美国总数的百分比	2.0%	1.6%	2.1%	
在美国非法移民来源地的序位		第六位	第五位	
全美无证移民总数	350	700	1100	214.3%

2000年数据：U.S. Dept. of Homeland Security, Office of Immigration Statistics, 2002 Yearbook of Immigration Statistics；2006年数据：Jeffrey. S Passel. 2006；U.S. INS. Estimates of the Unauthorized Immigrant Population Residing in the US: 1900 to 2000. http://www.uscis.gov/graphics/shared/aboutus/statistics/Ill_Report_1211.pdf

附图1 进入美国的中国大陆非正规移民：2000年的路线与数量

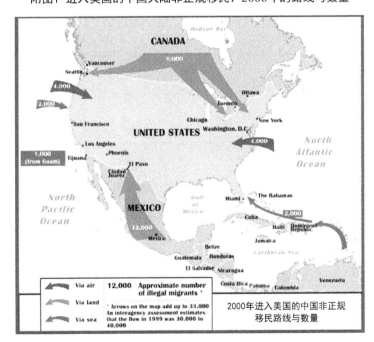

附图2 契约华工的合同原件

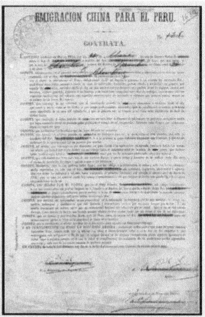
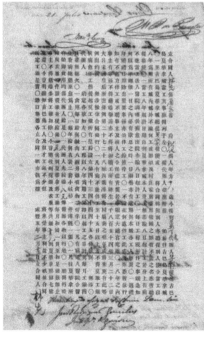

龙登高·人力资本跨国流动及其融资网络

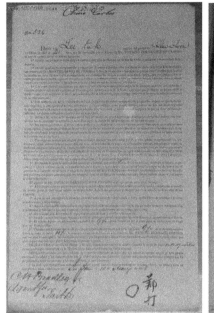

附图3 契约白奴 Indenture 原件

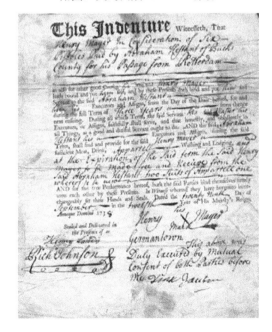

20世纪"文化中国"的再展演
侨乡与海外华人社会的社区节日

蔡志祥[*]

摘要

社区性节日展陈了社会群体的整体。在20世纪，中国和海外华人的社区性节日受到了很多挑战，到了近年才"复兴"起来。作为周期性的活动，社区性节日定期庆祝，因此是社区成员已知和共享的活动。然而，仪式细节以及对节日的解释总是会根据不断变化的宏观环境而进行调整。20世纪是华侨身份由旅居者向定居者转变的时期。这是一个华侨与祖籍地疏远、在东道国定居，以及与中国重新联系的时期。本文将使用三个典型的节日来讨论中国社区性节日作为一种全球现象的延续，特别是探索节日在海外华人社会中仪式结构的演变及其与祖先家乡之间的相互作用。本文认为，中国传统文化，尤其是持续庆祝的社区性节日，不仅是华侨华人建立华人身份认同的工具，有助于重建与祖籍的联系；更重要的是，它们是海外华人利用的一种文化资源，在在地化过程中，塑造为在生活国家中的重要"他者"的身份。"中华文化"是一种生存策略，考验着地方当局的宽容度；同时，通过标准化的仪式，缓和华侨华人的内部差异。

关键词：社区性节日、文化中国、华侨华人、侨乡、文化资源

---

[*] 蔡志祥，香港中文大学历史系，goatlionc5@gmail.com。

本文原刊于《华人研究国际学报》，第14卷，第1期，2022年6月，页1–18。经授权转载。

This is an Open Access chapter published by World Scientific Publishing Company. It is distributed under the terms of the Creative Commons Attribution-NonCommercial-NoDerivatives 4.0 (CC BY-NC-ND) License which permits use, distribution and reproduction, provided that the original work is properly cited, the use is non-commercial and no modifications or adaptations are made.

Reenacting "Cultural China" in the Twentieth Century:
Communal Festivals in Emigrant and Overseas Chinese Communities

CHOI Chi-cheung

Abstract

Communal festivals have always been a representation of the community. Throughout the twentieth century, communal festivals in China and among Chinese people living in overseas communities came under many challenges, but have been "revived" with great success in recent years. As periodic event, a communal festival is celebrated regularly therefore is an event known and shared by members of the community. Yet, ritual details as well as interpretation of the event are always adjusted in response to the changing macro-environment. The twentieth century was a period when the status of the Chinese overseas changed from sojourners to settlers. It was a period when the overseas Chinese delinked with their ancestral hometown, settled in their host countries, and reconnected with China in the last quarter of the century. This paper will use three exemplar festivals to examine the continuation of Chinese communal festivals as a global phenomenon, exploring, in particular, the interplay of ceremonial structures evolving in overseas Chinese settings and their ancestral hometown. It argues that traditional Chinese culture, particularly continuously celebrating Chinese communal festivals, are not only serve as a tool for establishing Chinese identity and instrumental to re-establish connection with their ancestral hometown, they are, more importantly, a cultural facade that the overseas Chinese employ to indigenise, to project themselves as a significant "other" in their adopted country. "Chinese culture" is a survival strategy testing the tolerance of local authorities and, with standardised ritual, mitigates internal differences among the overseas Chinese.

Keywords: Communal Festival; Cultural China; Overseas Chinese; Emigrant Community; Cultural Resources

前言

"文化中国"的论述最晚可以追溯到19世纪中叶,当作为一个政治实体的中国面临着帝国和殖民列强威胁的时候。同治、光绪时期(1862–1874年),"中体西用"的意涵在政治家和知识分子的思想和讨论中占据主导的地位。[1] 虽然危机中的中国是一个政治问题,但19世纪末和20世纪初的思想家指出中国文化的弱点阻碍了中国的现代化。[2] 民国政府重建中国的努力导致试图与中国传统价值观或实践保持距离,并倾向于采用西方文化作为"正确"的生活方式。在这种自我探究的大环境中,1928年国民党统一中国时,制定了新的规定、限制宗教活动。[3] 在1950年代和1960年代,当"新"中国在中国之外的意识形态的基础下建立时,寻找在铺天盖地的压力下一瞬间幻灭的、支撑中国作为政治实体、生存了数千年的文化基础的探索,吸引着很多学者。这一时期的研究强调了诸如科举、[4] 农村行政[5] 和法律[6] 等国家制度;或农村市场、[7] 家庭和

---

[1] Mary Clabaugh Wright, *The Last Stand of Chinese Conservatism: The Tung-chih Restoration, 1862–1874* (Stanford: Stanford University Press, 1957).

[2] Lin Yusheng, *The Crisis of Chinese Consciousness: Radical Antitraditionalism in the May Fourth Era* (Madison: University of Wisconsin Press, 1979).

Chow Tse-tsung, *The May Fourth Movement: Intellectual Revolution in Modern China* (Cambridge: Harvard University Press, 1960).

[3] Rebecca Nedostup, *Superstitious Regimes: Religion and the Politics of Chinese Modernity* (Cambridge: Harvard University Asia Center, 2009).

Poon Shuk-wah, *Negotiating Religion in Modern China: State and Common People in Guangzhou, 1900–1937* (Hong Kong: The Chinese University of Hong Kong Press, 2011).

[4] Ho Ping-ti, *The Ladder of Success in Imperial China: Aspects of Social Mobility, 1368–1911* (New York: Columbia University Press, 1962).

[5] Hsiao Kung-chuan, *Rural China: Imperial Control in the Nineteenth Century* (Seattle: University of Washington Press, 1960).

[6] Chu Tung-tsu, *Local Government in China under the Ch'ing* (Cambridge: Harvard University Press, 1962).

[7] George William Skinner, "Marketing and Social Structure in Rural China," Parts 1-3, *Journal of Asian Studies*, Vol. 24, No. 1–3, pp. 3–43; 195–228; 363–399.

宗族、[8] 民间信仰[9] 以至儒家文化的再审视[10] 等社会和地方制度。同时，人类学家在中国本土以外进行的田野调查研究，挑战了从上而下的观点。[11] 1970年代末中国的改革开放和海外华人经济实力几乎同时崛起，促使人们重新审视中国文化的灵活性和柔韧性。从1982年到1990年代中期，由美国学术研究委员会（American Council of Learned Society）和社会科学研究委员会（Social Science Research Council）组成的中国研究联合委员会（Joint Committee on Chinese Studies），资助并出版了28册的会议论文集。这些研究进一步支持了边缘和多样性对理解中国文化的重要性。[12] 这里的边缘性是指地理上远离中央的地域社会或海外华人社区；它也指涉挑战官方认可的文化行为正确性的、多样的生活方式。

"中国性"和"文化中国"的问题源于对大一统挑战的离心力。[13] 然而，关于"中国性"和"文化中国"的讨论总是假设人们最终会有

---

[8] Maurice Freedman, *Lineage Organization in Southeastern China* (London: University of London; Athlone Press, 1965).

Maurice Freedman, *Chinese Lineage and Society, Fukien and Kwangtung* (London: University of London; Athlone Press, 1966).

[9] Arthur Wolf, "God, Ghost and Ancestor," Arthur Wolf (ed.), *Religion and Ritual in Chinese Society* (Stanford: Stanford University Press, 1974), pp. 131–182.

[10] Joseph Richmond Levenson, *Confucian China and its Modern Fate: A Trilogy* (Berkeley: University of California Press, 1968).

[11] David Faure, Helen F. Siu (eds.), *Down to Earth: The Territorial Bond in South China* (Stanford: Stanford University Press, 1995).

[12] 例如：David Johnson, Andrew J. Nathan, Evelyn S. Rawski (eds.), *Popular Culture in Late Imperial China* (Berkeley: University of California Press, 1985).

James L. Watson, Evelyn S. Rawski (eds.), *Death Ritual in Late Imperial and Modern China* (Berkeley: University of California Press, 1988).

Rubie S. Watson, Patricia Buckley Ebrey (eds.), *Marriage and Inequality in Chinese Society* (Berkeley: University of California Press, 1991).

[13] Wang Gung-wu, "Greater China and the Chinese Overseas," Special Issue: "Greater China," *The China Quarterly*, No. 136 (1993), pp. 926–948.

Tu Wei-ming, "Cultural China: The Periphery as the Center," Special issue: "The Living Tree: The Changing Meaning of Being Chinese Today," *Daedalus*, Vol. 120, No. 2 (1991), pp. 1–32.

强调中国人的身份或与中国联系的倾向。[14] 虽然边缘性是理解"文化中国"的关键，但本文将从"中国性"的"最基本层面"，即地理边缘、移民和海外华人社区[15] 以及社会边缘、习俗和节日[16] 重新审视"文化中国"的问题。

20世纪末以来，华侨华人及其与祖先家乡联系的研究，迅速从关注经济和政治转向文化的问题。然而，这些研究时常将联系视为一种单向的流动，强调华侨华人对家乡的建设以及如何在祖籍故乡中，促进"中国性"。然而，宗教节日的研究，显示家乡联系的实践和解释是双向。中国不仅是一块磁石，吸引着海外华人回国、联系他们祖先的文化遗产和传统，也是第二、三代华侨华人在生活国中，建构"中国性"和自我意识的文化资源。[17] 换言之，"中国性"、"文化中国"是华侨华人在异国、他乡建立一种"显著的他者"（significant others）的文化手段；而这种文化手段，通过节日文化而实践。

---

[14] Yeh Wen-hsin (ed.), *Becoming Chinese: Passages to Modernity and Beyond* (Berkeley: University of California Press, 2000).

Wang Gung-wu, "Greater China and the Chinese Overseas," Special Issue: "Greater China," *The China Quarterly*, No. 136 (1993), pp. 926–948.

Leo M. Douw, Peter Post (eds.), *South China: State, Culture and Social Change during the 20th Century* (Amsterdam: Royal Netherlands Academy of Arts and Sciences, 1996).

Leo M. Douw, Cen Huang, Michael R. Godley (eds.), *Qiaoxiang Ties: Interdisciplinary Approaches to "Cultural Capitalism" in South China* (London & New York: Kegan International; Leiden & Amsterdam: International Institute for Asian Studies, 1999).

[15] Tu Wei-ming, "Cultural China: The Periphery as the Center," Special issue: "The Living Tree: The Changing Meaning of Being Chinese Today," *Daedalus*, Vol. 120, No. 2 (1991), pp. 1–32.

[16] Wang Gung-wu, "Greater China and the Chinese Overseas," Special Issue: "Greater China," *The China Quarterly*, No. 136 (1993), pp. 926–948.

[17] Kenneth Dean, "Renewed Flows of Ritual Knowledge and Ritual Affect within Transnational Networks: A Case Study of Three Ritual Events of the Xinghua (Henghua) Communities in Singapore," Bernardo E. Brown, Brenda S. A. Yeoh (eds.), *Asian Migrants and Religious Experience: From Missionary Journeys to Labor Mobility* (Amsterdam: Amsterdam University Press, 2018), pp. 71–100.

随着二次大战后东南亚地区的独立运动和民族国家的建设，对九皇诞、[18] 丧葬仪式、[19] 仪式戏剧[20] 和乩童灵媒[21] 等华人宗教活动来思考文化中国在华人在地化过程中的兴趣勃增。这些研究探讨了华人移民到东

---

[18] Cheu Hock Tong, *The Nine Emperor Gods: A Study of Chinese Spirit-Medium Cult* (Singapore: Times Books International, 1988).

Cheu Hock Tong, "The Festival of the Nine Emperor Gods in Peninsular Southeast Asia," Cheu Hock Tong (ed.) *Chinese Beliefs and Practices in Southeast Asia* (Petaling Jaya: Pelanduk Publications, 1993), pp. 17–57.

[19] Tong Chee Kiong, *Chinese Death Rituals in Singapore* (London & New York: RoutledgeCurzon, 2004).

[20] 龙彼得著，王秋桂、苏友贞译〈中国戏剧源于宗教仪典考〉，《中外文学》第7卷第12期（1979），页158–181。Piet van der Loon, "Les Origines rituelles du théâtre chinois," trans. Wang Chiu-kui, Su Yu-tseng, *Chung-Wai Literary Monthly*, Vol. 7, No. 12 (1979), pp. 158–181.

容世诚《戏曲人类学初探：仪式、剧场与社群》（台北：麦田出版，1997）。Yung Sai-shing, *The Anthropology of Chinese Drama: Ritual, Theater and Community* (Taipei: Rye Field Publishing Company, 1997).

容世诚、张学权〈南洋兴化的目连戏与超度仪式〉，《民俗曲艺》第92期（1994），页819–852。Yung Sai-shing, Ken Cheong, "Mulian Play in Southeast Asia and the Ritual Deliverance," *Journal of Chinese Ritual, Theatre and Folklore*, No. 92 (1994), pp. 819–852.

田仲一成《中国祭祀演剧研究》（东京：东京大学东洋文化研究所，1981）。Issei Tanaka, *Ritual Theatres in China* (Tokyo: Institute for Advanced Studies on Asia, Tokyo University, 1981).

田仲一成《中国の宗族と演剧》（东京：东京大学东洋文化研究所，1985）。Issei Tanaka, *Lineage and Theatre in China* (Tokyo: Institute for Advanced Studies on Asia, Tokyo University, 1985).

余淑娟〈逢甲大普度：新加坡九鲤洞的中元祭典〉，《田野与文献：华南研究资料中心通讯》第44期（2006），页1–8。Yee Sok Kiang, "Decennial Universal Salvation: *Zhongyuan* Ritual of Kiew Lee Tong Temple in Singapore," *Fieldwork and Documents: South China Research Resource Station Newsletter*, No. 44 (2006), pp. 1–8.

余淑娟〈新加坡九鲤洞甲申年目连戏概述〉，《南洋学报》第60卷（2006），页76–94。Yee Sok Kiang, "Mulian Play Performed in the Kiew Lee Tong Temple, Singapore in the Year of Jiashen (2004)," *Journal of the South Seas Society*, Vol. 60 (2006), pp. 76–94.

余淑娟《新加坡九鲤洞的目连戏：中国宗教仪式剧个案研究》，博士论文（新加坡：新加坡国立大学中文系，2010）。Yee Sok Kiang, "The Mulian Play in Singapore Kiew Lee Tong Temple: A Case Study of Chinese Ritual Theatre," PhD Dissertation (Singapore: National University of Singapore, 2010).

[21] Margaret Chan, *Ritual is Theatre, Theatre is Ritual: Tang-ki Chinese Spirit Medium Worship* (Singapore: Wee Kim Wee Centre, Singapore Management University, 2006).

Jean DeBernardi, *The Way That Lives in the Heart: Chinese Popular Religion and Spirit Mediums in Penang, Malaysia* (Stanford: Stanford University Press, 2006).

南亚后所面临的同化压力中的种族团结运动,在表述华人方言群宗教节日实践的同时,也透过文化的共同性,凝聚了不同方言的群体。在东南亚的华人民间宗教的研究时常被放在政治和经济框架内。DeBernardi在对槟城中元节的分析中,认为传统的华人的宗教节日被社区精英巧妙地运用。他们通过强调共同的"中国"身份,消融以及整合乡土和方言群体的差异和冲突。DeBernardi指出尽管在19世纪末、20世纪初的华人精英一直热衷支持宗教节日,可是在1970年代和1980年代,这些华人精英认为宗教节日是"农民的封建迷信"活动而对之疏离。[22] 然而,到了1990年代,华人精英又重新支持宗教节日活动,希望通过支持这些活动,创造一个共享的公共文化环境、动员群众从而获得他们在政治上的回报。曾玲在新加坡坟山管理组织(广惠肇碧山亭)的研究中也同样的认为宗教仪式是达至民族团结的重要手段。[23]

如果节日和政治如此紧密联系,那么节日作为海外华人共同的文化就值得进一步的仔细研究。下文将以新加坡的华人社区节日为例,进一步的探索这个问题。

社区节日:新加坡的例子

民间宗教就像钟摆一样,借助人群的来回移动、通过节日的实践而跨越地域的制限。海外成员不仅为祖乡带来了现代化,而且重新强

---

[22] Jean DeBernardi, *Rites of Belonging: Memory, Modernity, and Identity in a Malaysian Chinese Community* (Stanford: Stanford University Press, 2004), p. 180.

[23] 曾玲《越洋再建家园:新加坡华人社会文化研究》(南昌市:江西高校出版社,2003)。Zeng Ling, *Rebuilding Homeland in Overseas: Socio-Cultural Studies of Singapore Chinese* (Nanchang: Jiangxi Universities and Colleges Press, 2003).

曾玲、庄英章《新加坡华人的祖先崇拜与宗乡社群整合:以战后三十年广惠肇碧山亭为例》(台北:唐山出版社,2000)。Zeng Ling, Chuang Ying-chang, *Chinese Ancestral Worship and Integration of Lineage and Territorial Societies in Singapore: A Case Study of the Singapore Kwong Wai Siew Peck San Theng in the 30 Years after WWII* (Taipei: Tonsan Publications Inc., 2000).

固了传统。[24] 如果没有内部或外部刺激，它就会停止摆动而集中于服务地域社区。社区节日是海外华人实践本土化过程中的文化手段。他们利用这一文化活动将自己塑造成为他们居住国家中的"显著的他者"。中国文化是海外华人用来考验地方当局容忍度的生存策略。通过规范的仪式和礼仪实践，社区节日是缓解海外华人内部差异的有效方式。华侨华人对"文化传统"，在不同的世代有着不一样的理解和实践。他们在回应国家（中国和居住地）政策和宏观环境的过程中，对"文化中国"的认识和实践，在不同的社会阶层和方言群中有着不同的方式和手段。

周期性的社区宗教节日可以视为一种仪式性的生态系统。他有自身的仪式序列、有执行仪式的专家、有组织和融资体系。社区通过周期性的宗教节日，让有份的成员共同分享文化习俗和传统，通过节日的活动确定社会身份和社区的界线。海外华人社区不仅通过展现"中国性"与中国联系，社区宗教节日所展现的"中国性"更可以是一种本土化的工具：和祖乡的联系、断裂和再联系、在居住地的融合以及建立不同层级的身份认同，他们通过社区的实践，回应在地国家的政策、对祖乡文化的想象，同时回应宏观环境对民间宗教的挑战和赋予的机遇，如：（1）19世纪末以来的科学与反迷信的思潮；（2）19世纪末20世纪初的鼠疫引发的卫生危机；（3）20世纪中期的太平洋战争与战后的悼念与忘却；（4）1949年以后中国的封关和1970年代末的改革开放与再联系，以及（5）20世纪末以来的非物质文化遗产的动力等等。

换言之，在讨论社区节日的时候，我们必须要注意不同社群所庆祝的节日的同时，也要注意不同社会阶层在不同世代之间的差异。

下文以新加坡为例，进一步探讨社区节日自19世纪末以来所展演的"文化中国"的摆动。

---

[24] James L. Watson, *Emigration and the Chinese Lineage: The Mans in Hong Kong and London* (Berkeley: University of California Press, 1975).

James L. Watson, "Presidential Address: Virtual Kinship, Real Estate, and Diaspora Formation: The Man Lineage Revisited," *The Journal of Asian Studies*, Vol. 63, No. 4 (2004), pp. 893–910.

曾经在1850年代当过新加坡警察总长（Police Magistrate）的华汉（J. D. Vaughan）在1879年出版了一部关于英国海峡殖民地华人的风俗习惯的书。[25] 华汉在书中罗列了三类新加坡华人庆祝的节日。第一类为华人普遍庆祝的节日如农历新年、天公诞（一月初九）、元宵（一月十五）、清明、端午（五月初五）、中元（农历七月初一到三十）、中秋节（八月十五）以及年底十二月二十四的送神。第二类是在庙宇里举行、并非所有华人都会庆祝的节日，如二月十九（Virgin of Lotus Flower，按：即金花诞）；四月初八（Day of the First Priest，按：即佛诞）、三月十三（Charitable Commander in Chief，按：可能是指农历三月十五的保生大帝诞）和六月十九（Priests Who Died in Celibacy，按：可能是指观音菩萨诞）。还有三月初三（Inventor of Letters' Day，按：即文昌诞）、四月十一（孔诞）和六月十三（鲁班诞）。第三类的节日庆典是潮州人每年一次从十月二十六到十一月，以及福建人三年一次的游神活动。其中华汉着墨最多的是春节、中元，以及游神活动。他指出很多时候，会馆会出钱赞助让群众观赏在节日时上演的街戏（wayang）。[26] 关于游神，华汉有这样的描述：

>……潮州人抬着他们的神像，从泰陵的坟场（Cemetery at Tanglin，按即泰山亭义山）巡游到在 Philip Street（菲立街）的庙（按：即粤海清庙）观赏戏剧。神像停放在那里到十一月才抬回原来的义山。……福建人三年一次也有举行类似的巡游。他们从 New Harbour Road 的坟场（按：大概是恒山亭）经过大坡的福建人聚居的地方后，抬到在直落亚逸街（Teluk Ayer Street）的福建庙（按：即天福宫）。在那里稍停后抬回在坟山的庙宇。巡游非常壮观，用了福建社群不少的金钱。巡游队伍由苦力扛抬旗帜、锣伞、饰物、神舆以及喧闹的乐队。[27]

---

[25] Jonas Daniel Vaughan, *The Manners and Customs of the Chinese of the Straits Settlements* (Kuala Lumpur & Singapore: Oxford University Press, 1971).
本书是由新加坡 Mission Press 于1879年发行版本的再版。
[26] 同上，页44–45。Ibid., pp. 44–45.
[27] 同上，页49。Ibid., p. 49.

华汉以警察总长的身份，通过关于人群管制的工作、人脉关系以及日常的观察，介绍他所认识的华人节日。从华汉的描述，我们可以注意到19世纪中后期的华人节日和族群、行业的关系，同时也注意到华人如何通过游神，一方面划分方言群体的界线，另一方面接连了方言群体对生活祈求的神圣地方（如福建人的天福宫和潮州人的粤海清庙）以及灵魂安顿的地方（如福建人的恒山亭和潮州人的泰山亭）。也就是说，游行的范围是连接了代表"生"和"死"的华人的神圣地域。华汉的描述中，也显示了华人社区节日中如何一方面挪用华人原乡的文化传统，另一方面突出了在地性。大抵，在海外华人的社区节日中，可以分为三个类别：第一类是汉族共同庆祝的、代表"文化中国"的节日。[28] 在这一类别中，海外华人尤其注重有关生和死的节日，以及与他们关联的在定居和确立公民身份的过程中，对生活庇佑的期待和对死有所依的关怀。这些节日包括农历新年的庆祝活动，给祖先的节日（即清明和重阳节）以及救赎无祀孤魂的节日（如中元、普度和万缘会）。第二类是随着华人移民带到海外的节日，并且为不同的族群或方言群体庆祝。这些节日包括妈祖-天后信仰、潮州善堂执行的仪式和法会、兴化莆田人举办的九鲤洞逢甲普度等。第三类社区节日是海外华人社区以传统文化的名义，举办的富有在地特色的活动，并且从一个特定的地方和/或方言群体传播到其他地方，并为不同的方言群体共享。这些节日包括起源于

---

[28] Wolfram Eberhard, *Chinese Festivals,* ed. Lou Tsu-k'uang (Taipei: The Orient Cultural Service, 1972).

Joan Law, Barbara E. Ward, *Chinese Festivals in Hong Kong* (Hong Kong: South China Morning Post, 1982).

李露露《中国节：图说民间传统节日》（福州市：福建人民出版社，2005）。Li Lulu, *Chinese Festivals: Illustration of Traditional Folk Festivals* (Fuzhou: Fujian People's Publishing House, 2005).

普吉岛的九皇诞、[29] 从马来西亚柔佛的一座寺庙开始的链接不同华人方言群的游神活动[30] 以及源自华南的万缘会[31] 等。

我们尝试从三个华人社区节日的例子，进一步思考在漫长的历史发展过程中海外华人社会和祖乡的关系：

一、中元祭祀

农历七月中元节（盂兰节）是中国人普遍都会度过的节日。这是一个普施救赎，安抚亡魂的节日。我们可以从两个角度来说明新加坡华人的中元节。

---

[29] 参考：Cheu Hock Tong, *The Nine Emperor Gods: A Study of Chinese Spirit-Medium Cult*. Cheu Hock Tong, "The Festival of the Nine Emperor Gods in Peninsular Southeast Asia," pp. 17–57.

Ho De Wei Dawin, "*Nine Vessels, One Festival: The Nine Emperor Gods Festival*," Bachelor's Thesis (Singapore: School of Art, Design and Media, Nanyang Technological University, 2020).

[30] 莫家浩〈战时游神：日据时期《昭南日报》有关新山柔佛古庙游神报道析读〉，白伟权主编《2017年新山华族历史文物馆年刊》（新山：新山华族历史文物馆，2018），页37–44。Bak Jiahow, "Procession of Deities during the War time: Analysis of Reports in *Syonan Jit Poh* on the Procession of Deities of the Johor Ancient Temple during the Japanese Occupation Period," Pek Wee Chuen (ed.), *Annals of Johor Bahru Chinese Heritage Museum, 2017* (Johor Bahru: Johor Bahru Chinese Heritage Museum, 2018), pp. 37–44.

庄仁杰〈传统的创新与发明：以新山柔佛古庙游神为例〉，《2017年新山华族历史文物馆年刊》（新山：新山华族历史文物馆，2018），页44–50。Chong Ren Jie Henry, "Innovation and Creation of Traditions: A Case Study on the Procession of Deities of the Johor Ancient Temple," Pek Wee Chuen (ed.), *Annals of Johor Bahru Chinese Heritage Museum, 2017* (Johor Bahru: Johor Bahru Chinese Heritage Museum, 2018), pp. 44–50.

[31] 蔡志祥〈从反迷信到万缘会：广州到东南亚的城市救赎仪式〉，李孝悌、陈学然编《海客瀛洲：传统中国沿海城市与近代东亚海上世界》（上海：上海古籍出版社，2017），页30–42。Choi Chi-cheung, "From Anti-Superstition to Grand Salvation Ritual: Salvations Rituals of the Cities from Canton to Southeast Asia," Li Hsiao-ti, Chan Hok Yin (eds.), *China and Overseas Chinese: Traditional Chinese Coastal Cities and the Maritime World of Modern East Asia* (Shanghai: Shanghai Chinese Classics Publishing House, 2017), pp. 30–42.

（一）从灵魂救赎到庆赞中元的在地化过程[32]

对于19世纪初新加坡开埠之后，大部分是单身南来的华人来说，客死异乡意味着死后没人供养、灵魂没有归属的忧虑；同时，无所依归的幽魂对生者来说是一种威胁，慰藉无主幽魂，是解消怨灵危害人间的方法。因此，中元节祭祀孤魂是新加坡华人各个方言群、精英和群众都同样重视的活动。英国殖民政府也理解到控制中元节是管治华人的有效方法。1887年因为华民护卫司被刺，一度禁止中元祭祀。[33]然而，政府一方面理解民众对无祀幽魂的恐惧，禁制华人济幽的活动非常困难；另一方面也警觉到民众的祭祀活动与私会党的密切关系。因此，在1887年以后，政府的政策是容许民众在依循严格法规的前提下，进行祭祀幽魂的活动。规定祭祀必须拿到政府的准证，并且规定"昔年曾因普度演剧

---

[32] 本节主要参考：蔡志祥〈从鬼戏到歌台：中元普度的娱乐、表演与仪式〉，蔡志祥、横山广子编《在世俗与神圣之间：近代亚洲的盆会、中元和七月的节日》专号，《节日研究》第14辑（2019），页3–22。Choi Chi-cheung, "From Ghost Theatre to *Getai*: Entertainment, Performance and Ritual of the *Zhongyuan* Hungry Ghost Festivals," Choi Chi-cheung, Hiroko Yokoyama (eds.), Special Issue: "Ritual Between Other World and This World: Bon, *Zhongyuan*, and the Seventh Month Celebration in Modern Asia," *Festival Studies*, No. 14 (2019), pp. 3–22.

蔡志祥〈葬与祭：19世纪末20世纪初新加坡英国殖民政府对华人节日与坟山的管治〉，陈俊强、洪健荣主编《台北州建州百年：在地化与国际化的视角》（新北：台北大学海山研究中心、新北市立图书馆，2021），页229–257。Choi Chi-cheung, "Burial and Ritual: Governance of Chinese Festivals and Burial Ground by the British Colonial Government of Singapore in the Late 19th and Early 20th Century," Chan Chun Keung, Hung Jian-rong (eds.), *Centennial of the Establishment of Taipei State: Perspectives of Localisation and Globalisation* (New Taipei: Center for Haishan Research, National Taipei University; New Taipei City Library, 2021), pp. 229–257.

[33] 蔡志祥〈葬与祭：19世纪末20世纪初新加坡英国殖民政府对华人节日与坟山的管治〉，页236–237。Choi Chi-cheung, "Burial and Ritual: Governance of Chinese Festivals and Burial Ground by the British Colonial Government of Singapore in the Late 19th and Early 20th Century," pp. 236–237.

蔡志祥〈从鬼戏到歌台：中元普度的娱乐、表演与仪式〉，蔡志祥、横山广子编《在世俗与神圣之间：近代亚洲的盆会、中元和七月的节日》专号，《节日研究》第14辑（2019），页10。Choi Chi-cheung, "From Ghost Theatre to *Getai*: Entertainment, Performance and Ritual of the *Zhongyuan* Hungry Ghost Festivals," Choi Chi-cheung, Hiroko Yokoyama (eds.), Special Issue: "Ritual Between Other World and This World: Bon, *Zhongyuan*, and the Seventh Month Celebration in Modern Asia," *Festival Studies*, No. 14 (2019), p. 10.

酬，发生过打架之街，均不许其再事演剧。"[34] 然而，19世纪末的海外华人精英既要配合政府反对私会党的政策，也受到科学和反对迷信的大思潮的影响，故此在理解草根群众对无祀鬼神的恐惧和不安的同时，对于祭祀采取了新的诠释和实践方法。在华人精英的推动下，限制祭祀活动的规模。华文报章在19世纪末以后，也指摘中元祭祀的迷信和奢侈的元素，强调了中元祭祀活动的娱乐、慈善和孝道成分。在20世纪初，新加坡华人精英提出改良民俗、反对迷信的方法："即（1）推动改良在华校的教育方法；（2）取消妆艺游行（Chingay）；及（3）限制祭祀幽鬼的日数，从30天缩短到1天。这些建议要到1930年代初，在林文庆等大力推动下，才在华人社会实施下来。妆艺游行完全取消了，个别家户虽然仍然在中元时祭祀恶鬼，但是规模显然没有以前的盛大。"[35] 因此，新加坡的中元节是在强调"庆赞中元"的表象下进行普度幽魂的宗教仪式。灵魂救赎以至对死者的孝思是一种非迷信的宗教慈善活动，有很强烈的对生者服务的意义。20世纪中叶以来，新加坡的中元节是把原来的中国祭祀文化，通过歌台等表演演绎为服务新加坡华人、强调世俗化的节日。"中元节的娱乐盛宴，较诸超幽度亡更为重要。"[36]

（二）断裂与再联系：九鲤洞的逢甲普度[37]

本土化并不意味着与祖乡关系的完全割裂。文化延续、断绝和再

---

[34] 〈警厅对于中元演剧酬神之办法〉，《南洋商报》，1927年8月9日，第3页。
"The Police Department's Approach to *Zhongyuan* Theatre," *Nanyang Siang Pau*, 9 Aug 1927, p. 3.
[35] "Chinese Topics in Malaya," *The Straits Times*, 10 December 1931, p. 16.
[36] 蔡志祥〈从鬼戏到歌台：中元普度的娱乐、表演与仪式〉，蔡志祥、横山广子编《在世俗与神圣之间：近代亚洲的盆会、中元和七月的节日》专号，《节日研究》第14辑（2019），页12–16。
Choi Chi-cheung, "From Ghost Theatre to *Getai*: Entertainment, Performance and Ritual of the *Zhongyuan* Hungry Ghost Festivals," Choi Chi-cheung, Hiroko Yokoyama (eds.), Special Issue: "Ritual Between Other World and This World: Bon, *Zhongyuan*, and the Seventh Month Celebration in Modern Asia," *Festival Studies*, No. 14 (2019), pp. 12–16.
[37] 本节主要参考：蔡志祥〈阴阳过度：2004年新加坡九鲤洞逢甲普度中的仪式与剧场〉，《南洋学报》第61卷（2007），页1–12。Choi Chi-cheung, "Yin-yang Transition: Ritual and Theatre in the 2004 Decennial Universal Salvation Ritual of Kiew Lee Tong Temple in Singapore," *Journal of the South Seas Society*, Vol. 61 (2007), pp. 1–12.

联系是与宏观环境的变化有很大的关系。新加坡九鲤洞的逢甲普度是一个很好的例子。[38] 福建省的兴化移民在1930年代把家乡的信仰移植到新加坡。20世纪中以来,属于兴化人的九鲤洞每逢甲年的农历七月会举行一次大型的"逢甲普度"仪式。逢甲普度不仅包括道教、佛教和琼瑶法教的仪式,而且包括演出肉身目连戏(人戏而非傀儡戏)。九鲤洞庙里1954年的碑记指出,第一次的逢甲普度在1944年开始举办。然而,据1943年《昭南日报》的记载,九鲤洞在该年的农历七月十五日至十九日"……中元佳节,第三年度大普度,演兴化得月大班,练习目连救母戏,并延僧道诵经,设醮超度前方忠勇英灵及孤滞幽魂,祈祷圣战完遂,东亚共荣,合岛平安……。"[39] 报导指出,1943年是第三年度普度、也有演出目连救母戏。[40] 因此,也许九鲤洞在太平洋战争和日占期间都有举行普度,而且规模应该不小。碑记所说的1944年第一次举办十年一次的肉身目连的普度戏剧,大概是由在新加坡的兴化移民练习演出的。大抵无论是宗教仪式或仪式戏剧,在1974年以前主要

---

[38] 关于逢甲普度,可以参考注20各书及文,以及:

蔡志祥〈阴阳过度:2004年新加坡九鲤洞逢甲普度中的仪式与剧场〉,《南洋学报》第61卷(2007),页1–12。Choi Chi-cheung, "Yin-yang Transition: Ritual and Theatre in the 2004 Decennial Universal Salvation Ritual of Kiew Lee Tong Temple in Singapore," *Journal of the South Seas Society*, Vol. 61 (2007), pp. 1–12.

田仲一成《中國の宗族と演劇》,页1024–1090。Issei Tanaka, *Lineage and Theatre in China*, pp. 1024–1090.

野村伸一〈事例5:シンガポールの目連戯と塔懴〉,野村伸一编著《東アジアの祭祀伝承と女性救済:目連救母と芸能の諸相》(东京:风响社,2007),页237–265。Shinichi Nomura, "Case 5: Mulian Play and the Ritual of Pagoda Repentance in Singapore," Shinichi Nomura, *Ritual Heritage and Female Salvation in East Asia: Various Perspectives on the Mulian Saving His Mother Play and Performance* (Tokyo: Fukyosha Publishing Inc., 2007).

[39]〈昭南岛九鲤洞公建普度,祈祷圣战完遂东亚共荣〉,《昭南日报》,1943年8月10日,第二版。

"Salvation Ritual of the Kiew Lee Tong Temple in Syonan-to, Praying for the End of the Holy War and the East-Asia Co-Prosperity," *Syonan Jit Poh*, 10 Aug 1943, p. 2.

[40] 1954年距离二战结束不久,撰写碑记者和庙宇、族群关系的人不可能忘记了1944年以前已经有进行普度,并且上演肉身目连戏。碑记指出1954年是第二届的逢甲普度,大抵是因为从1954年开始,兴化移民把上演"肉身目连"的普度仪式常规化,每十年进行一次。其余年份则上演傀儡戏。

都是由在新加坡的兴化移民执行和演出的。1974和1984年因为本地的兴化道士凋零，他们聘请了在马六甲的兴化道士执行仪式。然而，目连救母戏仍然是由本地的兴化移民练习演出。1994年开始，随着中国的改革开放以及新加坡和中国的再联系，九鲤洞开始聘请中国的道士、和尚和戏班来新加坡执行仪式和演戏。目连救母一类的所谓"鬼戏"虽然在中国的文化大革命时因为迷信而被禁止在祭祀时演出。然而，"目连救母"戏仍然以戏曲研究、教学和戏曲表演的名义，以民俗的内部表演形式而存在。[41] 1980年代中国改革开放以来，乡村的民间宗教活动逐渐回复，目连戏也由学院走到民间，并且再次进入海外的华人社会中。一方面因为本地仪式、戏班的凋零，另一方面因为祖乡的开放，新加坡的九鲤洞从1994年开始，每十年的逢甲普度都从福建莆田聘请兴化僧人、道士和剧团来新加坡执行仪式和演出戏剧。余淑娟指出这是因为"……适逢大陆开放，加以新加坡当地演员凋零，九鲤洞便聘请中国莆仙戏一团的陈金兴前来执导，与本地演员合作完成演出。2004年第七届逢甲大普度，九鲤洞同样请来莆仙戏班前来演出。唯上一届是国家剧团，这一届是民间戏班。"[42] 余氏的研究，反映了"目连戏"在20世纪末从中国国家演艺到民间民俗的一个发展过程，把被国家标签为迷信的"鬼戏"重新嵌入人民的宗教生活中。更重要的是中国国家认可的非物质文化遗产这样的国际语言，给予宗教演戏重新嵌入祭祀仪式一个合理的根据。在这样的背景下，九鲤洞的祭祀和演剧也在断绝了半个世纪以后，重新和祖乡文化连接起来。

---

[41] 〈文化部党组织关于停演"鬼戏"的请示报告〉（1963年3月16日），中华人民共和国文化部办公厅编《文化工作文件资料汇编（二）》（北京：内部出版，1988）。
"The Party Organization of the Ministry of Culture's Report on the Request to Suspend 'Ghost Play,'" (16 March 1963), General Office of the Ministry of Culture of the People's Republic of China (compile), *Collection of Documents Relating to Cultural Works, Vol. 2* (Beijing: Internal Reference, 1988).

[42] 余淑娟〈新加坡九鲤洞甲申年目连戏概述〉，《南洋学报》第60卷（2006），页78。
Yee Sok Kiang, "Mulian Play Performed in the Kiew Lee Tong Temple, Singapore in the Year of Jiashen (2004)," *Journal of the South Seas Society*, Vol. 60 (2006), p. 78.

二、天后－妈祖信仰[43]

文化中国的断裂和再连接的可能性，无疑与祖乡中国的宏观政治经济环境有关。同时，也和华人生活地的政治经济环境相关。新加坡的天后－妈祖信仰可以进一步说明这样的关系。文化中国的选择，也和地域阶级有关。从1980年以来，中国政府以莆田湄洲的天后祖庭为中心，积极地以宗教分香关系来推动和平统一。但是在新加坡，从湄洲祖庙分灵的关系，仅仅在中层的社会群体中达成。上层的族群组织（如福建、潮州等）以及下层的坛庙强调的是地域帮群、乡村组织的关系，而非湄洲分灵或地域结盟的关系。以天福宫为例，庙宇的天后金身据说是在1840年自福建兴化府湄州天后宫迎请而来，同年的天后诞，举行盛大的迎神仪式，并且决定每三年举行一次盛大的绕境活动。[44] 天福宫为战前福建帮领袖和福建商人议事之所。游神绕境的范围，也是福建系船务公司、九八行和米行，以及闽人聚居的范围。妈祖不仅保护在新加坡居住和营商的福建人，天福宫也很快地成为福建系领导人和商人讨论政治和业务的地方。在新的福建大厦落成以前，福建会馆就在天福宫右侧，庙宇原来就是闽帮总机构的所在地。[45] 1907年（光绪三十三年）获得光绪皇帝御赐的"溟南靖波"匾额。金碧辉煌的匾额提醒人们庙宇的皇朝国家地位。庙宇的妈祖神像，不时地护送到福建湄洲祖庙，为其宗教的灵

---

[43] 本节主要参考：Choi Chi-cheung, "Beyond Hegemony and Sisterhood: Transnational Tianhou-Mazu cult in East Asia," Special Issue: "Ethnicity, Ritual and Festivals in Asia," Oscar Salemink, Siu-woo Cheung (eds.), *Asian Education and Development Studies*, Vol. 9, No. 1 (2019), pp. 26–36.
[44] 林源福〈战前的天福宫与闽帮社会〉，杜南发主编《南海明珠：天福宫》（新加坡：新加坡福建会馆，2010），页368–387。Lim Guan Hock, "Thian Hock Keng Temple and the Fujian Community Before the WWII," Toh Lam Huat (ed.), *Pearl of the South Sea: Tian Fu Gong* (Singapore: Singapore Hokkien Huay Kuan, 2010), pp. 368–387.

宋旺相（Song Ong Siang）在《新加坡华人百年史》中引述Cameron在1840年4月发表的关于华人市区举行第一次迎神庙会的记载，他指出"这次迎神庙会是为庆贺从中国运来的第一尊女神雕像而举行的。"

参见：宋旺相著，叶书德译《新加坡华人百年史》（新加坡：新加坡中华总商会，1993），页42。

Song Ong Siang, *One Hundred Years' History of the Chinese in Singapore*, trans. Ye Shude (Singapore: Singapore Chinese Chamber of Commerce and Industry, 1933), p. 42.

宋旺相原书由John Murray于1923年在伦敦出版。

[45] 道光三十年"建立天福宫碑记"中称庙为"唐人议事之所"。碑立于庙内。

力重新充电。每三年一次的绕境巡游不仅提醒人们，天福宫妈祖的湄洲分灵的关系，还定义了新加坡福建人的行业和居住范围。1915年福建会馆改组，天福宫乃成为会馆的附属机构。"改组后的福建会馆也致力移风易俗。……为了破除迷信，改组后不久，委员会在征得五股头的同意下，决定废除天福宫三年一度的盛大的迎神赛会。……1935年5月17日议决废除所属的迎送香亭……天福宫天后神像于1936年3月30日，由十多名善男信女护送回福建湄洲省亲，5月11日回銮。原来计划是要举行盛大迎接天后回銮仪式，后来顺从福建会馆的意愿而取消"[46] 1840年至1935年之间天福宫周期性的游神绕境活动在1936年以后完全废止。也就是说，新的领导阶层决定履行移风易俗、破除迷信的信念。他们取消了盛大的游行，也停止了"回娘家"的进香活动。决定疏远与迷信相关的宗教活动导致了会馆决定让佛教组织来管理庙宇。直到2006年，福建会馆是天福宫的"不在地主"，疏远庙宇的任何宗教仪式。2006年福建会馆重新取回天福宫的管理权。从该年开始，每年在农历三月廿三日妈祖诞前举行三天的佛教法会，以及在妈祖诞当天举行一天的道教的平安清醮。[47] 会馆自2000年以后，积极推动闽南文化的活动，出版与在新加坡的福建人和天福宫相关的书籍。天福宫的女神保护在新加坡的福建人，也维护了在新加坡的福建文化和加强了福建人的族群认同。也就是说，天福宫天后的灵力，在1936年以后，并非来自湄洲，而是来自世俗国家，即从清朝皇帝御赐匾额到新加坡政府在1970年代赋予的文化遗产

---

[46] 〈废止所属神庙年例迎送香亭〉，《南洋商报》1935年10月19日，第7版。"Abolish the Annual Procession of Incense Pavilion of Temples Belongs to the Singapore Hokkien Huay Kuan," *Nanyang Siang Bao*, 19 October 1935, p. 7.
　林源福〈战前的天福宫与闽帮社会〉，杜南发主编《南海明珠：天福宫》，页378。Lim Guan Hock, "Thian Hock Keng Temple and the Fujian Community Before the WWII," Toh Lam Huat (ed.), *Pearl of the South Sea: Tian Fu Gong*, p. 378.
[47] 必须注意的是活动的名称随时间而添加。如2012年佛教的三天仪式为"梁皇宝忏大法会"及"消灾祈福大法会"，道教的一天仪式为"平安请醮法会暨祈安礼斗法会"。这四天（从三月廿日到廿三日）统称为"庆典活动"、而妈祖诞正日举办的福建提线木偶戏和歌台为"文化活动"。2013年增加了妈祖诞"文化展览"。根据2006、2012及2013年调查，并参考：
　黄文车《闽南信仰与地方文化》（高雄：春晖出版社，2013），页159–194。
　Huang Wenju, *Belief and Local Culture of Southern Fujian* (Kaohsiung: Chun Hui Press, 2013), pp. 159–194.

身份。她的力量是由福建会馆的领导人定义。直到1930年代为止，天福宫一方面联系着祖庭、祖乡，另一方面建立本地福建群体的生、死联系的地域界线。1990年代以后，随着中国的改革开放，福建群体以天福宫为中心，透过如福建傀儡戏和南音的表演等，在新加坡建立福建文化的中心。2006年妈祖信俗列入第一批中国国家级非物质文化遗产，2009年更成为联合国教科文组织的世界非物质文化遗产。随着天后－妈祖信仰先后成为中国国家级及联合国教科文组织的非物质文化遗产项目，湄洲妈祖成为世界非物质文化遗产"妈祖信俗"的祖庭的时候，新加坡的上层架构的方言群体并没有因此而重新嵌入祖庙分灵的层级系统里。对于一些新加坡的地方坛、庙来说，神明的威力来自村落人脉的共同分享和建立，皇朝国家以及祖庭的灵力也只是遥远的、想象的存在。新加坡的下层社会群体的坛、庙横向和纵向联系，也只是建基于岛内过去的地域和方言关系。从而，湄洲祖庙并非这些地域神明灵力的来源。然而，湄洲祖庙在20世纪80年代初的重建，重新确立祖庙的地位，并且作为一种强力的摄石，吸引海外分灵庙宇的重新朝圣。妈祖信仰先后在21世纪成为中国国家的和世界的非物质文化遗产，提供了海外华人与祖庙再联系的动力。在新加坡，我们观察到祖庙对于地方的中间层级的会馆和庙宇尤其具备吸引力，提供了他们在新加坡本地的神明灵力来源的根据。[48]

三、万缘胜会[49]

文化中国的学习与调整有着模仿与创新的过程。新加坡广惠肇碧山亭举办的万缘胜会可以说是在模仿中国文化过程中的一种在地的创新。

---

[48] Choi Chi-cheung, "Beyond Hegemony and Sisterhood: Transnational Tianhou-Mazu cult in East Asia," Special Issue: "Ethnicity, Ritual and Festivals in Asia," Oscar Salemink, Siu-woo Cheung (eds.), *Asian Education and Development Studies*, Vol. 9, No. 1 (2019), pp. 26–36.

[49] 本节主要参考：蔡志祥〈从反迷信到万缘会：广州到东南亚的城市救赎仪式〉，李孝悌、陈学然编《海客瀛洲：传统中国沿海城市与近代东亚海上世界》，页30–42。Choi Chi-cheung, "From Anti-Superstition to Grand Salvation Ritual: Salvations Rituals of the Cities from Canton to Southeast Asia," Li Hsiao-ti, Chan Hok Yin (eds.), *China and Overseas Chinese: Traditional Chinese Coastal Cities and the Maritime World of Modern East Asia*, pp. 30–42.

Choi Chi-cheung, "Ancestors Are Watching: Ritual and Governance at Peck San Theng, a Chinese Afterlife Care Organization in Singapore," *Religions*, Vol. 11, No. 8 (2020).

万缘胜会原来是清末民初华南地方为对应科学和反迷信的思潮发展出来的、以悼念、纪念国家英雄的名义,透过僧、道、尼的法力来进行灵魂救赎的宗教慈善仪式。万缘会透过移民和移民网络,很快地为广府人的侨乡社会接受、并且在他们的居住地生根。这些原来在侨乡社会举办的万缘会,是乡民以国家认可的语言,在"反迷信"的巨潮下,有效地解决乡民灵魂信仰的需要。然而,这样的祭祀语言,在东南亚的华人社会里,一方面用作解决安抚幽魂的精神需要,解决安顿祖先、使之不沦为无主孤魂的仪式工具;另一方面,有效地筹集资金、成为社会的、慈善的和政治的工具。虽然渡亡依然是仪式的主体,然而它们各自对应不同的地方社会的发展轨迹,调整与仪式相关的功能和作用。

1920年代开始,新加坡的为广惠肇碧山亭,以纪念的形式,在坟山清理后,举办万缘会,进行灵魂救赎的仪式。从1922年到2017年,碧山亭共组织了14次大型的万缘胜会和5次规模较小的超度幽魂胜会。这些仪式,从不定期举行,发展到21世纪以后,大概五年举办一次。仪式由僧、道、尼执行,[50] 短的是1日2夜,长的是7日8夜。每一次万缘胜会都是因为碧山亭遇上财政困难或需要扩展服务而举行。例如1922年万缘会的盈余用作建立碧山庙、茶亭、公所和学校。1943年虽然在日占时举行,仍然有盈余来成立一个基金,并且建立一个地方的市集。1946年举行的第三次万缘会的盈余用作购买七片新坟地安葬日占时的死者,同时建立一所新的办事处和学校。战后随着新加坡华人人口的增加,以及中国政权的转移,运柩回乡的可能性减低,新的坟地的需求也增加。1952年的万缘胜会的利润,便是用作迁葬早期坟墓的费用。1958年的万缘会的盈余则作为购买新坟地的资金。碧山亭的常规性收入主要来自坟墓的租金、香油捐助和坟地内的种植园的租金。可是,1973年开始新加坡政府在新市镇发展的计划下,禁止土葬、并且迁走种植园。面对新的时代,碧山亭分别在1976和1978年举行万缘胜会,筹集资金兴建安置骨灰的灵灰阁、一座大楼以及将来扩展的费用。从碧山亭举办的万缘胜会,也许我们可以这样的理解:作为一个坟山管理组织,

---

[50] 2017年增加了来自马来西亚的,属于客家香花传统的斋姑执行的仪式。

在1970年代以前，举行万缘会主要有两个目的，那就是安抚亡魂以及筹集资金作为扩展坟地和教育及社会福利的用途。1970–1980年代以后，万缘胜会举行的目的是建立服务死者的灵灰阁。1990年代以后，碧山亭的领袖，积极推动碧山亭成为敬宗追源的祖先祭祀以及弘扬中国文化的中心。因此，把万缘胜会从非常规性的仪式活动，改为五年一届的常规活动，从而藉此得到固定的收入来源，用以推动碧山亭作为仁孝的儒家文化的基地。从组织者的角度，万缘胜会无疑满足了碧山亭领袖服务生者与死者的伦理目的。万缘胜会贯彻他们固守的儒家伦理、慈善和反迷信的信念。我们必须同时注意的是碧山亭的万缘胜会的祭祀对象并非一般的游魂野鬼，而是一些原来是有主的祖先。万缘胜会不过是把有主的个人祖先，通过仪式，成为会馆的、集体的共同祖先。万缘胜会是碧山亭的三个标识性的服务范围之一。[51] 根据碧山亭的官方网页，万缘胜会是碧山亭"……弘扬孝道与饮水思源价值观的旗舰活动，由和尚、尼姑和道士集体诵经，收入除了用来资助坟山庙宇，维修建路外，也捐助各类社会慈善活动。"[52] 在碧山亭文物馆的"守候"展厅，强调了在21世纪万缘胜会的跨越广惠肇族群，是以孝道促进"各族群籍贯人士和谐共处"的活动，配合了新加坡建国以来，小心慎重维系的种族和谐政策。

要言之，从1920–1930年代开始，万缘胜会因为封建迷信的关系在中国被禁止了。但是，在东南亚的华人社会，万缘胜会则被赋予宗教慈善和孝道的新解释而继续下来。在新的解释与实践下，新加坡的广惠肇碧山亭不仅延续了灵魂救赎的中国文化，而且配合了在地国家的种族和谐的政策，给予文化中国在海外华人社会的新意涵。

---

[51] 碧山亭的网址的首页，列出三个服务范围：骨灰灵塔、广惠肇碧山亭文物馆和万缘胜会。见：

"新加坡广惠肇碧山亭"，新加坡广惠肇碧山亭官网，https://sgpecksantheng.com/（最后访问日期：2020年6月23日）。

"Singapore Kwong Wai Siew Peck San Theng," Offical Website of Singapore Kwong Wai Siew Peck San Theng, https://sgpecksantheng.com/ (Accessed: 23 June 2020).

[52] "万缘胜会"，新加坡广惠肇碧山亭官网，https://sgpecksantheng.com/grand-universal-salvation-ritual/（最后访问日期：2022年5月15日）。

"Grand Universal Salvation Ritual," Offical Website of Singapore Kwong Wai Siew Peck San Theng, https://sgpecksantheng.com/grand-universal-salvation-ritual/ (Accessed: 15 May 2022).

小结

19世纪中期，华人人口急剧增加。这些远赴重洋的华人大部分是单身的男性，他们依赖团体提供的生活的保护以及死后的祭祀。对于社团的依赖也导致了团体之间的竞争，导致种种的治安问题。19世纪中叶以来，新加坡政府制定连串的法规（如危险社团法）和建立政府机构（华民护卫司）来管治华人。一方面在理解到七月中元节对华人的重要的同时，政府也采用一些临时的规定（如禁止中元普度或演剧），试图通过规范葬地和限制华人的宗教节日活动来控制会党和群众。另一方面，为了处理卫生和都市扩展而制定的坟山政策，鼓励了合法的社会群体和灵魂安顿的结合关系。19世纪末20世纪初的华人领袖，在面对政府管治华人的葬和祭的政策，以及19世纪末以来反对迷信的思潮下，强调纪念和追悼国家英雄的万缘胜会，强调中元祭祀的慈善、孝道和世俗性，从而淡化了宗教节日活动的封建迷信性质及其与私会党的关系。[53] 中元祭祀和天后－妈祖信仰展示了海外华人在回应在地政府的政策与环球思潮的同时，一方面强调社区节日的"中国元素"，另一方面赋予新的诠析和意涵以作为在异乡生活的文化策略。

太平洋战争后的社会重建以及新中国的建立，使得华人对中国文化从实在的联系发展到从经验和想象中实践社区节日，从而也加强了社区节日的在地性。为了配合地域民族国家的建立和对社会的重建，华人的祭祀方式也有所改变。就如1946年新加坡政府设立战争纪念委员会（War Memorial Committee），提出两个纪念方案：由新加坡协会（Singapore Association）倡议，扶轮社（Rotary Club）支持的建立肺结核医院以及社会福利局（Social Welfare Council）倡议的建立社区中心。[54] 政府的立场是倾向服务生者的公益和福利。在1960–1970年代以

---

[53] 蔡志祥〈葬与祭：19世纪末20世纪初新加坡英国殖民政府对华人节日与坟山的管治〉，陈俊强、洪健荣主编《台北州建州百年：在地化与国际化的视角》，页229–257。
 Choi Chi-cheung, "Burial and Ritual: Governance of Chinese Festivals and Burial Ground by the British Colonial Government of Singapore in the Late 19th and Early 20th Century," Chan Chun Keung, Hung Jian-rong (eds.), *Centennial of the Establishment of Taipei State: Perspectives of Localisation and Globalisation*, pp. 229–257.

[54] "The Living and the Dead," *The Straits Times*, 30 October 1946, p. 4.

前，新加坡政府极力发展建设、推动民族融和。城市发展也征用了不少的坟山土地。因此也令民众祭祀的场所有所限制，从而也影响到祭祀悼念方式的改变。

总言之，华人的节日，在新加坡经历了不同的发展轨迹。

20世纪中叶以后，随着中国的重新开放，中国政府借助文化推动经济投资和发展，同时也像摄石一样，牵起了海外华人的寻根热潮和文化溯源远动。华人回乡建设祖坟、祠堂以至戮力捐输建设宗教庙宇的祖庭，中国再次成为吸引华人回乡回国的摄石。华人的故国、祖乡希企凭借文化和宗教节日的联系，加强华人回国回乡投资建设的意欲。改革开放，令人群相互流动的可能性增加，也带动了中国的文化再输出。如钟摆一样，海外华人社会和祖乡相互撞击互动。20世纪末、21世纪初的非物质文化遗产，更加促了这样的钟摆互动关系。九鲤洞和潮汕善堂的例子，说明了宗教节日如何从摄石作用发展到钟摆作用。也就是说，从1990年代开始，华人更进一步强调在地宗教节日的中国性，并且因为非物质文化遗产的溯源而强调原乡族群的文化源流。如妈祖、广泽尊王、莆田兴化九鲤洞等原乡庙宇祖庭积极地进行祖乡文化的再输出。因此，对于海外华人来说，在再次建立华人共同文化的同时，也加强了族群、方言群的文化差异。这样的共同性和差异性的"文化中国"的表现，显现了海外华人的帮群性以及在不同种族共同生活的环境中，以"文化中国"建立一个"显著的他者"的身份。文化中国既是联系祖乡的工具，也是以海外华人社会的特殊关系在居住国家容许的范围内，回应中国的文化再输出。

20世纪海外华人的宗教性社区节日可以说是在想象与实践"文化中国"的时候展演的一种文化策略。不断地被重新演绎的"文化中国"，在不同的时代既满足不同阶级、不同族群的诉求，对应在地国家的社会政治的发展，也回应了祖乡国家的文化宗教政策以及环球思潮的冲击。

跨界连结
论华侨银行战时发展策略（1938–1945年）

杨妍[*]

摘要

本文聚焦于1938至1945年间，通过银行内部文档、刊物，报章新闻，员工口述历史和传记等资料，讨论新加坡华侨银行战时的发展策略。身处复杂多变的政治环境中，华侨银行以危为机，通过建立东南亚、中国和欧美澳之间的跨界联系，再增设民信部抢占侨汇市场、创办《华侨经济》及合办南洋企业公司来促进贸易投资、通过多重网络进行海外转移这三方面，于实践中探索如何改善运作方式、扩大业务范围、规避风险，在满足战时需求的同时，扩大影响力，提高声誉，使其转变成为比西方银行、华人传统金融机构更受欢迎的华人银行中的巨擘。该案例有助于探究跨界连结对华人银行发展的重要性，亦能从华人银行史的语境中反思现代性议题。

关键词：战时、新加坡、华侨银行、海外华人、跨界、侨批

---

[*] 杨妍，新加坡国立大学中文系，chsyang@nus.edu.sg。

本文原刊登于《华人研究国际学报》，第14卷，第1期，2022年6月，页1-18。经授权转载。

This is an Open Access chapter published by World Scientific Publishing Company. It is distributed under the terms of the Creative Commons Attribution-NonCommercial-NoDerivatives 4.0 (CC BY-NC-ND) License which permits use, distribution and reproduction, provided that the original work is properly cited, the use is non-commercial and no modifications or adaptations are made.

Building Transboundary Connections:
The Development Strategies of Oversea-Chinese Banking Corporation during Wartime, 1938-1945

YANG Yan

Abstract

Focusing on the period from 1938 to 1945, this article highlights the wartime development strategies employed by the Oversea-Chinese Banking Corporation (OCBC) in Singapore using primary sources such as internal bank documents, journals and publications, newspapers, oral histories and biographies of its staff. In a complex and volatile political environment, the OCBC successfully transformed its crisis into an opportunity to expand its business and boost its influence by establishing transboundary connections across Southeast Asia, China, Europe, North America and Australia by the mid-20th century. Three innovative ways were implemented, including: a) setting up the Department of Remittances and collaborating with the Postal Remittances & Savings Bank of China to capture the overseas remittance market; b) publishing the magazine titled "The Oversea-Chinese Economics" and creating an interlocking partnership with the Nanyang Development & Finance Corporation to promote trades and investments across Southeast Asia and China; as well as c) re-registering the bank and transferring the capital abroad through multiple transboundary networks. These efforts allowed the bank to expand its service coverage, reform its corporate structure and optimise its operation process in order to meet wartime needs of the overseas Chinese communities. In doing so, the bank also extended its influence and global reach, eventually gaining a reputation of being more popular than Western banks and other traditional Chinese financial institutions that had existed in the same era. This research seeks to provide insights on the dynamics of the transboundary connections that contributed towards the bank's success during the turbulent years and explore issues related to modernity in the context of the overseas Chinese banking history.

Keywords: Wartime, Singapore; Oversea-Chinese Banking Corporation (OCBC); Overseas Chinese; Transboundary; Remittance

一、引言

海外华人银行的发展史一直以来因资料匮乏而乏人问津。[1] 银行作为一种西式现代金融机构,如何在处于传统与现代之间的海外华人社会运作实践,如何被华人群体包括银行从业者、顾客等理解应用,为何能匹敌甚至胜出同时期的传统中式金融组织和西方现代银行,这些问题值得思考。特别是在20世纪上半叶政经局势动荡之中,以南洋为腹地、以跨界华侨为受众的华侨银行(Oversea-Chinese Banking Corporation,简称OCBC)的脱颖而出,格外引人瞩目。

本文将以华侨银行为个案,聚焦于1938–1945年间,讨论该行的战时跨界策略,剖析其如何通过建立、发展东南亚与中国及其他地区之间的连结,优化运作,多元发展,险中求生,从而成为华人金融界的巨头。关于二战时期新马银行的研究从缺,主要因为该阶段银行的内部档案尽已销毁或散轶。[2] 然而,得益于这期间多样的跨界流通,本地缺失的资料却能在香港、上海、厦门觅得,包括银行与合作机构的信件、文档等。通过这些一手史料,结合银行的期刊、报章的报道广告、银行人员的口述历史和传记等,本文试图拼绘出二战时华侨银行

---

[1] 目前的银行史研究主要以国家和银行类型为单位,讨论不同国家的银行和各类型如商业银行等的发展史。由海外华人创办的银行数量不多,且较集中在东南亚地区,相关研究较少,见:

Tan Ee-Leong, "The Chinese Banks Incorporated in Singapore & the Federation of Malaya," *Journal of the Malaysian Branch of the Royal Asiatic Society*, Vol. 42, No. 1 (1969), pp. 256–281.

Rajeswary Ampalavanar Brown, *Capital and Entrepreneurship in South-East Asia* (Houndmills, Basingstoke, Hampshire: The Macmillan Press Ltd; New York: St. Martin's Press, 1994), pp. 160–172.

杨妍《危与机:论新加坡早期华人银行之生存发展1903–1945》,硕士论文(新加坡:新加坡国立大学中文系,2013)。Yang Yan, "Crises and Changes: The Development of Overseas Chinese Banks in Singapore during 1903–1945," Master's Thesis (Singapore: National University of Singapore, 2013).

[2] 该阶段的原始资料经历了两次浩劫,在日本占据新加坡1942年前后,为了保护银行和客户,银行主动销毁了部分文件。之后于1990年代因公司改革,原欲捐出的银行史料由于涉及到资料保密和客户隐私等法律原因,最终选择销毁。前人学者在论述新马银行史时均略过1941–1945年这一段,而分为战前和战后及其他阶段,见:

Lee Sheng-Yi, *The Monetary and Banking Development of Singapore and Malaysia*, 3rd Edition (Singapore: Singapore University Press, 1990), pp. 34–49.

的跨界图景，填补研究空白，探讨银行如何在现实环境中把握机遇，改革创新，通过跨界的机制来获取最大利益，反映出海外华人银行的现代化特征和独特进程。

二、跨界连结的基础

华侨银行是由华商银行（Chinese Commercial Bank，1912–1932）、和丰银行（Ho Hong Bank，1917–1932）、旧华侨银行（Oversea Chinese Bank，1919–1932）于1932年合并而成。[3] 从广告（图1）可见，分行众多是该行的主要卖点。[4]

图1：大华银行、华侨银行、中国银行广告并排对比（从左至右）

---

[3] 本文以"旧华侨银行"指称合并之前的华侨银行，三行合并的过程及合并前后的改变见：
杨妍〈1933之变革：论新加坡早期华人银行发展——以华侨银行为例〉，《华人研究国际学报》第4卷第2期（2012），页53–82。
Yang Yan, "The Transformation in 1933: How Did the Early Overseas Chinese Banks in Singapore Develop? A Case Study of Oversea Chinese Banking Corporation Ltd.," *The International Journal of Diasporic Chinese Studies*, Vol. 4, No. 2 (2012), pp. 53–82.

[4] 〈大华银行广告〉、〈华侨银行广告〉、〈中国银行广告〉，《南洋商报》，1939年1月25日，第12版。
"Advertisement of United Overseas Bank," "Advertisement of OCBC," "Advertisement of Bank of China," *Nanyang Siang Pau*, 25 January 1939, p. 12.

如滨下武志对汇丰银行 (Hongkong and Shanghai Banking Corporation) 分行网络的评价，[5] 华侨银行的分行也充分利用了华侨商人、华侨经济及华侨汇款，但其受众更遍及中小华商和中下阶层的民众，体现在更多设于华人聚居地的分行。与汇丰相比，华侨银行在马来半岛的分行数量更多，占据华人众多的各埠（图2）。[6] 相较英资银行如汇丰银行、有利银行（Mercantile Bank）、渣打银行（Chartered Bank）因原料出口贸易倾向在马来亚东岸设点，华侨银行选择渗入华人较多的西岸。

图2：华侨银行分行在马来亚和荷属东印度分布图

---

[5] 滨下武志著、马宋芝译《香港大视野：亚洲网络中心》（香港：商务印书馆，1997），页111–116。

　Takeshi Hamashita, *Hong Kong's Great Perspective: Asian Network Centre*, trans. Ma Songzhi (Hong Kong: The Commercial Press, 1997), pp. 111–116.

[6] 根据〈华侨银行各地分行〉，《华侨经济》第1卷第1期（1941），页4，和其他关于分行设立的报章信息整理。图3亦同。

　"Branches of OCBC," *The Oversea-Chinese Economics*, Vol. 1, No. 1 (1941), p. 4.

20世纪初,西方银行通过买办(Comprador)和华人鸿商富贾接触,少数中下阶层的华人则通过印度高利贷债主(Chettiar)借款,如同饮鸩止渴。[7] 因此,华侨银行则为民众带来了新气象。中下阶层人数可观的华侨成为银行的目标对象。如银行总经理陈延谦在分行开幕时介绍,新人开户只需五百元存入,不满五百元者仍可凭店铺介绍开户。[8] 相比高高在上的西方银行,华侨银行更贴近侨胞的日常活动。对比传统金融组织如当铺、钱庄,华侨银行大规模的分行网络(图3)跨越了地域,连接东南亚各埠和中国,有助于资金的跨界运转。

图3:华侨银行亚洲地区分布图

---

[7] 陈延谦〈新加坡华人银行发达史〉,《华侨经济》第1卷第1期(1941),页18–19。
Tan Ean Kiam, "A History of Chinese Banking in Singapore," *The Oversea-Chinese Economics*, Vol. 1, No. 1 (1941), pp. 18–19.

[8] 〈怡保华侨银行开幕日总理陈延谦与本报驻怡记者一席谈〉,《南洋商报》,1933年9月19日,第7版。本文中的货币除特别说明外,均以叻币为单位。
"An Interview with Managing Director Tan Ean Kiam by Our Special Correspondent in Ipoh on the Opening Day of OCBC's Ipoh Branch," *Nanyang Siang Pau*, 19 September 1933, p. 7.

除了主要商埠如槟城、马六甲、吉隆坡、柔佛，华侨银行在马来半岛其他分行的建立均早于汇丰。这归功于银行吸收了其前身在1917至1920年代设置的多处分行。早前，和丰、旧华侨的董事包括了分行所处各地的知名华商，如马六甲的曾江水、峇株巴辖的陈瑞和、麻坡的张顺兰和黄亚四、爪哇的黄仲涵和黄奕注等，董事的人际网络开拓了银行的分行网络。[9] 此外，银行也在1933至1941年间派经理去各地考察，根据当地商业活动和货币走势来判断时机，继续在东南亚开设分行，如泗水、海防、曼谷、安顺、昔加末等。[10]

时间之早，地点之多，意味着华侨银行较其他银行，更能占据先机，接触到广大华人社群，成为一个有跨界影响的、属于华侨群体的本土银行。每个分行都独立运作，业务范围（见表1）与总行一样，相互之间直接交流，并能与其他合作机构直接沟通，无须通过总行，提高了行政效率。[11]

---

[9] 陈维龙《新马注册商业银行》（新加坡：新加坡世界书局有限公司，1975），页27–34。
　 Tan Ee Leong, *Registered Commercial Banks in Singapore and Malaya* (Singapore: The World Book Company, 1975), pp. 27–34.

[10] 〈华侨银行分行分布各地〉，《南洋商报》，1972年10月31日，第28版。"Branches of OCBC Over the World," *Nanyang Siang Pau*, 31 October 1972, p. 28.
　 狄克·威尔逊著，译者不详《安如磐石：华侨银行四十周年纪念册》（新加坡：华侨银行有限公司，1972），页49。Dick Wilson, *Solid as a Rock: The First Forty Years of the Oversea-Chinese Banking Corporation*, trans. Unknown (Singapore: OCBC, 1972), p. 49.
　 〈华侨银行总理陈延谦明日出游棉兰并欲巡视马来亚各分行〉，《南洋商报》，1937年7月14日，第6版。"OCBC Managing Director Tan Ean Kiam Will Make His Visit to Medan and Branches in Malaya," *Nanyang Siang Pau*, 14 July 1937, p. 6.

[11] 华侨银行在1939年特发通告给各分行，要求分行在战时通讯中断的情况下自主运作，无须联络总行。
　 Grace Loh, Goh Chor Boon, Tan Teng Lang, *Building Bridges, Carving Niches: An Enduring Legacy* (Singapore: Oxford University Press, 2000), p. 88.

表1：上海分行业务说明[12]

一	收受普通活期定期存款
二	办理各种放款或贴现
三	票据承兑
四	办理国内汇兑
五	经中央银行特许办理国外汇兑
六	代理收付款项
七	买卖公债库卷及公司债券
八	办理与业务有关之仓库或保管业务
九	投资于生产工用或交通事业
十	代募公债公司债及公司股份
十一	收受外国货币或买卖生金银

分行的员工相互调转，互动频繁。如原为厦门分行要员的孙清喜，后调任麻坡分行经理，再转调曼谷分行副经理。[13] 分行人员除了日常业务，也负责调查当地商情、政治、社会，与总行和其他分行及时分享。[14] 分行人员也与当地华人商会交好，时常联欢。[15] 更关键的是，分行还以所在市镇为据点，辐射到周边商港。例如荷属东印度的

---

[12] 上海市社会局关于华侨银行股份有限公司登记问题与经济部的来往文书，上海市档案馆藏，Q6-1-3952。
Correspondences between Shanghai Social Bureau and Ministry of Economic Affairs Regarding the Registration of OCBC in China, Shanghai Municipal Archives, Q6-1-3952.

[13] 〈麻坡华侨银行现任经理孙清喜君将调任曼咯华侨银行要职〉，《南洋商报》，1934年8月13日，第9版。
"General Manager Sun Qingxi of OCBC's Muar Branch Will Be Posted to OCBC's Bangkok Branch," *Nanyang Siang Pau*, 13 August 1934, p. 9.

[14] 如占碑分行：徐笃谦〈"占碑"的近况〉，《友声》第1卷第1期（1935），页19–22。
Xu Duqian, "Updates about Jambi," *The OCBC Echo*, Vol. 1, No. 1 (1935), pp. 19–22.
巨港分行：吴仲瑜〈巨港情报〉，《友声》第1卷第1期（1935），页22–26。Wu Zhongyu, "Information about Palembang," *The OCBC Echo*, Vol. 1, No. 1 (1935), pp. 22–26.

[15] 〈怡保华侨银行举行联欢之盛况华侨银行即侨胞之银行〉，《南洋商报》，1933年10月18日，第7版。
"OCBC's Ipoh Branch Held a Celebration and Announced That OCBC Serves for All Overseas Chinese," *Nanyang Siang Pau*, 18 October 1933, p. 7.

四间分行在当地如望加锡、巴东、万隆、实武牙、民那多等港口,设立代理处。[16] 这说明银行有能力通过分行的延伸进一步覆盖东南亚大部分地区。

所有分行由总行副总经理周福隆监察。周和掌管外汇的柯守智紧密合作,被誉为承托银行发展的两巨擘。[17] 由此可见分行拓展对银行而言的重要性。这些分行布局在华人聚居地,既是金融网络的节点,又是商业网络的枢纽。这些点连结成一个复线联系的网络,处理跨界活动,如汇兑、贸易、投资等。覆盖广阔的分行,为这个网络提供了各种外汇、设施、资金和资讯的流通,帮助银行提高效率,把握商机。这些跨界活动同时也不断巩固这个网络,增加经济活动的体量、频率和效率,增强银行的跨区域实力及影响力。下文将通过三个例证来说明跨界连结的操作和影响。

三、抢占跨界侨汇

华侨银行从1938年起直接经营侨批业务,极短时间内占据市场大部分份额。如此大动作却未引起足够重视,目前的研究因资料局限,出现

---

[16] 〈华侨银行新景象增加购买及代换国币港币〉,《南洋商报》,1937年2月3日,第8版。
"OCBC Recently Buys in Chinese Currency & Hong Kong Dollar and Offers the Exchange Service," *Nanyang Siang Pau*, 3 February 1937, p. 8.

[17] 口述历史资料,资料来源应提供者要求保密,银行的管理架构见:杨妍《危与机:论新加坡早期华人银行之生存发展1903–1945》,硕士论文,页44–47。
Yang Yan, "Crises and Changes: The Development of Overseas Chinese Banks in Singapore during 1903–1945," Master's Thesis, pp. 44–47.

了史实差误。[18] 从新发现的文档结合当时新闻来看，华侨银行不仅开拓了新市场，更简化了侨汇运作的流程，堪称行业变革者。

银行意识到，战时的侨汇市场是一个难得的商机。1938年初，日军入侵中国东南沿海一带，侨批运送极不稳定，款项遗失、信差被劫时有发生。原本的市场主导者民信局、侨批局因此常破产、歇业。[19] 但是，战时的侨汇金额有增无减，不仅包括赡家性侨汇，还有大量捐资性侨汇和投资性侨汇。据统计，"自抗战开始以来，华侨汇款极为踊跃，去岁尤突破历年纪录，超过常年3倍……"[20]

银行瞄准这个机会，由周福隆与中国邮政储金汇业局（简称储汇局）局长刘攻芸博士联络。[21] 两人同为福建祖籍，刘攻芸曾前往新加

---

[18] 如：Rajeswary Ampalavanar Brown, *Capital and Entrepreneurship in South-East Asia*, p. 155.

蚁健〈抗战期间及战后初期海外华侨银行的侨批〉，王炜中主编《首届侨批文化研讨会论文集》（汕头：潮汕历史文化研究中心等，2004），页118–130。Yi Jian, "The Remittance of OCBC during the War and the Early Post-war Period," Wang Weizhong (ed.), *Proceedings of the First Symposium on Overseas Chinese Remittance Culture* (Shantou: Center for Historical and Cultural Studies of Chaoshan, 2004), pp. 118–130.

刘伯挚〈华侨银行的侨批业务〉，《福建金融》第6期（2016），页70–72。Liu Bozi, "The Remittance of OCBC," *Fujian Finance*, No. 6 (2016), pp. 70–72.

Liu Bozi, "The Operating Modes of the *Qiaopi* Trade and Impact on the *Qiaopiju*: A Case Study of the Oversea-Chinese Banking Corporation (OCBC)," Gregor Benton, Liu Hong, Zhang Huimei (eds.), *The Qiaopi Trade and Transnational Networks in the Chinese Diaspora* (London: Routledge, 2018), pp. 130–143.

一些研究未能准确说明华侨银行和储汇局的关系，或将华侨银行误认为广东省银行海外分支，或将华侨银行、储汇局联手推出的民信业务与侨批局通过银行分行之间汇兑的操作混为一谈。

[19] 李小燕《中国官方行局经营侨汇业务（1937–1949）》，博士论文（新加坡：新加坡国立大学中文系，2010），页97–101。

Li Xiaoyan, "A Study of Overseas Chinese Remittance through Chinese National Banks and Post Offices, 1937–1949," PhD Dissertation (Singapore: National University of Singapore, 2010), pp. 97–101.

[20] 〈国内要闻：去岁闽侨汇款回国创新纪录〉，《银行周报》第24卷第12期（1940），页22–23。

"Domestic News: Remittances from Overseas Hokkiens in Last Year Hit a New High Record," *The Bankers Weekly*, Vol. 24, No. 12 (1940), pp. 22–23.

[21] Oral History of Renee Chew, *Special Project*, National Archives of Singapore, File No. 002005, Reel No. 2.

刘攻芸原名刘驷业，署名S. Y. Liu。

坡考察汇业，由华侨银行和民国总领事馆接待。²² 储汇局方面，该局听从国民党政府指令，吸收侨汇，以免外流至日伪政府或黑市。²³ 考虑到华侨银行是南洋颇具规模的机构，储汇局希望能利用其东南亚的网络来管控侨汇。银行方面，该行向来与民国政府金融界关系密切，其董事先有中国银行新加坡代表黄柏权，后有中国银行总经理张嘉璈的妹夫朱文熊。²⁴ 银行希望能与官方建立联系，从而获得经营侨汇的正当性，并能通过储汇局在中国国内的分处派发侨汇，更为稳妥。双方各取所需，一拍即合，签署了协议。²⁵

为了推广这项业务，银行增加人手，于1938年9月设立了民信部。银行一开始便放眼整个南洋，竭力宣传：

> 自从祖国抗战军兴，因种种关系，至此民信汇款大受影响，华侨银行新设立之民信部，凡福建广东广西大小各市镇，均能通汇，且手续简便，汇价公平，保障安全……播音台特分五种方言，将此重要消息广播，俾全马华侨得以周知，外埠各地之华侨银行分行，如峇都巴辖、麻坡、马六甲、芙蓉、吉隆坡、

---

[22] 〈我邮政储汇局长刘攻芸南来考察邮汇业〉，《南洋商报》，1938年7月29日，第5版。
"The Director-General of Postal Remittances and Savings Bank S. Y. Liu Visited Nanyang for Investigating the Postal Remittance Industry," *Nanyang Siang Pau*, 29 July 1938, p. 5.

[23] 李小燕〈侨汇争夺战：国民政府官方行局与日伪、港府的侨汇争夺〉，黄贤强主编《族群、历史与文化：跨域研究东南亚和东亚》（新加坡：新加坡国立大学中文系、八方文化创作室，2011），下册页574。
Li Xiaoyan, "The Battle for Remittances: The Competitions among the Chinese National Banks and Post Offices, the Japanese Government and the Hong Kong Government," Wong Sin Kiong (ed.), *Ethnicity, History and Culture: Trans-regional and Cross-disciplinary Studies on Southeast Asia and East Asia* (Singapore: Department of Chinese Studies, National University of Singapore; Global Publishing Co., 2011), p. 574.

[24] 〈华侨银行去年所获纯益七十余万元〉，《南洋商报》，1938年5月7日，第7版。
"OCBC Gained a Net Profit of More Than 700k Last Year," *Nanyang Siang Pau*, 7 May 1938, p. 7.

[25] 华侨银行有限公司《华侨银行有限公司第二十一周年纪念册》（新加坡：华侨银行有限公司，1954），页13–14。OCBC, *Twenty-first Anniversary Souvenir Magazine of OCBC* (Singapore: OCBC, 1954), pp. 13–14.
叶渊〈民信汇款与祖国经济〉，《华侨经济》第1期（1941），页25。Yeh Yuan, "Overseas Chinese Remittance and the Economy of China," *The Oversea-Chinese Economics*, No. 1 (1941), p. 25.

槟城、吉兰丹、仰光、暹罗、安南、以及荷属各地分行亦同样次第设立……[26]

各分行负责收理当地的汇款和家书,交予储汇局香港处,经储汇局内地分处投送、兑支,回执转回华侨银行。回执使用银行附送之信封信纸,无须贴邮。由银行担保汇款送达,若因地址更改未能投交,按原汇价算回叻银或原来货币,汇款人得有保证。[27]

和一般民信局相比,华侨银行覆盖范围广阔且密集。得益于储汇局的内地网络,如广告(图4)所示,仅泉州就有47个通汇点,三省多达400余个,甚至连荒僻山区都设有站点。[28]

图4:华侨银行增设民信部广告

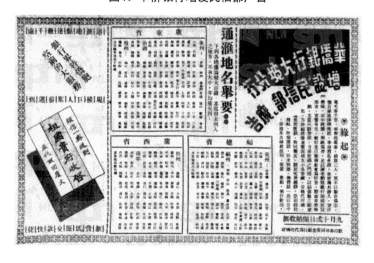

---

[26] 〈华侨银行有限公司民信部今日开幕通汇处遍设闽粤桂各地〉,《南洋商报》,1938年9月12日,第11版。
"Today is the Opening of OCBC's Department of Remittances which Serves the Purpose of Remittance All over Fujian, Guangdong and Guangxi," *Nanyang Siang Pau*, 12 September 1938, p. 11.

[27] 〈华侨银行民信部各地汇款从未间断〉,《南洋商报》,1938年12月9日,第7版。
"OCBC's Remittances to All Places Have Never Been Interrupted," *Nanyang Siang Pau*, 9 December 1938, p. 7.

[28] 〈华侨银行大坡分行增设民信部广告〉,《南洋商报》,1938年9月20日,第13版。
"Advertisement of OCBC's Newly Setup Department of Remittances," *Nanyang Siang Pau*, 20 September 1938, p. 13.

起初，银行仅通汇传统侨乡。后来考虑到市场需求，范围扩大，凭借储汇局的"一万二千余处邮务机关"，[29] 开辟云南、四川、贵州、陕西、浙江、江西、江苏等新市场（图5），[30] 吸引侨胞子弟求学汇款、投资西南汇款等，令其他侨批机构望尘莫及。[31]

图5：华侨银行民信部每日汇率

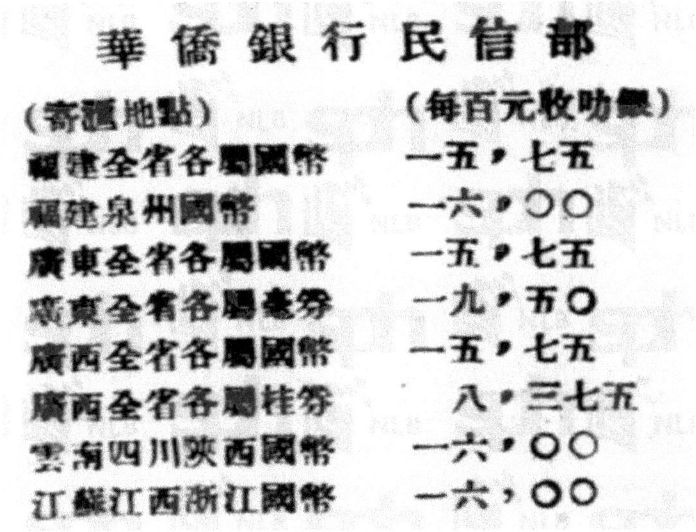

華僑銀行民信部	
（寄匯地點）	（每百元收叻幣）
福建全省各處國幣	一五，七五
福建泉州國幣	一六，〇〇
廣東全省各處國幣	一五，七五
廣東全省各處毫券	一九，五〇
廣西全省各處國幣	一五，七五
廣西全省各處桂券	八，三七五
雲南四川陝西國幣	一六，〇〇
江蘇江西浙江國幣	一六，〇〇

战况愈烈，更多民信局停汇，而华侨银行不断登报告知通汇信息，公开透明：

---

[29] 叶渊〈民信汇款与祖国经济〉，《华侨经济》第1期（1941），页25.
　Yeh Yuan, "Overseas Chinese Remittance and the Economy of China," *The Oversea-Chinese Economics*, No. 1 (1941), p. 25.
[30] 〈汇兑〉，《南洋商报》，1939年9月13日，第28版。
　"Remittance and Exchange Rate," *Nanyang Siang Pau*, 13 September 1939, p. 28.
[31] 〈华侨银行民信部独对海南岛各区银信照常收汇并扩充滇川陕民信〉，《南洋商报》，1939年3月5日，第6版。
　"OCBC Remittance Service to Hainan as per Normal and Expands the Remittance Service to Yunnan, Sichuan and Shanxi," *Nanyang Siang Pau*, 5 March 1939, p. 6.

> ……敝行接到二月廿二日封发之回文后，曾再继续受到二月尾及三月九日封寄者共数包，昨美多利轮到叻，又接到三月十三日在琼山封寄者一包，其中回文，尚有未领去者，请查阅可也，至于昨日收到之回文将再择一制版刊登以慰侨琼，对战区不嫌麻烦，设法收汇。[32]

该行仍能送汇，主要因为中国已加入万国邮政联盟（Universal Postal Union），邮政属于国际事务，且牵涉外籍人员，日军不敢妄动。[33] 此时，华侨银行和储汇局的联手，使其成为战时海外最安全的通道之一。因此，银行得以吸引北美、欧洲、澳洲等地的金融机构进行转汇。[34] 可见，银行通过侨汇，与亚洲以外的地区加强互动，形成了更广的跨界网络。

作为市场的后来者，银行积极与当地各批局合作，利用批局的在地网络，快速增加市场份额。[35] 以吉兰丹为例，该分行民信部开幕时，举办茶会邀请当地中华商会要员和各汇兑同业，商讨合作。[36] 一个月后，

---

[32]〈华侨银行民信部琼岛银信可照通汇〉，《南洋商报》，1939年4月1日，第7版。
"OCBC's Department of Remittances Continues Sending Remittance to Hainan Island," *Nanyang Siang Pau*, 1 April 1939, p. 7.

[33]〈我邮政储汇局长刘攻芸南来考察邮汇业〉，《南洋商报》，1938年7月29日，第5版。
"The Director-General of Postal Remittances and Savings Bank S. Y. Liu Visited Nanyang for Investigating the Postal Remittance Industry," *Nanyang Siang Pau*, 29 July 1938, p. 5.

[34] "Remittance Applied for by Mr. Shum Leun Bill of Vancouver, B. C. Canada, 31 Oct 1940," "Remittance from Netherlands," "Remittance of I.149. Sydney," and etc, Government Records Service of Hong Kong, HKMS175-1-1949～1972.

[35]〈华侨银行民信部各地汇款从未间断〉，《南洋商报》，1938年12月9日，第7版。
"OCBC's Remittances to All Places Have Never Been Interrupted," *Nanyang Siang Pau*, 9 December 1938, p. 7.
笔者于2012年6月在厦门考察发现，当地收藏家陈亚元等所藏华侨银行的批信有些仅盖银行分行的收汇印章，有些盖有当地信局和银行分行的收汇印章，更多图片参考：
蚁健〈抗战期间及战后初期海外华侨银行的侨批〉，页118–130。
Yi Jian, "The Remittance of OCBC during the War and the Early Post-war Period," pp. 118–130.

[36]〈吉兰丹华侨银行添办民信部〉，《南洋商报》，1938年11月13日，第11版。
"OCBC's Kelantan Branch Sets up Department of Remittances," *Nanyang Siang Pau*, 13 November 1938, p. 11.

该地民信局纷纷与银行订约,将批款通过华侨银行送出。[37] 民信局之所以愿意合作,因为银行约定利润分半,且由银行承担风险。[38] 而储汇局也发出通告,力推华侨银行。[39]

银行自身也为吸引顾客不断改良,如推出定期家用民信汇款等新方法:

> 此种汇款系用电报传送,故非常快捷。电费由本行担负,但为节省电费并利便办事起见,特规定每月发电一次,每次汇款须在国币五十元以上,汇价与(本行)普通民信汇款相同……汇款人如欲避免每月缴款之麻烦,可按数月或一年汇款约数将应缴之款,全数预先交存本行(由本行发给收条为凭,并将该款按周息三厘计息),每月十日本行即代汇款人依照申请书上所载发电付款。汇价照当日最佳者计算,汇出若干,余存若干及应得利息若干,逐月由本行报告汇款人……[40]

这不仅为顾客提供方便节约费用,也为银行争取到更多资金。银行因此吸引更多民众前来开户、存款。民信部成为了银行的门面。银行特聘通晓多种方言、英文、巫文的文员,希望令不同方言群的顾客感到亲

---

[37] 〈吉兰丹华侨银行民信部扩充业务〉,《南洋商报》,1938年12月16日,第32版。
"The Department of Remittances at OCBC's Kelantan Branch Expands Its Service," *Nanyang Siang Pau*, 16 December 1938, p. 32.

[38] 〈缅甸华侨银行筹设民信部〉,《南洋商报》,1938年12月19日,第14版。
"OCBC's Burma Branch Sets up Department of Remittances," *Nanyang Siang Pau*, 19 December 1938, p. 14.

[39] 〈中华邮政储金汇业局重要启事〉,香港政府档案处藏,HKMS175-1-1970。
"Important Announcements from the Postal Remittances and Savings Bank of China," Government Records Service of Hong Kong, HKMS175-1-1970.

[40] 〈华侨银行有限公司民信部定期家用民信汇款简章〉,香港政府档案处藏,HKMS175-1-1948/1958/1970。
"Instructions for the Customers Subscribing to Regular Service Provided by OCBC's Department of Remittances," Government Records Service of Hong Kong, HKMS175-1-1948/1958/1970.

近。⁴¹ 总经理陈延谦亦训示：

> 民信部亦为本行之新兴业务，顾客多为劳动界人士，办事人绝不可以彼等系工友或汇款不多，而有轻慢之表示；反之，办事人对此部顾客之应接方式，更应客气有礼，因此等侨胞将其血汗所得之金钱，寄回国内养家属，其精神本至为可佩，且当此国难时期，此种汇款与祖国经济极有裨益，故凡汇客有所询问，或对回文未到而有怨言者，亦应以极和悦之态度，说明理由，如或有因与外汇条例抵触不能收汇者，亦须详细陈述，并指示合法之手续，不应断然拒绝而不说明理由。⁴²

周福隆也频繁与储汇局沟通，亲笔致函刘攻芸，讨论如何根据顾客投诉来改进。周认为，顾客的反馈是另一种形式的宣传。当顾客认为服务周到，才会帮助银行建立声誉，有助宣传。反之则有负面效果。他要求储汇局方面对顾客投诉做出书面回应。他代表顾客反映的问题包括：一、汇款应送至收款人地址，但并未送抵，而是由收款人去15英里外的邮局领取，不符合顾客利益，这段路程对收款人或有危险；二、邮局方面要求抵押品或担保人，而银行建议取消，以便利收款人；三、邮局员工私自抽佣，银行已经偿还顾客，但要求邮局注明"银信齐交不得扣佣"或"银信齐交不折不扣"等字眼，以免顾客受骗；四、信款运送

---

⁴¹ 〈吉兰丹华侨银行民信部扩充业务〉，《南洋商报》，1938年12月16日，第32版。
"The Department of Remittances at OCBC's Kelantan Branch Expands Its Service," *Nanyang Siang Pau*, 16 December 1938, p. 32.

⁴² 《总理陈延谦先生向总行及大小坡支行全体同人训词》（新加坡：华侨银行有限公司印发，1941），页15–16。
A Briefing about Staff Discipline by Managing Director Tan Ean Kiam to All Staff in OCBC Branches in Singapore (Singapore: OCBC, 1941), pp. 15–16.

延迟，银行要求邮局25天内必须送抵；五、收款人没有回信，银行要求邮局主动向收款人要求回信，以方便确认。[43]

各分行也和储汇局香港处直接沟通，处理投诉。银行将投诉记录在档，追查原因，商讨处理方法。一封投诉甚至引起银行和储汇局之间数十回讨论，希望找出纰漏，从本质上改善。银行也时常帮助顾客处理侨汇诈骗，并建议顾客选用更合适的汇款方式。[44]从上千封信件往来可见，华侨银行强调人性化服务，为顾客着想，与储汇局进行了相当多的沟通，确保战时业务的成功。

和一般侨汇（图6）[45]相比，银行与储汇局的合作，分别使其在东南亚段内、中国段内，简化了流程，从六步减为四步（图7），提高了效率，缩短时间且降低风险。

对银行而言，这一业务不仅扩大了其在东南亚、中国的影响力，更使其与欧美澳的华人社群和金融机构增进联系。银行经手的资本量也剧增，不止有民用汇款，还吸引了民众认购公债，东南亚各地救国

---

[43] "Letter from Mr. Chew Hock Leong to The Director-General of Postal Remittances and Savings Bank, Hong Kong, 13 Dec 1938," Government Records Service of Hong Kong, HKMS175-1-1958 & 1970.

[44] 〈储汇局香港通讯处致华侨银行及其分行业务公函〉，香港政府档案处藏，HKMS175-1-1403；HKMS175-1-1949～1958；HKMS175-1-1970～1977。

"Letters from the Postal Remittances and Savings Bank to OCBC and Its Branches," Government Records Service of Hong Kong, HKMS175-1-1403; HKMS175-1-1949～1958; HKMS175-1-1970～1977.

[45] 据戴一峰、城山智子分别绘制的流程图制成，参见：戴一峰〈网络化企业与嵌入性：近代侨批局的制度建构（1850s–1940s）〉，《中国社会经济史研究》2003年第1期，页73–74。Dai Yifeng, "Network Enterprises and Its Embeddedness: Overseas Chinese Post Office and Its System Constructure in the Modern Times, 1850s–1940s," *The Journal of Chinese Social and Economic History*, No. 1 (2003), pp. 73–74.

Tomoko Shiroyama, "Overseas Chinese Remittances in the Mid-Twentieth Century," Choi Chi-Cheung, Takashi Oishi, Tomoko Shiroyama (eds.), *Chinese and Indian Merchants in Modern Asia: Networking Businesses and Formation of Regional Economy* (Leiden; Boston: Brill, 2019), p. 82。

赈灾委员会也通过该行汇款。[46] 这些业务亦推动了银行存款额增加，使其掌控更多的流动资金（图8）。[47] 银行也因此吸收了多种货币，有利于外汇盈利。合约显示，银行和储汇局之间的所有资金往来户头设立在银行，兑换以银行利率为准。[48]

除了与储汇局合作，银行自身也通过香港、上海、厦门分行处理东南亚和中国之间的汇兑。这类汇兑以商人商号、回国投资、银号信局委托的汇款为主，包括电汇、票汇、信汇、押汇、旅行汇款、代收期票等，图6中第四步金融机构的资金承转即包括了两地分行之间的汇款。这些业务从其前身的和丰、旧华侨银行已开始，日趋成熟。[49] 和

---

[46] 〈暹罗筹赈祖国难民委员会献金由华侨银行汇香港中国银行核收〉，香港政府档案处藏，HKMS175-1- 104。"Donations from Siam to the Committee for Relief of Refugees in the Motherland via OCBC to Bank of China's Hong Kong Branch," Government Records Service of Hong Kong, HKMS175-1-104.
〈香港华侨银行星洲总行经收救债款债票〉，香港政府档案处藏，HKMS175-1-113。"National Debts and Bonds of China via OCBC's Singapore Head Office to OCBC's Hong Kong Branch," Government Records Service of Hong Kong, HKMS175-1-113.
〈香港华侨银行泗水分行汇寄捐款〉，香港政府档案处藏，HKMS175-1-117。"Donations via OCBC's Surabaya Branch to OCBC's Hong Kong Branch," Government Records Service of Hong Kong, HKMS175-1-117.
〈香港华侨银行向财政部咨询华侨筹赈祖国难民委员会款项〉，香港政府档案处藏，HKMS175-1- 123。"Inquiries to China's Ministry of Finance from OCBC's Hong Kong Branch Regarding the Donations from Overseas Chinese to the Committee for Relief of Refugees in the Motherland," Government Records Service of Hong Kong, HKMS175-1-123.
〈香港华侨银行办理捐款事项的发票及有关文件〉，香港政府档案处藏，HKMS175-1-1403。"Invoices and Other Documents Related to the Donations via OCBC's Hong Kong Branch," Government Records Service of Hong Kong, HKMS175-1-1403.

[47] 根据：狄克·威尔逊著，译者不详《安如磐石：华侨银行四十周年纪念册》，页72–73的资料整理，1941–1945年资料因战争原因从缺。
Compiled from: Dick Wilson, *Solid as a Rock: The First Forty Years of the Oversea-Chinese Banking Corporation*, trans. Unknown, pp. 72–73.

[48] "Regards Agreement with Oversea-Chinese Banking Corporation Ltd., 18 July 1938," "To The Director-General of Postal Remittances and Savings Bank, Hong Kong, Our Firm Offers to You, 7 Nov 1938," Government Records Service of Hong Kong, HKMS175-1-1958.

[49] 林其仁〈银行业务概述〉，《友声》第1卷第1期（1935），页38–39。Lin Qiren, "An Overview of Banking Services," *The OCBC Echo*, Vol. 1, No. 1 (1935), pp. 38–39.
〈华侨银行汇兑部广告〉，《南洋商报》，1938年2月15日，第12版。"Advertisement of OCBC's Department of Remittance and Exchange," *Nanyang Siang Pau*, 15 February 1938, p. 12.
陈维龙《新马注册商业银行》，页28–32。Tan Ee Leong, *Registered Commercial Banks in Singapore and Malaya*, pp. 28–32.

储汇局签约时,华侨银行注明,在中国的三间分行仍处理原本的汇兑业务,不受合约限制。⁵⁰

总体来看,银行分行与储汇局、分行之间形成的跨界连结,利用战时求稳的机遇,扩大了业务范围,简化了侨汇流程,增强了银行的资本实力和业务能力,获得了广泛民众基础。但须指出的是,尽管侨汇为银行带来利益和声名,⁵¹ 但因资料原因,具体数额难以考察,估为每月总量千万元(国币)以上。⁵² 竞争对手的怨言亦从侧面证实了银行的影响。⁵³

四、促进跨界经济

银行作为新式金融机构,究竟什么功用,华商为何需要华侨自己的银行?这些概念是由银行业者灌输传达至客户民众。华侨银行有意突出其与传统金融组织的差别,强调银行不止有存款、放款、汇兑等功能,更是整个社会经济活动的总枢纽,是人体的心脏,左右经济活

---

[50] "Regards Agreement with Oversea-Chinese Banking Corporation Ltd., 18 July 1938," "To The Director-General of Postal Remittances and Savings Bank, Hong Kong, Our Firm Offers to You, 7 Nov 1938," Government Records Service of Hong Kong, HKMS175-1-1958.

[51] Oral History of Renee Chew, *Special Project*, National Archives of Singapore, File No. 002005, Reel No. 2.

狄克·威尔逊著,译者不详《安如磐石:华侨银行四十周年纪念册》,页50。Dick Wilson, *Solid as a Rock: The First Forty Years of the Oversea-Chinese Banking Corporation*, trans. Unknown, p. 50.

Oral History of Victor Chew Chin Aik, *Urban Planning in Singapore Project*, National Archives of Singapore, File No. 002786, Reel No. 3.

一位银行要员也指出,侨汇业务为银行带来巨大资金量和知名度,资料来源应提供者要求保密。

[52] 〈华侨银行有限公司民信部今日开幕通汇处遍设闽粤桂各地〉,《南洋商报》,1938年9月12日,第11版。

"Today is the Opening of OCBC's Department of Remittances which Serves the Purpose of Remittance All over Fujian, Guangdong and Guangxi," *Nanyang Siang Pau*, 12 September 1938, p. 11.

[53] 〈南洋华侨汇兑最近半年来之非常转变情形〉,《泉州日报》,1938年11月22日,转引自:李良溪主编《泉州侨批业史料》(厦门:厦门大学出版社,1994),页46。

"The Remittances from Overseas Chinese in Nanyang Has Drastic Changes Over the Past Half Year," *Quanzhou Daily*, 22 November 1938, Quoted from: Li Liangxi (ed.), *The Historical Materials about the Remittance in Quanzhou* (Xiamen: Xiamen University Press, 1994), p. 46.

动,有如人体的血液循环。[54] 对于华侨而言,跨界的经济至关重要,蕴藏着属于华侨的商机:

> 中国与南洋之经济关系,除我侨本身外,一向缺乏直接之联系,此层亦应设法加以促进。以我侨之地位言,前者乃吾人之祖国,后者乃吾人之第二故乡,尽一种联络媒介之责任,实义无可辞。故南洋之物产情形如何,既必须加以精密之调查,何者可以供给祖国,而祖国何种产品可以畅销南洋,凡足增进彼此间贸易之工作者,我侨均须唯力是视。目前祖国正在抗战建国之过程中,经济建设之规模甚大,将来极易成为南洋物产之最大顾客,能达到此目的时,实足以维持今后南洋无数代之繁荣;换言之,我侨此时多费一分力量促进祖国与南洋之经济联系,即可使南洋经济基础多稳固一分,而我侨今后之经济地位,亦并随之愈形稳定矣。[55]

如何促进跨界经济,华侨银行通过出版期刊、合办公司,推动信息、资本、商品的跨界流通。银行于1940年设立经济调查室,次年起出版季刊《华侨经济》,在各分行、中国及东南亚各大书店销售,每册二角五分。[56] 期刊的定位是为华人中小工商业者提供资讯和建议。[57] 因此,这份刊物集合了东南亚、中国、欧美宗主国,特别是跨界两地之间的信息和评论(表2),与之后汇丰银行创办的《远东经济评论》相似。

---

[54] 林其仁〈银行业务概述〉,《友声》第1卷第1期(1935),页35。Lin Qiren, "An Overview of Banking Services," *The OCBC Echo*, Vol. 1, No. 1 (1935), p. 35.

李俊承〈银行业与华侨社会〉,《华侨经济》第1卷第3期(1941),页1–7。Lee Choon Seng, "Banking Industry and the Overseas Chinese Society," *The Oversea-Chinese Economics*, Vol. 1, No. 3 (1941), pp. 1–7.

陈延谦〈新加坡华人银行发达史〉,《华侨经济》第1卷第1期(1941),页18–22。Tan Ean Kiam, "A History of Chinese Banking in Singapore," *The Oversea-Chinese Economics*, Vol. 1, No. 1 (1941), pp. 18–22.

[55] 〈发刊词〉,《华侨经济》第1卷第1期(1941),页3。"Preface," *The Oversea-Chinese Economics*, Vol. 1, No. 1 (1941), p. 3.

[56] 〈信息〉,《华侨经济》第1卷第1期(1941),封底页。"Information," *The Oversea-Chinese Economics*, Vol. 1, No. 1 (1941), back cover page.

该刊于1942年1月因日军入侵新加坡停刊,战后复办,但总出版期数不详。

[57] 〈发刊词〉,《华侨经济》第1卷第1期(1941),页3。"Preface," *The Oversea-Chinese Economics*, Vol. 1, No. 1 (1941), p. 3.

表2：《华侨经济》首三期篇目分类[58]

南洋 （60%）	中国 （11.4%）	跨界中国与南洋/中国与外界/南洋与外界（28.6%）
新加坡华人银行发达史	我国十五年来之财政思潮	抗战以来之交通
银行业与华侨社会	重庆银行业近况（重庆通信）	民信汇款与祖国经济
马来亚渔业与华侨	中国西南之经济发展	华侨汇款与抗建资源
马来亚树胶业与华侨	中国工业化之前途	抗战以来南洋华侨筹赈汇款统计
南洋黄梨业与华侨		战时中国之外汇管理
马来亚锡矿业与华侨		银行界与实业界合作问题
马来亚之椰子业		1941年首季滇缅路货运统计
荷印糖业与华侨糖商		现代银行制度之类型
论南洋华侨之经济危机		1940年马来亚对外贸易统计
马来亚人口估计表		欧美各国投资马来亚树胶园统计
荷印华侨之人口及财富		
菲律宾华侨人口统计		
越南华侨经济概况		
荷印经济与马来亚		
英属北婆罗洲经济概况		
海峡殖民地战税条例全文		
马来亚遗产税条例全文		
海峡殖民地战时货物保险条例		
马来亚战时经济与物价管理		
马来亚国防金融条例全文		
马来亚粮食统制条例		

[58] 笔者根据《华侨经济》1941年出版第1-3期的文章内容整理分类。
Compiled from: *The Oversea-Chinese Economics*, Vol. 1, No. 1-3 (1941).

银行汇总这些资料观点，通过纸本为载体，传播至东南亚和中国各商埠，促进了资讯的跨界流传，有助于读者掌握跨界商机。

该刊邀请报人冯列山[59]主持，除了登载调查室的一手报告，由银行董事主席李俊承、陈延谦和各部门经理撰述专论之外，还请来中国经济学家和金融界名人执笔，如张嘉璈、贾士毅、许性初、丁洪范、俞寰澄等。[60] 该刊的调查和分析均展现出专业水准。

调查室出品的一系列考察报告是该刊的亮点，主题包括南洋各区域各行业、各地华人人口与财富、中国与东南亚之间、东南亚各埠之间的跨界贸易统计等。调查人员从各地政府公报、杂志报章中采集数据，并与当地业界人士交流，收集一手讯息分析。[61] 考察涵盖了历史渊源、发展现状、特点优劣、前景展望、与殖民商人当地土人的合作与竞争等多方面。值得注意的是，报告多采用了当时流行的西方经济学分析方法，进行统计、归纳、修正和解释。对于数据缺乏的情况，

---

[59] 冯列山为中国获得新闻学博士第一人，1935年获慕尼黑大学博士学位，曾任《申报》驻欧记者，后南下香港、新加坡，1939年担任胡文虎收购《总汇新报》后之主编。

[60] 〈华侨银行经济调查室组辑华侨经济季刊第一卷第一期今日出版〉，《南洋商报》，1941年4月30日，第9版。"The Inaugural Issue of the Oversea-Chinese Economics Quarterly Edited by OCBC's Economic Research Office is Published Today," *Nanyang Siang Pau*, 30 April 1941, p. 9.

俞寰澄〈银行界与实业界合作问题〉，《华侨经济》第1卷第2期（1941），页1。Yu Huancheng, "Cooperation Issues between Banks and Industries," *The Oversea-Chinese Economics*, Vol. 1, No. 2 (1941), p. 1.

[61] 如：本行经济调查室〈南洋黄梨业与华侨〉，《华侨经济》第1卷第1期（1941），页84。OCBC's Economic Research Office, "Pineapple Industry in Nanyang and the Overseas Chinese," *The Oversea-Chinese Economics*, Vol. 1, No. 1 (1941), p. 84.

本行经济调查室〈马来亚树胶业与华侨〉，《华侨经济》第1卷第1期（1941），页60。OCBC's Economic Research Office, "Rubber Industry in Malaya and the Overseas Chinese," *The Oversea-Chinese Economics*, Vol. 1, No. 1 (1941), p. 60.

本行经济调查室〈1941年首季滇缅路货运统计〉，《华侨经济》第1卷第2期（1941），页109。OCBC's Economic Research Office, "Freight Statistics on the Yunnan-Burma Road in the First Quarter of 1941," *The Oversea-Chinese Economics*, Vol. 1, No. 2 (1941), p. 109. （该文数据整理于缅甸官方发表之《缅甸贸易月报》。）

戴英士〈荷印经济与马来亚〉，《华侨经济》第3期（1941），页32。Dai Yingshi, "Economy of Dutch East India and Malaya," *The Oversea-Chinese Economics*, No. 3 (1941), p. 32. 以及其他。

调查人员通过比较、推算，建立了原创数据，并评估其客观程度，得出有针对性的结论。例如，对马来亚锡矿业内欧人与华侨不同产锡方式的产量、投资额、成本、收益的估算等。[62] 该刊也将一些官方英文数据译成中文，建立中文的经济指标数据，并评价数据的准确性和意义，如"马来亚战时工程用品价格指数表"、[63] "1941年首季我国经滇缅路输入货物统计"[64] 等。不同于过去的口耳相传，这些属于专业化制度化的资讯传播，为跨界贸易投资提供了宝贵情报。

分享资讯之余，该刊也宣扬银行促进经济的功用。提供的建议均从现实出发，介绍欧日的跨界投资经验、战时欧美工商业的经验，为同样处于战局的华商提供参考。例如，该刊建议华侨将小资本汇成大资本，吸收游资投资在农工矿业、交通业等，提升规模，才能解决生产技术、跨界产销、与欧日竞争等一系列问题。[65] 如何汇集资本，关键在于运用资本市场，手段之一便是通过银行。如李俊承对银行与实业关系的评论：

---

[62] 本行经济调查室〈马来亚锡矿业与华侨〉，《华侨经济》第1卷第2期（1941），页44。
OCBC's Economic Research Office, "Tin Mining Industry in Malaya and the Overseas Chinese," *The Oversea-Chinese Economics*, Vol. 1, No. 2 (1941), p. 44.

[63] 冯少琛〈马来亚战时经济与物价管理〉，《华侨经济》第1卷第3期（1941），页28–31。
Feng Shaochen, "Economics and Price Management in Wartime Malaya," *The Oversea-Chinese Economics*, Vol. 1, No. 3 (1941), pp. 28–31.

[64] 本行经济调查室〈1941年首季滇缅路货运统计〉，《华侨经济》第1卷第2期（1941），页109–116。OCBC's Economic Research Office, "Freight Statistics on the Yunnan-Burma Road in the First Quarter of 1941," *The Oversea-Chinese Economics*, Vol. 1, No. 2 (1941), pp. 109–116.

[65] 葛青凡〈论南洋华侨经济之危机〉，《华侨经济》第1卷第2期（1941），页16–17。Ge Qingfan, "On the Crisis of the Overseas Chinese Economy in Nanyang," *The Oversea-Chinese Economics*, Vol. 1, No. 2 (1941), pp. 16–17.

本行经济调查室〈马来亚树胶业与华侨〉，《华侨经济》第1卷第1期（1941），页60–74。OCBC's Economic Research Office, "Rubber Industry in Malaya and the Overseas Chinese," *The Oversea-Chinese Economics*, Vol. 1, No. 1 (1941), pp. 60–74.

本行经济调查室〈南洋黄梨业与华侨〉，《华侨经济》第1卷第1期（1941），页79–84。OCBC's Economic Research Office, "Pineapple Industry in Nanyang and the Overseas Chinese," *The Oversea-Chinese Economics*, Vol. 1, No. 1 (1941), pp. 79–84.

现代工商业发达，贸易已具国际性质，商场情况日趋复杂，一般工商业家多侧重其所经营之本业部门，未能全盘兼顾；且过于注意生产，致常忽略市场之容纳量，一旦销路停滞，价格暴跌，事业便感维持困难。银行之地位不同，产销双方兼顾，对于每业之风险，无不特别留心，故银行如将所收集之资料以及对市场变化之预测，时常提供其顾客（工商业家）作为参考之用，相信此举可使工商业家知所戒备，减低损失。其次，经营现代经济事业，因同业间竞争甚烈，欲求发展已非单靠经验所能生效；银行规模较大，可聘经济学识经验丰富之专门人才从事研究工作，凡与银行往来之工商业家，如需要改进其事业之组织或管理时，银行均应随时贡献意见，促进工商业之合理化。再次，银行成为工商业之顾问机关后，则彼此联系便趋密切，无论经营放款或贴现业务，均易进行，毋须另费一番调查手续，是则此举又具有促进银行发展业务之效能也。[66]

华商个人也能通过银行得益。譬如，针对马来亚高额遗产税的征收，作者建议华人充分运用银行，不要急于贱卖产业来付税，而应将产业抵押于银行兑现，在后人经济情况良好时赎回，减低损失，以防破产。[67]

该刊的实际影响难以衡量，但不可否认的是，其提供的实例和建议开拓了读者的眼界和观念，令其了解银行的作用，增大了通过银行推展多元经济活动的可能性。另一方面，华侨银行也从实作出发，由中国区的董事朱文熊，与中国金融界实业界合资，创办南洋企业公司（Nanyang Development & Finance Corporation）。公司于1940年5月成立，朱文熊任总经理，金城银行主席周作民、华侨银行主席李光前任正副董事长。华侨银行出资52万元国币，占公司股份20.8%。尽管出资不多，但却是东

---

[66] 李俊承〈银行业与华侨社会〉，《华侨经济》第1卷第3期（1941），页7。
Lee Choon Seng, "Banking Industry and the Overseas Chinese Society," *The Oversea-Chinese Economics*, Vol. 1, No. 3 (1941), p. 7.

[67] 葛青凡〈论南洋华侨经济之危机〉，《华侨经济》第1卷第2期（1941），页21。
Ge Qingfan, "On the Crisis of the Overseas Chinese Economy in Nanyang," *The Oversea-Chinese Economics*, Vol. 1, No. 2 (1941), p. 21.

南亚唯一代表。[68] 公司以沟通南洋与中国的资金、原料、商品、信息、人才，推广工商贸易，促进实业为目的（业务范围见图9）。[69]

图9：南洋企业公司概况

南洋企業公司概況

地址：總公司設上海江西路二四六號。香港辦事處設雪廠街荷蘭行六〇一號，電話二一二八一號。

資本：國幣二百五十萬元。

宗旨：發展國民經濟，策進實業建設，推廣工商貿易，并爲南洋僑胞服務。

業務：農鑛實業工廠之投資事項；公私企業之輔助合作事項；進出口貿易之經營事項；地產證券之投資介紹及經理事項；公私財產之受委管理事項。

組織：董事長周作民，副董事長李光前，總經理朱文熊，協理徐致一，高事恒。下分企業，貿易，信託三部。在國內外要地分設辦事處。

往來銀行：華僑銀行，金城銀行及中外各大銀行。

業務：（一）出口貿易，該公司受各大國貨工廠委託，獲有在南洋之獨家經銷權，其品目如下：棉布、綢緞、恤衫、內衣、呢帽、鞋襪、毛巾、被單、皮件、搪瓷、鋼精、五金、電扇、電筒、電泡、樂器、茶葉、紙烟、烟具、熱水瓶、調味品、化裝品、絲織圖畫、文房用品、科學儀器、運動器具、兒童玩具、罐頭食品、中西藥材、建築材料、衛生器具、五金材料、鋼鐵材料、各種雜貨。該公司印有「國貨出品詳細目錄」，函索即寄。凡各地商行委託該公司代辦上項國貨出品及國內所產原料者，可開列種類及擬辦價格，致函該公司。該公司雖取少許手續費，而價格悉照廠盤，較之直接批購，尤爲合算。

（二）進口貿易：南洋各地產品不論原料製品，該公司一律可以代辦進口，僑胞委託在國內推銷者亦可。

（三）企業投資：代僑胞設計調查，依照指定範圍投資。亦可將款存放該公司，由該公司負責代爲投資。

（四）購置代辦：代僑胞在國內置買產業證券。

（五）信託保管：代僑胞投保各險，收付款項，經租房地，或經營工商實業。

服務工作 其他不收費用之服務工作如下：（一）答覆僑胞對國內各方事件之諮詢，（二）負責代僑胞調查國內事件，（三）招待返國旅行僑胞，並派員負傳譯介紹之責，（四）介紹僑胞與國內工商業通訊交易或參觀，（五）介紹僑胞子弟回國求學，代辦擇校繳費手續，負責照料。（六）僑胞需要國內人才，及僑胞人才願返國服務者，可由該公司代爲介紹。

对抗日本的政治局势，使得南洋与中国之间涌现更多商机。华人拒绝购买、销售日货，转而支持国货出口到南洋。另一边厢，中国战时物资紧缺，由南洋提供原料、商品，或投资设立工厂，不仅能满足中国国内需求，亦为祖国建设出力。对于中国工商界而言，他们倾向从南洋进

[68] 南洋企业公司档案，上海市档案馆藏，Q373-1-537；Q373-1-1222；Q373-1-1522。

Company Records of the Nanyang Development & Finance Corporation, Shanghai Municipal Archives, Q373-1-537; Q373-1-1222; Q373-1-1522.

[69] 〈南洋企业公司概况〉，《国货与实业》第1卷第5号（1941），页60–61。

"An Overview of the Nanyang Development & Finance Corporation," *Industrial and Chinese Products*, Vol. 1, No. 5 (1941), pp. 60–61.

口原料，而华侨生产的商品也被归为国货。⁷⁰ 南洋企业公司的业务（图10）便由此展开，甚至形成双重跨界的供应链，如第五类。公司也代客户买卖货物，并提供运输、报关、保险等服务。⁷¹

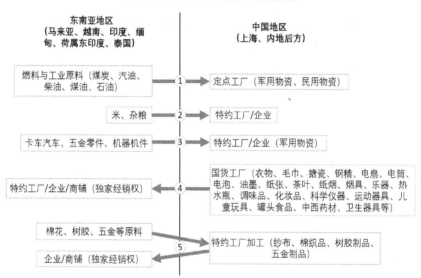

图10：南洋企业公司跨界贸易类别

---

⁷⁰ 庄仁杰《中国国货运动：中国和英属马来亚的比较研究，1912–1941》，硕士论文（新加坡：新加坡国立大学中文系，2009），页75。

Chong Ren Jie Henry, "A Comparative Study of Chinese National Product Movements: China and British Malaya, 1912–1941," Master's Thesis (Singapore: National University of Singapore, 2009), p. 75.

⁷¹ 整理自：南洋企业公司档案，上海市档案馆藏：Q373-1-499；Q373-1-528；Q373-1-534。

Compile from: Company Records of the Nanyang Development & Finance Corporation, Shanghai Municipal Archives, Q373-1-499; Q373-1-528; Q373-1-534.
南洋企业公司贸易部业务方案，上海社会科学院经济研究所中国企业史资料研究中心藏。

Business Solutions Offered by the Trade Department of the Nanyang Development & Finance Corporation, *Archival Collection of the Research Center for Chinese Enterprise History*, Institute of Economics, Shanghai Academy of Social Sciences.

进口到中国时，南洋企业公司的供应对象多是有政府背景或当地知名的厂商，侨商通过南洋企业公司为这些厂商供货，确保了销路和收益。出口到海外时，与南洋企业公司合作的是颇有名气的国货工厂，如康元制罐厂、华生电器厂、美亚织绸厂、中国化学工业社、上海乳品厂、金龙热水瓶厂、永昌钢精厂、中华珐琅厂等。[72] 这些产品质量有保障，加上独家经销权，使得华侨商家顺利销货。

南洋企业公司之所以能与这些厂商合作，主要因为其背后靠山——金城银行、华侨银行。中国区内的金城银行和遍布南洋的华侨银行，为货品的采购、生产、销售提供了在地的商业网络、充裕的周转资金和便利安全的结算手段。公司也扮演了中国工商业者与银行之间的中间人角色，有时协助实业工厂获得银行的押汇垫款，加速工厂的资金周转；有时则从银行透支借款，直接投资工商企业或提供融资，以此获得企业的部分管理权或独销权。[73]

对于华侨银行来说，由合办的南洋企业公司来经营跨界贸易投资，一方面能赚取交易的利息与汇率差，一方面通过与其他机构联手，筹集更多资金却能分散风险。据资料显示，南洋企业公司贸易部每月与华侨银行结账，金额从24.8万元至152万元国币不等，平均每月80万元。[74] 同时，银行为自身的客户——东南亚的中小华商和南洋企业公司牵线，这些贸易往来通过银行来操作，也使三方共利。

---

[72] 南洋企业公司董事会议事录，上海社会科学院经济研究所中国企业史资料研究中心藏。Minutes of the Board Meetings of the Nanyang Development & Finance Corporation, *Archival Collection of the Research Center for Chinese Enterprise History*, Institute of Economics, Shanghai Academy of Social Sciences.

[73] 南洋企业公司贸易部业务方案，上海社会科学院经济研究所中国企业史资料研究中心藏。Business Solutions Offered by the Trade Department of the Nanyang Development & Finance Corporation, *Archival Collection of the Research Center for Chinese Enterprise History*, Institute of Economics, Shanghai Academy of Social Sciences.

南洋企业公司档案，上海市档案馆藏，Q373-1-528。Company Records of the Nanyang Development & Finance Corporation, Shanghai Municipal Archives, Q373-1-528.

[74] 南洋企业公司华侨银行结册（1941–1942），上海市档案馆藏，Q373-2-130。Transaction Records between the Nanyang Development & Finance Corporation and OCBC (1941–1942), Shanghai Municipal Archives, Q373-2-130.

五、迁移与重生

1942年2月日军攻占新加坡，日本军政府立即控制了新加坡的金融系统。华侨银行因此大受打击，经营呈现颓废之态。此时的跨界业务亦陷入停顿，多处分行受战事影响关闭。[75] 但是，银行没有坐以待毙，而是通过跨界连结向海外转移、重新注册，使其能保存部分实力，劫后重生。

这期间担当重任的是因战时布局而升任董事经理的陈振传。他在银行内部是陈延谦、周福隆等的后辈，年轻但资历不浅，17岁起获聘华商银行书记，随后并入华侨银行。和前辈们不同，他在新加坡出生，与殖民政府关系密切（见表3）。[76] 银行支持陈振传在多个公共事务委员会中担任要职。[77] 主席李光前也受政府委任加入了因战事设立的民防委员会和撤退委员会。

1941年，银行预估日军入侵将造成冲击，因此提前部署，减少放贷，累增储备金，计划将资金和文件转移海外。陈振传作为政府委员会要员，受殖民地货币局主席韦斯伯格（H. Weisberg）委托，将财政部保险库内的新钞焚毁，以免落入日军之手。陈振传寻求他熟识的长辈、华社领袖陈嘉庚的帮助，征集工人焚烧新钞。华侨银行也效仿财政部的做法，把银行的新钞焚毁，并由官员当场记录钞票编码，之后将总值结算到银行账目中。除了新钞，银行也将其存款储蓄在英国财政部，将所持现金换成英镑，存放在银行的合作机构——英国米兰银行（Midland Bank）。另外，陈振传也代表银行，寻求澳洲的合作机构新南威尔士银行（Bank of New South Wales）帮忙，将公司的文件备份

---

[75] 狄克·威尔逊著，译者不详《安如磐石：华侨银行四十周年纪念册》，页60。
Dick Wilson, *Solid as a Rock: The First Forty Years of the Oversea-Chinese Banking Corporation*, trans. Unknown, p. 60.

[76] 整理自：Lee Su Yin, *British Policy and the Chinese in Singapore, 1939 to 1955: The Public Service Career of Tan Chin Tuan* (Singapore: Talisman Publishing, 2011), pp. xvi–xvii.
表格仅罗列1939–1946年间陈振传的部分公共职务，并非全部。

[77] Grace Loh, Goh Chor Boon, Tan Teng Lang, *Building Bridges, Carving Niches: An Enduring Legacy*, pp. 38, 40.

表3：陈振传1939-1946年参与的公共事务委员会（部分）

年份	委员会	职位
1939	海峡英籍华人公会 Straits Chinese British Association	委员 Committee Member
1939	新加坡市议会 Singapore Municipal Commission	委员 Commissioner
1941	民防委员会 Passive Defence Council	副委员长 Assistant Commissioner
1941	撤退委员会 Evacuation Committee	委员 Committee Member
1942	马来亚人公会（澳洲） Malayan Association (Australia)	委员 Committee Member
1943	华侨公会（印度） Oversea-Chinese Association of India	副主席 Vice President
1945	马来亚人公会（印度） Malayan Association (India)	主席 President
1945	英国军政府咨询委员会 British Military Administration Advisory Council	委员 Council Member
1946	新加坡咨询委员会 Singapore Advisory Council	委员 Council Member

交与保管。[78] 与1932年遇到危机银行合并时不同，此时华侨银行不再依赖个人网络，而是以非个人网络，通过与其市场互补的跨界代理，转移资金文件。而银行与英国财政部的联系，一方面是由陈振传作为海峡华人的多重身份和社会网络促成，另一方面华侨银行也被视为归属殖民地的银行，因此得到财政部协助。

殖民地网络的影响也反映在银行最终选择在印度重新注册。鉴于日军逼近，银行决定仿效欧洲公司1940年应付德国闪电战而采取的自救措施，将总部迁至外国注册，以便继续管理资产和未受影响的分行。因此1942年2月初，陈振传被升为董事经理，与陈延谦同等职位。陈延谦留守本地消极应对的同时，陈振传赴海外重新注册。在韦斯伯格协助下，

---

[78] Ibid, pp. 41–42.

陈振传获得优先权，前往巴城再准备飞往仰光转赴重庆，将银行移至重庆注册。[79] 但是受战争影响，陈在巴城未能转飞。他选择前往澳洲，在当地新南威尔士银行设立了一个华侨银行办事处。[80] 在澳洲滞留一年半后，陈决定再前往重庆。此时，日本已占据缅甸，银行仰光分行的主要职员和文件已转至重庆。重庆是中国战时首都，国民党政府邀请海内外银行家相聚该地商讨策略。因此，移至重庆仍然可行。[81]

由于东亚和东南亚均被日军侵占，因此只能从南亚赴渝。陈振传于1943年8月抵达印度。但他得知民国政府财政枯竭，可能会施压令银行将资产转入中国，使银行利益受损。因此，陈决定不赴重庆，转在英殖民地印度注册。[82] 这一转变可见，银行仍以经济利益为重，而海外华人的多重身份使其能在中国和殖民帝国之间流动、选择。陈振传根据《国防法令（公司暂将注册地址更动）》，先在孟买开设办事处，后于1945年1月注册成功，并召开流亡股东大会，召集了海外分行的若干职员。[83]

这期间，陈振传在印度的社会参与也强化了他的英籍身份认同，并因此得到英政府的信任，有助于银行战后的发展。陈抵达印度后，被

---

[79] Grace Loh, Goh Chor Boon, Tan Teng Lang, *Building Bridges, Carving Niches: An Enduring Legacy*, p. 43.
〈南洋华侨银行内移〉，《战地工合》第2卷第7-8期（1942），页179。"OCBC Relocating to Inland China," *Chinese Industrial Cooperatives in Wartime China*, Vol. 2, No. 7-8 (1942), p. 179.

[80] Grace Loh, Goh Chor Boon, Tan Teng Lang, *Building Bridges, Carving Niches: An Enduring Legacy*, p. 56.

[81] Ibid, p. 58.

[82] Ibid, p. 62.
图3中，重庆处以X表示该分行曾登记，但并未开业，缘因其计划注册，但最终撤销，转至印度。
〈经济部公告（卅三）参字第16675号〉，《经济部公报》第7卷第6期（1944），页260。
"Announcements from the Ministry of Economic Affairs, Vol. 33, No. 16675," *Bulletin of the Ministry of Economic Affairs*, Vol. 7, No. 6 (1944), p. 260.

[83] 狄克·威尔逊著，译者不详《安如磐石：华侨银行四十周年纪念册》，页56。
Dick Wilson, *Solid as a Rock: The First Forty Years of the Oversea-Chinese Banking Corporation*, trans. Unknown, p. 56.

要求按照《外籍人士登记法令》登记为在印度居留的外籍人士，包括出生时是日本、中国或泰国公民。陈在新加坡出生，是华人，也是英籍公民，持马来亚签发的英国护照。陈认为自己并非外籍人士，便写信向登记处解释，并请律师上诉。德里政府仍坚持要求英籍华人登记。陈发动了在印度的马来亚人社群，向伦敦的殖民大臣上诉。他也向有交往的、在马来亚的英国官员求援，通过他们与殖民地驻孟买特别代表艾亨（C. D. Ahearne）联络。艾亨回复肯定了英籍华人不应登记。陈振传以此为据，令当地政府收回命令，并修改规定。[84]

从一开始未被当作英籍人士，陈按照英国人的做法由律师上诉争取权益，并通过他与殖民官员的人际网络得到协助，确立了他的英籍身份。这一过程既反映出他对殖民国的认同，也强化了他的效忠，并被殖民官员界定为对英帝国忠诚，因而得到了殖民者的青睐。陈在印度注册的做法也使银行更进一步嵌入殖民地的跨界网络。这些交织影响，使得陈和华侨银行在战后被英政府赋予重任，将其视为推动殖民地经济计划、与帝国合作的在地代理人。1945年9月，陈振传和他的银行助手被视为本土银行的代表，和英国银行代表一起作为民政官员登乘军机，优先返回新加坡。[85]回新后，由于渣打银行管理者未能及时抵达，华侨银行被赋予过渡时期财政部的角色，发行新马来亚货币以取代战时日本货币。华侨银行还协助其他华人银行分获新货币，以便自身降低风险。[86]至此，华侨银行不仅成为本土银行的巨头，更胜出西方银行，抢占了英政府与华人金融界之间的中间人位置。

---

[84] Grace Loh, Goh Chor Boon, Tan Teng Lang, *Building Bridges, Carving Niches: An Enduring Legacy*, pp. 60–61.

[85] 狄克·威尔逊著，译者不详《安如磐石：华侨银行四十周年纪念册》，页63。
Dick Wilson, *Solid as a Rock: The First Forty Years of the Oversea-Chinese Banking Corporation*, trans. Unknown, p. 63.

[86] Grace Loh, Goh Chor Boon, Tan Teng Lang, *Building Bridges, Carving Niches: An Enduring Legacy*, p. 73.
狄克·威尔逊著，译者不详《安如磐石：华侨银行四十周年纪念册》，页66。Dick Wilson, *Solid as a Rock: The First Forty Years of the Oversea-Chinese Banking Corporation*, trans. Unknown, p. 66.

六、结语

正如银行1933年合并时设计的标志（图11），扬帆而起的帆船作为跨界工具，象征银行的客户群——华侨，寓示了华人移民的跨界性、流动性。"华侨"被形塑为一种共同体，超越方言群、地域。与之相应，银行的业务、市场、机遇也是跨界的、流动的，从不限于一个地区，而是生于多点多线连结的网络中。在战时环境下，跨界、流动的机制提供了新的机会和可能。银行把握多地华人社群的需求，通过跨界复线的金融网络和商业网络，在东南亚各地、中国、英帝国、澳洲之间运转，增加业务、扩大客户群、提升实力和影响力，对银行的发展起到了关键作用。

图11：华侨银行标志

这一案例也显现了海外华人的现代性实践。银行同时借镜西方现代银行和传统侨批局的经验、长处，因应战时环境和客户需求，运用多种资源灵活创新，通过个人网络及非个人网络协作，促进了资本、市场、信息、人员的互通和流动，优化运作，规避风险，从而成为金融界的领军。这样的现代性生成于其身份的多重性、跨界性、流动性，因而能同时嵌入两个网络——跨国华人的网络和殖民帝国的社会网络，汲取多种资源，糅合各方优势。这些跨界网络和策略，在1970年代银行国际化扩张时仍被沿用，为其提供了根基。本文的发现，有助于修正该行从1970年代才跻升跨国银行等认知，[87] 凸显了跨界机制在华人银行发展过程中的历史脉络和深远意义。

---

[87] Grace Loh, Goh Chor Boon, Tan Teng Lang, *Building Bridges, Carving Niches: An Enduring Legacy*, pp. 155, 165.

传统与嬗变：华侨华人慈善事业新发展

邢菁华*、张洵君**

摘要

中华慈善文化渊澄取映，赓续绵延，当代华侨华人慈善事业关乎慈善与中国"现代性"议题。文章通过对华侨华人慈善缘起、捐赠领域、捐款动因、新老慈善家的代际差异比较，论述了从传统中嬗变是当代华侨华人慈善事业的主脉络。当代华侨华人的慈善事业体现了一种新的中西文化综合。在公益慈善领域，当代华侨华人为疫情下呈现的现代性危机贡献出了华人智慧和华人方案。

关键词：慈善、华侨华人、代际差异、文化认同

---

* 邢菁华，清华大学华商研究中心研究员，致公党党史研究与党务工作委员会委员，致公党北京市委侨海工作委员会副主任，主要从事华侨华人、产业史与商业史领域的研究。
** 张洵君（通讯作者），清华大学华商研究中心研究员，贵州财经大学特聘教授。

Tradition and Evolution:
New Development of Overseas Chinese Philanthropy

XING Jinghua, ZHANG Xunjun

Abstract

Chinese charity culture has a long history, and contemporary overseas Chinese charity is related to charity and China's "modernity" issues. This paper illustrates that the main vein of contemporary overseas Chinese philanthropy from the tradition evolution by comparing the causes of philanthropy among overseas Chinese, philanthropic giving field, donation motivation, the generational differences between old and new philanthropists. The philanthropy of contemporary overseas Chinese reflects a new integration of Chinese and Western culture. In the field of philanthropy, contemporary overseas Chinese have contributed Chinese wisdom and Chinese solutions for the crisis of modernity under the epidemic.

Keywords: Philanthropy; Overseas Chinese; Generational Differences; Cultural Identity

中华传统文化源远流长、博大精深，在五千年连绵不断的中华民族文明史上产生了重大而深远的影响。慈善事业是慈善文化的延续，慈善文化是一种内在的理念，代表着一种精神层面，而慈善事业则通过内生动力，经过制度、组织和程序所呈现出外在的行动。中华慈善事业的存在与发展，是与中华慈善文化的传承与创新紧密相连的；换言之，没有中华慈善文化的传承与创新，也就没有中华慈善事业的存在与发展。[1] 中华文明的核心价值是"责任先于自由，义务先于权利，社群高于个人，和谐高于冲突。"[2] 中华文明核心价值所强调的仁爱原则、礼教精神、责任意识、社群取向，以及对王道世界的想象与实践，贯穿于两千多年的历史实践，彰显出中华文明对关联性、交互性伦理的特别重视，以及对多样性和谐的特别推崇。中国文化的特征是以群体为本位，以家庭为中心，由小及大，由近及远，由亲及疏，延伸拓展形成社会人际网络。[3]

慈善文化作为中华传统文化的瑰丽一章与重要组成部分，经过几千年的积淀与演进，形成了自身独特而精到的核心概念及思想体系。《周易》是"群经之首，大道之源"，《易传》是诠释《易经》的经典著作。《易传·文言传·坤文言》有云："积善之家，必有余庆，积不善之家，必有余殃"。中华传统慈善文化以其人性的宗旨、和谐的架构，形成了各个流派、各种学说的基本内核：儒家主张的"仁爱"，道家主张的"为善"，佛家主张的"慈悲"，墨家主张的"兼爱"，以

---

[1] 周秋光〈中华慈善文化及其传承与创新〉，《史学月刊》2020年第8期，页105–113。
　Zhou Qiuguang, "Chinese Charity Culture and Its Inheritance and Innovation," *Journal of Historical Science*, No. 8 (2020), pp. 105–113.
[2] 陈来《中华文明的核心价值：国学流变与传统价值观》（北京：生活·读书·新知三联书店，2015）。
　Chen Lai, *The Core Value of Chinese Civilization: The Evolution of Sinology and Traditional Values* (Beijing: SDX Joint Publishing Company, 2015).
[3] 费正清著，郭晓兵译《中国的思想与制度》（北京：世界知识出版社有限公司，2008）。
　John King Fairbank, *Chinese Thought and Institutions*, trans. Guo Xiaobing (Beijing: World Affairs Press Co. Ltd., 2008).

及那些流芳百世的"老吾老以及人之老,幼吾幼以及人之幼"、"恻隐之心,仁之端也"、"积德累功,慈心于物"、"善者吾善之,不善者吾亦善之"、"天下兼相爱则治,交相恶则乱"、"从善如登,从恶如崩"、"勿以恶小而为之,勿以善小而不为"等等千古智慧的结晶。[4] 近代慈善主体发生了新的变化,随着中西慈善文化的交流碰撞,特别是国际红十字会的人道主义精神与西方新的社会福利公益思想传入中国,以民间社会为主体的慈善群体出现,民间社会开始在慈善救助中发挥作用。现代慈善是继传统古代慈善和近代慈善文化基础之上的一种新理念新思路,它早已超越财富的世俗含义本身,社会责任、乡土情结、民族精神都在其中熠熠生辉。弘扬慈善文化所要达到的境界是构建全社会浓郁的人文关怀,减少冲突,调和矛盾,使社会呈现一种稳定和谐的状态。这与推动构建人类命运共同体的中华民族使命理路相通,逻辑内在统一。

海外华侨华人的慈善溯源

华人移民是中国近现代史不可分割的组成部分,华人向外移民不仅是一种超越地域、跨越国界的社会现象,而且是一种经济和文化相结合的实践行为和建构跨国社会场域的动态过程。[5] 早在一个世纪之前,移居海外的华商、华工以及难民通过侨汇、投资等方式救济家乡的亲人、支持家乡公共事业的发展。这种现象一直持续到当代,即使在祖籍地中国已经成为当今世界第二大经济体,侨乡也已经成为发达地区

---

[4] 李济慈〈慈善文化:以传统为根时代为翼〉,新华网,http://www.xinhuanet.com/gongyi/2017-02/16/c_129480631.htm(最后访问时间:2021年12月30日)。

Li Jici, "Charity Culture: Tradition as The Root and Era as the Wing," http://www.xinhuanet.com/gongyi/2017-02/16/c_129480631.htm (Accessed: 30 December 2021).

[5] 孔飞力著,李明欢译《他者中的华人:中国近现代移民史》(南京:江苏人民出版社,2016)。

Philip Alden Kuhn, *Chinese Among Others: Emigration in Modern Times*, trans. Li Minghuan (Nanjing: Jiangsu People's Publishing House, 2016).

的时候，华侨华人的慈善捐赠也依然在持续发展。[6] 海外华侨华人社会对慈善文化的传承，也表明了中华文化的蓬勃生命力。华人在海外重建了各种文化认同与社会网络，以华商与侨领为核心形成了各种华人社团，组织多种活动，互帮互济，处理群体内部事务及与当地社会的关系，形成了以血缘为纽带的宗亲会、以地缘与方言为纽带的同乡会馆、以业缘为纽带的商会、以信仰为纽带的各种宗教团体等。"达则兼济天下"，成功华商勇于担当社会责任，不仅承担着华人社会的公益与公共事业，而且反哺当地社会，或回馈家乡与祖籍国。特别令人感动的是，各地的华文教育就是在他们完全自发组织下发展起来，形成华文基础教育、职业教育乃至高等教育的体系，却不需要当地政府出一分钱一分力。海外华人社会形成了富有生机和内在活力的自发秩序与自生机制。华商弘扬中华慈善文化，彰显社会责任与情怀，对世界繁荣与和平贡献卓著。[7]

香港大学管理学院院长 S·戈登·雷丁说："一个典型的海外华人的肖像可以被描绘成一个合成体，它的每个部分在现实生活的事例中都可见到。"[8] 海外华人有共同的文化传统、共同的理想范型、共同的社会行为准则，同样的优势和同样的弱点。换句话说，都属于一种独特的文化类型，保持了多少世纪不变。闽籍学者林其锬教授提出"五缘文化说"，就是对以亲缘、地缘、神缘、业缘和物缘为内涵的五种

---

[6] 景燕春〈华人移民慈善的动力机制：以广东侨乡顺德为例〉，《华侨华人历史研究》2018年第4期，页68-75。
Jing Yanchun, "The Dynamic Mechanism of Chinese Diaspora Philanthropy: A Case Study of Shunde in Guangdong Province," *Journal of Overseas Chinese History Studies*, No. 4 (2018), pp. 68–75.
[7] 龙登高〈中华慈善文化源远流长〉，《金融博览》2018年第6期。
Long Denggao, "Chinese Charity Culture Has a Long History," *Financial View*, No. 6 (2018).
[8] S·戈登·雷丁著，谢婉莹译《华人的资本主义精神》（上海：上海人民出版社，2009）。
Stanley Gordon Redding, *The Spirit of Chinese Capitalism*, trans. Xie Wanying (Shanghai: Shanghai People's Publishing House, 2009).

关系的文化研究。[9] 亲缘，就是宗族、亲戚关系，它包括了血亲、姻亲和假亲（或称契亲、如金兰结义等）；地缘，就是邻里，乡党等关系，即通常所说的"小同乡"和"大同乡"；神缘，就是共同的宗教信仰的关系，如对关羽、妈祖等的信仰，共奉的神祇结合着的人群；业缘就是同学、同行之间的关系，有共同的利益和业务关系，有切磋和交流的需要和愿望，由此组合而成的人群，其组织形式便是同学会、学会、协会、研究会等等；物缘，就是因物（如土、特、名、优等产品）而发生的关系，因物而集合的人群，也会出现诸如行会、协会、研究会之类的组织。赵红英认为"五缘文化理论是从文化角度分析研究地域间中国人相互关系的一种理论概括，也是研究华侨华人社会结构与人际网络的一种视角。五缘文化理论的一大特点是，它特别重视动态的中华民族人际间的关系，是对中华民族在流动迁徙、开拓创业、适应涵化过程中社会结构和人际网络特征的概括。"[10]

慈善文化作为一种观念形态，有着极其深刻的哲学背景和社会因素。从早年移民成立的"宗亲会"、"会馆"等互助组织，到如今的现代慈善事业多元化发展，华侨华人的慈善公益事业日渐成熟。从捐款方向看，慈善形式越来越多元化，实现了从实物到资金、再到基金会的专项捐款的转变；捐款地域从以侨乡为主变为向全国辐射，特别向中西部贫困地区倾斜；捐款领域从以教育为主，变为逐步涉及医疗、灾难、重大事件、社会民生等各个方面。

---

[9] 林其锬〈"五缘"文化与亚洲的未来〉，《上海社会科学院学术季刊》1990年第2期，页118–127。

Lin Qitan, "The Culture of Five Ties and the Future of Asia," *Quarterly Journal of Shanghai Academy of Social Sciences*, No. 2 (1990), pp. 118–127.

[10] 赵红英、宁一，"五缘文化与华侨华人社团"，〈"五缘文化与现代文明"笔谈〉，《东南学术》2013年第5期，页272。

Zhao Hongying, Ning Yi, "Five Ties Culture and Overseas Chinese Association," in "Comments on Five Ties Culture and Contemporary Civilisations," *Southeast Academic Research*, No. 5 (2013), p. 272.

慈善捐赠的行为与动因

一、当代华侨华人的公益慈善现状

华人慈善组织长期以来在华人社区和当地民众中开展助危济困、关爱融入、公益回馈和社会服务等有意义的活动，彰显了华侨华人之间的帮扶互助形象。[11] 如：2008年汶川特大震灾，据不完全统计，五大洲45个国家和地区的华侨华人以及港澳台同胞参与了捐款灾区的行动，捐款超过13亿元人民币；多年来正大集团为中国社会公益事业累计捐款金额超过5亿元人民币；澳大利亚华人慈善事业"光明之行"每年派遣志愿医疗队到中国贫困地区，开展义诊和扶贫助学等公益活动；来自102个国家和地区的35万海外华侨华人及港澳台同胞向北京奥运会合计捐款9.3亿元人民币建设奥运会场馆"水立方"等。[12]

根据国务院侨办统计数据显示，目前海外华侨华人社团约有2.5万个，2017年度各级政府侨务部门共受理华侨华人、港澳同胞向中国国内的慈善捐款总额合计29.71亿元人民币，同比增长38.83%，捐赠总额比上年增加8.31亿元人民币。捐助领域主要集中在教育（41.82%）、社会事业（35.83%）、医疗卫生（10.49%）和生产生活设施建设（8.45%）等。[13] 由此可见华侨华人及港澳同胞的捐赠偏好，教育仍然是他们关注并捐赠的最主要领域，其次为社会事业、卫生医疗和生产生活。

---

[11] 人民日报海外版〈华人"善二代"真情滋润社会〉，http://m.haiwainet.cn/middle/3543452/2018/0705/content_31346903_1.html（最后访问日期：2022年5月15日）。

People's Daily Overseas Edition, "The Second Generation Chinese Philanthropists' Read Dedication for Society," http://m.haiwainet.cn/middle/3543452/2018/0705/content_31346903_1.html (Accessed: 15 May 2022).

[12] 张秀明〈改革开放以来华侨华人对中国慈善事业的贡献探析〉，《华侨华人历史研究》2018年第4期，页23–33。

Zhang Xiuming, "The Contribution of Overseas Chinese to China's Philanthropy Since the Reform and Opening-up," Journal of Overseas Chinese History Studies, No. 4 (2018), pp. 22–33.

[13] 慈善公益报（网络版）〈2017年华侨华人等慈善捐赠29.71亿〉，http://csgyb.com.cn/news/yaowen/20180514/18465.html（最后访问时间：2021年12月30日）。

China Charity Federation, "Overseas Chinese Donated RMB 2.971 Billion to Charity in 2017," http://csgyb.com.cn/news/yaowen/20180514/18465.html (Accessed: 30 December 2021).

改革开放40年以来，广大华侨华人及港澳同胞向中国国内社会公益事业的捐赠从2003年的600亿元人民币，到2017年累计增长已超过1000亿元人民币（因数据可获得性，这里是华侨华人与港澳同胞的捐赠额合计数）。[14] 其中，仅捐建中国内地中小学、职业教育、大学等各类教育项目即占慈善捐赠的一半以上。根据中国国务院侨办统计的2017年接受华侨华人、港澳同胞捐赠的16个省份金额，闽、粤、浙、沪4个省（市）受赠均超亿元，其受赠金额合计占全国总额的85.93%，捐赠资金为地方民生改善和社会发展提供了有力支持。[15]

中国从国家层面长期倡导通过传播慈善文化，发扬慈善精神，弘扬传统美德，践行社会主义核心价值观。海外侨胞的捐赠行为与政府对慈善的态度密切相关。[16] 这些年慈善事业快速发展，很大程度上弥补了政府在社会保障投入上的不足。例如国务院侨办成立了"侨爱工程"；中国侨联发起"中国华侨公益基金会"；福建省侨联发起中国第一个省级华侨公益基金会——福建省华侨公益基金会等等，反映了中国政府对慈善的重视程度越来越高，海外华侨华人慈善意愿也随之增长。

---

[14] 该数据来源：许又声〈国务院关于华侨权益保护工作情况的报告〉，第十三届全国人民代表大会常务委员会第二次会议，2018年4月25日。
Xu Yousheng, "Reports of State Council on the Overseas Chinese Rights Protection," Presented on the Second Meeting of the 13th National People's Congress of the People's Republic of China Standing Committee, 25 April 2018.

[15] 中国国务院侨务办公室〈2017年侨务部门受理华侨华人、港澳同胞慈善捐赠29.71亿〉，http://www.gqb.gov.cn/news/2018/0207/44334.shtml（最后访问时间：2021年12月30日）。
Overseas Chinese Affairs Office of the State Council of China, "The Overseas Chinese Affairs Office Received Charitable Donations of RMB 2.971 Billion from the Overseas Chinese and Compatriots in Hong Kong and Macao," http://www.gqb.gov.cn/news/2018/0207/44334.shtml (Accessed: 30 December 2021).

[16] 邓国胜〈中国富人捐款水平及其变化原因〉，《中国行政管理》2013年第2期，页71–74。
Deng Guosheng, "The Level of Donations from Wealthy People in China and the Reasons for the Changes," *Chinese Public Administration*, No. 2 (2013), pp. 71–74.

二、当代华侨华人慈善捐赠的动因

海外华侨华人捐款大体上经历了由非理性捐赠向理性捐赠转变的过程。他们在中国兴办公益事业，此前主要是为了报效桑梓、刻碑留名、纪念先人等目的。现在，捐款的目的则更加务实，有着经济和政治方面的追求和愿望，希望能在某一方面有所回报或者提高影响力，与祖籍国建立更深层次的合作关系等。慈善成为了沟通海内外最快捷有效的阳光桥梁。当然，单纯以慈善作为眷恋故土、回报社会方式的慈善家也不在少数。

根据2011年《亚洲家族慈善调研报告》[17]关于家族慈善事业的主要激励因素所示，在对100多位华侨华人受访者进行调研中发现，家族价值观与传承、长辈教育与鼓励、家族事业领域、家族传统、强化家族的联系、家族管理或税收为主要考虑因素（见图1），特别是第一代慈善家对家族所属的地区、种族和文化更具有认同感和责任感。

图1：华侨华人家族慈善事业的主要激励因素

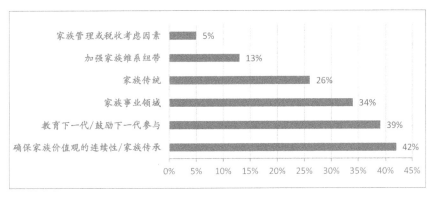

数据来源：瑞银集团，欧洲工商管理学院《亚洲家族慈善调研报告》（2011）。
UBS, INSEAD, "UBS-INSEAD Study on Family Philanthropy in Asia," (2011).

---

[17] UBS, INSEAD, "UBS-INSEAD Study on Family Philanthropy in Asia," (2011), http://gife.issuelab.org/resources/15222/15222.pdf (Accessed: 15 May 2022).

亚洲的华侨华人慈善最核心的关键词是"家族",这是中华传统文化中"家国同构"、"家国情怀"儒家思想的当代体现。家族企业,家族传承和家族财富管理,体现了中国传统文化的基因图谱。自公元前500年孔孟思想萌芽开始,家族的观念就已深深烙印在中华民族的文化信仰之中。相比西方社会,中国人对于家族更加重视,也更利于营造家族成员和谐相处的环境。根据2017年中国工商银行私人银行调研数据显示,74%的超高净值家族依靠实业经营积累财富,其家族财富规模分布在5000万到5亿元人民币的区间。92%的受访家族当前介入了实业经营。以实业经营致富的家族多数仍保有实业经营,通过非实业经营致富的家族也将家族财富再投资于创立实业,说明超高净值家族普遍将实业经营视为创富之源。中国家族一代的成功形象与刻苦耐劳的事业精神,潜移默化地形成二代对一代的尊敬与对家族的认同。超过80%的受访者以身为家族一分子为荣,并乐于投身家族事业。

而北美华人方面,在美国洛杉矶亚美公义促进会（Asian Americans Advancing Justice-Los Angeles）发起的《全球华人慈善行动》首期报告中指出,三大因素是美籍华人慈善家的捐款动因：一是出于行业兴趣、从属关系、实用性、影响力；二是宗教、经历和家庭的影响；三是社会影响成为慈善事业的考虑因素。

通过上面的比较可以发现,华侨华人从事慈善的动因是非常多元的,不能一概而论。身处不同的国家,受其文化差异的影响,捐款动因自然不同。缺乏对不同国家文化方面和地缘因素的考虑,就很难判断价值观的形成,从而对慈善动因的判断过于片面。但一般而言,家庭、兴趣以及人生经历是多数慈善家捐款的共同动机。

从投向中国的捐赠款看,人民币进账目前还是主流,虽然捐赠方主要来自于广大华侨华人及港澳同胞,但事实上许多款项出自于他们在中国的投资或资产。同时,捐赠呈现三个特点：一是在自己的家乡捐赠,回馈父母、家乡对他们的养育之恩；二是在事业所在地捐赠,回馈当地对个人事业上的支持；三是奖教助学也比较多。

汉密尔顿认为中国社会是由制度化的社会关系网组成的，这些网络的参与成员只承认与他们有私人义务关系的人群，[18] 家族之间的情谊、信任和义务是海外华侨华人群体捐款时经常考虑的因素。

华侨华人捐赠群体希望所捐的钱能全部用在项目建设上，他们不仅关注项目的结果，而且重视项目实施的过程，关心项目后期的运行及发展。一些慈善家通过基金会已经有着成熟的运作和管理经验，他们希望能够了解和掌握资金的用途，实现效率最大化。西方国家慈善事业发展早，且规范和成熟。中国慈善事业处于起步阶段，伴随着中国《慈善法》的颁布及社会的关注，近些年，慈善事业的透明度、规范化等方面也得到很大的改善，这对于海外捐款的持续性至关重要。

慈善文化视域下的新老代际差异

美国知名亚裔研究学者，加州大学洛杉矶分校（UCLA）的周敏教授认为，当代国际移民虽然种族背景和社会经济地位不同，看起来还保持着自己的族裔身份认同、文化传统以及与祖籍国的联系，但是他们及其后裔有着强烈的融入移居国主流社会和被其接纳的意愿，[19] 这反应了新一代华人慈善家们具有不同的社会融入价值观，从而影响着现代慈善事业的新发展动向。海外新生代不同于期待"落叶归根"的父辈、祖辈。华裔新生代的父辈、祖辈们是"他者的华人"，是一部中国近现代移民史，"从殖民统治者到被奴役的臣民，从独立后民族国家执掌大权的统治集团到洋溢民族主义激情的知识精英；从颐指气使的大富豪到埋头养家糊口的升斗小民，'华人'与周边'他者'之

---

[18] Gary G. Hamilton (ed.), *Asian Business Networks* (Berlin: Walter de Gruyter GmbH, 1996), p. 6.
[19] 周敏、刘宏〈海外华人跨国主义实践的模式及其差异：基于美国与新加坡的比较分析〉，《华侨华人历史研究》2013年第1期，页1–19。
Zhou Min, Liu Hong, "Changing Patterns of Overseas Chinese Transnationalism: The United States v. Singapore," *Journal of Overseas Chinese History Studies*, No. 1 (2013), pp. 1–19.

间呈现出错综复杂的互动关系。"[20] 而在住在国出生的华裔虽然是华人的一部分，但不属于国际移民。特别是华裔新生代，更是"我者建构"、"落地生根"的一代，生活观念、价值取向、社会体验、个人行为选择等方面有着与前辈不同的特征。海外新生代的观念已由老一辈的"落叶归根"转变为"落地生根"。他们更加注重改善生存环境，提升社会经济地位，拓展生存发展空间。投资时更加理性务实，注重生态、经济、社会的三重效益，不再受制于本土观念的牵制，世界各地都是他们视野中的选择目标。

在改革开放四十多年期间，新华侨华人和华裔新生代中涌现出一批科技人才和企业家，他们正在不同行业崭露头角，活跃于世界的舞台。老一代华侨华人企业家往往是白手起家，经历了艰难打拼的创业过程，大多没有机会接受系统完整的高等教育。而新一代华裔慈善家往往成长于优越的家庭环境中，大多接受过西方教育，具有国际化视野，将慈善作为塑造家族企业社会责任形象的重要手段。[21] 在进行慈善行动的过程中，他们不仅仅限于简单的捐款捐物，而是像经营企业一样对待慈善，以慈善事业吸纳专业化人才，进行专业化管理，熟练应用新技术新工具，主动积极参与慈善进程，以各自兴趣点出发，找到慈善带给自己的成就感和满足感。海外华裔新生代的创新与开拓，与父辈的言传身教密不可分，同时也刻上了自身成长经历和时代变迁的烙印。一些华人企业专项成立了家族慈善基金会、慈善信托，将家族理念、价值观等体现在慈善事业中，让其家族精神在后代中得以长期弘扬及有效传承。如励媖中国联合创始人及总裁、新加坡华裔陈玉馨表示，2013年，她创办励媖中国，致力于在教育、技术、企业家精神等方面帮助女性提

---

[20] 孔飞力著，李明欢译《他者中的华人：中国近现代移民史》，页38-39。

Philip Alden Kuhn, *Chinese Among Others: Emigration in Modern Times*, trans. Li Minghuan, pp. 38-39.

[21] 陆波《行善天下：一个公益经理人的跨国札记》（北京：中国社会出版社，2016），页27。

Lu Bo, *Doing Good Across the World: Personal Reflections by a Chinese Philanthropy Executive* (Beijing: China Social Publishing Ltd, 2016), p. 27.

升自我发展能力。美国南加州大学职能科学与职能治疗学部的华裔助理教授陈文扬表示，作为美国华裔的一员，他对智能科学和智能治疗学颇有兴趣，正在美国积极与世界顶尖的大学合作，开展对残疾人的帮扶。美国唐仲英基金会执行董事梁为功在近日的采访中表示，与老一代的华侨华人相比，新一代华侨华人和华裔新生代更善于运用数据、科技、媒体等现代化技术，并将资产管理、项目管理、风险管理等专业化知识应用到现代慈善事业中。[22] 鉴于这些年中国经济的持续发展，越来越多的海外华裔新生代积极与中国合作，中国也通过各种政策吸引他们回祖籍国发展和投资，并开展交流与合作。

新冠疫情中的慈善与人类命运共同体

大疫如大考，如何应考，值得深思。但毋容置疑，这次重大公共卫生事件为慈善事业的创新提供了契机。只有在疫情中，我们才有可能更加全面细致地观察并思考慈善公益的起源和作用。这是因为，突如其来的疫情从某种程度上将整个社会最大可能地还原到"自然状态"。在这种状态下，我们看到了人性的各种写真，看到了各类组织的真实能力。在这个特定的时空下，我们才能在"看得见的"之外，思考和发现更多"看不见的"。

从主客观两方面而言，慈善公益在现代社会生活中已经成为一支推动社会进步的重要力量。虽然从整体而言依旧是一种边缘性的力量，但正是这种边缘性力量，带来新的视野和实践。这里，我们将扶贫济困，抢险救灾，突发事件中的应急施救等慈善行为，称之为传统慈善。如1998年大洪水，2008年汶川大地震等超强自然灾难中的慈善救助、捐赠行为。这次在中国乃至全球发生的新冠疫情，是历史上罕见的灾难。

---

[22] 邢菁华〈善二代的新视角和新作为〉，《金融博览》2018年第8期，页20–21。
　Xing Jinghua, "New Perspectives and New Actions of the Second Generation Philanthropists," *Financial View*, No. 8 (2018), pp. 20–21.

虽然它与传统的自然灾难同样具有突发性和严重的危害性，但又有许多不同的内容和特点。自然，与之相适应的慈善行为也呈现出不同的特征。海外华侨华人跨越国界的慈善行为，更是具有其鲜明的特点，主要表现在以下几个方面：

一是筹募形式发生新的变化。传统的筹募，一些慈善机构和社会公益团体，在事件发生的第一时间，往往通过举办大型文艺晚会、社会名流餐会、拍卖会等，广泛动员社会力量，唤起和激发人们的捐赠热情。这次疫情的暴发，由于受援对象和环境的特殊性，这类活动和形式自然不是首选。为适应外部环境的变化，大多数华侨华人和侨团采用"线上募捐方式"。事实证明，这一新形式同样取得了不逊以往的成绩。

二是捐赠的地域、范围广泛且分散。这与传统慈善捐赠的情况有很大不同。一般情况下，捐赠地域范围比较局限。而这次疫情范围既广泛又多变，使组织慈善捐赠遇到了新的难题。可能昨天位于不同国家的华侨华人还在支援中国，而很快他们所处的地域或者国家就成了需要被援助的对象。这种多变性让人一下子很难适应，更何况海外华侨华人分布广，所以跨越国界的救助在此次救援中体现得淋漓尽致。仅中国华侨公益基金会就收到捐款累计折合超过2.7亿元人民币，捐赠者覆盖六大洲。[23]

三是捐赠物品和捐赠渠道的特殊性。口罩等防疫物资成为了各国主要稀缺资源。中国疫情暴发初期，防疫物资紧缺，广大华侨华人为了采购到防护用品和医疗器械，他们全球扫货，既有满街搜罗，也有重金购买。国际运输不畅，海外华侨华人便想方设法、千方百计地把防疫物资运送回国，有的利用航空及国际物流等运输渠道，有的甚至采用蚂蚁搬家的方式，先将物资集中到机场，再委托来华人员以随身行李的方式

---

[23]〈2020中国公益年会｜乔卫：华侨华人在公益慈善事业中发挥着独特作用〉，《公益时报》，2020年12月30日。

"Qiao Wei: Overseas Chinese are Playing a Unique Role in Public Welfare and Charity," *China Philanthropy Times*, 30 December 2020.

"人肉护送"。"史上最长行李托运单"、"最美带货人"、"口罩航班"层出不穷，不一而足，一系列感人事迹令人动容。[24]

四是慈善公益的模式呈现多元化。当国际疫情蔓延时，海外华侨华人自发组建SOS互助群，联系中国的专家帮助海外华侨华人在线解答疑难问题、提供心理疏导，向留学生等困难群体提供免费爱心餐、设立轻症患者隔离点、24小时紧急救助电话等。许多海外当地民众在自家门外的信报箱内惊喜地发现了华侨华人邻居投放的口罩和精心编译的防疫小贴士；许多海外当地医院、学校、警察局、养老院陆续收到了华侨华人捐赠的防疫物资；许多国家的侨团主动请缨，帮助当地政府与中国医疗器械生产企业对接；一些华商通过经营模式的创新开展对当地困难群体和生态环境的救助等等。华侨华人力挺住在国的用心用情，一如当初他们支援祖籍国的尽心尽力。

这些新的慈善变化在以往的经历中不曾有过，这也是外部环境影响下的首次慈善创新。慈善事业作为全世界的社会服务提供者、社会发展重要力量、社会治理现代化的重要参与者，伴随着中国改革开放四十多年的不断深化得到迅速发展，也是全球治理体系中民间交往、民生项目、民心相通和构建人类命运共同体的重要载体。

结语

慈善是全世界人类共通的语言，慈善文化渗透在经济和社会发展中。中华慈善文化呈现多元一体的格局，从长时间维度看经历了从传统走向现代的过程，而华侨华人与中华慈善文化相伴相生。以侨领为核心形成的各种海外华人社团，或互济互助，或施善教化，促进了华

---

[24] 邢菁华、龙登高、张洵君〈抗击新冠疫情中的海外华侨华人：基于行动者网络理论的分析〉，《民族研究》2021年第1期，页66—76。
　Xing Jinghua, Long Denggao, Zhang Xunjun, "The Research of Overseas Chinese in Combating the COVID-19 Epidemic: Analysis Based on Actor-Network Theory (ANT)," *Ethno-National Studies*, No. 1 (2021), pp. 66–76.

人与当地文明交流、社会融合及经济发展。从传统中嬗变，是当代华侨华人慈善事业的主脉络。随着工商文明的崛起，西方文化的冲击，当代华侨华人从理念到实践，在捐赠领域、捐款动因、与老一代慈善家的代际差异等方面呈现出了新的慈善特征。当代华侨华人的慈善事业体现了一种新的中西文化综合。当今时局下的新冠疫情凸显了全球公共卫生治理的脆弱性。在公益慈善领域，当代华侨华人为疫情下呈现的现代性危机贡献出了华人智慧和华人方案。

区域华文文学的越界、跨国与主体解/构
以旅台马华文学为例

朱崇科[*]

摘要

区域华文文学的产生和发展自有其阶段性和因为时代语境差异带来的不同进度与特色，文学生产的主体性及其身份认同也在发生着巨大变化，尤其是网络媒体的强势崛起也部分消解了固有的身份政治，毋庸讳言，个体物理空间的迁移、身份的转换、宏阔（文化）政治语境的影响等等自然也确立了作者个体及区域文学生产的某种边界乃至界限感，同时也有可能的世界眼光（如李永平），但作者对更大文学场的影响力或名利的追逐又部分消解同时又建构了创作主体新的身份认同（如黄锦树）。

关键词：旅台马华文学、李永平、黄锦树、华人性

---

[*] 朱崇科，中国中山大学中文系（珠海），zhuchk@mail.sysu.edu.cn。

本文原刊登于《华人研究国际学报》，第14卷，第1期，2022年6月，页63 - 74。经授权转载。

Cross-border, Transnationalism, and De-construction of the Subject in Malaysian Chinese Literature within Taiwan

ZHU Chongke

Abstract

The emergence and development of Area Chinese literature has its phase progress or even characteristic features. Meantime the subjectivity and identities of the authors are changing much, considering new media is partly smearing out boundary of old identity politics. If we explore into the subjectivity of Malaysian Chinese Literature within Taiwan field, we can find that on the one hand the sense of boundary does exist, but on the other hand excellent authors can cross the borders: Li Yongping has its pursuit of being a cosmopolitan novelist, while Ng Kim Chew has a worldly tendency for accepting mainland China as his new market. Thus, the subjectivity can be both constructed and deconstructed at the same time.

Keywords: Malaysian Chinese Literature within Taiwan; Li Yongping; Ng Kim Chew; Chineseness

某种意义上说，不同时空、代际更迭的华人其属性特征（Chineseness）或身份认同（identities）也往往与时俱进，而新老移民之间的关系既有传统的磨合性/竞争性矛盾，又可能产生新的联系与冲突，而重大历史事件或思潮又会对他们产生新的冲击或影响，比如全球化（globalisation）或跨国主义（trans-nationalism），这些元素一方面增加了身在其间的人的身心流动感，同时另一方面却又可能强化了其日益累积的在地主义痕迹，导致了可能的本土全球化。

更值得关注的是，新媒体/媒介的崛起（比如微信/Wechat、Facebook等）会让旧有的交通不便、沟通不畅难度大大降低，这就让某些本土化进程变慢，而某些重大事务的席卷全球（比如迄今为止世界范围内依然如火如荼的新冠疫情）却又大大改变了个体的工作、学习与生活习惯，甚至堪称风格突变，比如云留学（线上课程）、在家办公、严重依赖快递等，毫无疑问，这都让某些新移民的移入国认同变弱，而采取更务实、灵活的策略。

类似地，不同区域的华文文学也因了华人社会的历史变迁、现实撞击、创作主体的流散与跨越而与常规套路（文学史上的某些规律）不太吻合，产生了值得我们认真探勘的新质与繁复张力。比如新移民文学（尤其是以北美为中心）的延续与嬗变（变更为他国护照只是为了出行与活动方便，他们更多还是在移出国——中国活动，不管是创作语言还是发行与评论市场），此中当然也会有各种各样的危与机。[1]

---

[1] 朱崇科〈论新移民文学生产的危与机〉，《暨南学报（哲学社会科学版）》2020年第3期，页1–9。
Zhu Chongke, "On New Immigrants Literature's Challenges and Opportunities," *Jinan Journal (Philosophy and Social Sciences)*, No. 3 (2020), pp. 1–9.

耐人寻味的是，为了论述的集中性与有效性，即便是我们把视野缩小到旅台马华文学[2]的场域中来，其中的复杂变化也值得我们认真总结与反思。在此视阈中，越界、跨国实践中所彰显的丰富意蕴令人眼界大开，尤其是，它也折射出华人写作主体的从个体到群体的自我解/构。这里所选的个案分别是李永平（1947–2017）与黄锦树（1967– ）。李横跨了英殖民者统治时期和马来西亚独立，黄则经历了台湾的解严节点（1987年7月15日）；他们都有自己的执念，李不愿承认自己是马华作家，黄对中国性浓烈的中国大陆颇多意见，但吊诡的是，他们最终都与之和解，乃至趁势飞扬。

一、向他者要强者

正如华人移出中国、漂泊海外的复杂动因主线清晰（更多是生计或工作需要），旅台马华作家留学台湾亦是原因繁复但又有迹可循。简单而言，可用推拉的张力理论加以解释。在大马国内，因为同化需要而实际上相对歧视华人的教育政策使得不少优秀华人学子选择留洋，而上一两代"返唐山"的叮咛浸润言犹在耳，这是赴台的推力；在拉力方面，打着中华民国旗号的台湾更需要借助华侨华人子弟充实力量"反攻大陆"实现光复大业或春秋大梦。这边厢李永平留学时期的中国大陆正在轰轰烈烈搞文革（1966–1976），想回而不能；黄锦树的大学时期则是中国大陆改革开放的前十年内，彼时的台湾（亚洲四小龙之一）生龙活虎、意气风发，明显更有吸引力。

---

[2] 目前的研究专著主要有：陈大为《最年轻的麒麟：马华文学在台湾（1963–2012）》（台湾：台湾文学馆，2012）。Chen Tah Wei, *The Youngest Kylin: Malaysian Chinese Literature in Taiwan, 1963–2012* (Taiwan: National Museum of Taiwan Literature, 2012).

温明明《离境与跨界：在台马华文学研究（1963–2013）》（北京：中国社会科学出版社，2016）。Wen Mingming, *Off-shore and Cross-border: Studies of Malaysian Chinese Literature in Taiwan* (Beijing: China Social Sciences Press, 2016).

朱崇科《大马"南洋"叙述中的台湾影响及其再现模式》，《厦门大学学报》2015年第3期，页87–95。Zhu Chongke, "Representative Modes of Taiwan Experiences in Malaysia's 'Nanyang' Narration," *Journal of Xiamen University (Arts and Social Sciences)*, No. 3 (2015), pp. 87–95.

（一）强化中国性

如果从新马华文教育背景来看，语言政治视野下的英校生们多选择前往欧美（尤其是英美加国等），至少也是大洋洲（澳大利亚、新西兰）留学，而华校生除了本地南洋大学以外，往往都是台湾，毕竟中国与新马的关系交往自有其节奏（与大马1974年5月31日建交，与新加坡则是1990年10月3日）才逐步正常化，1990年代以后留学中国大陆的马来西亚学生才开始增多。但是李、黄的留学皆在此之前，只能选择为侨生优质服务一条龙且有奖学金的台湾。

从拉力角度思考，台湾当局更希望把侨生培养成为海外华人效忠中华民国且协助祖国建设的有生力量或至少是同盟；而从文化主导权的角度思考，台湾虽然偏安于一隅，却又要和中国大陆竞争文化的宰制权和正统地位（尤其是中华文化传统的嫡系传承人身份），这都意味着无论是李永平还是黄锦树都必然被浓烈的中国性所包围，而更耐人寻味的是，作为彼时身为青年学子的李与黄对这种中国性却又是热烈拥抱的，惟其如此，才能够壮大与强化大马华族文化与文学创作的谱系与根脉。

李永平最直接的表现其实是他的"文字修行"。[3] 来台湾留学之前，他已经是一个小有所成的青年作家（1966年以中篇小说《婆罗洲之子》参加了由婆罗洲文化局举办的征文比赛独占鳌头），关注的议题更多是大马（尤其是婆罗洲）故事，而赴台后的李日益精进，台大外文系的训练让他更能够从比较的视野对中华文化及文字展开精心探索，通读李永平的文字表述，不像1949年后中国大陆的规范化文字——现代汉语的白话化那么准确、简单却又枯干，李笔下的文字、场景更显得文白夹杂、中西混融，有一种明清气质加民国风度的杂糅感。而表现在重大主题或事务上，他的《海东青》（1992）出版于台湾解严之后却弘扬了蒋介石"出埃及记"的精神，这种出力不讨好的操作却也可视为中国性延迟（belated Chineseness）的再现。

---

[3] 黄锦树〈流离的婆罗洲之子和他的母亲、父亲：论李永平的"文字修行"〉，《中外文学》第26卷5期（1997），页119–146。

Ng Kim Chew, "The Exiled Son of Borneo and His Mother & Father: On Li Yongping's 'Character Practice'," *Chung-wai Literary Monthly*, Vol. 26, No. 5 (1997), pp. 119–146.

从台湾"惨绿的中文系"（从本科到博士分别是台大、淡江大学、清华大学）毕业的黄锦树则是另外一番光景。他的视阈或研究对象被限定在1949年以前，而焦点之一其实就是中国性。不只是探勘中华文化（尤其是晚清为中心）中的中国性，比如他1998年的台湾清华大学博士论文题目为《近代国学之起源1897-1927》，而硕士论文则研究章太炎；而且他也研究现代的中国性，并出版了专著《文与魂与体》（台北：麦田出版，2006），甚至他还爱屋及乌、举一反三，借此反思马华文学的中国性，并成为这方面的一流专家，《马华文学与中国性》（台北：元尊出版社，1998）则是集中代表。正是建基于对强大的中国性的热烈拥抱和研究，他才洞察了马华文学中中国性的表演性与依附性特征，甚至为了强大马华而提出或拥护"去中国性"的概念，[4] 如断奶论、经典缺席等等，乃至演化成令人瞩目也侧目的"黄锦树现象"。

（二）拥抱本土性

这里的本土主要是指台湾，当然也部分兼及大马。长期的旅台让李永平、黄锦树对台湾的本土性呈现出复杂的拥抱态度。简而言之，他们更加拥抱或热爱包容时期的台湾本土，而与过度民粹，比如台独（也是本土性的一种）保持距离和深切反思，因为作为侨生的他们更是国民党政府政策下的产物或获益者，而成为了民进党执政时期的外来人、牺牲品与贱视者。

李永平留台时期的台湾经济繁荣、活力四射，即便是文学创制上亦有其独特性和高度，包括台湾现代诗、现代小说及其现代派批评自

---

[4] 朱崇科〈"去中国性"：警醒、迷思及其它：以王润华和黄锦树的相关论述为中心〉，《亚洲文化》第27期（2003），页164–177. Zhu Chongke, "'De-Chineseness': Awareness, Myths and Others: Centering on Wong Yoon Wah's and Ng Kim Chew's Essays," *Asian Culture*, No. 27 (2003), pp. 164–177.

后收入：朱崇科《"南洋"纠葛与本土中国性》（广州：广东人民出版社，2014），页206–225。

Also included in: Zhu Chongke, *"Nanyang" Obsession and Native Chineseness* (Guangzhou: Guangdong People's Publishing House, 2014), pp. 206–225.

有其本土韵味,同时又接续了1930年代的中国现代文学、横向移植或对话了彼时的欧美文学潮流,李永平在这样的环境里堪称如鱼得水。可以理解的是,在李永平超过一半的小说创作主题中,台湾都是不折不扣的中心,不只是人物活动的场域,还包括了引领者朱鸰,重大事件等等皆有台湾风骨。当然,李永平视野开阔、气势恢宏,在其创作的首尾也有涉及大马本土的状描,二者也有交叉,包括书写二战时期被日本侵略者派到南洋的台湾籍士兵以及相关生活(包括妓女、慰安妇等)。李永平对台湾的反思也相对深入全面,令人读后可感知其拳拳之心。

黄锦树对台湾本土的拥抱显而易见。正是台湾严格的学术训练与犀利的问题意识让他在回望大马时既显得胸有成竹、杀气腾腾,同时又恨铁不成钢以台湾的标尺丈量现实大马。而此时的台湾成为黄锦树学术批评的资源宝库,同时台湾的活跃、包容和良好文学生态也成为黄锦树得以快速成长的温床,他凭借此上佳平台一跃成为优秀青年作家。关键的是,黄本身的方言——闽南语与台湾交流的主流话语对接顺利。

二、对抗诗学与"承认的政治"

东南亚华人身份认同的复杂性或多重性(multiple identities paradigm)[5]不只是源于多种元素的角力,政治、经济、文化、族性与现实关怀,而且还可能蕴含了个体内部的冲突——撕裂与长期的对抗,当然也可能是个体超越自我的痛苦升华成卓越。从个人品性而言,李永平相对简单纯粹,但也显得执着与激烈;黄锦树复杂敏感、安全感低,容易被激怒、攻击性强,他们在书写实践中呈现出不同的追求。当然,

---

[5] 有关论述可参:王赓武〈东南亚华人的身份认同之研究〉,《王赓武自选集》(上海:上海教育出版社,2002),页238–266。

Wang Gungwu, "Studies on Southeast Asia Chinese Identity," *Selected Works of Wang Gungwu* (Shanghai: Shanghai Educational Publishing House, 2002), pp. 238–266.

我们也可理解为这是不同作家对个体文学身份地位"承认的政治"（the politics of recognition）[6]的不同类型的探索。

（一）提纯中华性

李永平自有其高远追求，而其人生经历也部分成就了他。离开台湾后，他继续赴美深造，从一个区域中心位移到世界第一强国——美国取经，获美国纽约州立大学比较文学硕士、圣路易华盛顿大学比较文学博士，而台北和纽约的差异想必让他感触颇深。作为学者的李永平和作为华人作家的李永平在身份感受上明显有别，前者为追求学术可以忽略他的复杂华人身份，后者则难以摆脱类似的纠葛。如今看来，已经成为李之经典名作的《吉陵春秋》彰显出李前所未有的创造力高度与意义指涉，从这个角度看，他既传承了鲁迅，某些层面甚至部分超越了鲁迅。

李永平以其别致的笔触建构了一个纸面上的文化中国象征——吉陵，它是一个具有四不像哲学内涵的恶托邦（dystopia），它既有台湾、南洋、中国大陆南方省份的影子，然而又都不是，它和鲁镇、湘西、山东高密一起成为华语文学圈文学地理学上虚构出来的精神原乡地标。李的超越性不只是体现在此长篇结构的精妙与精致文字的提纯上，而且还呈现出它对"中华性"的丰富与挖掘宽度，李永平对国民劣根性的批判从中国人扩大为世界范围内的华人，而其笔下的吉陵作为半开放的场域结构（小城加山坳围绕），实际上隐喻了转型中的城乡同质性，它代表了乡村、小城、大城，实际上等于否认了未来各种救赎（知识、宗教、自我等等）的不可能性，其内在深切的悲剧性有很强的原罪意识、高远的批判性和悲悯情怀。

---

[6] 最精彩的代表性论述来自：查尔斯·泰勒著，董之林、陈燕谷译〈承认的政治〉，汪晖、陈燕谷编《文化与公共性》（北京：生活·读书·新知三联书店，1998），页290–337。Charles Taylor, "The Politics of Recognition," trans. Dong Zhilin, Chen Yangu, in Wang Hui, Chen Yangu (eds.), *Culture and Publicity* (Beijing: SDX Joint Publishing Company, 1998), pp. 290–337.
英文版参见：Charles Taylor, *Multiculturalism and "The Politics of Recognition"*, ed. Amy Gutmann (New Jersey: Princeton University Press, 1992).

颇耐人寻味的是，李永平再也未能写出类似《吉陵春秋》的高远作品，或许是他身居美国时相对单一强势的语言——英语的刺激和诱引让他的中国书写有了更大的世界性眼光和强大的超越性。类似的书写还体现在王润华先生（1941–）的《内外集》（台北：国家出版社，1978）中的"象外象"创作上，这组诗原本是在美国威斯康辛大学麦迪逊校区攻读博士的王跟随周策纵教授等老师修习古文字和古代文学的副产品，这种时空的超越性引发了他回归古代文化中国原点的再现与反思，他之后的类似书写（新马诗人）都未曾超越此类诗作，甚至包括王润华自己。[7] 李的其他作品往往落实到台湾或记忆/神话中的南洋之上了。

（二）"坏孩子"全面开弓

被王德威视为"坏孩子"[8]的黄锦树兼具作家和学者双重身份，而在作家身份中，他又长于书写中短篇小说、文学批评及散文，堪称是多面手。或许是由于性格问题，或许是过于敏感地感悟到了身份游移的尴尬，他也近乎全面开弓，为自己多头身份得到全面确认而对许多人提出批评。

身为作家，即使黄锦树日益在台湾文坛上建立了自己的地盘且扬名立万，但黄从未放弃他的大马本土根据地或桥头堡，和某些立志返回中国的华侨类似，他似乎要返回大马。他首先拿来祭旗的其实是长期盘踞大马文坛的马华现实主义（他所谓的"本土老现"），而其批

---

[7] 朱崇科〈论王润华放逐诗学的三阶段〉，《香港文学》2015年第11期，页18–29。
Zhu Chongke, "On Three Phases of Wong Yoon Wah's Exile Poetics," *Hong Kong Literature*, No. 371 (2015), pp. 18–29.

[8] 王德威〈序论：坏孩子黄锦树——黄锦树的马华论述与叙述〉，黄锦树《由岛至岛》（台北：麦田，2001），页1。
David Der-wei Wang, "Prelude: Bad Boy Ng Kim Chew - Ng Kim Chew's Narration and Discussion on *Mahua*," Ng Kim Chew, *From Island to Island* (Taipei: Rye Field Publishing Co., 2001), p. 1.

评具体对象之一就是曾担任会长、德高望重的老作家方北方;[9] 其次，他也不断在大马文坛放火"烧芭"，包括断奶论、清算本土评论者，努力建立起（后）现代主义的声威与抢占地盘，和他论争过的新马本土论者比比皆是，包括陈雪风、许文荣等等；第三，他还将批评指向了中国大陆学者：言其缺乏良好的问题意识、得当的学术规范以及充分的本土知识（local knowledge），所写文章往往是肤浅的表扬修辞学或是标签式套用。

平心而论，黄锦树的上述批判自有其合理性，马华本土现实主义的固步自封的确部分阻碍了大马华文文学的更新换代与整体提升，但现实主义并未过时，黄锦树不该错误地一棍子打翻一船人；大马文学评论界整体含金量不够，原本他可以发挥所长，但他的惹火烧身、四面树敌却又强化了这种土法炼钢批评里残存的意气用事与不合理性。而对其他场域的有关研究者，他不懂得惺惺相惜，缺乏"理解之同情"，不能并肩作战，提升马华文学批评及研究的国际影响力，而是肆意践踏。

从宏阔的层面上讲，黄锦树及其马华文学情结似乎具有很强的不安全感，尽管马华文学已经是东南亚华文文学中整体实力最强的一支，但主体性成长困厄于中国大陆与马华本土的双重夹击中，黄具有很强的危机感和对抗意识，一方面是因为他视自己为马华文学的传薪者，另一方面则是因为他的喜欢批评、不善团结有生力量壮大集体，这恰恰是他应该向他的批判对象所认真深入学习的强项部分：团结牺牲、坚韧不拔、他者视角。对抗诗学如果从内部整合或超越的角度来看，它可以变成一个别致的突破路径，甚至产生上佳的效果，如李永平的《吉陵春秋》；但如果控制不好，原本是弱者争取权益的合理合法合情的"承认的政治"就变成重复霸权逻辑，这往往是两败俱伤或同归于尽的套路。

---

[9] 朱崇科〈方北方的文学本土转型及其限制〉，《西南民族大学学报》2014年第6期，页176–183。

Zhu Chongke, "Local Transformation and Limitations in Fang Beifang's Literary works," *Journal of Southwest Minzu University (Humanities and Social Science)*, No. 6 (2014), pp. 176–183.

三、共谋的双赢？

时间总是流逝，后继的我们总可以看到历史的结尾或至少是部分发展。作家们一代代老去"各领风骚数十年"，新一代强势崛起虎视眈眈，哪怕是个体作家也会随着现实的推演而衰老，甚至发生了出人意料的翻转。

（一）李永平：与全世界和解

有情有义的李永平终究入籍台湾，而他对大马的感情也是相对复杂。在接受访谈时，李永平说自己"同时拥有三位母亲：生育我的婆罗洲和收养我的台湾，加上一个遥远的、古老的、打我有记忆开始，就听爸爸不时叨叨念念的'祖国'——唐山"，但当被问到他是哪里人时，却终其一生面临认同的困惑，既无法认同自己是马来西亚人，也认为自己始终客居台湾，最终只回答："我是广东人！"[10]

可以理解的是，由于他出生在1947年的英属婆罗洲砂拉越邦古晋市，十年后马来西亚才宣告独立，而东马和西马的龃龉关系始终非常复杂，所以长期以来，他并不承认自己是马华作家，但退休后的李也在发生变化，他终于肯承认自己是马华作家，他的《吉陵春秋》早已进入大马华文教材（无论是中学还是大专院校），而他晚年创造的《大河尽头》（月河三部曲之一）已经成为他安妥大马及自我灵魂的长篇巨制，历史、神话、现实、自我、异族等等，和谐并存、纵横交错，他无论从文学创作还是身份认同上都指向了大马。

颇有意味的是，在纸面上建构文化中国的李永平也和中国大陆结缘了，不只是他的优秀长篇逐步在大陆面世，在临终的前几年，他终于踏上了"祖国"的土地。2014年11月11–12日，第三届"中山杯"华侨华人文学奖颁奖仪式和华文文学与"中国梦"座谈会在广东省中

---

[10] 高嘉谦〈迷路在文学原乡：李永平访谈〉，高嘉谦编《见山又是山：李永平研究》（台北：麦田出版，2017），页269–270。
  Gao Jiaqian, "Lost in Literary Homeland: An Interview with Li Yongping," Gao Jiaqain (ed.), *The Mountain is the Mountain: Studies on Li Yongping* (Taipei: Rye Field Publishing Co., 2017), pp. 269–270.

山市举行。经过评委会认真评审,李永平的长篇小说《大河尽头》(上、下卷)、加拿大作家张翎的长篇小说《阵痛》摘得评委会大奖并共享30万元奖金。据新闻报道说,李永平对获此华侨华人文学大奖感到十分意外,此次文学奖之旅也助年过花甲、一生漂泊无居的他首次踏上祖国大陆。

从更终极的意义上说,李永平实现了他的文学世界、个体身份与现实世界之间的和解,无论是大马、台湾、中国大陆都是他念兹在兹的原乡、故乡或他乡,作为漂泊一生的浪子,2017年被病魔纠缠多年的他终于回归了大地母亲的怀抱,不必纠结于身份的撕裂与对抗,而实际上他无论是在大马、台湾,乃至整个华文文学圈都已经是当之无愧的经典小说家了。

(二)黄锦树:实用主义

四面出击乃至树敌不少的黄锦树也在发生重大变化,身体抱恙[11]让他更依赖他人,而他在风格上似乎变得更通达乃至圆滑了,毕竟也是年过半百之人了。

黄锦树所做的第一件出人意料却又可想而知的事情就是入籍台湾。当年在他大杀四方时他也将矛头指向了台湾,包括他获取硕士博士学位风波、论文发表审查等等都认为自己受到了不公正待遇,但他终究务实地变成了台湾人。而旅台马华文学作家中依然持有大马护照的陈大为、钟怡雯夫妇,他们的态度却相对平和而稳健,虽然陈大为也曾为此为黄锦树辩护,认为黄从皮到骨都是大马人。耐人寻味的是,黄和他最倚重、一度并肩作战、理论功力最强的马华同乡旅台学者林建国博士也分道扬镳了。有些时候,表面上看是学术观点不同,而内在的则是性格差异带来的人情撕裂。

---

[11] 马华学者张惠思在2017年为黄锦树的《乌暗暝》(上海文艺出版社,2020)写序〈我们的南洋摩罗〉时提及"发现我们的南洋摩罗已老。才不过四十九岁。坐在机场高速道路往吉隆坡奔驰的车子前座,因为身上的病,他仿佛真的是一位已经完全透支的疲惫旅人在返乡。在不停的瞌睡如梦中和我们断断续续的闲话家常"。

或许更令人惊讶的是，黄锦树对他一贯不满的中国大陆（从中国性批判到言论出版自由，比如《南洋人民共和国备忘录》出版风波等等）逐步高调回归乃至抢占了。一开始只是参加少数学术会议，如去他所在台湾就职单位（暨南国际大学）名称相当的广州暨南大学开会演讲，而后他又开始拿取大陆颁给他的大奖，根据新闻报道，2018年4月25日上午，首届"北京大学王默人－周安仪世界华文文学奖"颁奖典礼在北京大学英杰交流中心阳光厅举行。本届评奖通过两轮评选，最终确定贾平凹《极花》和黄锦树《雨》获得评委会大奖。与此同时或之后，黄不断在大陆连续出版他的文学创作——《雨》、《乌暗暝》等等，不少大陆读者恍如发现出土文物般惊讶不已，而实际上，远比这些作品丰富的黄锦树还有待继续挖掘。[12]

总结黄锦树的变化，我们不难发现贯穿不变的是他的实用主义和功利主义：在他才华横溢却名实未符时，年富力强的他打开了强烈攻击之门，这是建功立业的捷径，虽然也难免不少误伤；但当他年老力衰、相对虚弱却已功成名就时他选择了连纵策略，把自己包装成愿意为人所见到的不羁才子形象，继续扩大战果，这是黄的随机应变，抑或锐气尽失？我们或许称之为共谋的双赢吗？

21世纪以来，华人作家或华人的价值动向似乎日益难以归类，尤其是有才华的个体更易变得原子化，令人悲哀的是，李永平这一类型的纯粹性情中人作家似乎已成绝响，而功利性或实用型追求似乎日益甚嚣尘上。我们不妨开阔眼界，把视线投放到马华本土作家黎紫书身上，她的最新一部长篇《流俗地》虽有一些变化，但在我看来，并未真正超越其处女长篇《告别的年代》，但此书却在大马、台湾、中国大陆近乎同步发行，风生水起，关键是宣传广告先声夺人，甚至超越了严肃作家该有的严肃而变得产业性浮夸。某种意义上说，这也同时更凸显出中国大陆文化产业及广阔市场的强势崛起，甚至已经回到中心地位。

---

[12] 朱崇科《争夺鲁迅与黄锦树"南洋"虚构的吊诡》，《暨南学报》2015年第10期，页1–11, 116。

Zhu Chongke, "Paradoxes in Ng Kim Chew's Nanyang Fiction," *Jinan Journal (Philosophy and Social Sciences)*, No. 10 (2015), pp. 1–11, 116.

结论

从历史的眼光去探勘族群的发展与界限设定,我们往往会发现:变,似乎才是主旋律。即便是以旅台马华作家中的两位优秀作家李永平、黄锦树为例,我们依然可以察觉其重大变化。从一开始找寻自我的学习过程中强化中国性、拥抱台湾性,到确立自我过程中的提纯中华性或四面出击存在,再到名利双收后选择与世界和解或实用主义取向,越到后面似乎差异越大,或许不变或交叉之处恰恰是永恒的利益:有的人选择了精神,有的人选择了名利、物质。新冠疫情依然如火如荼,后疫情时代的华人社会何去何从值得关注,但变是永远的,这或许是我们目前为止唯一可以肯定的东西,毕竟我们可以或不得不因应时代并且勠力建设一个新世界。

鲁迅木刻思想的马来亚传播

胡星灿[*]

摘要

1930年，马来亚青年戴隐郎负笈北上，求学于上海艺术专科学校西画科。在校期间，他与鲁迅结识，并在其感召下积极参与"新兴木刻运动"。归返南洋后，他将鲁迅木刻思想刊载于《南洋商报》的副刊《文漫界》和《今日艺术》，"马来亚木刻运动"随之展开。可以说，鲁迅从未到过南洋，却无意中促成了马来亚现代木刻的萌芽，他被称为"马来亚木刻之父"可谓当之无愧。然而，戴隐郎在引介鲁迅时，虽对其有所继承，却亦会根据本土情境进行"反叛"。在继承与"反叛"之间，鲁迅木刻思想的马来亚传播全貌得以呈现，"马来亚"的主体性与能动性也对鲁迅的选择、修改、塑造中得以凸显。

关键词：鲁迅、新兴木刻运动、戴隐郎、马来亚、后殖民

---

[*] 胡星灿，中国中山大学中文系（珠海），*huxc3@mail.sysu.edu.cn*。

The Dissemination of Lu Xun's Woodcut Theories in Malaya

HU Xingcan

Abstracts

In 1930, Tai In-long, a Malayan young fellow, went China to study in the western painting department of Shanghai Art College. While in school, he got acquainted with Lu Xun, and under his inspiration, he actively participated in the ascendant "Modern Woodcut Movement" at that time. After returning to Nanyang, he introduced Lu Xun's woodcut theories in art supplements *Wenman Jie* and *Today's Arts* of *Nanyang Siang Pau*, and hence the "Malayan Modern Woodcut Movement" launched continuously. It can be said that although Lu Xun has never been to Southeast Asia, he inadvertently induced the germination of modern woodcuts in Malaya, and he is well-deserved to be titled as the "Father of Malayan Modern Woodcut". Of course, the dissemination of Lu Xun's woodcut theories in Malaya is not progressing smoothly, as the recipient, Malayan Art Circle also screened, misread and even reshaped Lu Xun according to actual needs and local circumstances. And by outlining the dissemination of Lu Xun's woodcut theories in Malaya, not only can we see Lu Xun's influences on the Nanyang Chinese Community in terms of spiritual guidance, identity aggregation and paradigm reference, but we can also see the peculiarity, subjectivity and agency of "Malaya" as a unique "chronotope". Besides, this paper is a response to so-called "Colonist-Lu Xun".

Keywords: Lu Xun; Modern Woodcut Movement; Tai In-long; Malaya; Post-colonialisation

一、引言

鲁迅作为蜚声国际的中国作家与公共知识分子，在东南亚的传播可谓其来有自，"东南亚鲁迅研究"也自有其史。从目前研究成果看，"东南亚鲁迅研究"成果斐然、规模可观，但其研究范式却相对固定，研究目的也不外乎"重申鲁迅在东南亚的影响"、"考证鲁迅影响真确性"两种。此类研究容易使我们产生刻板印象，即：鲁迅对于东南亚华人社群的影响是宏大的、强势的，甚至不容置疑的。

而该刻板印象最终造成"东南亚鲁迅研究"走入"歧途"。特别在冷战思维、"后学"浪潮的影响下，越来越多海外学者借助"后殖民"理论将鲁迅打造成阻滞了东南亚华文文学/文化自如发展的"文化殖民者"，甚至有学者通过"遮蔽鲁迅"以实现"去中国性"（de-chineseness）的政治表达。此时，破除鲁迅"文化殖民者"身份、恢复鲁迅在东南亚的真实位置显得格外迫切。

事实上，鲁迅从未到过东南亚，他的作品、思想、精神都是经过"传播"（transmission）来到南洋的，"传播"预示着鲁迅难免要受到具体情境的检阅、透视与塑造。换言之，鲁迅在东南亚的传播充满着被动性与不确定性，其声望固然宏大，但仍需受到诸多宰制，因此，其"文化殖民者"身份是经不起推敲的。基于此观点，本文便以"鲁迅木刻思想的马来亚传播"为例，对"殖民者鲁迅"略作回应。

马来亚现代木刻艺术滥觞于1936年，在这一年，马来亚木刻从"复制型"（duplicate）艺术转向"创作型"（create）艺术，而在其中起到承前启后作用的即为鲁迅。当然，鲁迅无法直接传经送宝，鲁迅的"文艺嗣子"、马来亚归侨戴隐郎便承担了这一职责。戴隐郎（Tai In-long），又名戴英浪，祖籍广东惠阳，1906年出生于英属马来亚沙戥埠。1930年左右，在上海求学的戴隐郎与彼时推行"新兴木刻运动"的鲁迅结识，两人有了实质上的师承关系。1932年后，戴隐郎归返南洋，他高举鲁迅大纛，将鲁迅木刻思想带到马来亚，"马来亚木刻运动"由此展开。[1] 必须指出，戴隐郎在传播鲁迅木刻思想时有着自己的立场与坚持，故而鲁迅木刻思想遭到"反叛"，呈现出与本源思想截然不同的异质性色彩。

二、史前史：鲁迅与戴隐郎交游考

追溯"马来亚木刻运动"的起源问题，不得不提到戴隐郎与鲁迅的交游，正是基于此，戴隐郎与鲁迅的师徒关系才得以明确，"马来亚木刻运动"才得以发生。可遗憾的是，由于互动的当事人均未留下书面的相交记载，所以这段交游史逐渐被遗忘。但是，根据两人共同居住于上海"北四川路"这一事实，加上同代文人也留下的口述、回忆等材料，可推敲出两人间存在着确凿且密切的互动往来。

（一）以鲁迅为中心的"北四川路"交游圈

1927年，来自全国各地的知识分子汇聚上海，而作为政治、经济、文化"中间地带"的北四川路（今称四川北路）则接纳了他们的到来。此后三年，各种报刊书局、文艺社团来此安营扎寨，各色知识分子游走于此，北四川路逐渐成为中国最重要的文化场所，同时也成为一个不可忽视的"文化生产空间"。需要说明的是，身处北四川路的知识分子与该空间保持着紧密关联，且该关联是双向的、互动的：一方面是知识分子积极参与了空间的文化建设；另一方面是空间中犬牙交错的意识形态、话语观念、文化结构也制约、影响着知识分子。

而鲁迅的到来，则进一步强化了北四川路的"文化生产"意义。1927年10月3日，鲁迅目睹广州由"革命策源地一变而为反革命策

---

[1] 1939年，戴隐郎受"四君子事件"牵连，被英国殖民者驱逐出境，此后"马来亚新兴木刻运动"遭到破坏。见：孙孺〈纪念英浪〉，《回音壁》第1期（1987），页35。
Sun Ru, "Memoirs of Ying Lang," *Echo Wall*, No. 1 (1987), p. 35.

源地"，² 在悲愤之余离开广州，抵达上海。在共和旅馆短暂停留后，他随周建人搬进了位于北四川路附近的景云里（横滨路35弄），之后又迁居拉摩斯公寓（北四川路194号），最终在大陆新村（施高塔路）度过其生命的最后历程。相比此前对文学的关注，北四川路时期的鲁迅更关心"图像"（尤其是木刻）的引介与宣传。仅在1927–1928年间，他便搜集了包括《版画を作る人へ》、*The Woodcut of Today*、*The Woodcut of Today at Home and Abroad*、*The Modern Woodcut* 在内的20余种木刻书籍。在此基础上，他还编辑《奔流》、《艺苑朝华》，大量"输入外国版画"，并搭建木刻理论。在他的凝聚和影响下，北四川路成为"新兴木刻运动"的前沿阵地，不仅"一八艺社"、"春地美术研究所"、"野风画会"、"MK木刻研究会"在此建社，"一八艺社习作展览会"、"春地画展"、"木刻·摄影展览会"等展览在附近举办，胡一川、李桦、陈烟桥、黄新波、刘岘等一批木刻青年也时常往来于此。各个艺文界人士的交游往来，也共同构建了以鲁迅为中心的"北四川路"交游圈。

可见，在戴隐郎到来前，北四川路已成为任何一个有志于实现文艺抱负的木刻青年必须朝圣的殿堂，他们"沉溺"此处，迫切地希望与鲁迅、与这个象征着"新兴"、"进步"、"左翼"的交游圈发生联系。1930年，参加"上海艺术专科学校"³ 开学典礼的戴隐郎，抱着同样的愿望，在北四川路永安里的一所亭子间安顿下来，该处距离鲁迅居住的拉摩斯公寓步行距离不过四百余米，离鲁迅流连的内山书店也只有

---

² 许广平《鲁迅回忆录·厦门和广州》（北京：作家出版社，1961），页76。
   Xu Guangping, *Memoirs of Lu Xun: Xiamen and Guangzhou* (Beijing: The Writers Publishing House, 1961), p. 76.
³ 1930年，刚从东京美术学校毕业的王道源接手不堪办学的人文艺术大学，创办了上海艺术专科学校，并开设了西画、音乐、建筑、工艺等学系，新校舍位于北四川路附近的江湾天通庵路。

三百余米。⁴ 彼时，戴隐郎就读"西画科"，⁵ 师从王道源、陈抱一，但入学不久后，他对油画、水彩的兴趣寥寥，却对木刻兴致高昂。适逢上海艺专在江湾路校舍举办学期绘画展览会，戴隐郎顺利见到了前来参会的鲁迅，⁶ 借着这次机缘，在展览过后，他与同学温涛、梁锡鸿等人频繁前去同样位于江湾"上海一八艺社研究所"，并就木刻问题数度求教鲁迅。⁷ 不仅如此，由于居住便利，他也时常前往内山书店，聆听鲁迅讲学。此后，他更是参加鲁迅举办的三次木刻展览：德国作家版画展、俄法书籍插画展览会、德俄木刻展览会，进一步与鲁迅交流，并由此奠定了他对木刻的终生兴趣。⁸ 根据笔者考察，上海时期的戴隐郎实际上一直追随着鲁迅，两人相遇的机会非常多，但实际记录在案的交往只有5次（见表1）。当然，除了直接交往外，"北四川路"交游圈的文化生产作用也无疑强化了鲁迅影响力向戴隐郎的流动与渗透。

---

⁴ 戴铁郎口述〈爱国画家、抗日老战士戴英浪的坎坷一生〉，上海市历史博物馆主编《都会遗踪》第5辑（上海：学林出版社，2012），页160。
  Dai Tielang, "The Struggling Life of Dai Ying Lang: A Patriotic Painter and Anti-Japanese Aggression Veteran," Shanghai History Museum (ed.), *Cultural Heritage of Cities*, Vol. 5 (Shanghai: Academia Press, 2012), p. 160.

⁵ 小谷一郎著，王建华译〈关于王道源及"青年艺术家联盟"的事〉，《上海鲁迅研究》第1期（2013），页146–174。
  Ichiro Kotani, "The Things About Wang Daoyuan and 'Young Artists League'," trans. Wang Jianhua, *Shanghai Lu Xun Study*, No. 1 (2013), pp. 146–174.

⁶ 鲁迅〈1931年6月29日〉，《鲁迅全集》第16卷（北京：人民文学出版社，2005），页259。
  Lu Xun, "29 June 1931," *The Complete Work of Lu Xun*, Vol. 16 (Beijing: People's Literature Publishing House, 2005), p. 259.

⁷ 广东美术馆编《遗失的路程：梁锡鸿》（广州：岭南美术出版社，2006），页12。
  Guangdong Museum of Art, *Lost Landscape: Sikhung Leung* (Guangzhou: Lingnan Fine Arts Publishing House, 2006), p. 12.

⁸ Lim Cheng Tju, "Political Prints in Singapore," *Print Quarterly*, Vol. 21, No. 3 (2004), pp. 266–281.

表1：戴隐郎与鲁迅的五次直接交往

时间	方式	场合	地点
1931	直接会面	上海艺专学期绘画展览会	江湾路
1931	直接会面	上海一八艺社研究所	江湾路
1932–1933	直接会面	德国作家版画展	静安寺路
		俄法书籍插画展览会	武进路
		德俄木刻展览会	千爱里40号

1934年左右，戴隐郎离开上海，折返马来亚。[9] 途径香港时，他与温涛、刘火子、李育中、张一弘组成"深刻版画研究会"，并通过温涛向鲁迅写信求教，鲁迅收到信后予以回复（信件已佚失）——这也是他与鲁迅的最后一次交流。[10] 但显然，鲁迅对戴隐郎的影响是终生的，自鲁迅去世后，他自觉以鲁迅文艺嗣子自居，继续在新马、香港、台湾等地传播鲁迅火种，在回到中国大陆后，他还就职于延安鲁迅艺术学院华中分院和中央美院华东分院（现中央美术学院），将鲁迅木刻研究视为毕生事业。

（二）"暑期木刻讲习会"余絮

如上所言，戴隐郎曾于1931年前往位于江湾路的"上海一八艺社研究所"聆听鲁迅讲课。而根据记载，鲁迅前后两次到过"一八艺社"（分别是：1931年8月24日和1931年9月19日），而且只在8月24日上午为一八艺社成员讲解过所藏画册，由此判断，戴隐郎求教于鲁迅的时间正是这一日。[11] 需要指出的是，鲁迅之所以会于8月24日前往"一八艺

---

[9] 关于戴隐郎何时到香港暂无明确定论。庄华兴认为戴隐郎是1935年到达香港，陈国球则认为他应于1934年（或更早）抵港，因为1934年由他主编的《今日诗歌》就已经面世，由他组织的诗歌团体"同社"也已形成。

[10] Tang Xiaobing, *Origins of the Chinese Avant-Garde: The Modern Woodcut Movement* (Berkeley: University of California Press, 2007), p. 148.

[11] 鲁迅〈1931年8月24日〉，《鲁迅全集》第16卷，页266。
Lu Xun, "24 August 1931," *The Complete Work of Lu Xun*, Vol. 16, p. 266.

社",是应社团成员之邀,弥补部分成员未能参加8月17日至8月22日间的"暑期木刻讲习会"之憾。可见,8月24日的讲课实际上是"暑期木刻讲习会"的延续与补充。

图1:暑期木刻讲习会结业合影

"暑期木刻讲习会"是中国木刻发展进程的一个里程碑,自它以后,中国木刻正式由复制艺术转为艺术创作,大量木刻社团由此涌现,"新兴木刻运动"也至此展开。[12] 更重要的是,讲习会上,除了内山嘉吉"介绍了刻刀的种类、用法,着色的刷子,印版画用的马连等实物,并用图解说明制作方法、印刷、用纸等"之余,[13] 鲁迅还提纲挈领地强调木刻的方法论与创作观:[14]

---

[12] 木刻讲习会后,由学员或相关人士牵头创立的木刻社团大量涌现,比如,讲习会学员江丰、李岫石、黄山定、倪焕之等在上海成立"春地美术研究所";成员顾鸿干、倪焕之等发起了"野风画会";成员钟步青、陈铁耕创建"M·K木刻研究会";冯雪峰、于海等人发起"现代木刻研究会"。

[13] 内山嘉吉、奈良和夫著,韩宗琦译《鲁迅与木刻》(北京:人民美术出版社,1985),页11。

Uchiyama Kakitsu, Kazuo Nara, *Lu Xun and Woodcut*, trans. Han Zongqi (Beijing: People's Fine Arts Publishing House, 1985), p. 11.

[14] 尽管鲁迅在日记中只谈到在讲习会上担任翻译的经历,但考察内山嘉吉、江丰、陈卓堃等人的回忆,鲁迅实际上在翻译的同时也补充了大量木刻知识。

1. "直干"法

鲁迅第一次提到"直干",是在《近代木刻选集(一)》的"小引"中:"所谓创作底木刻者,不模仿,不复刻,作者捏刀向木,直刻下去……这放刀直干,便是创作底版画首先所必须,和绘画的不同,就在以刀代笔,以木代纸或布。"[15] 据他所言,所谓"直干",便是"捏刀向木,直刻下去",而根据奈良和夫解释,"直干"同时还蕴含一种坦率直截、"入木三分"的创作精神。[16] 在讲习会上,"直干"显然也是鲁迅传递的重要观点。陈卓堃(陈广)在回忆讲习会时就说:"我们当时一般都是用铅笔在木板上大体构图之后,用刀在木板上'直干'的。刻的时候也不受草草构成的画稿的限制。"[17] 可见,"直干"在会上就已被学员完全接受;

2. "创作版画"

鲁迅对中国"创作版画尚无所知"[18] 的现状实感忧心,因此讲习会的核心内容除了讲授"创作版画的作法"外,还意在扭转学员思维,使他们认识到"创作版画"绝非"复制版画",他表示"创作版画"是"一种由画家一手造成的版画,也就是原画,倘用木版,便叫作'创作木刻',是艺术家直接的创作品,毫不假手于刻者和印者的"。[19]

---

[15] 鲁迅《近代木刻选集》第1期(上海:上海合记教育用品社,1929),页3–4。
Lu Xun, *The Selection of Modern Woodcut*, Vol. 1 (Shanghai: Shanghai He Ji Education Supplies Press, 1929), pp. 3–4.

[16] 内山嘉吉、奈良和夫著,韩宗琦译《鲁迅与木刻》,页114–116。
Uchiyama Kakitsu, Kazuo Nara, *Lu Xun and Woodcut*, trans. Han Zongqi, pp. 114–116.

[17] 王观泉〈木刻讲习会习作初窥〉,韦尔申编《时代变革中的美术》(沈阳:辽宁教育出版社,2010),页630。
Wang Guan Quan, "A Glimpse of Woodcut Workshop", Wei Er Shen(eds.), *Art in the Changing Times* (Shenyang: Liaoning Education Press, 2010), p. 630.

[18] 内山嘉吉、奈良和夫著,韩宗琦译《鲁迅与木刻》,页18。
Uchiyama Kakitsu, Kazuo Nara, *Lu Xun and Woodcut*, trans. Han Zongqi, p. 18.

[19] 鲁迅〈《木刻创作法》序〉,《鲁迅全集》第4卷,页625。
Lu Xun, "The Preface of *Woodcut Creation*," *The Complete Work of Lu Xun*, Vol. 4, p. 625.

3. "实际应用"

鲁迅在讲习会上曾介绍过凯绥·珂勒惠支的《农民战争》,[20] 他对这位"和颇深的生活相联系"、"被周围的悲惨生活所动"的艺术家表示敬佩,同时他也指出木刻在反应、表达与介入现实时的"实际应用"。此后他将木刻与现实结合的思想,在1936年的《〈凯绥·珂勒惠支版画选〉序目》中予以呈现:"只要一翻这集子,就知道她以深广的慈母之爱,为一切被侮辱和损害悲哀,抗议,愤怒,斗争;所取的题材大抵是困苦,饥饿,疾病,死亡,然而也有呼号,挣扎,联合和奋起。"[21]

4. "图像=叙事"

早在留学日本时期,鲁迅就已意识到图像与"立人"、"启蒙"话语间的连结,[22] 比如,在1906年创办的《新生》上,他刊登瓦支的《希望》以"表明了自己由此生存下去的信念",[23] 又曾尝试用威勒须却庚的《骷髅塔》、《革命家的公开处刑》"想向那些志在改革中国现状的留学生提醒这一点(牺牲)"。[24] 到了1927年,接受左翼美术后的鲁迅更是注意到图像在配合、辅助"革命"时的效用。[25] 此后,他逐渐摆脱

---

[20] 江丰〈鲁迅先生与"一八艺社"〉,人民美术出版社编辑《回忆鲁迅的美术活动》(北京:人民美术出版社,1981),页6–10。
Jiang Feng, "Mr. Lu Xun and 'Yi Ba Art Club,'" People's Fine Arts Publishing House (ed.), *Memoirs of Lu Xun's Art Activities* (Beijing: People's Fine Arts Publishing House, 1981), pp. 6–10.

[21] 鲁迅〈《凯绥·珂勒惠支版画选》序目〉,《鲁迅全集》第6卷,页487–488。
Lu Xun, "The Preface of *Selection of Käthe Kollwitz's Woodcut*," *The Complete Work of Lu Xun*, Vol. 6, pp. 487–488.

[22] 鲁迅〈科学史教篇〉,《鲁迅全集》第1卷,页35。
Lu Xun, "The Article of Scientific History Education," *The Complete Work of Lu Xun*, Vol. 1, p. 35.

[23] 内山嘉吉、奈良和夫著,韩宗琦译《鲁迅与木刻》,页79。
Uchiyama Kakitsu, Kazuo Nara, *Lu Xun and Woodcut*, trans. Han Zongqi, p. 79.

[24] 周作人〈关于鲁迅〉,《宇宙风》第29期(1936)。
Zhou Zuo Ren, "About Lu Xun," *The Cosmic Wind*, No. 29 (1936).

[25] 从1925年开始,鲁迅就系统地阅读左翼美术观书籍,其中包括《新俄罗斯美术大观》、《无产阶级艺术论》、《革命艺术大系》、《马克思主义艺术论》等。由此,他认识到艺术的社会作用。

"为文作图"的理念,走上"以图代文"的新路径。因此,鲁迅在讲习会上所起的作用,绝不是展览木刻、作些补充、翻译日语那么简单,他对图像叙事性的思考无疑丰富了木刻的内涵,也为"新兴木刻运动"成为全国范围内的社会运动(而不仅仅是美术运动)奠定了基础。

而诚如上文所言,8月24日鲁迅的讲课内容与讲习会相差无几,那么在侧旁听的戴隐郎自然也接收到上述木刻思想。所以,戴隐郎这一时期的木刻作品、文艺观念皆打上了鲜明的鲁迅印记:比如,他在"1935年全国木刻联合展览会"上展出的木刻《瞠目》便体现了"放刀直干"、"有力之美"的特点,其"刻力"尤其受到称赞,[26] 唐弢更誉之为"刚健"之作;[27] 又如,他创作的"香港最早出现,论点最完整的现代诗论文"——《论象征主义诗歌》,[28] 在谈论欧外鸥、李金发、施蛰存、林英强等人的象征主义诗歌外,也兼论了诗歌的"美育"、"立人"主张。

三、继承与"反叛":鲁迅木刻思想的马来亚传播

1935年,戴隐郎返回马来亚,同时也将鲁迅木刻思想带到南洋,"马来亚木刻运动"由此开启。必须指出,此时东北亚局势不稳,中国战事随时爆发,加之戴隐郎先后加入中共与马共,因此无论基于现实考量抑或情感逻辑,他在接收/表达文艺时必然会兼顾现实需求与政治立场。在归返南洋初期,他所作的诗论、杂文(以《诗人的态度和动向》、《抬头,举目,开步走》为代表)即可看出他向左翼美学靠

---

[26] 中外通讯社〈全国木刻展览开幕〉,《山西国术体育旬刊》第34期(1935)。
Zhong Wai News Agency, "Opening of National Woodcut Exhibition," *Shanxi Guo Shu Sports Journal*, No. 34 (1935).

[27] 唐弢《海天集》第一辑(上海:新钟书局,1936),页128。
Tang Tao, *Hai Tian Collection*, Vol. 1 (Shanghai: Xin Zhong Bookshop, 1936), p. 128.

[28] 陈国球〈浮城书写与香港文学史:论叶辉的《书写浮城》〉,《文学世纪》第21期(2002)。
Tan Kok Kew, "Floating City Writing and the History of Hong Kong Literature: On Ye Hui's *Writing The Floating City*," *Literary Century*, No. 21 (2002).

拢，²⁹ 而他本人参与"马华巡回剧团"的"救亡剧"、"街头剧"、"筹赈剧"表演亦可看出他对左翼运动的支持与实践。³⁰ 所以，他固然称得上是鲁迅的文艺嗣子，但他在传播鲁迅木刻思想时也会根据具体情境对其作出筛选、修改。换言之，鲁迅木刻思想的马来亚传播伴随着戴隐郎对鲁迅的继承与"反叛"。

（一）忠实的继承者

1936年，戴隐郎在《南洋商报》的副刊《文漫界》（1936年5月24日至1936年12月20日）担任主编一职。在设计副刊时，他注意到南洋缺乏木刻艺术，"在目前的南洋，木、漫这问题之被提出，似乎还嫌太早。从以往的出版物看来，曾刊载过木刻创作的，固属凤毛麟角；而漫画的踪影，也是寥若晨星"，因此，他有意扩大鲁迅木刻思想在马来亚的影响，并试图以此开启马来亚木刻运动，"木刻的表现强而有力，漫画的取材便捷而多面，两者所负的任务，都是不离暴露黑暗、批判现实、散播光明的。因此，凡是站在南洋文化范畴里的文化人，都有立即提倡和动员制作之必要！"³¹ 具体来看，戴隐郎主要从以下三方面传播鲁迅及其木刻思想：

1. "具象化"鲁迅

鲁迅去世后，戴隐郎曾用三期篇幅纪念鲁迅（见图2），它们分别谈到鲁迅精神、民族意涵以及木刻遗产（见表2）。此外，他还刊

---

²⁹ 杨松年编《大英图书馆所藏战前新华报刊》（新加坡：新加坡同安会馆，1988），页140、143。

Yeo Song Nian (ed.), *The Pre-war Singaporean Chinese Newspapers in British Library* (Singapore: Tung Ann District Guild, 1988), pp. 140, 143.

³⁰ 朱绪《新马话剧活动四十五年》（新加坡：文学书屋，1985），页17。

Zhu Xu, *Forty-Five Years of Modern Play Activities in Singapore and Malaysia* (Singapore: Literature Book House, 1985), p. 17.

³¹ 戴隐郎〈木漫在南洋〉，《南洋商报·文漫界》，1936年5月31日，第11版。

Dai Ying Lang, "Woodcut and Cartoon in Nanyang," *Nanyang Siang Pau*, 31 May 1936, p. 11.

登两幅以鲁迅肖像为主题的木刻：英浪（戴隐郎笔名）所刻的《导师鲁迅》强调明暗对比，彰显鲁迅的沉郁顿挫、忧国忧民；而尘漫侥刻的《悼念鲁迅先生》则以"精神不死"为题，突出鲁迅刚健不屈的风骨（见图3、4）。必须说明，此前鲁迅在新马华人社群通常以文学、戏剧、口头宣扬的方式传播，而肖像木刻的出现则使鲁迅以视觉化（visualisation）的方式呈现，这使鲁迅传播不再是抽象精神的传播，而是具象、直观的形象传播。这种由"精神"到"形象"的变化自然在传播时更为便捷、快速，也能使鲁迅的影响从南洋"文化界"扩散到基数更多的"大众"（the commons）中去，但以"形象"取代"精神"也造成了鲁迅的内核被抽空——鲁迅变得单薄、片面，甚至其最具价值的思想可被随意建构——这直接的影响便是此后鲁迅的"造神运动"（idolisation movement）在南洋上演。

图2：1936年10月25日《文漫界》刊头

表2："鲁迅与木刻"的介绍文章

年份	刊物	日期	刊数	文章	
1936	文漫界	10月25日	24	致敬	记念著述过劳而逝的鲁迅
1936	文漫界	11月1日	25	中国木刻运动之母——鲁迅	
1936	文漫界	11月8日	26	鲁迅先生的遗教	鲁迅先生在全国木刻展会场里

图3:《导师鲁迅》英浪(戴隐郎)刻　　图4:《悼念鲁迅先生(一)》尘漫侥刻

2. "转述"鲁迅木刻思想

《文漫界》大部分文章是戴隐郎对鲁迅木刻思想的转述(见表3),比如,《论题材》系列文章便转述自鲁迅的《记苏联版画展览会》、《〈引玉集〉后记》、《〈近代木刻选集〉小引》等文,而《论木刻艺术》则转述自鲁迅给中华艺术大学作的演讲。[32] 这里之所以称为"转述"而非"援引",是因为戴隐郎并没有原封不动地搬运,而是基于上文提到的"私心"对原文进行了部分拣选,这一问题下文会有所讨论,此处暂且不表。

3. "绘制"鲁迅木刻思想光谱

在《文漫界》中,戴隐郎并未只聚焦于鲁迅,他还周详呈现了鲁迅木刻思想的起源与后续:在《苏联版画集》、《苏联印行普式庚画册》和《世界名刻介绍》中,他展示了西欧和苏俄的木刻成就及现状

---

[32] 戴隐郎〈论木刻艺术(3):木刻作者应有的认识和决定〉,《南洋商报·文漫界》,1936年9月13日,第12版。

Dai Yinglang, "On Woodcut Art (3): The Understanding and Decision of Woodcut Authors," *Nanyang Siang Pau*, 13 September 1936, p. 12.

（见图5）；在《第二回全国木刻流动展览会筹备的经过》、《第二回全国木刻流动展览会在杭州》中则跟踪报道了中国木刻联合展览会的举办情况；而在《来自中国的木运作者》、《上海木刻作者协会成立宣言》中，他推荐了鲁迅木刻的继承者们，其中包括了李桦、段青干和芝冈等木刻青年。

图5：1936年7月5日《文漫界》刊头

当然，作为文艺副刊，《文漫界》也刊载了许多中国、本地的木刻作品，其中包括了《推进》、《怒视》、《逃荒》、《工厂一角》、《小憩》、《缝衣妇》等。而这批作品的涌现一方面说明鲁迅木刻思想已被本地接受（至少从技术层面可以看出），另一方面也看出"马来亚木刻运动"正在勃兴，胡贵宏就指出"文漫界"后，不仅木刻数量有所增多，而且木刻已经摆脱以往作为文学"附庸"的地位，成为独立的艺术形式。[33]

---

[33] 胡贵宏《战前新加坡卡通与木刻运动（1900–1941）》，硕士论文（新加坡：南洋理工大学国立教育学院，2005），页57。
  Foo Kwee Horng, "Cartoon and Woodcut Movements in Pre-war Singapore, 1900–1941," Master's Thesis (Singapore: National Institute of Education, Nanyang Technological University, 2005), p. 57.

(二）可被理解的"反叛者"

　　1937年，《文漫界》停刊，《南洋商报》重新开辟《今日艺术》（1937年1月10日–1937年6月26日）取而代之，而重新调整副刊的主因是中国抗日战争爆发，作为在东南亚华人社群中颇具影响力的《南洋商报》势必要积极响应中国战事。[34] 因此，在内容上，《今日艺术》仍承担宣扬木刻、刊载作品、动员制作等职责，但在立意上，《今日艺术》则以左翼美学为中心，将木刻视为宣传、斗争的工具。此外，在对待鲁迅的态度上，身为主编的戴隐郎也因时局变化从此前相对保守的继承变成颇为适度的"反叛"。当然，所谓的"反叛"意不在否定，而是因时制宜的权宜修改，所以此举不单可以被理解，甚至值得被"同情"。

1. "文艺先行" / "政治先行"

　　鲁迅在面对"文艺与政治"的问题时，始终保持着一个文艺工作者该有的操守与信仰，他既反对"文艺"为"政治"的"容器"或"宣传品"，也反对"文艺"脱离政治。所以，在"两个口号"论争中，他认为当"国防文学"成为文学创作的唯一创作标准与价值尺度时，文学便与政治等量齐观，其独立价值便不复存在。基于此，他并不认同"国防文学"的提法。但显然，戴隐郎没有延续该观念。从《文漫界》开始，戴隐郎就透露出向"国防文艺"靠拢的趋势，比如，在1936年12月6日，他刊登了渠明然的《论国防绘画》。该文言辞激烈地将绘画与"国防"划上等号，并认为绘画"应当属于最多数民众的教育的工具"，所有画家应当"在行人道上，墙壁上"，"积极地表现出国防绘画的目的与任务的"。[35] 到了《今日艺术》，戴隐郎愈加频繁地刊登强调文艺与政治相结合的文章，比如《木刻的第一课》、《时代艺术》、《艺术界应立刻猛醒》、《漫谈国防艺术》等文皆明确了文艺

---

[34] 1937年，《南洋日报》创立了"今日文化"、"今日科学"、"今日教育"、"今日青年"、"今日妇女"、"今日电影"和"今日艺术"七种副刊，戴隐郎仍旧出任主编一职（直至同年6月卸任）。

[35] 渠明然〈论国防绘画〉，《南洋商报·文漫界》，1936年12月6日，第12版。
Qu Ming Ran, "On National Defense Paintings," *Nanyang Siang Pau*, 6 December 1936, p. 12.

配合中国国内战斗需要的必要性与急迫性。特别在《新兴艺术之动向》中，作者广略还倡议"一切艺术家们起来朝着新兴艺术之动向，以艺术家之力去完成革命的救亡的伟大任务"，认为只有"政治宣传画"才是中国艺术的唯一出路。[36] 可见，戴隐郎将"国防"的需求逾越文艺的追求，放弃了鲁迅适度中和的"文艺与政治"观。

2. "写实主义"/"表现主义"

鲁迅的美术思想来源驳杂，他曾广泛接受象征主义、印象派、未来派、直觉主义、立体主义等美术思潮的影响，而在形成明确的木刻理论前，他还集中接触过表现主义的相关书籍、画作。[37] 所以，尽管鲁迅偏好"清醒健康"的写实派，强调"紧握着世事的形相"，[38] 但仍不可忽视表现主义思潮对他的影响。然而，对西方现代美术并不陌生的戴隐郎却只保留了鲁迅"紧握世相"的一面。比如，在《文漫界》中，他强调木刻家要多关注"现在"而不是"细腻玲珑的风景或什么无谓的东西"，[39] 虽然鲁迅也提出过类似观念，但前提是鲁迅认可风景木刻并认为木刻的发展规律是由相对简单的风景木刻向"紧握世相"的木刻过渡，他并没有质疑风景木刻存在的合理性。而在《今日艺术》中，"追踪现实"更是被视为当前最重要的诉求，不仅风景木刻就此"绝迹"，而所有发表的木刻也多倾向于"有血有肉表现现实生活的作品"，其中《凭吊》、《囚人》、《浓烟》就是典型。所以，当"写实"作为唯

---

[36] 广略〈新兴艺术之动向〉，《南洋商报·今日艺术》，1937年3月6日，第22页。
Guang Lve, "Modern Art Trends," *Nanyang Siang Pau*, 6 March 1937, p. 22.

[37] 早在1912年，鲁迅就开始接触表现主义美术，到了1924年，他更是通过翻译厨川白村、山岸光宣、板垣鹰穗等人的作品，系统接受表现主义理论。

[38] 鲁迅〈《凯绥·珂勒惠支版画选集》序目〉，《鲁迅全集》第6卷，页488。
Lu Xun, "The Preface of *Selection of Käthe Kollwitz's Woodcut*," *The Complete Work of Lu Xun*, Vol. 6, p. 488.

[39] 戴隐郎〈论木刻艺术（3）：木刻作者应有的认识和决定〉，《南洋商报·文漫界》，1936年9月13日，第12版。
Dai Yinglang, "On Woodcut Art (3): The Understanding and Decision of Woodcut Authors," *Nanyang Siang Pau*, 13 September 1936, p. 12.

一标准被提出时，马来亚木刻在艺术纵深性的开采上便多有怠懒，比如，同样是以"牺牲"为主题，珂勒惠支的《牺牲》通过粗犷的线条和细致的明暗对比，表现了母亲的悲伤、痛苦、愤怒等复杂情感，[40] 而《凭吊》虽脱胎于鲁迅的《药》，但在表现上却显得朴拙、稚嫩。（见图6、图7）

图6：牺牲

图7：凭吊

3."内容" / "形式"

鲁迅对木刻的形式问题并未具体展开，但并不意味他对此毫无关注。事实上，鲁迅在《拟播布美术意见书》中就提出了"形美"的概念，此后在搜集外国木刻时，他也曾对"法国技巧很高的佳作"表示赞叹。[41] 在木刻运动中，他更是提出要兼顾木刻的形式美，因为"木刻是一种作某用的工具，是不错的，但千万不要忘记它是艺术"，[42] 反

---

[40] 李欧梵〈鲁迅、珂勒惠支和毕亚兹莱〉，陈子善编《比亚兹莱在中国》（北京：生活・读书・新知三联书店，2019），页130。
Leo Lee, "Lu Xun, Käthe Kollwitz and Aubrey Beardsley," Chen Zishan (ed.), *Aubrey Beardsley in China* (Beijing: SDX Joint Publishing Company, 2019), p. 130.

[41] 增田涉著，龙翔译《鲁迅的印象》（香港：天地图书有限公司，1980），页80。
Wataru Masuda, *The Impression of Lu Xun,* trans. Long Xiang (Hong Kong: Cosmos Book Ltd., 1980), p. 80.

[42] 鲁迅〈致李桦〉，《鲁迅全集》第13卷，页303。
Lu Xun, "To Li Hua," *The Complete Work of Lu Xun,* Vol. 13, p. 303.

之，木刻便会"堕落和衰退"，"如新剧之变为开玩笑的'文明戏'一样"。[43] 可见，鲁迅重视木刻形式，诚如他重视木刻内容一样。然而，戴隐郎在《文漫界》便对形式问题关注较少，在《今日艺术》中更是鲜有提及。

必须承认，戴隐郎的"反叛"对马来亚文艺界而言是有益处的，当一种全新的能够替代"文以载道"的补偿方案出现时，对于那些尚不熟稔白话写作或者在中国经典作家影响下束手束脚的马华文艺工作者而言，强调政治性、现实性的木刻未尝不是一种创作"捷径"。但"反叛"所带来的对木刻艺术性的解构，最终也造成了马来亚木刻并没有得到预期的发展。

四、溯因与反思："马来亚"的影响/干预

戴隐郎在鲁迅木刻思想的传播过程中所表现出的偏离，固然可以用接受美学的"影响与焦虑"说或经典心理学的"弑父"理论来解释，但是，"马来亚"作为一个相对自如的、独立的"时空体"（chronotope）亦应该对传播的偏离"负起相应的责任"。

（一）延迟的否定

1. 迟到的马来亚

中国与马来亚隔着广阔海域，这片海域作为一个缓冲区使得"中国－马来亚"的传播并不是直接的，而是间接的、相对阻滞的。而这个巨大的传播距离也导致马来亚华人社群总是处于一种"迟到"的状态——无论是中国的文学、戏剧、电影等文化产品，还是政治、思潮等社会事件，总会间隔一段时间才落地马来亚。而"迟到"除了带来信息传递的延宕，更在一定时间内形成了"阐释真空"——信息缺乏明确的阐释标尺、亦无占据绝对阐释权的"话语机器"的阻遏。比如，鲁迅的新马传播就很能说明"迟到"与"阐释真空"的关联。

---

[43] 同上。Ibid.

事实上，鲁迅在马来亚的传播从一开始就处于迟到的状态：1918年，鲁迅发表《狂人日记》闻名全国，此时的马华文学却尚未萌芽，直到1927年，马华社群才首次接触鲁迅创作；到了1930年，鲁迅已接触共产主义理论，成为左联盟主，但马华文坛仍有"革命文学家"打着"打倒鲁迅"的口号；甚至1936年鲁迅逝世，"两个口号"争论业已平息，马华文坛反对"民族革命战争的大众文学"的声浪还未停歇。可以说，尽管马华社群与中国保持高度一致，但受制于"迟到"的状态，鲁迅的马来亚传播相较于中国始终晚了一步。而鲁迅的迟到直接导致马华社群对鲁迅的认识是悬置的、耽搁的，甚至是误读的。比如，《阿Q正传》于1927年才传入马来亚，但此时马华社会的反帝反殖民呼声高涨，马华文坛也在创造社、太阳社影响下掀起"新兴文学"运动，因此，传递启蒙思想的《阿Q正传》自然无法与当地产生联结，鲁迅便被冠以"迂腐"、"陈旧"的帽子遭到抨击、非议。[44] 但众所周知，1927年的鲁迅已经向"左转"，他的思想、创作进入了新的阶段，然而这一转变并未被马华社会察觉。彼时彼地的鲁迅受到此时此地情境的透视，必然造成鲁迅被严重误读。

而戴隐郎对鲁迅的木刻思想的"反叛"也是"迟到"作用下的产物。鲁迅木刻思想建构于1930年左右，但时隔六年才经由戴隐郎传至马来亚。六年间，时移势迁，"抗日"、"反殖"已逐渐成为华侨社会的首要任务，所以戴隐郎自然无需全盘引介鲁迅木刻思想，而只用挑选部分适用于斗争的内容即可。

2. 滞缓的启蒙

如果将1919年第一篇马华新文学的诞生视为开端，那么马华社群的启蒙运动在理论上应该皆与中国同步发展，但事实上，马华社群内

---

[44] 章翰《鲁迅与马华新文艺》（新加坡：风华出版社，1977），页4–5。
Zhang Han, *Lu Xun and Malaysian Chinese Modern Literature and Art* (Singapore: Feng Hua Press, 1977), pp. 4–5.

部语种复杂（闽南、潮汕、粤府、琼州等地方言杂糅）、文化多样，导致外生性（并具有转译性）的启蒙运动极难穿刺结构稳定的华人社群，比如，作为启蒙文学载体的白话文的使用和推广就进展缓慢。因此，当马来亚共产党（简称马共）在共产国际的授意下成立时，[45] 它所面对的是一个殖民势力根深蒂固、封建思想积重难返、语言惯习壁垒森严的华族社会，其"民族解放斗争、反帝反封建斗争、马来亚苏维埃共和国的建设"的宏愿极难推进。因此，深化启蒙、宣传左翼思想便成为马共不得不解决的实际问题。

此时，已是中国共产党员的戴隐郎，[46] 凭借其丰富的文艺实践成为马共外围组织"马来亚抗敌后援会"（AEBUS）的五个常委之一。[47] 考虑到当前马华社群白话普及的滞后，他索性用戏剧（街头剧、筹赈剧、独幕剧等）、绘画（漫画、木刻）替代文学创作，承担起宣传作用。因此，戴隐郎在马来亚传播鲁迅木刻思想，与其说是个体自发的审美活动，倒不如说是马共一次有组织、有计划的文艺实践，其作用是承担起本应由新文学创作为主导的启蒙运动，塑造华族子弟的启蒙思维，聚拢他们的抗敌意识。所以说，戴隐郎在《文漫界》的继承与《今日艺术》的"反叛"看似互相抵牾，其内在的思考逻辑却一脉相承。但此时的戴隐郎多少还顾及了鲁迅的真实意图，并未将"反叛"贯彻得十分彻底，到1939年日军入侵马来亚前夕，戴隐郎的"反叛"才走向激烈，他在《向马华美术工作者召告》中甚至强力宣告："由于当前马华美术界的主观力量仍是那么地散漫、薄弱，使整个美术界掉在马华救亡的后面……马华美术工作者，直到今天还有绝对多数游离于为

---

[45] 南岛丛书编辑委员会编《马来亚风云七十年》（新加坡：南岛出版社，2000），页12。
Editorial Committee of South Island Series (ed.), *Seventy Years of Malaya* (Singapore: Nan Dao Press, 2000), p. 12.

[46] 杨松年〈戴隐郎与新马华文文学〉，《亚洲文化》第14期（1990）。
Yeo Song Nian, "Dai Yinglang and Chinese Literature of Singapore and Malaysia," *Asian Culture*, No. 14 (1990).

[47] 五名常委分别是：（黄）耶鲁、洪涛、吴天、（戴）隐郎、（王）厌之。

艺术而艺术的范畴……支付出每个美术工作者最大的力量，献给马华救亡统一战线，献给中华民族，献给祖国！"[48]

（二）现实主义的扩张

1. 无边的现实主义

马华文学史家方修曾断言："尽管几十年来马华文艺运动有时高涨，有时低沉；作品的产量有时多，有时少；作品的质量有时很高，有时很差；但现实主义的精神却始终像一根红线一样，贯串着全部的创作历史，体现在所有重要的作品里面，成了文学创作的主流，从未间断过。"[49] 诚哉斯言。事实上，在马华文艺场域里，文艺最初的形态就是现实主义的，此后现实主义传统便延续下来：1910年代末期，"五四"运动传至马来亚，运动中对人的重视、对"除旧迎新"的拥抱，以及对启蒙的关注都被本地作家采纳；进入1920年代，在左翼力量的介入下，现实主义作为一种进步的方法论/世界观被文艺界奉为圭臬；到了1950年代，在本地殖民主义和左翼势力的斡旋中，现实主义创作也时常被视为战斗工具。换句话说，现实主义传统在马华文艺界可谓根深蒂固。

当然，以现实主义传统囊括整个马华文艺不仅显得粗鲁武断，而且也必然遭致东南亚本土学者以及在台马华文学研究者的不适，比如，张锦忠、黄锦树等人就尝试用"复系统"、"经典缺席"等论述推翻现实主义在马华文坛的主流位置。诚然，他们的研究固然观点明确、材料扎实，但其背后也暗藏着剔除"中国性"、抗拒"左翼传统"的野心以及对政治话语偷龙转凤的操弄。但此类研究也确实带出了一个被忽视的命题——现实主义在马华文艺场域的主流地位离不开背后群体性的认同与政治力量的加持。

---

[48] 英浪〈向马华美术工作者召告〉，方修编《马华新文学大系》第8卷（新加坡：星洲世界书局有限公司，1972），页519。
　　Ying Lang, "To Malaysian Chinese Artists," Fang Shiu (ed.), *The Collection of Modern Malaysian Chinese Literature* (Singapore: Sin Chew World Bookshop Company, 1972), p. 519.
[49] 方修《评论五试》（沈阳：辽宁教育出版社，1997），页140。
　　Fang Shiu, *Five Methods of Ping Lun* (Shenyang: Liaoning Education Press, 1997), p. 140.

实际上，在马来亚独立前，马华文艺场域多数青年文艺工作者都是左翼的，他们不仅将现实主义视为创作方法论，还将之视为品行、道德、精神的规范。于是，对现实主义的维护更像是"进步的"人生观、价值体系的追求，比如1950年代，左翼青年对"现代主义思潮"的批驳就多用"颓废"、"灰黄"、"堕落"等负面字眼。而且随着马来亚左翼阵营的扩大，现实主义还与政治成为姻亲，与革命成为盟友，原本作为文艺思潮的现实主义的外延已经无限散播，成为了淹没一切的"无边的现实主义"。[50] "无边的现实主义"强势浩大，使得马华文艺工作者有意/无意地回避其他文艺形态。戴隐郎身处其中也不能例外。事实上，戴隐郎对现实主义外的其他文艺形态是有感知能力的，在就读上海艺术专科学校时，他便广泛接触包括毕加索、特朗、佛拉芒克、马谛斯等在内的西方现代主义画家，从他前期的木刻作品中亦可发现表现主义木刻的影响。但显然，在他介绍木刻时，并没有点出木刻背后的文艺现代性追求，比如，在刊载《世界名刻介绍》、《现代匈牙利的木刻艺术》、《法国二月革命与平民画》等西方现代美术时，他只谈到了木刻作为"弱小民族"、"劳工大众"的"武器"，具有强大的战斗力、革命力。此外，马华文艺工作者高举现实主义大纛，实际上还是一种政治表态，拒绝提及现代主义，亦是表明与"颓废落后"的资本主义、殖民主义割席。

2. 理性主义盲视

"无边的现实主义"的撒播实际上还预示着绝对理性在马华社群的主导地位。事实上，从新文化运动在新马地区展开以来，无论是启蒙思想还是左翼逻辑都试图基于"进化论"/"进步历史观"承诺一个渐进的、现代的未来，而这两种思维也多展现出对"崇高理性"的狂热膜拜。然而，正如孔多塞认为的，当理性成为唯一的价值标尺时，那

---

[50] 张锦忠〈张锦忠答客问：马华文学与现代主义〉，《南洋商报·南洋文艺》，2010年11月29日。
  Tee Kim Tong, "Tee Kim Tong's Answers to Guests' Questions: Malaysian Chinese and Modernism," *Nanyang Siang Pau*, 29 November 2010.

么其内部便滋生出对"差异者"的暴力,"他们除了自己的理性就不承认有任何其他的主人……"。[51] 换言之,理性固然蕴含着透视知识、建构现代性的潜能,但却不是唯一方式,特别在美学实践领域,"审美活动并不是理性化的活动,也不是受理性支配的感性活动,而是超理性活动。……这不仅体现为审美的直觉性、非逻辑性、幻想性、极度的动情性,更由于它实现了人的超越性追求,即成为审美理想的创造。"[52] 因此,当绝对理性的触角伸到木刻领域时,马来亚木刻便成为理性主体用以传递知识/真理、搭建启蒙意识、宣扬革命理想的器具,其既无法突破工具/实用理性的规范,也难以超越意识形态的圈囿。

很显然,戴隐郎便是在理性思维驱使下传递鲁迅木刻思想的,他将鲁迅木刻思想简化为单纯的用于勾连启蒙、革命、战斗的技术,从而收缩了探索鲁迅木刻思想审美面向的可能性。当然,戴隐郎的偏离也未必是自发性行为,鲁迅对理性主义难以理顺的态度也是其中原因。

可以看出,戴隐郎对鲁迅木刻思想的继承与"反叛"需要结合"马来亚"特殊时空才能予以解释。而"马来亚"作为一个影响/干预鲁迅传播的闯入者,将鲁迅的木刻思想"马来亚化",至此,鲁迅及其木刻思想不同程度地产生变异。

五、结语

在"东南亚鲁迅研究"场域,有一种研究倾向得到许多学者的拥趸,那就是将鲁迅视为阻滞了东南亚华文文学/文化自如发展的"文化殖民者",将承袭鲁迅衣钵的南洋子弟视为被斩断自由意志的"被殖民者"。

---

[51] 孔多塞著,何赵武等译《人类精神进步史表纲要》(北京:生活·读书·新知三联书店,1998),页182.
Marquis de Condorcet, *Sketch for a Historical Picture of the Progress of the Human Mind*, trans. He Zhaowu et al. (Beijing: SDX Joint Publishing Company, 1998), p. 182.
[52] 杨春时《走向后实践美学》(合肥:安徽教育出版社,2008),页5.
Yang Chunshi, *Towards Post-practicalism Aesthetics* (Hefei: Anhui Education Press, 2008), p. 5.

但是众所周知,鲁迅从未踏足南洋,无论是作为施加影响的影响者抑或阻碍本地文学/文化建构的干预者,皆非其本意。而这也恰好说明,在鲁迅的东南亚传播过程中,作为当事人的鲁迅极为被动,他必然要受到本土文化、政治、社会等诸多情境的修改与选择,本文所举出的"鲁迅木刻思想"的马来亚传播就是一个鲜明例子。因此,"东南亚鲁迅"不仅与"本体鲁迅"会有一定距离,甚至判断"东南亚鲁迅研究"是一门关于鲁迅的建构论研究(而非本体论研究)也未尝不可。

而与鲁迅"交谊至深、感情至洽"的郁达夫也曾做过此类判断,他告诫南洋子弟不必事事模仿鲁迅,"不必这样的用全副精神来对付",不提鲁迅在南洋有多少讹传,况且"鲁迅也不会再生,则讨论了,终于有何益处?"[53] 可见,鲁迅并不是以强势的、不容申辩的殖民姿态来到南洋的,因此称其为"殖民者"不仅不准确,还暴露了部分学者对南洋本土文学/文化资源的不自信以及对政治话语的过度滥用。

---

[53] 郁达夫〈几个问题〉,《星洲日报・晨星》,1939年1月21日,第8版。
Yu Da Fu, "Some Questions," *Sin Chew Daily*, 21 January 1939, p. 8.

隐形宣传与友联出版社：
从亚洲基金会档案(1955–1970) 看纯文艺期刊《蕉风》[*]

许维贤[**]

摘要

本文运用亚洲基金会(The Asia Foundation)档案，探讨美国中央情报局(CIA)自1955年起暗中资助友联出版社在新马的文化活动和《蕉风》创办的始末；通过解读双方协议、信函和报告以及《蕉风》内容，并跟友联高层在晚年的回忆进行比较，从而辨证友联高层回忆美援历史及刊物自主性的虚实。研究发现美方多次审查友联账务、刊物内容和工作效益，对友联和《蕉风》进行干预和批评。《蕉风》编辑方针被设定为不谈政治的纯文艺刊物，实际是要实现美方的"隐形宣传"策略，读者一般看不到友联成员参与文化冷战的宣传行为，而是看到《蕉风》以自由文化的纯文艺理念，大力散播现代主义，以防读者被共产主义影响。最后本文从文艺的"自主法则"和"他律法则"来反思友联与《蕉风》的主流论述，并指出友联成员及其刊物在冷战时空跟马华左翼刊物相比，前者在本土经济和政治场域佔有很大优势，更多时候显然受利于他律法则，而不是主流论述所宣称的自主法则。

关键词：友联出版社 《蕉风》 纯文艺 亚洲基金会 "隐形宣传"

---

[*] 本文是笔者冷战研究计划（编号CACRG-2201）的部分成果，获得新加坡华族文化中心"华族艺术与文化研究资助金"支持，谨致谢忱。作者所发表的任何看法、研究结果及建议，皆不代表新加坡华族文化中心立场。本文初稿曾受邀分别宣读于大坂大学、立教大学、马来亚大学、台湾中央研究院、台湾大学和南洋理工大学的研讨会，感谢上述主办方的邀请，亦感谢史丹福大学胡佛研究所图书档案馆职员们、舛谷锐教授、宫原晓教授、沈双教授、杜汉彬、黄玉君和贺淑芳曾提供部分协助、资料或意见。本文原载于《二十一世纪》（许维贤：〈文化冷战中的"隐形宣传"：论友联出版社与《蕉风》在新马的经营（1955–1970）〉，《二十一世纪》(香港中文大学中国文化研究所)，2022年10月号）。感谢《二十一世纪》同意授权转载。本文对原载论文的题目和内容进行了部分的修改和更新。

[**] 许维贤，新加坡南洋理工大学人文学院中文系长聘副教授。

Unattributable Propaganda and the Union Press: On the Pure Literature and Arts Magazine *Chao Foon* in the Archives of the Asia Foundation (1955-1970)

HEE Wai Siam

Abstract

This article utilizes The Asia Foundation archives to explore the covert funding by the United States CIA of Union Press cultural activities in Singapore and Malaysia since 1955, as well as the founding of *Chao Foon*. By analyzing agreements, letters, reports, and *Chao Foon*'s content, and comparing them with the recollections of Union Press's leaders in their later years, the article seeks to discern the truth about the recollections of US aid history and the autonomy of the publications. The research reveals that the US conducted multiple reviews of Union Press's finances, publication content, and performance, and intervened in and criticized Union Press and *Chao Foon*. The editorial policy of *Chao Foon* was set to avoid political discussions and present itself as a purely literary publication, but in reality, it aimed to fulfill the American strategy of unattributable propaganda. Readers generally did not see Union Press members engaging in propaganda activities of the cultural Cold War; instead, they saw *Chao Foon* promoting pure literary freedom, vigorously spreading modernism to prevent readers from being influenced by communism. Finally, the article reflects on the mainstream discourse of Union Press and *Chao Foon* from the perspectives of the autonomous principle and the heteronomous principle of literature. It points out that compared to leftist publications in the Malayan Chinese community during the Cold War era, Union Press members and their publications had significant advantages in the local economic and political spheres, often benefiting from the heteronomous principle rather than the autonomous principle claimed by mainstream discourse.

Keywords: Union Press; *Chao Foon*; Pure Literature and Art; Asia Foundation; Unattributable Propaganda

一、文化冷战、亚洲基金会和友联出版社

冷战是以美国为首、标榜资本主义的自由世界，跟以苏联为领导、标榜社会主义的共产世界，在全球各地的政治、经济、军事、艺术、教育、文学、娱乐以及生活形态上展开争取人心的"战役"，宣传自由世界和共产世界各自在社会制度、价值系统和生活方式孰优孰劣的竞赛。美国总统杜鲁门（Harry S. Truman）于1947年在国会宣布杜鲁门主义（Truman Doctrine）外交政策，启动对外经济援助的"马歇尔计划"（Marshall Plan），正式掀开全球冷战序幕之际，也启动国内外宣传媒体展开"文化冷战"。亚洲冷战起源则可以追溯到1948年英国殖民政府宣布马来亚进入紧急状态，它掀开了亚洲冷战的帐幕，把亚洲推向国际冷战的前沿地带[1]。在马来亚启动的紧急状态是热战和冷战的并驾齐驱，一方面，英方正式对马来亚共产党宣战，发动长达十二年的全国剿共热战，这是对第二次世界大战前后新马数十年间多次主要由左翼发起的全国工人罢工运动和学生运动的暴力解决行动；另一方面，英方联合美国进行文化冷战，共谋策划针对新马的反共文化宣传政策和行动，强制推行"马来亚化"政策并严厉取缔来自中国和苏联等国并在各地流通的左翼书刊，同时全面启动政治宣传机构的各种反共媒介，对日益影响民心的共产主义意识形态进行围堵和封锁，并高举民主和自由世界的旗帜，组织各种抵制左翼的学生活动，亦制作或资助各种反共文本（例如刊物、书籍、广播和影视等）以赢取人心。为了对抗和消灭共产主义在东南亚华人社会的影响，英美协商多时，透过美方的亚洲基金会（The Asia Foundation, TAF）进行赞助和协调，秘密安排香港的友联出版社（以下简称"友联"）进入新马逐步开展各种文化业务，包括创办书局、杂志社、发行社、印务公司、文学出版社和教材出版社等，以及在各地设立大大小小的青年康乐部，并在友联（也泛指1960年代在香港重组的友联集团"友联文化事业有限公司"）通讯部的领导下组织各种面向华校生的文化与文学活动，蕉风出版社和《蕉风》正是友联众多业务的重要分支之一。

---

[1] Karl Hack, "The Origins of the Asian Cold War: Malaya 1948", *Journal of Southeast Asian Studies* 40, no. 3 (2009): 473.

TAF是1954年成立的非政府组织，前身是自由亚洲委员会（Committee for a Free Asia，CFA），从属于美国中央情报局（CIA）于1951年创设和命名为"DTPILLAR"的反共计划[2]。它当初成立的其中两大宗旨是反共和反对其他极权主义，最重要的目标是全球海外华人[3]。TAF作为美国官方权力的中介，在亚洲寻找"在地中介"执行文化宣传任务[4]。友联正是它在香港和东南亚进行幕后合作的"在地中介"。

友联于1951年4月5日在香港成立[5]，创社主要成员包括燕归来（Maria Yen，原名邱然）、陈思明（Jefferson Chen See-ming，又名陈维瑭、陈濯生）、徐东滨（William Hsu Tung-pien）和史诚之（Anderson Shih，又名史刚毅）等人。这四人均是当时香港流亡组织"民主中国青年大同盟"（以下简称"同盟"）成员。同盟是自外于国共政治体制的"第三势力"，其目标是"在国共两党之外创造一种新的政治影响，一种追求政治民主、经济公平和文化自由的理想中国的民主事业"[6]。同盟秘书长燕归来是首个与TAF建立业务关系的人，她是北京大学外文系学生，其父亲是北大教育系教授邱椿，她在父亲好友桂中枢的介绍下认识了TAF在香港的负责人艾伟（James T. Ivy）[7]。桂中枢当时是TAF的特约顾问，艾伟游说旧金山总部资助同盟的反共活动和刊物，得到TAF的鼎力支持，友联于1952年6月3日在确定得到TAF赞助的一个月后即开始出版《中国学生周报》[8]。

---

[2] "Committee for a Free Asia, Program & Planning" (28 September 1951), CIA, DTPILLAR, www.archive.org/details/DTPILLAR, vol. 1, no. 0040, 1.

[3] "Committee for a Free Asia" (1950), DTPILLAR, vol. 1, no. 0001, 1-4.

[4] 王梅香：〈冷战时期非政府组织的中介与介入：自由亚洲协会、亚洲基金会的东南亚文化宣传（1951–1959）〉，《人文及社会科学集刊》，第32卷第1期（2020年3月），页129。

[5] 王延芝（徐东滨）：〈漫谈"周报"和友联〉，《星岛日报》，"灌茶家言"专栏，1988年11月1日，第10版。

[6] 傅葆石：〈文化冷战在香港：《中国学生周报》与亚洲基金会，1950–1970（上）〉，《二十一世纪》，2019年6月号，页57。

[7] 奚会暲：〈奚会暲（1929–）〉，载卢玮銮、熊志琴编著：《香港文化众声道》，第一册（香港：三联书店，2014），页65–66。

[8] 傅葆石：〈文化冷战在香港：《中国学生周报》与亚洲基金会，1950–1970（上）〉，页59。

友联显然不满足于仅以香港为中心，它也在新马地区建立起东南亚的反共／非共枢纽。根据一封徐东滨写给艾伟的信函，早在1951年初，友联成员王安娜（Anna Wang）已被派往马来亚调查是否有可能在该地区发展项目，当时马来亚的局势似乎比较稳定和平静，一直到1954年5月新加坡发生动乱，友联高层审度局势之后决定采取行动[9]。友联通过王安娜的引介跟梁宇皋建立联系[10]，并邀请他担任友联的首席顾问[11]。梁宇皋是马来亚剿共计划的重要一员，曾被委任为联邦战争理事会（Federal War Council）的成员，也是马华公会的发起人之一，先后担任过马六甲州元首和马来亚司法部长[12]。TAF档案显示，友联最初是被马来亚联合邦的一位部长邀请到当地进行特定任务，马来亚内政安全部则在英殖民政府心理战部门的指导下紧密监督友联[13]。1954年11月《中国学生周报》社长余德宽（John Paul Yu Tak-foon）被派往新加坡进行初步调查后，1955年1月草拟"新马文化项目"计划书，向TAF倡议启动八个项目，包括在各地成立组织中心和通讯部等。同年4月燕归来亲自到新马视察，最后友联决定强化新马文化项目[14]。《蕉风》和《学生周报》都是新马文化项目的产物。

二、美援、纯文艺与《蕉风》的由来

1955年11月创刊于新加坡的《蕉风》是1950年代以降东南亚最重要的华语文艺期刊之一，新马文坛最具影响力的两场华语现代主义运动均跟友联成员和《蕉风》的大力推动有关（下详）。1959年《蕉风》社址

---

[9] "William Hsu to James Ivy" (27 February 1956), Asia Foundation Records（以下简称AFR），Box P-135, IMG_4388, 1, Hoover Institution Library & Archives, Stanford University.

[10] 何振亚：〈何振亚（1925–2009）〉，载卢玮銮、熊志琴编著：《香港文化众声道》，第一册，页21。

[11] "L. Z. Yuan to John F. Sullivan" (15 March 1960), AFR, Box P-135, IMG_ 4773, 1.

[12] 陈中和：〈梁宇皋〉，载何启良主编：《马来西亚华人人物志》（八打灵：拉曼大学中华研究中心，2014），页754–56。

[13] "William T. Fleming to John F. Sullivan" (18 June 1962), AFR, Box P-322, IMG_6580-6581, 1-2.

[14] "William Hsu to James Ivy" (27 February 1956), AFR, Box P-135, IMG_4388, 1.

迁往吉隆坡，1999年暂时休刊，前后出版共488期；2002年由马来西亚南方学院马华文学馆复刊，接续出版至今。《蕉风》被林春美称为"世界上出版历史最悠久的中文刊物"[15]。该刊的创办人和第一任社长是余德宽，首任主编是方天（张海威），1956年底方天去职后主要由姚拓、白垚和彭子敦分工主编《蕉风》，1960年黄思骋执掌编务，一年后由黄崖接手主编工作，直到1969年姚拓和白垚重新担任主编，并邀请李苍（李有成）和牧羚奴（陈瑞献）共同主编《蕉风》。后来不少马来西亚华人（马华）作家包括张锦忠和林春美等人均主编过《蕉风》，众多新马的老中青作家皆在此刊发表作品，《蕉风》也俨然成为马华文坛最具代表性的纯文艺刊物。

仅管TAF在幕后资助友联和《蕉风》的档案早已解密，至今学者对友联和《蕉风》的论述却并没有全面结合档案进行探究。大部分研究不是缄口不提就是避重就轻，仅有少数论者如庄华兴直面"它背后的文化政治与冷战的关系"[16]。林春美宣称早期《蕉风》"寻求华文文学在马来亚的政治和文化的自由"[17]，被英国学者戴杰铭（Jeremy E. Taylor）批评为"罔顾了殖民政府和其在地同盟在《蕉风》幕后所扮演的推动角色"，他结合小部分相关英美冷战档案，揭露正当作为竞争对手的左翼书刊被政府取缔，《蕉风》却得以顺利创办并可持续出版，原因是殖民政府和TAF"命令《蕉风》不得批判殖民政府和联盟（马华公

---

[15] 林春美：〈我在蕉风休刊的最后日子〉，《蕉风》，第488期（1999年2月），页1。此说不实，因为台湾有两份刊物略早于《蕉风》的创刊时间，分别是1954年2月创刊的《皇冠》和3月创刊的《幼狮文艺》，而且《皇冠》从未停刊并出版迄今。感谢台湾国家图书馆的馆员从旁协助查询馆藏资料核实此说。参见应凤凰：〈文艺杂志、作家群落与六〇年代台湾文坛〉，载东海大学中国文学系编著：《苦闷与蜕变：六〇、七〇年代台湾文学与社会》（台北：文津出版社，2007），页150。

[16] 庄华兴：〈战后马华（民国）文学遗址：文学史再勘察〉，《台湾东南亚学刊》，第11卷第1期（2016年4月），页13。

[17] Choon Bee Lim, "Imagining and Practising a Pure Malayanised Chinese Literature", in *Intersecting Identities and Interculturality: Discourse and Practice*, ed. Regis Machart et al. (Newcastle: Cambridge Scholars Publishing, 2013), 159.

会和巫统[UMNO]）的政策"[18]。纵然林春美承认TAF资助友联和《蕉风》的历史事实，然而在没有掌握和引述TAF档案的研究状况下，只能选择性地探讨《蕉风》的纯文艺作品有否逃离反共和马来亚化的政治议程，更关注"辨析其中可能的衍变"[19]。

《蕉风》在友联的经营下从创刊初期宣扬"纯马来亚化文艺"，发展到1950年代末和1960年代标榜刊物的"纯文艺"特性，甚至在第143期革新号至第173期（1964年9月至1967年3月）的封面直接打出"纯文艺月刊"口号，后人提起《蕉风》"一般上比较倾向于把重点放在它的'纯文艺'上"[20]。这种"纯文艺"预设可以轻易超越政治化的论述，在没有参照历史档案所设定的政治议程之前未免是"非历史化"和有待检证的。

不少论者从纯文艺角度出发，选择性地解读《蕉风》那些不问政治的作品，从而反驳或淡化该刊曾在冷战时期配合美方宣传的运作和策略。美方有关冷战文化外交的文件把"宣传"界定为"举凡在支持国家宗旨的设计下能影响任何群体的意见、情绪、态度或行为的传播，无论这些传播是直接或间接，只要它能为赞助方带来好处即可"[21]。此广义的界定赋予宣传机器间接的传播功能，这正是美方冷战意识形态的特点，即"隐形宣传"（unattributable propaganda）。宣传行为往往被

---

[18] Jeremy E. Taylor, "'Not a Particularly Happy Expression': 'Malayanization' and the China Threat in Britain's Late-Colonial Southeast Asian Territories", *The Journal of Asian Studies* 78, no. 4 (2019): 801–802.

[19] 林春美：〈非左翼的本邦：《蕉风》及其"马来亚化"主张〉，《世界华文文学论坛》，2016年第1期，页71。

[20] 林春美：《蕉风与非左翼的马华文学》（台北：时报文化出版企业股份有限公司，2021），页36。

[21] The Senate Select Committee on Intelligence Activities, *Final Report of the Select Committee to Study Governmental Operations with Respect to Intelligence Activities, United States Senate Together with Additional, Supplemental, and Separate Views*, bk. 1, Foreign and Military Intelligence (Washington, DC: U.S. Government Printing Office, 1976), 627.

巧妙掩盖，看似从未进行过一样[22]，而这会否是论者在研究友联和《蕉风》与TAF的关系时往往轻易忽略或没有意识到的盲点？TAF档案重复强调《蕉风》是"一份纯文学刊物"[23]，这跟《蕉风》标榜刊物的"纯文艺"特性是内外呼应的。美方在宣传策略上要让《蕉风》看起来纯粹是纯文艺刊物，不涵盖美方政治宣传，最好被外界理解为现代作家自发追求的纯文艺梦想，以便更有效地跟左翼政治宣传文学进行势不两立的切割，最终成功建构纯文艺（现代主义）和左翼政治宣传文学（现实主义）在新马的二元对立规范框架话语。麦都哈特（Martin J. Medhurst）和布兰德斯（H. W. Brands）指出"冷战是一种修辞建构"，强调"为了能够更新对冷战的思考方式，理解冷战修辞的面向将能提供其他路径无法提供的重要视角"[24]。本文有意揭示纯文艺和左翼政治宣传文学的二元对立正是冷战修辞在新马场域的建构。而《蕉风》的"纯文艺"立场在多大程度上体现了美方的"隐形宣传"策略？这无疑值得深究。

　　至今马华文坛包括不少写作人对于《蕉风》创刊前后的美援历史一般所知不多。例如早期在《蕉风》发表不少作品的马华资深作家菊凡在2008年《蕉风》第500期的专题撰文，引述姚拓生前向媒体宣称已赔掉一栋大楼来贴补《蕉风》多年亏损的说法，并自言"没有姚老的出钱出力，绝对不会有《蕉风》的诞生、茁长、壮大与延续"[25]。姚拓历任马来西亚友联总编辑，以及《蕉风》和《学生周报》社长兼主编长达三十余年。菊凡把《蕉风》诞生归功于姚拓的"出钱出力"，显然并不知道《蕉风》创刊前后均有美援背景，甚至把创刊人余德宽误以为是姚拓。《蕉风》由余德宽于1955年在新加坡创办并出任社长，姚拓于1957年

---

[22] Andrew Defty, *Britain, America and Anti-Communist Propaganda 1945–53: The Information Research Department* (New York: Routledge, 2004), 227; Frances S. Saunders, *The Cultural Cold War: The CIA and the World of Arts and Letters* (New York: New Press, 2000), 3.

[23] "Introduction", in *Union Press Organization: Annual Report 1965* (1965), AFR, Box P-322, IMG_6838, iv.

[24] Martin J. Medhurst and H. W. Brands, "Introduction: The Rhetorical Construction of History", in *Critical Reflections on the Cold War: Linking Rhetoric and History*, ed. Martin J. Medhurst and H. W. Brands (College Station: Texas A&M University Press, 2000), 6–7.

[25] 菊凡：〈愿蕉风永远不老〉，《蕉风》，第500期（2008年12月），页29。

2月才来到新加坡加入阵营[26]。这个失误归根究底不能归咎菊凡一人,因为新马媒体一直普遍把姚拓视为"蕉风之父"或"摇篮手",姚拓在生前也一概否认友联活动和旗下刊物得到美国资助。他于1964年就撰文宣称友联"绝对"不受任何国家和政党的补助[27]。这种斩钉截铁的否认延续到晚年他在自传《雪泥鸿爪:姚拓说自己》中对美援历史只字不提,有异于其他友联高层如徐东滨和奚会暲等人在晚年坦承这段美援历史。

可是,TAF对友联的资助是否会为友联带来限制或干预其业务?那些当年直接跟TAF交涉的友联高层晚年接受采访时均异口同声否认。1950年代就友联及旗下刊物包括《蕉风》之出版跟TAF签署多项协议的友联总编辑徐东滨晚年撰文,对外宣称友联是绝对独立自由的组织:"友联的一切政策、立场、人事、业务,绝对独立自由,向来不受任何外人支配,包括对友联支持了二十多年的'亚洲协会'〔亚洲基金会〕在内。"[28] 其他友联高层亦几乎重复徐东滨的说辞,例如曾担任友联总经理的何振亚声称TAF对友联"从来不干预,甚至批评也不批评"[29]。沈双研究《中国学生周报》时亦认同上述说法,并认为绝大部分友联高层之所以在印象中都不觉得TAF干预他们在《中国学生周报》的日常工作,那是基于以下事实:TAF不怎麽关注刊物内容,仅在刊物内容对TAF的网络造成麻烦、威胁到TAF结构的平稳或导致各网络交点出现沟通障碍和误解时,它们才会在TAF档案中被详细论及,而且TAF只会选择寥寥几位友联成员进行沟通[30]。王梅香则进一步强调友联文化人"作为主体的自主性",虽然她承认"友联文化人被各种结构性的力量形塑",美方也"掌握文化发展的大方向",但认

---

[26] 姚拓:《雪泥鸿爪:姚拓说自己》(吉隆坡:红蜻蜓出版有限公司,2005),页570。
[27] 姚匡(姚拓):〈事实是最好的说明〉,《学生周报》,第419期(1964年7月29日),页8。
[28] 王延芝(徐东滨):〈漫谈"周报"和友联〉,第10版。
[29] 何振亚:〈何振亚(1925–2009)〉,页30。
[30] Shen Shuang, "Empire of Information: The Asia Foundation's Network and Chinese-Language Cultural Production in Hong Kong and Southeast Asia", *American Quarterly* 69, no. 3 (2017): 604–605.

为友联文化人在友联细部的发展中有展现其"自主性"[31]。上述说法已在坊间形成主流话语。

然而，TAF是否真的"从来不干预"友联业务和"不怎么关注"友联刊物内容？这是直接牵涉到友联自主性的大哉问。本文充分调动和细读史丹福大学胡佛研究所图书档案馆（Hoover Institution Library & Archives）、CIA等有关友联的多种档案资料，探讨TAF如何在幕后赞助友联高层在新马创办《蕉风》和蕉风出版社，并结合冷战时期双方协议、信函、报告，友联高层晚年的回忆以及《蕉风》内容，从而辩证友联高层回忆美援历史及刊物自主性的虚实。

三、《蕉风》与亚洲基金会签订的协议

1955年6月28日，TAF与友联签订有关蕉风出版社和《蕉风》的协议。该协议由友联代表甲方，TAF代表乙方，由徐东滨和艾伟共同签署，双方同意以下协议条款[32]：

1. 乙方主要为甲方提供两大方面的财务资助，其一是承担蕉风出版社成立经费；其二是蕉风出版社和其项目所有财务赤字将由乙方承担，资助将从1955年7月1日开始。
2. 乙方没有持续性的责任为甲方提供财务资助；
3. 倘若甲方没有履行协议或蕉风出版社在社会的影响力不足，乙方有权终止资助甲方；

---

[31] 王梅香：〈香港友联与马华文化生产：以《蕉风》与《学生周报》为例（1955–1969）〉，载张锦忠、黄锦树、李树枝编：《冷战、本土化与现代性：〈蕉风〉研究论文集》（高雄：国立中山大学人文研究中心，2022），页29–30。王梅香没在文中论证她所谓"友联细部的发展中有展现其'自主性'"指的是什么，没分析友联跟TAF签署的合约条款，全文只掌握和引述1955年的五条TAF档案，也没论证友联文化人"作为主体的自主性"究竟在TAF档案和友联经营中如何显现出来。要厘清友联文化人是否有展现"作为主体的自主性"，至少要分析友联跟TAF签署的合约条款，并且要掌握和引述TAF从1950至1960年代的档案进行不同阶段的比较和分析。王梅香只引述五条TAF档案不但不足，而且也无法论证出友联文化人有在细部展现"作为主体的自主性"。

[32] "Agreement" (28 June 1955), AFR, Box P-135, IMG_3696, 1-3.

4. 甲方将全力促使蕉风出版社日益成为社会有效的交流和传播媒介，强化华裔学生认识自由世界的真相、理念、理论和结论；此外，甲方必须全力建立和维持《蕉风》在报导工作的最高水准，并加强对证据可靠性、报告准确性和分析谨慎性的重视；
5. 甲方将持续提高《蕉风》销量，让刊物财务收支达到理想状态，并在尽可能最早的时段内让刊物迈向自力更生；
6. 甲方必须在接受资助期间，每月提交相关的账目报表予乙方，并全面向乙方报告所有与出版社有关的主要发展和更新的政策；
7. 甲方必须与乙方保持紧密联系，在维护双方的利益下提高蕉风出版社的品质和有效性；
8. 如果蕉风出版社停止营运或被迫停止营运，这项协议将会失效，所有资助将宣告终止；
9. 甲方成立蕉风出版社和发展其业务是在乙方认为纯属值得和自愿支援的情况下得到资助，这些资助并不表示乙方是甲方的合伙人、负责人、代理人或独立承包商。甲方必须承担蕉风出版社和其项目各种索款、要求和承诺的责任；
10. 甲方同意维护和保障乙方不在商标、品牌、版权、文字、艺术或产权上受到任何个人、公司或企业的任何索赔和侵犯，甲方也需负起（包括但不限于）任何涉及到诽谤成份的出版内容所导致的法律责任；此外，甲方同意保障，员工或公众一旦受伤或死亡，乙方将免于一切索赔；
11. 为了确保蕉风出版社作为一个真正华人组织的特性可以得到有效彰显，即没有得到任何非华人资金的资助或被任何非华人势力控制，甲方和乙方将全力对这项协议的真相和性质完全保密。

TAF与友联于1956年9月18日签署更新协议，主要内容与上述协议大同小异，主要不同在于把香港《中国学生周报》、《大学生活》、新加坡学生周报社与蕉风出版社涵盖进来,以及添加此条款:"如果协议条款出现争端,这应交由香港民事诉讼庭委任的独立仲裁员进行仲裁。无论协议任何部分的争端发生在哪里,该名仲裁员都具备相关审判权。"[33] 这明显意味着友联跟TAF签署的协议是具有法律约束力的契约,友联如未能履行协议条款,则形同违约,双方谈判失败的最终解决方案就是友联需在香港面对TAF的法律诉讼。

从协议看来,TAF是根据合约有条件地支持友联,友联必须每年重新向TAF申请拨款,若其表现达到TAF提出的条件和指标,拨款才会下达。TAF对友联的资助有否附带条件,以至限制或干预友联业务?那些当年直接跟TAF交涉的友联高层在晚年都一口否认,例如何振亚的答覆是"绝对没有";王健武也说"没有附带条件,没有说拿了钱就要替你做什么";林悦恒甚至澄清"'友联'不附属于他们,不是依他指示做事";奚会暲则乾脆回应这些问题"事实上是不存在的"[34]。然而,TAF资助友联的每个项目,从协助刊物宣传、资助组织各种活动的各大组织中心和通讯部到《蕉风》,双方都会签署各种协议。从上述双方签署的协议看来,每个条款的要求都几乎是附带条件的体现,亦为TAF干预友联的业务提供法理基础。协议内容写得很详细,修辞很明确,并且很具体地详列友联必须承担各种法律责任。这些协议形同契约,具有一定的法律约束力,以确保友联履行协议;而且每次TAF拨款予友联和《蕉风》之前,均会在上述协议的基础上再按照每年的出版业绩和不同情况增添额外条款,并要求友联签署文件确认。要管窥这些协议内容有否真正落实,每次友联和《蕉风》顺利领款和签署上述协议信函即是佐证之一。另外一个佐证即在友联每年、每半年或每三个月提交给TAF的报告中,会详细列出哪些刊物内容和活动落实了协议条款。

条款1阐明《蕉风》如有任何亏损,TAF都会全额补偿,并不是1999年《蕉风》编委会编辑和顾问在暂时休刊启事宣称的"《蕉风》

---

[33] "Agreement" (18 September 1956), AFR, Box P-135, IMG_3598, 1-4.

[34] 何振亚:〈何振亚(1925–2009)〉、王健武:〈王健武(1929–)〉、林悦恒:〈林悦恒(1935–)〉、奚会暲:〈奚会暲(1929–)〉,载卢玮銮、熊志琴编著:《香港文化众声道》,第一册,页27、164、190、66。

每期亏损的款项，一向都由吉隆坡的友联文化事业有限公司负担"[35]，至少在TAF幕后支持友联的1955年至1970年代初期并不是如此。换言之，在那段长达超过十四年接受美援的出版时期，蕉风出版社和《蕉风》完全是不需赔钱的生意[36]。条款3规定倘若友联没有履行协议或蕉风出版社在社会的影响力不足，TAF有权终止资助。所谓"履行协议"，主要指所有项目必须维护和促进自由世界的原则，若友联无法在这个反共主旨上在社会发挥其影响力，TAF也没有必要继续资助友联。这些条款的要求显然带有很强的威慑性和约束力，达不到指标的话，幕后合作关系就宣告瓦解；友联一旦违约，就必须承担随时会被终止资助的风险。条款6 要求友联每月具体地向TAF报告业务主要发展，正好说明TAF和友联幕后的关系实质上是上级和下级的从属关系，下级有责任每月向上级交代业务表现，并接受上级的监督和批评，因此在这个体现上下阶层的结构体制下，TAF不太可能不监督或不干预友联的业务。而条款11要求友联对TAF资助和性质"完全保密"，根本是在掩盖美方的宣传行为，完全贯彻了美方的"隐形宣传"策略。

四、亚洲基金会对友联和《蕉风》的监督和干预

CIA的机密报告显示美方要求TAF必须把所有由其资助出版的书刊

---

[35] 《蕉风》编委会编辑和顾问们：〈蓄足精力，再次奔驰：《蕉风》暂时休刊启事〉，《蕉风》，第488期（1999年1月／2月），页3。根据《蕉风》休刊号主编林春美近来说法，此启事是当时姚拓以"蕉风编委会编辑和顾问们"的名义所写的。参见林春美：《蕉风与非左翼的马华文学》，页14。

[36] 从目前收集到的档案显示，TAF对友联的资助可能在1970年7月31日停止。然而根据曾在友联工作的金千里的说法，1976年美援对友联的支持才逐渐递减。参见金千里：〈50–70 年代香港的文化重镇：忆"友联研究所"〉，《文学研究》，2007年第7期，页175。由于部分TAF有关友联的档案包括1970年代的文件尚未解密，笔者不但不排除金千里之说，反而认为他的说法值得相信，因为当年跟TAF签署协议的友联总编辑徐东滨也承认TAF资助友联长达"二十多年"。友联从1952年开始接受资助，按此推算，TAF估计在1976至1981 年间才渐渐停止资助友联。参见王廷芝：〈漫谈"周报"和友联〉，第10版。

都送交CIA进行审查和评估，友联出版的书刊当然也不例外[37]。TAF驻新马代表平均每星期接触在新马的友联成员至少一次[38]，密切监督友联所有活动业务，包括蕉风出版社和《蕉风》的编辑方针和内容。

有别于《中国学生周报》及其新马版旗帜鲜明的反共倾向，《蕉风》总体内容的反共倾向并不鲜明，这跟它的策略是要争取大批无组织、徘徊于左翼和右翼的中间派学生群体有关。根据监管该项目的TAF代表致旧金山总部主席的信函，《蕉风》由蕉风出版社出版，起初与友联的关系完全不能公开，但由友联及《中国学生周报》的领导密切监管。友联把新马华裔学生分成三大群体，第一大群体是激进共产主义份子，他们擅于组织并扩大影响力；第二大群体是少数不太擅长组织的反共份子，相对之下影响力有限；第三大群体是大批无组织的中间派学生，他们日益感受到被共产主义威胁的压力。蕉风出版社和《蕉风》有意强化、组织和招收的对象就是那些中间派学生，最终目标是让他们远离共产主义份子，成为非共群体一员。蕉风出版社按照1955年6月28日与TAF签订的协议设定六条《蕉风》出版编辑方针：其一，在创刊初期不应有太明显的反共意识或讨论任何政治议题；其二，不应批评或表达对当地政府的愤懑；其三，应提倡民主精神和人类自由的原则；其四，应主要包含由当地华裔学生、教师和作家提供的文学与教育性质内容，而且也应把马来亚特色的相关资料翻译成华文；其五，内容除了取材新马，也应包含国外其他优秀作品；其六，应谨慎和低调组织对新马社会发展建设有益和强化自由世界的学生活动[39]。

首条编辑方针即是在实践美方的"隐形宣传"策略，以便创刊初期在不触怒那些普遍同情共产主义的学生群体的前提之下，第一时间有效争取到大批无组织的中间派学生纳入友联和《蕉风》阵营，支持他们进行一切非共活动，让他们不知不觉跟共产主义保持距离并乐意成为非共群体一员后，才循序渐进地指导有领导才能的学生低调组织反

---

[37] "Project Outline" (1955), DTPILLAR, vol. 2, no. 0029, 15.

[38] "John H. Tallman to John F. Sullivan" (27 October 1958), AFR, Box P-135, IMG_4959, 5.

[39] "Robert D. Grey to the President, TAF" (29 June 1955), AFR, Box P-135, IMG_3694, 1-2.

共活动。换言之，非共和反共在TAF和友联的活动原则中并不冲突，而是相辅相成的政治收编论述。反共论述明显是要拉拢那些愿意站在前线进行反共的群体；非共论述则只是要收编那些愿意跟共产主义切割的群体，包括被指为"非共左翼"（non-Communist left）的进步知识份子或作家，他们对共产主义感到幻灭但依然信仰社会主义理念，这也是美援文化部署和支援对象，《蕉风》首任主编方天和其父亲张国焘在某种程度上即是"非共左翼"[40]。至于第二和第三条编辑方针更是匪夷所思，既要求《蕉风》宣扬民主精神和自由理念，却不允许它批评或表达对当地政府的不满，明显违背民主精神和自由理念主张的批判思维和独立思考，更与友联宗旨理念的三大口号"政治民主、经济公平、社会自由"有所抵触[41]。显然，这些幕后操作的出版编辑方针自相矛盾，但也印证了友联和《蕉风》并非超然于政治党派。

TAF通过双方签署的协议操控友联的出版编辑方针和政治倾向，蕉风出版社和《蕉风》可以自主的空间其实被友联成员的回忆夸大，双方协议开宗明义要求蕉风出版社在编辑所有书刊包括《蕉风》和组织新马华裔学生活动的过程中，所有项目的基本理念和决策必须维护和促进自由世界的原则和自由华人（free Chinese）的信念[42]。换言之，蕉风出版

---

[40] 参见Frances S. Saunders, The Cultural Cold War, 62-63. 张国焘是中国共产党创始人之一，1938年投奔国民党，1948年移居台北，翌年移居香港，曾任《中国之声》社长，友联成员孙述宇在晚年接受采访时表示"张国焘大概是由美国人给钱养活"（参见孙述宇：〈孙述宇（1934–）〉，载卢玮銮、熊志琴编著：《香港文化众声道》，第一册，页121）。张海威在上海交通大学就读期间因参加学生运动被国民党以"共产党嫌疑"罪名拘留，狱中他跟其他被捕学生绝食，父母探狱携带蛋炒饭劝他进食被拒（参见邵有民：〈黎明前的狱中斗争岁月〉，《上海史与党建》，2009年第3期，页15），后来估计是在父亲跟国民党周旋后很快被释放。张海威先是在香港被友联聘为《中国学生周报》编辑，后来才被派往新马编辑《蕉风》。他担任《蕉风》编辑的时间估计仅一年左右，但在《蕉风》发表了质量俱佳的小说，蕉风出版社也于1957年推出他的短篇小说集《烂泥河的呜咽》。有研究者指出他的小说"同情劳工的立场相当鲜明"，但又回避了"马共与华教的问题"，"文学书写体现出非共左翼作家的社会主义写实主义理念，甚且也不无包含具有批判意味的现代主义"（参见贺淑芳：〈《蕉风》创刊初期（1955–1960）的文学观递变〉〔新加坡：南洋理工大学博士论文，2017〕，页115）。

[41] 何振亚：〈何振亚（1925–2009）〉，载卢玮銮、熊志琴编著：《香港文化众声道》，第一册，页11。

[42] "Agreement"(28 June 1955), 1; "Agreement" (18 September 1956), 1.

社和《蕉风》的所有书刊和活动必须宣扬美方资本主义主导的自由世界意识形态，不能涉及同情或支援共产主义阵营的内容。

《蕉风》创刊号甫出版于1955年11月10日，TAF即委託三名评审全面审查《蕉风》的编辑方针和内容。这三名评审是TAF驻香港的华裔顾问袁伦仁（L. Z. Yuan）、Raymond Hsu 和 M. H. Su（中文名字不详）。袁伦仁在11月16日迅速提交审查评论，他认为《蕉风》提倡的"纯马来亚化文艺"宗旨值得称道，并引证刊稿如许云樵撰写的〈新嘉坡掌故谈〉，认为其对本地色彩的传达做了很好的示范。不过，他指出刊物还有进步的空间，以争取更广阔的目标读者群，并提醒刊物的基调应是面向大众，因此没必要只刊登长文；《蕉风》更需要强化读者和编者的关系，增设一个可供读者和编者交流和讨论青年问题的栏目，读者提问范围可以涵盖各大领域，编者则在专家的协助下回答读者的来函询问，他甚至说编者当然也可以经常自己编造问题，然后以有趣的方式回答[43]。

另外一篇由 Raymond Hsu 提交的评论则措辞比较强烈，他批评刊物封面刻意标明《蕉风》为"纯马来亚化文艺半月刊"是不适当和荒唐的，应交由读者自行判断该刊是否"纯马来亚化"，不然只会更让人们怀疑。这显然就是要《蕉风》贯彻美方的"隐形宣传"策略，不要让外人一眼看穿该刊的官方色彩。此外，虽然封面设计相当不错，内页排版也还过得去，但他批评封面颜色显得不太协调。接着，他对作品进行评论，首先批评校阅做得不好，有些作品用的是水平很低劣的中文，语法不通，并提醒大众化不意味着要用拙劣的文字进行书写。他特别点名〈椰树下感怀〉文句不通，〈亚都拉和海盗〉读起来像一篇翻译文章。申青（余德宽）撰写的〈玉皇大帝发动细菌战〉隐含政治性，作者是在评论发生在新加坡的近闻，如果读者不清楚这一背景就会感到费解。其次他也批评刊登的散文太多，短篇小说太少，而且内容枯燥。《蕉风》创刊号收录三篇小说，其中包括方天的《胶泪》上集。Raymond Hsu 劝告说，如果还要续登友联成员的作品（暗指方天

---

[43] "Yuan to James T. Ivy" (16 November 1955), AFR, Box P-135, IMG_3683, 1-2.

《胶泪》上集），至少出版之前应邀请称职的作家润饰全文[44]，可见他不太满意《胶泪》的文笔。

最后一篇评论由M. H. Su撰写，是他在读了上述两篇评论后的再评论。他对袁伦仁肯定《蕉风》的"纯马来亚化文艺"出版宗旨表达赞同，《蕉风》主编也在实践此宗旨，此立场显然跟Raymond Hsu的评价不同。不过，他赞同后者对〈椰树下感怀〉的批评，认为此文只是在炫耀作者颇有造诣的中国古典文学知识，是全刊中写得最差的一篇文章[45]。

上述审查评论证明了何振亚所谓TAF"从来不干预，甚至批评也不批评"友联的说法是不能成立的，事实上每期《蕉风》均被TAF送审，因此有关TAF当年"不怎麽关注"友联刊物内容的说法不攻自破[46]。散文〈椰树下感怀〉被两名评审点名批评，表面上是针对该文的文法和遣词用句，其实是评审不耐烦于作者在全文流露眷恋故土中国的情怀，作者"山东佬"自称二十年前从中国来到南洋，至今依旧为自己"无能捍衞锦绣河山"和未能"到大后方干点救亡工作"，而只能到南洋"逃避现实"感到惭愧；文末还望天祈求有日能归国回乡："别无企望，只问青天，何事有家归不得！？"[47] 呼应了此文开头引述苏轼《水调歌头》"人有悲欢离合，月有阴晴圆缺"的"把酒问青天"之姿。这种故国黍离之思显然有悖于《蕉风》"纯马来亚化"的意识形态，因此不无意外地遭受评审批判。

三名评审相当严苛地审查《蕉风》创刊号几乎每篇作品，证明了TAF的确有干涉《蕉风》编辑方针之举，而且影响了该刊接下来的内容编排。创刊号因收录多达八篇散文而遭到评审批评，第2期《蕉风》散文数量就减了一半，仅剩四篇。第3期的短篇小说数量应评审要求大量增加，从创刊号的三篇，翻倍增加至六篇。另外，上述评审批评

---

[44] "Raymond Hsu to James T. Ivy" (17 November 1955), AFR, Box P-135, IMG_3685, 1-2.

[45] "M. H. Su to James T. Ivy" (18 November 1955), AFR, Box P-135, IMG_3687, 1.

[46] 1965年袁伦仁在致TAF驻马代表的信函里报告他已审查每期《蕉风》。参见"L. Z. Yuan to William T. Fleming" (22 March 1965), AFR, Box P-322, IMG_6451, 2。

[47] 山东佬：〈椰树下感怀〉，《蕉风》，第1期（1955年11月），页17。

《蕉风》封面刻意标明的宣传文案"纯马来亚化文艺半月刊"也在第37期（1957年5月）被拿下，也许是友联内部与TAF和英殖民政府经过多番交涉和讨论后的决定[48]。这不意味《蕉风》放弃了"马来亚化"主张，按照该期编者比较间接和委婉的解释，那是应合读者来函的提醒——虽然《蕉风》在进行"马来亚化的文艺拓植工作"，但"一地的文化提高不能只靠关起门来埋首苦干，也应该吸收外地的精华"[49]。也是从第37期开始，《蕉风》增设署名"现代佳作选"栏目，每期选登中西著名现代作家作品，包括沈从文、徐志摩和李金发翻译法国现代派诗人魏尔伦（Paul Verlaine）的作品，这也渐渐启动《蕉风》对现代主义文艺的观照。

曾担任《蕉风》和《学生周报》主编多年的白垚于1959年3月发表在《学生周报》的《麻河静立》，一般被友联成员誉为马华文坛的第一首现代诗。他于同年4月发表于《蕉风》第78期的文章〈新诗的再革命〉被誉为马华现代诗的现代主义宣言，这期也是编者自称《蕉风》从外貌到内容的重大改版，从"原是综合性的文艺刊物"，朝向"纯文学方面发展"，并且申明"我们反对以政治标准来代替艺术标准"[50]。

---

[48]《蕉风》提倡"纯马来亚化"，隐含对当时马华左翼圈热衷把"马来亚化"和现实主义艺术创作的根本原则相提并论的"马来亚化"论述的批评，暗指马华左翼圈提倡的是"不纯正的马来亚化"，恐怕还掺杂对"中国化"诸种元素的承担（参见庄华兴：〈战后马华（民国）文学遗址〉，页17）。在这场左右阵营借"马来亚化"议题的话语争夺或交锋过程中，TAF更多是基于美方"隐形宣传"策略，不希望《蕉风》太明显地介入这些论争。另一方面，TAF和英殖民政府在监督友联业务方面时有分歧，前者比较不希望看到友联的反共旗帜太明显，后者却相反。例如TAF抱怨友联过于被英殖民政府官员影响，参见"The Representative (Malaya/Singapore) to John Sullivan, Director, Programs Department" (29 July 1959), AFR, Box P-57, 1。TAF从友联和英殖民政府签订的备忘录中得知政府部门有权控制友联，并有责任指导友联活动，而且要确保友联能宣传有利于政府的活动，可是TAF又不希望友联成为政府属下机构或心理战部门的分支，这种短期的政治要求在TAF看来太危险。参见"John F. Sullivan to William T. Fleming" (11 June 1962), AFR, Box P-322, IMG_6582, 1。

[49] 编者：〈一张新的菜单〉，《蕉风》，第37期（1957年5月），页4。

[50] 编者：〈读者・作者・编者〉，《蕉风》，第78期（1959年4月），页24。根据白垚回忆录，此话出自该期编者姚拓。参见白垚：《缕云起于绿草》（八打灵：大梦书房，2007），页74-75。

白垚在其晚年的回忆录津津乐道当年由他发动的"新诗再革命":"马华文坛的文学反叛,始于现代诗,五十年代的新诗再革命,始于《蕉风》……在历史的深层,'新诗再革命'与'播散现代主义',无不与《学生周报》有关……没有《学生周报》,就不会有《蕉风》的现代文学。"[51] 白垚这一锤定音的追溯,被张锦忠视为"马华文学的第一波现代主义运动"[52]。白垚在〈新诗的再革命〉提出的五点主张,诚如他在晚年承认,除了"横的移植"外,其余四点是借中国五四火把,把胡适〈文学改良刍议〉的部分主张笼统地再说一遍;他亦自认其现代诗观主要来自于中国五四现代诗人如梁宗岱等人[53]。换言之,第一波现代主义运动的启蒙源头更多是来自民国那些提倡纯诗和纯文学的现代派作家,而不是直接来自欧美的现代主义作家。

当年TAF是如何看待和评价《蕉风》于1959年4月改版后所主张的"纯文学"宗旨呢?11月30日TAF对《蕉风》进行审查的田野报告,批评《蕉风》编辑的心理仍然更重视"纯文学目标",而忽略了该刊更为广阔的社会政治目的。该报告不满《蕉风》倾向于以中华文化和文学性来替代该刊的长期社会政治目标,不满编辑过于重视把现代中华的新诗和散文风格以及美学价值灌输给一般读者和土生土长的马来亚作者,严重忽略了如何表达新马华人对于马来亚国族的忠诚,而这在TAF看来才是当务之急。该报告认为《蕉风》需要协助新马华人的马来亚化,因此有必要带头回应新马两地政府的主要政策,并要求《蕉风》推动本地作家以马来亚人的惯用语、腔调和背景来进行文学创作,而相应地减少关注和刊登香港和台湾作家的作品[54]。

上述评述再一次让我们看到TAF不但干涉《蕉风》的编辑方针和内容,对其远离政治的"纯文学"主张也划下了范围底线。它要求《蕉

---

[51] 白垚:《缕云起于绿草》,页83。
[52] 张锦忠:《马来西亚华语系文学》(八打灵:有人出版社,2011),页57。
[53] 白垚:《缕云起于绿草》,页90-94。
[54] "Chao Feng Society (8501): Field Report" (30 November 1959), AFR, Box P-135, IMG_3652, 1.

风》的政治倾向有必要靠向当地政府设定的方向，并要确保《蕉风》创刊时所被赋予的"马来亚化"政治功能能够被后来的《蕉风》成员延续。TAF的主张是遵照美国国务院官员的指示，即其任务是协助东南亚华人融入当地，倘若TAF过度引导东南亚华人支持台湾，恐怕会让东南亚华人与当地产生疏离[55]。虽然《蕉风》对于"纯文学"的追求，并不能让TAF"百分之百放心"[56]，但更让它不放心的是其"纯文学"理念不是直接来自欧美文学，而是来自中华民国（台湾）那些对中国还怀有眷恋的五四作家，这在TAF看来恐怕会强化新马作家对中国文学的嚮往，不利于马来亚政府所推广的"马来亚化"政策。

无论如何，由于TAF总部主席布鲁姆（Robert Blum）明确指示必须採取一切措施，以减少友联成员及其刊物内容涉及政治的可能性[57]，这让《蕉风》可以更心安理得地沉醉于纯文学的世界，标榜"纯文艺"来定位自身在马华场域的位置，把纯文艺和左翼政治宣传文学进行二元对立的切割，启动了马华场域有关现代主义和现实主义的二元对立规范框架话语。当时其他友联刊物如《学生周报》刊登的《蕉风》广告，也经常以"纯文艺"来作为《蕉风》品牌的宣传文案[58]。当然这一切不意味着《蕉风》远离政治，它提倡的"纯文艺"在美方幕后"隐形宣传"策略的指引下，演变成有效而隐蔽地通行于自由世界的"政治宣传"和"品牌宣传"。

第一波现代主义运动比较倚重中台港作家对西方现代文学的译介，未能比较全面、直接地通过本土翻译活动引进欧美现代文学，这项未竟之业被《蕉风》1969年8月至1970年代初期发展到顶峰的第二波现代主

---

[55] "Memorandum for the Record: Meeting with Messrs. Strong and MacKnight of the Department of State" (22 May1953), DTPILLAR, vol. 2, no. 0043, 1.

[56] 沈双：〈背叛、离散叙述与马华文学〉，《二十一世纪》，2016年12月号，页44。

[57] "Robert Blum to John Gange" (18 April 1960), AFR, Box P-135, IMG_4756, 2.

[58] 有关《蕉风》宣传文案出现"纯文艺"的广告，刊登于《学生周报》第138期（1959年3月13日），页11、第169期（1959年10月16日），页2、第176期（1959年2月4日），页7。

义运动继承和实践。期间《蕉风》编委由牧羚奴、李苍、白垚和姚拓所组成，此波运动顺利汇合了1967年以降由牧羚奴和梁明广等人在《南洋商报》副刊"文艺"引领风气的"高蹈现代主义"（high modernism）译介和创作队伍，通晓英文、法文、中文和马来文的牧羚奴直接把欧美现代作品翻译成中文，亦亲身示范创作各种现代作品，让《蕉风》提倡的"纯文艺"发展到顶峰。

五、亚洲基金会对《蕉风》的资助

TAF给友联的拨款大致分成以下九大项目：第一，拨款予活动中心，这部分往往最多，主要供新马友联总部，以及各地组织中心和通讯部缴付租金、薪金，购买办公用品，举办各种活动等；第二，拨款予发行部，供其发行友联所有书刊包括《学生周报》和《蕉风》等；第三，拨款予学生周报社及《学生周报》作日常营运；第四，拨款予蕉风出版社及《蕉风》作日常营运；第五，拨款予新加坡艺联剧团和吉隆坡剧艺研究会；第六，拨款予生活营和野餐会等青年活动；第七，补助成立新马的华文书局；第八，资助年轻作家计划；第九，其他额外拨款，如奖学金、图书出版费和作文比赛等[59]。

为了向TAF申请经费，友联每年都要重新提交详细的来年预算案报告予TAF，列出《蕉风》的年度预算费用。受限于部分档案尚未解密或公开，表1仅列出《蕉风》从1955至1970年的数据。这些数据来源主要出自友联和TAF每次领款双方签订的协议信函、报告或通信记录等。需要注意的是，TAF提供给《蕉风》的总经费不限于以下资助金额，因为部分供《蕉风》发行与进行活动和宣传的经费通常计算在上述活动中心、发行部和其他额外拨款的项目中。

---

[59] "William T. Fleming to Chen See Ming" (1 August 1965), AFR, Box P-286, IMG_5305-5306, 1-2.

表1 亚洲基金会对《蕉风》的资助金额，1955至1970年

年度期限	资助金额（叻币、马币、美元）	美元（折算）
1955.11.1–1956.3.31	ST$21,130	~US$7,043
1956.4.1–6.30	ST$11,720	~US$3,907
1956.7.1–1957.6.30*	ST$81,548 + ST$4,000 = ST$85,548	~US$28,516
1957.7.1–1958.6.30#	ST$45,600 + ST$83,600 = ST$129,200	~US$43,067
1958.7.1–30	M$3,167	~US$1,056
1958.8.1–1959.7.31	M$18,000	~US$6,000
1959.8.1–1960.7.31△	M$16,860	~US$5,620
1960.8.1–1961.7.31	M$12,970	~US$4,323
1961.8.1–1962.7.31	M$11,396	~US$3,799
1962.8.1–1963.7.31	M$12,000	~US$4,000
1963.8.1–1964.7.31	M$14,100	~US$4,700
1964.8.1–1965.7.31+	M$14,100	~US$4,700
1965.8.1–1966.7.31+	M$14,100	~US$4,700
1966.8.1–1967.7.31+	M$14,100	~US$4,700
1967.8.1–1968.7.31	US$3,500	US$3,500
1968.8.1–1969.7.31	US$1,500	US$1,500
1969.8.1–1970.7.31	US$1,500	US$1,500
总拨款（推算）		~US$132,631

资料来源："Basic Agreement Dated 28 June 1955 between James T. Ivy and William Hsu" (28 June 1955), Asia Foundation Records（以下简称AFR）, Box P-135, IMG_3699- 3700, 1-2, Hoover Institution Library & Archives, Stanford University; "Attachment No. 2 to Basic Agreement Dated 28 June 1955" (27 March 1956), AFR, Box P-135, IMG_3674, 1; "Attachment No. 2 to Basic Agreement Dated 1 July 1956" (10 September 1956), AFR, Box P-135, IMG_3604, 1; "The Representative, Malaya/Singapore to the President, TAF" (3 January 1958), AFR, Box P-135, IMG_4982,1; "The Representative, Malaya/Singapore to the President, TAF" (16 July 1958), AFR, Box P-135, IMG_4975, 1; "John H. Tallman to Chen See Ming" (22 September 1958), AFR, Box P-135, IMG_3668, 1; "The Representative, Malaya/Singapore to the President, TAF" (1 October 1958), AFR, Box P-135, IMG_4968, 1; "John H. Tallman to Chen See-ming" (28 September 1959), AFR, Box P-135, IMG_4895, 1; "William Fleming to Chen See-ming" (2 December 1959), AFR, Box P-135, IMG_4834-4835,1-2; "William T. Fleming to the President, TAF: Enclosure-Regular

Program Monthly Budget-August 1960-July 1961" (9 September 1960), AFR, Box P-135, IMG_4668, 1; "The Representative, Malaya/Singapore to the President, TAF" (28 April 1961), AFR, Box P-135, IMG_4542,1; "The Representative, Malaya/Singapore to the President, TAF" (16 June 1961), AFR, Box P-135, IMG_4537,1; "William T. Fleming to Chen See Ming" (9 August 1961), AFR, Box P-135, IMG_4523-4524, 1-2; "Union Press-Malaysia-Written Agreements" (1961), AFR, Box P-322, IMG_6456-6459, 2-3; "William T. Fleming to Chen See Ming" (1 August 1962), AFR, Box P-322, IMG_6633-6634, 1-2; "William T. Fleming to Chen See Ming" (15 August 1963), AFR, Box P-322, IMG_6630, 1; "William T. Fleming to Chen See Ming" (4 February 1964), AFR, Box P-322, IMG_6623-6624, 1-2; "William T. Fleming to the Chen See Ming" (5 November 1964), AFR, Box P-322, IMG_6619, 1; "The Representative, Malaysia to the President, TAF" (12 November 1964), AFR, Box P-322, IMG_6479, 1; "William L. Eilers to Jefferson Chen See Ming" (29 October 1965), AFR, Box P-322, IMG_6461, 1; "The Representative, Malaysia to the President, TAF" (2 November 1965), AFR, Box P-322, IMG_6402, 1; "David Getzoff to Jefferson Chen See Ming" (21 October 1966), AFR, Box P-286, IMG_5378, 1; "The Representative, Malaysia to the President, TAF-Annex II: Three- Year Plan for Foundation, Assistance to UCO Projects Malaysia 1967/68 through 1969/70" (16 March 1967), AFR, Box P-286, IMG_5229, 1.

说明：（1）折算兑换率：ST\$3（ST指叻币）大约折合US\$1，参见"Robert D. Grey to the Representative, Malaya/Singapore" (12 March 1959), AFR, Box P-135, IMG_4146, 4; M\$3（M指马币）大约折合US\$1，参见"The Representative, Malaya/Singapore to the President, TAF" (6 February 1959), AFR, Box P-135, IMG_4942, 4。兑换率出自1959年档案记录，由于兑换率经常浮动，折算成美元的数据（以_显示）仅是推算。（2）"*"号标示的年度，TAF额外拨款ST\$4,000资助《蕉风》和《学生周报》主办的年度作文比赛。"#"号标示的年度，ST\$83,600是从友联活动中心基金账户调动过来补偿《蕉风》亏损的款项。"△"号标示的年度为每月资助M\$1,405，一年总共M\$16,860。在"+"号标示的三个年度里，资金在一年内分成四次付款，每次M\$3,525，四次总共M\$14,100。

  从1955年11月至1958年6月，友联的业务中心基本是在新加坡，因此TAF给友联的拨款是以海峡殖民地的叻币（ST\$）计算。在TAF资助下，友联于1958年8月在吉隆坡成立专属经营的印刷厂马来亚印务公司。TAF给友联的拨款从1958年7月以降开始以马币（M\$）计算，为友联的业务中心移向吉隆坡做好准备。《学生周报》于1958年8月由新加坡转到吉隆坡印刷[60]；1959年1月《蕉风》第75期的印刷开始由新加坡转到吉隆坡，同年4月《蕉风》社址也迁往吉隆坡。TAF最后三年资助《蕉风》的款项据笔者掌握到的档案账目均以美元计算。

  从表1看来，友联在大部分年度得到数额不一的拨款，这些拨款既包括补偿上一年度《蕉风》的亏损，有些年度也包括TAF对《蕉风》的

---

[60] 姚拓：《雪泥鸿爪：姚拓说自己》，页566。

额外拨款。可以推测，友联和《蕉风》在所有年度都基本达到了TAF提出的各种条件和指标、落实协议内容，否则不可能得到持续拨款。《蕉风》在1957年7月至1958年6月得到最多经费，除了补偿上一年度的亏损，额外的拨款是为了奖励《蕉风》历年业务蒸蒸日上。TAF驻新马代表在提呈给旧金山总部的年度预算报告中，解释了1955至1957年《蕉风》不但成功培养了一批年轻写作人、艺术家和有志之士进行群组活动，也在销量和收入上有所增加，预计接下来的几年中赤字会有所减少[61]。《蕉风》在1961年8月至1962年7月得到较少的经费，恐怕是受累于TAF从1959至1960年不时派专员对新马友联各地通讯部进行明察暗访而提呈予旧金山总部的负面调查结果，调查报告指控有些通讯部只是虚有其表，没有举办青年活动，其设立目的是要获取TAF的资助而已[62]。这导致TAF启动对友联的账目审查，动摇了彼此之间长期的信任关系，结果是TAF否决了友联于1961/62年度提出的部分总预算，最终衝击了该年度的拨款总额[63]。由上可见，TAF通过奖励和惩罚措施来监控友联业务。《蕉风》分别在1968年8月至1969年7月以及1969年8月至1970年7月得到最少经费，那是TAF计划逐步退出资助友联项目的结果。

值得注意的是，无论是1959年4月《蕉风》第78期改版号以降先后由白垚、黄思骋和黄崖启动的马华文学第一波现代主义运动，或者1969年8月《蕉风》第202期以降由牧羚奴、李苍、白垚和姚拓等人带动的第二波现代主义运动，都受惠于TAF的资助。笔者无意以美方资助金额来抹煞这两波现代主义运动对新马文学的重要贡献，仅是要指出现代主义在马华文坛的兴起其来有自，并非锺怡雯所以为"带着历史的偶然"[64]。

TAF对《蕉风》长达超过十四年（1955年11月至1970年7月）的资助金额，总拨款推算为132,631美元，仅佔新马友联得到的总拨款9%左

---

[61] "Budget Project Sheet: Chiao Feng Society, Amount: 1957–58" (1957), AFR, Box P-32, IMG_3160, 1.

[62] "Francis Cooray to the President, the Asia Foundation" (12 October 1959), AFR, Box P-135, IMG_4851, 1-2.

[63] "William T. Fleming to Chen See Ming" (1 February 1961), AFR, Box P-135, IMG_4249, 1.

[64] 钟怡雯：《马华文学史与浪漫传统》（台北：万卷楼图书股份有限公司，2009），页80。

右[65]。从1950至60年代新马的经济层面来看，当时人民的生活费用较低廉，相对之下，总体上TAF对友联活动和其旗下刊物的资助金额可谓庞大，并不是奚会暲所说的友联得到的资助"数字不是很大"[66]。单以《蕉风》为例，1955至1958年每本零售价仅是叻币两角（表2），然而1957至1958年TAF对《蕉风》的资助金额却超过叻币13万元（表1），1957至1958年《蕉风》每月平均销量大约4,000本，1964年最高可达8,000本（表3）。而且如前所述，《蕉风》若有任何亏损，TAF都会全额补偿，这已白纸黑字写在双方的出版协议里。

表2 《蕉风》的规格和售价转变，1955至1967年

年份和期数	开本	页数	零售价	出版周期
1955–1956（第1–18期）	32开	32	两角	半月刊
1956–1958：（第19–72期）	16开	24	两角	半月刊
1958.11–1959.3（第73–77期）	16开	36	三角	月刊
1959.4–1964.8（第78–142期）*	16开	24	三角	月刊
1964.9–1967.3（第143–173期）	16开	76	五角	月刊

资料来源：*Union Press Organization: Annual Report 1962* (1962), AFR, Box P-322, IMG_6718, 24; *Union Press Organization: Annual Report 1964* (1964), AFR, Box P-322, IMG_6784-6785, 31.
说明："*"号标示的期号均附赠32开以及32页的中篇小说。

从《蕉风》的规格和售价转变来看，它的页数不多，从24页发展到后来的76页，每本零售价仅从最初的叻币两角涨到后来的五角，高中学

---

[65] 根据友联和TAF领款双方每次签订的协议信函、报告和通信记录等，笔者统计和推算出新马友联从1955至1970年得到TAF的总拨款为1,438,535美元(参见许维贤：〈亚洲基金会在新马的文化冷战：以友联出版社和《学生周报》为例〉．《中外文学》，2023年第481期，页89–92)。这个总拨款还不包括TAF拨给香港友联和马来亚文化事业有限公司出版各种教材的其他巨额和零利息贷款。

[66] 奚会暲：〈奚会暲（1929–）〉，页67。

生佔65%的銷數[67]。《蕉風》低廉的售價足以讓廣大學子負擔,每月平均銷量非常亮眼。從1955至1958年每月平均銷量維持在4,000本上下,這跟1999年《蕉風》暫時休刊啟事所提供的數據頗有出入:"《蕉風》的銷數始終只有一千五百左右",最高的銷數是在1960年"銷出三千多份"[68]。對比表3的數據,《蕉風》在1960年的銷量卻是最差的,僅有3,500本,不過也高踞當時本地華文刊物銷量榜首[69]。這可能意味著要不當年友聯高層向TAF誇大《蕉風》銷量,要不友聯高層晚年的回憶可能夾雜虛構成份。

表3 《蕉風》每月平均銷量估算(本),1955至1965年

年份	1955	1956	1957	1958	1959	1960	1961	1962	1963	1964	1965
銷量	接近4,000	接近4,000	接近4,000	4,000		3,500		5,700			
下限					3,700		3,700		5,000	4,300	4,825
上限					超過7,500		5,000		5,700	8,000	6,000

資料來源:"The Representative, Malaya/Singapore to the President, TAF: Program Budget — Year 1958–59" (27 January 1958), AFR, Box P-134, IMG_3468, 27; "Chao Feng Society (8501): Field Report" (31 March 1959), AFR, Box P-135, IMG_3653, 1; "Robert D. Grey to the President, TAF" (29 June 1959), AFR, Box P-135, IMG_3694, 1; "The Chao Foon Monthly" (31 May 1960), AFR, Box P-135, IMG_3651, 64; "William T. Fleming to L. Z. Yuan: U.P.O. Programs & Activities in Malaysia" (8 October 1962), AFR, Box P-322, IMG_6569, 4; *Union Press Organization: Annual Report 1962*, 25; "L. Z. Yuan to the Record: Discussion with UPO leaders" (11 October 1963), AFR, Box P-322, IMG_6525, 4; *Union Press Organization General Review: 1956–1963* (1963), AFR, Box P-322, IMG_6696-6697, 17; "Yu Nan Shen to John F. Sullivan" (26 November 1964), AFR, Box P-322, IMG_6477, 4; *Union Press Organization: Semi-Annual Report January–June 1964* (1964), AFR, Box P-322, IMG_6819, 19; "Introduction", in *Union Press Organization: Annual Report 1964* (1964), AFR, Box P-322, IMG_6764-6765, vi; "A Summary of the Aims, Policies and Works of U.P.O in Malaysia" (18 November 1965), AFR, Box P-322, IMG_6670, 6; *Union Press Organization: Annual Report 1965* (1965), AFR, Box P-322, IMG_6858, 37.

說明:1964年的上限8,000本中,包括當年銷售到香港的2,000本《蕉風》。

---

[67] 另有15%賣給教師;新加坡、雪蘭莪和霹靂就佔了《蕉風》55% 的總銷數。參見 "Project Data Sheet: Chao Feng Society" (1961), AFR, Box P-134, IMG_3552-3553, 46–47。

[68] 《蕉風》編委會編輯和顧問們:〈蓄足精力,再次奔馳〉,頁3。

[69] "The Chao Foon Monthly" (31 May 1960), AFR, Box P-135, IMG_3651, 64.

六、友联在报告中对《蕉风》的反共功能和影响的陈述

友联在提交给TAF的1964年度报告中,阐明《蕉风》的宗旨乃是协助推动马来西亚青年对民主原则、西方现代文学、哲学和民主政府的认识,希冀年轻作家有能力吸收西方知识份子的知识和技能,并在这些有益的阅读启蒙和身处马来西亚的背景下创作他们自己的文学[70]。从创刊号开始,《蕉风》就刊登翻译自西方作家的小说。编者黄思骋在第92期(1960年6月)开始宣告"每期都刊出两篇世界著名小说家的短篇小说",当期就刊登了美国作家爱伦·坡(Edgar Allan Poe)和亨利(O. Henry)的短篇小说译文,并简介两位作家的背景。黄思骋在第103期(1961年5月)表示每期要"有系统的来介绍现代世界文学",当期开始连载艾略特(T. S. Eliot)长诗《荒原》(*The Waste Land*),并附有文章介绍和探讨《荒原》的价值[71]。随后《蕉风》大量引进和介绍欧美作家如福克纳(William Faulkner)、赛珍珠(Pearl S. Buck)、乔哀思(James Joyce)、毛姆(William S. Maugham)、汤玛斯·曼(Thomas Mann)和沙特(Jean-Paul Sartre)等人的作品。

上述情况一直延续到香港作家黄崖于1961年接手《蕉风》编务工作后。黄崖在《蕉风》第126期(1963年4月)透露接到不少读者来信,建议"减少介绍现代西洋文学的篇幅",原因有两点:"一、翻译的文字,读者不习惯;二、现代文学的表现方式和我们常看到的本邦作品距离太大。"即使如此,黄崖依旧坚持《蕉风》"介绍现代西洋文学的工作",仅是今后"尽量选刊比较精短的现代西洋作品"[72]。这番坚持背后当然是要贯彻《蕉风》要协助推动马来西亚青年吸收和学习西方现代文学的宗旨。

---

[70] *Union Press Organization: Annual Report 1964* (1964), AFR, Box P-322, IMG_6784-6785, 30.
[71] 编者:〈编者的话〉,《蕉风》,第92期(1960年6月),页1;编者:〈编者的话〉、叶逢生:〈简介艾略特和《荒原》〉、T. S. Eliot著,维廉译:〈荒原〉,《蕉风》,第103期(1961年5月),页1、3、4–5。《蕉风》创刊号就已刊登西方作家W. Menard著、钟剑雄译的小说《捕虎记》,参见该期页29–31。
[72] 编者:〈编者的话〉,《蕉风》,第126期(1963年4月),页1。

黄崖誓言要让该刊"沟通国内国外的文坛",并在第143期推出革新号,宣称广邀"全球各国"作家惠稿予《蕉风》[73]。来自台湾的诗人周梦蝶、痖弦、罗门、叶珊(杨牧)、余光中、洛夫、管管和周策纵等都有作品在《蕉风》发表,其中周梦蝶和痖弦等人的不少诗作都是首先在《蕉风》发表而并非转载,尤其是周梦蝶诗集《还魂草》的许多作品都是先刊登在《蕉风》。在《蕉风》革新号后,台湾诗人占据了《蕉风》的诗页,其次是香港,马华诗人敬陪末座[74]。《蕉风》在黄崖接手后大量刊登台湾作家的作品,除了希望开拓《蕉风》销路,其他原因不外是在回应当时美国对东南亚华人外交政策的调整,既要加强海外华人对在地国的认同,也要促进海外华人对台湾的喜爱,以阻止他们认同中国大陆政府[75]。上述台湾作家的作品的确掀起马华文坛对台湾文学的喜爱风潮,1970年代由马华作家温任平和温瑞安领军的天狼星诗社在马来西亚各地星罗棋布设立分社,影响力风靡一时,其成员作品无不受到台湾诗人如余光中、痖弦或叶珊的影响和薰陶,而该诗社成员的作品有不少正是在《蕉风》首发,后来温瑞安和一些成员均赴台深造,另外在台自立门户,创办神州诗社,也吸引当时不少台湾年轻作家参与,其中林耀德更是对该诗社"涉入颇深"[76]。综上所述,《蕉风》显然不仅是新马的地方杂志,其跨国跨界的面向也值得关注。此外,《蕉风》的订阅者来自国内外,友联在提交给TAF的年度报告中记录哈佛大学教授芮效卫(David Roy)也从美国来函订阅《蕉风》全册[77]。

在友联提交予TAF一份1956至1963年的总体报告中,《蕉风》和《学生周报》宣称已栽培超过三百名马来亚年轻作家,其中八十名表现卓越者已成为著名和流行作家,他们被广泛称为"蕉风派",并在

---

[73] 编者:〈编者的话〉,《蕉风》,第141期(1964年5月),页1;第143期(1964年9月),页16。

[74] 黄子:〈一份重构马华文坛版图的杂志:《蕉风》的"国际化"与"马来西亚化"〉,《蕉风》,第500期(2008年12月),页34。

[75] "Request for PP Project Renewal" (1958), DTPILLAR, vol. 2, no. 0003,2.

[76] 杨宗翰:〈从神州人到马华人〉,载陈大为、钟怡雯、胡金伦编:《赤道回声:马华文学读本II》(台北:万卷楼图书股份有限公司,2004),页164。

[77] *Union Press Organization: Annual Report 1965* (1965), AFR, Box P-322, IMG_6858, 36.

文坛形成一股强大势力以抵抗左翼的攻击[78]。单是在1963至1964年的两年内，友联自称已组织二百位本地年轻作家以对抗文坛上那些被共产主义份子影响的作家。这些"蕉风派"作家被左翼作家视为"首要敌人"[79]。从1963年一份报告可见，友联也向TAF"告状"左翼学生如何辱骂友联是"政府走狗"[80]。

友联每次上报TAF，几乎都会列出友联诸刊包括每期《蕉风》如何批判左翼出版商，以及其旗下作家怎样向读者灌输自由世界的理念。例如在1962年度报告中指出，《蕉风》1962年设定的方针即是组织年轻作家以抵抗来自香港和新加坡的左翼出版社。为了达致该方针，《蕉风》资助各地的年轻作家出版小型文学刊物，分别在北马出版《绿洲》、中马出版《荒原》、南马出版《新潮》，以及在全马出版《银星》[81]。上述这些文学刊物都是在"蕉风派"的旗帜下进行活动[82]。该报告也列出《蕉风》如何通过文艺批评来揭露新马左翼作家怎样以共产主义为标准来评判文学作品，并批判《南洋商报》的某篇文章不过是抄袭自毛泽东、周扬和刘少奇在《光明日报》发表的文学观点。此外，该报告也交代《蕉风》哪些文章具备"意识形态的训练"（ideological training），诠释自由竞争的意义，如何基于公平和正义捍卫民主原则，以及怎样推动年轻人理解自由的概念以免他们变得武断[83]。1963年11月，《蕉风》第133期增设"文艺沙龙"版，自此刊登了不少作者和读者来函，批判那些被共产主义份子影响的作家，例如指控这些反对现代派的作家"

---

[78] *Union Press Organization General Review: 1956–1963* (1963), AFR, Box P-322, IMG_6696-6697, 17–18.

[79] *A Summary of the Aims, Policies and Works of U.P.O in Malaysia* (18 November 1965), AFR, Box P-322, IMG_6670, 6.

[80] *Union Press Organization Report: Quarter July–September, 1963* (1963), AFR, Box P-322, IMG_6730, 1.

[81] 参见 *Union Press Organization: Annual Report 1962* (1962), AFR, Box P-322, IMG_6718, 25。这四本文学刊物由各自同名的文学社或诗社经营，云集一大批当年友联栽培的"蕉风派"作家群和编辑部团队，包括李苍、冰谷和周唤等人。

[82] *Union Press Organization Report: Quarter April– June, 1963* (1963), AFR, Box P-322, IMG_6650, 11.

[83] *Union Press Organization: Annual Report 1962*, 25–26.

都是一群"花言巧语"的撒旦！"[84] 而白垚一系列五篇反驳和批判现实主义的〈现代诗闲话〉也在较后期《蕉风》的"文艺沙龙"版连载。

友联在报告中陈述新马的左翼文坛情况以及哪些报刊被左翼份子控制，例如指控新马两大日报即《南洋商报》和《星洲日报》的文学版位拒绝刊登友联年轻作者的作品[85]。在1964年度报告中，友联向TAF投诉左翼份子控制了《南洋商报》、《星洲日报》、《通报》和《星槟日报》的文学版位，而吉隆坡《中国报》和槟城《光华日报》的文学版位则愿意协助刊登友联阵营下年轻作家的作品。报告分析指出左翼势力依旧凌驾友联实力，但友联的出版和活动与左翼阵营还是平分秋色，只要继续努力，假以时日会击败他们[86]。报告仔细列出和比较友联文学刊物和左翼文学刊物在1964年每月平均的估计销量（表4）：

表4 友联和左翼文学刊物每月平均销量比较（本），1964年

友联刊物及其销量	左翼刊物及其销量
《蕉风》：6,000	《南洋文学》：3,000
《海天》：2,000	《文艺世纪》：2,000
《荒原》：2,000	《文艺季风》：2,500
《新潮》：1,000	《十字路口》：2,000
《银星》：1,000	《1960年代》：1,000
	《南桥》：1,500
	《保山》：2,500
总计：12,000	总计：14,500

资料来源：*Union Press Organization: Annual Report 1964*, 32.

---

[84] 高弓：〈一个请教：致《大学青年》叶长楼君〉，《蕉风》，第133期（1963年11月），页13。
[85] *Union Press Organization Report: Quarter July–September, 1963* (1963), AFR, Box P-322, IMG_6730, 12.
[86] *Union Press Organization: Annual Report 1964* (1964), AFR, Box P-322, IMG_6784-6785, 32-33.

虽然当时《蕉风》的6,000本销量超越任何一份左翼文学刊物，但友联文学刊物的总体销量仅是12,000本，还是比不上左翼文学刊物的14,500本。友联以上述数据和分析来暗示TAF必须继续加大幅度资助友联。《蕉风》和一批被友联培养出来的马来西亚年轻作家大力揭露左翼作家如何对青年知识份子造成污染和破坏，他们正与这些左翼作家持久陷入一场激烈的意识形态斗争中。为了强化《蕉风》的整体实力，友联决定自革新号起增加刊物页数，从原来的24页增加到76页（表2），以便扩大内容范围，促进当地的历史和文化研究，打造真正的马来西亚文学，并坚持仅刊登第一流作品[87]。

TAF驻马代表坦承基金会对友联众多项目都有参与兴趣，但唯独《蕉风》是"最难评估的项目"，他可以接受《蕉风》的说明——该刊的意义在于组织年轻作家和防止那些青年才俊涉及颠覆势力的活动，然而却不相信那些倾向于反对势力的报刊能在马来亚联合邦政府的控制下得以存在[88]。言下之意是，他认为友联往往在报告中夸大了友联和《蕉风》如何跟那些倾向于左翼势力的报刊及其文人群体进行斗争的过程，因为凡是出现左翼势力苗头的报刊在当时都会被马来亚联合邦政府取缔，友联那种夸大的叙述反而让他对《蕉风》的反共影响力产生怀疑。

七、结论："自主法则"和"他律法则"

美方的文化冷战策略是希望《蕉风》看起来是纯文艺刊物，不涵盖美方政治宣传，"纯文艺"是掩盖早期《蕉风》亲美政治立场的屏障，呼应了CIA冷战意识形态宣传特点所主张的"隐形宣传"——上乘的宣传就是要看起来完全不像宣传[89]，这跟冷战时期在自由世界流通的纯文艺理念不谋而合。

---

[87] *Union Press Organization: Annual Report 1964* (1964), AFR, Box P-322, IMG_6784-6785, 31.

[88] "William T. Fleming to the President, TAF" (21 October 1963), AFR, Box P-322, IMG_6519, 2.

[89] Frances S. Saunders, *The Cultural Cold War*, 1.

正如王绍光指出，CIA的宣传手法十分灵活，不像共产党国家的宣传那么生硬、呆板[90]。美方冷战文件把"最有效的宣传"界定为"主体沿着你所希望的方向前进，而这些主体还坚信是自身在决定方向"[91]。那些弘扬纯文艺的现代主义信徒把第三世界的政治元素从文学场域驱除后，往往以为是自身在决定文学比较高雅的方向，殊不知是在沿着美方所希望的"去政治化"方向前进。CIA不仅仅限于以抽象和纯实用的方式从事文化冷战，他们还有明确的美学目标，那就是他们追求的高雅文化。冷战时期由美方主导的现代主义运动即是这种高雅文化的其中一个化身，现代主义旗下的抽象表现主义（Abstract Expressionism）被CIA作为跟共产世界宣扬的社会主义现实主义（Socialist Realism）对立的反共武器大力推广；CIA拨巨款在幕后资助纽约现代艺术博物馆（The Museum of Moder Art, MoMA）巡回国内外展览和推广抽象表现主义画作。当时莫斯科对任何背离社会主义现实主义的作品都大力谴责，因此CIA认为凡是敌方反对的，都值得美方支持。美方文化官员认为抽象表现主义恰好可以作为一种反共意识形态、一种自由意识形态和创新精神的展现，它既不影射什么，也不作出政治表态，与社会主义现实主义背道而驰，这恰好是苏联人仇视的艺术[92]。

在中共鼓吹毛泽东〈在延安文艺座谈会上的讲话〉（以下简称〈讲话〉）提倡文艺必须服务政治的冷战语境下，社会主义现实主义一直是新中国文艺奉行的主旋律，其对立面就是主张文艺必须超越政治的纯文艺与现代主义方案。美方通过CIA在全球各地"秘密资助那些带有文学性与思想性的刊物与团体"[93]，TAF支持友联和《蕉风》的"纯文艺"立场不过是实践CIA冷战意识形态的"隐形宣传"组成部分。早期《蕉风》屡次组稿刊登反对毛泽东和鞭挞社会主义现实主义的文章，晚年

---

[90] 王绍光：〈中央情报局与文化冷战〉，《读书》，2002年第5期，页98。

[91] Frances S. Saunders, *The Cultural Cold War*, 4.

[92] Frances S. Saunders, *The Cultural Cold War*, 4, 234, 255–60.

[93] Frances S. Saunders, *The Cultural Cold War*, 410.

白垚撰文仍然乐此不疲揭穿〈讲话〉是皇帝新衣[94]。早期《蕉风》高举"纯文艺"旗帜,阻挡了读者发现《蕉风》在幕后为CIA背书的宣传行为。友联当然没有超越政治,但读者看到的不是友联成员参与政治的宣传行为,而是他们如何以自由文化的理念,用心良苦地握着纯文艺的防御针,为广大的新马读者群集体注射现代主义的剂药,以防他们感染共产主义的瘟疫。

林春美以文艺的自主法则(autonomous principle)高度评价黄崖近十年主编《蕉风》时期:"排除掉文学的政治功能、确立文学的自主法则,是这个时期最为激烈的"建立文学体制规范的斗争"……黄崖时期对文学自主法则的高度推崇,塑造了六〇年代《蕉风》的两个重要特质:一是现代主义文学的引入,二是作为"纯文艺"刊物的定位调整。这在很大程度上影响了其后的文学发展。"[95] 黄崖推广"纯文艺"的确促进了马华文学规范的体制化,但从分析档案和《蕉风》内容显示,他的编辑方针主张以及推广"纯文艺"和"马来西亚化",均是高度配合美方和当地政府为友联设定的指导原则。跟其他《蕉风》编辑相比,黄崖的名字比较多见于TAF档案中。除了由于他在任较久,也是因为他比其他编辑更落力参与和组织全马各种文艺和社会活动,本身也热心参与马华公会的政党活动[96]。正如德国理论家布尔格(Peter Bürger)支持哈贝玛斯(Jürgen Habermas)的观点,即文艺自主性在资产阶级社会的发展,其确立的先决条件是文化生产脱钩于政治和经济体系[97],友联和《蕉风》在冷战时空接受美援和当地政府政治意识形态的指导和支配,《蕉风》所标榜"纯文艺"的"文艺自主性"在没有具备经济和政治独立的先决条件下,究竟能在多大程度上让文艺"自主"起来?

---

[94] 章鉴:〈毛先生的文艺妙论〉,《蕉风》,第168期(1966年10月),页60;白垚:《缕云起于绿草》,页168。

[95] 林春美:《蕉风与非左翼的马华文学》(台北:时报文化出版企业股份有限公司,2021),页140–44。

[96] 庄华兴:〈战后马华(民国)文学遗址〉,页27。关于《蕉风》的"马来西亚化",参见黄子:〈一份重构马华文坛版图的杂志〉,页30–46。

[97] Peter Bürger, *Theory of the Avant-Garde*, trans. Michael Shaw (Minneapolis, MN: University of Minnesota Press, 1984), 24.

一如法国理论家布迪厄（Pierre Bourdieu）揭示，文化生产时刻是他律法则（heteronomous principle）和自主法则之间互相争斗的场域，那些能在经济和政治场域占有优势的艺术家往往能从他律法则中受益，而那些坚守自主法则、"非功利"的激进艺术家却以失败的生命告终来作为自身文艺尊严的捍卫，他们必须与官方政治和经济的他律保持距离，而且要对这些他律进行不断的斗争，方能在文艺自主场域得到高度评价[98]。友联成员和其刊物若在冷战时空跟马华左翼刊物相比，前者显然在本土经济和政治场域占有很大优势，更多时候受利于他律法则，而不是自主法则；后者在本土经济和政治场域则处于劣势，长期被官方取缔、压制或阻碍，刊物寿命不长[99]。

综上所述，友联的确配合美方和当地政府的指示，经常在年度报告里呈报刊物的意识形态效益和销量，显而易见这有违于文艺自主性所主张的"非功利"。而从美方在1950、60年代对友联进行意识形态效益的审慎评估和干预，以及对其账务和活动进行严密调查和计算的工作氛围来看，《蕉风》提倡的"纯文艺"和"文艺自主性"论述固然让人向往和肃然起敬，但这些理念在多大程度上停留在理论或"隐形宣传"的层面？或在多大的程度上升到实践的文学场域？而《蕉风》在接受美援和官方政策指导的同时，其成员和作家群还能在多大程度上在作品和言行中发挥自身的能动性、创造力和自我批判能力？这都是日后研究者可以进一步结合刊物内容和作家群来探讨和厘清的问题。

---

[98] Pierre Bourdieu, *The Rules of Art: Genesis and Structure of the Literary Field*, trans. Susan Emanuel (Stanford, CA: Stanford University Press, 1996), 214–23, 77–85.

[99] 庄华兴：〈冷战在马来与马华文学场域的介入与冲击（1950–1969)〉,《文化研究》，第32期（2021年4月），页55–56。

www.ingramcontent.com/pod-product-compliance
Lightning Source LLC
Chambersburg PA
CBHW061208250625
28437CB00004BA/21